LEGAL ISSUES IN

Property
Valuation
and Taxation

LEGAL ISSUES IN

Property Valuation and Taxation

CASES AND MATERIALS

With a new foreword by David Brunori

Joan Youngman

L LINCOLN INSTITUTE
OF LAND POLICY
CAMBRIDGE, MASSACHUSETTS

Lincoln Institute of Land Policy 2006

© 1994, 2006 International Association of Assessing Officers
Reissue licensed from International Association of Assessing Officers

Library of Congress Cataloging-in-Publication Data
Youngman, Joan
Legal issues in property valuation and taxation: cases and materials /
Joan Youngman, with a new foreword by David Brunori.
     p. cm.
Includes bibliographical references and index.
ISBN 1-55844-162-X (alk. paper)
    1. Real property—Valuation—United States—Cases.
2. Real property tax—Law and legislation—United States—
   Cases. I. Title.
KF6528.A7Y68 2006
343.7305'42—dc22   2005029926

Cover design by David Gerratt/DG Communications
Cover photo © Photodisc

Printed and bound by Webcom Limited in Toronto, Ontario, Canada.
The paper is Legacy Offset, a 100% recycled, acid-free sheet.

MANUFACTURED IN CANADA

CONTENTS

FOREWORD

The property tax in the United States has never been more important. Despite numerous attempts to limit its use, the property tax remains the most significant source of tax revenue for local governments. In 2005 cities and counties raised well over $300 billion—more than half of all local government own-source revenue—from this tax alone. This money pays for vital services such as education, public safety, and transportation.

Impressive as its fiscal role is, the importance of the tax goes far beyond the sheer dollars collected. The property tax has long been considered an effective and efficient method of financing local public services while promoting local financial and political autonomy. It is a stable and dependable revenue source, long appreciated by public finance scholars, but the public itself has rarely shared this positive view. Indeed, it has now become a staple of public finance lore that the property tax is viewed by voters as the "worst tax" due to its visibility, a history of poor administration, and the often stiff burdens it imposes on homeowners of low or fixed incomes.

The reissue of this casebook coincides with a long period of rapidly rising house prices that have increased property tax burdens in many areas, and renewed calls for reduction or even abolition of the tax, in a parallel to the property tax revolts of the 1970s and 1980s. The tax is challenged by businesses and homeowners, in ballot measures and state legislatures.

Understanding how the property tax works has never been more daunting or more critical. Rapid changes in the way property is assessed and valued test veteran and novice practitioners alike. But students in the field are lucky. This book will continue to assist anyone searching for a better understanding of how the property tax system works. This is the "go to" book that draws together important cases and materials on the fundamental legal issues concerning the property tax. Its reissue is proof of the enduring value of this volume, and its continued availability will help students and practitioners to understand concepts such as current use, comparable sales, and the income and cost approaches to valuation. Readers are introduced to the problems of taxation of long-term leases, subsidized housing, and fractional valuation. Like any good casebook, this one tells a story, and in the process it makes clear the complex legal issues involved in property valuation and taxation.

— *David Brunori*
Research Professor of Public Policy,
The George Washington University and
Contributing Editor, *State Tax Notes*

PREFACE TO THE 2006 EDITION

This volume presents significant cases illustrating fundamental legal principles of property valuation and taxation. It is intended to be useful to lawyers
and law students, and also to policy makers, practitioners, and others with a
special interest in the property tax. The original publication of this material
by the International Association of Assessing Officers (IAAO) signaled their
belief that a legal casebook would benefit tax professionals and administrators. The success of this collection led the Lincoln Institute of Land Policy
to reissue it in an effort to continue its availability and expand its reach still
further.

This compilation of judicial opinions builds on the pioneering work of
Professor James Bonbright. More than a half-century ago, he began his magis-
terial treatise *The Valuation of Property* with a chapter on "The Problem of
Judicial Valuation," taking as his starting point Justice Brandeis's observation that "value is a word of many meanings."[1] These cases consider which
of the many meanings of "value" may be relevant in a given instance and
which meaning of "property" fits the purpose of a specific valuation.

The cases themselves provide perhaps the best answer to an obvious
question: Why should the intensely practical property tax be analyzed
through the vehicle of judicial opinions? In fact, the property tax poses
many interpretive challenges in defining such basic concepts as property,
ownership, and value. The ordinary complexities of everyday life, which
include divisions of rights between landlords and tenants, distinctions
between business profits and property rents, and disputes over the current
use of property, require that courts provide operational definitions for these
abstract terms.

In such situations, legal opinions can do more than settle individual dis-
agreements between taxpayers and assessors. Ideally, they clarify the reasoning by which a solution is drawn from statutory language or general legal
principles, and help the reader understand how this result might change in
a different factual setting. An opinion can also address counterarguments,
whether in reasoning considered and rejected in the decision itself, or in an
explicit dissent by other judges hearing the same case. The most significant
"dissents" are sometimes found in contrary decisions on the same point by
two tribunals, whether they are courts in different states, courts of different
jurisdictions in the same state, or even the same court at different times.

---

1. *Southwestern Bell Telephone Co. v. Public Service Comm'n*, 262 U.S. 276, 310 (1923).

This volume thus presents alternate approaches to fundamental legal issues rather than snapshots of the evolving positions of courts in various jurisdictions. The new Appendix provides updated statistical information for the tables in chapter 1, which demonstrate the continuing importance of the tax to local governments. This is in many ways a natural development, because the property tax is uniquely suited to serve as an autonomous source of local government revenue. Immovable property does not shift location in response to taxation; it can be locally identified; and its value provides a relatively stable tax base. Local administration and control permit decentralized budget decisions and enhanced accountability and responsiveness. However, the decentralized nature of the tax can also disguise its cumulative importance. Today the property tax raises almost twice as much revenue as the federal corporate income tax, and more than ten times as much revenue as state corporate income taxes.

These cases have been edited to minimize procedural and technical details and to enhance their accessibility to readers outside the legal profession. The questions following the cases are generally intended for discussion, and often will not have one correct answer. Omitted text in legal opinions is indicated by ellipses. However, omitted citations to other opinions and omitted footnotes within the opinions are not marked. Because footnotes in the opinions retain their original numbering, not all case footnotes will be numbered consecutively. Footnotes to the author's own text are numbered consecutively within each chapter.

Many people contributed to the completion of this work. The cases were compiled originally for a course on state and local taxation offered with Professor Oliver Oldman of Harvard Law School. His comments and suggestions, together with those of Professor Richard Pomp of the University of Connecticut School of Law, were of great assistance. Dr. Joseph Eckert and the IAAO were interested in expanding the original work beyond a legal casebook format to address assessment and appraisal issues as well. At the IAAO Annie Aubrey edited the manuscript with great skill and care. Wayne Tenenbaum of the IAAO offered insightful comments from both legal and appraisal perspectives. Special thanks are due to Darcy Ryding, Brad Mitchell, and Tarrant Sibley for their able research assistance. At the Lincoln Institute, the expert editorial guidance of Emily McKeigue and Ann LeRoyer made this reissued volume possible.

1 INTRODUCTION

Property Taxation as a Field of Study

Property tax studies offer several perspectives on current political and economic developments in the United States. At the most basic level, they provide information on a stable, longstanding, and endlessly controversial revenue source that serves as a mainstay of autonomous local government finance in this country. More generally, any recurrent ad valorem tax raises assessment problems that yield rich material for the study of valuation principles critical to many areas of taxation, finance, economics, and commerce. Finally, this tax brings into sharp focus many political issues concerning payment for government services.

Two central characteristics shape the property tax in the United States: its local administration and its nature as an asset tax. A tax on real estate can be administered at the local level, and so provide a city, town, or school district with an autonomous revenue source. This contribution to independent local government is balanced, however, by the negative reaction of property owners to a tax levied on a nonliquid asset and collected in a small number of highly visible installments.

Political discontent with the property tax also has wider policy implications. The feasibility of taxing nonliquid assets is a particularly significant issue in an era of decreasing reliance on progressive taxation and increasing reliance on regressive consumption taxes and fees. Asset taxation, whether through a recurrent ad valorem tax or in another form, such as an estate tax, can mitigate the increasing concentration of wealth that accompanies a regressive tax structure. The history and travails of the property tax as a large-scale, functioning asset levy bear on the feasibility and acceptability of any form of wealth taxation. The practical political experience of property tax administration can also enrich abstract public finance analysis. For example, local tax officials are keenly aware that the theoretical virtue of visibility, or "transparency," in taxation has served to increase public discontent with property taxes relative to less apparent consumption taxes, payroll taxes, or income taxes withheld at the source.

Any ad valorem tax raises problems of tax base measurement or valuation. Valuation issues are critical to numerous governmental and commercial transactions, from business negotiations to the calculation of awards in eminent domain takings, from the measure of damages in tort claims to rate-setting for public utility services. In this way property tax cases can yield insights into the valuation process with utility far beyond the sphere of taxation alone. The annual assignment of market values to large numbers of taxable parcels provides courts with a vast array of disputes for consideration and decision.

Perhaps the most significant issue raised by the valuation process concerns the definition of property itself. Any calculation of fair market value relies, even if implicitly, on a prior decision as to which rights and interests constitute the property being valued. This inquiry can be confined to a single question, such as whether the provisions of an unfavorable lease affect valuation for tax purposes. It can also encompass a broad range of evolving issues concerning private rights and public restrictions, such as liability for remediation of toxic contamination, responsibility for historic preservation, or the effect of innovative planning techniques such as transferable development rights. As the concept of property as a social and political phenomenon changes, the process of valuing and taxing that property must change as well.

Many political issues connected with the property tax concern its role as the mainstay of independent local government finance. The property tax no longer supplies the major portion of local government funds from all sources, but it represents the largest single source of autonomous local revenue. The straitened state budgets of the 1980s helped dramatize the importance of this function, as states reduced local aid even as the federal government eliminated revenue sharing. Such measures impressed on localities their need for funding not contingent on decisions by another level of government.

More generally, the operation of the tax illuminates political choices about the distribution of the benefits and burdens of self-government. For example, by effectively freezing most valuations until property is sold, the California tax limitation measure known as "Proposition 13" provided a clear statement on the relative tax burdens to be borne by long-time residents and new arrivals. Throughout the nation, use of the property tax to finance education has sparked debate on the distribution and redistribution of wealth across jurisdictional and generational lines. The adoption of preferential tax systems for agricultural and open-space land in each of the fifty states represents a land-use decision, just as tax-relief measures for the elderly, for veterans, or for homeowners generally reflect community values. None of these elements is static, and their evolution through periods of changing fiscal, political, and even demographic patterns offers insight into civic culture as it develops over time.

The Property Tax as a Local Tax

The property tax is the primary local tax in the United States, providing the major portion of independent local government revenue in forty-eight of the fifty states.[1] The strengths of the property tax have kept it operative in various forms since colonial times. Its equally significant drawbacks have made it a focus of popular discontent, particularly during periods of heightened antitax sentiment. Both its advantages and its problems are closely related to the nature of a recurrent ad valorem tax, especially one limited to a specific asset.

A major advantage of a real property tax is the relative ease with which land and buildings can be located and identified, and their stability over time. The immobility of real estate compared, for example, to income or sales prevents simple migration to other jurisdictions in response to the tax, although in the long run investment can shift to other locations. Immobility also reduces the problem of tax-base allocation, which can become extremely burdensome to taxpayers and administrators alike when sales or income-producing transactions span numerous small jurisdictions. The problem of collecting tax for hundreds or thousands of local districts has been a powerful argument against requiring mail-order retailers to collect sales and use taxes for jurisdictions in which their customers live.[2] Similarly, local and state income taxes can require apportionment of income earned through work in multiple sites.[3]

Finally, an immovable asset also provides a source of collateral for taxes due from the owner. Unpaid taxes can be secured by a lien on the property, with potential foreclosure and sale to pay this debt. These features recommend the tax as a source of autonomous revenue for local governments, which often have neither the economic base nor the administrative capacity for efficient sales or income taxation.

Along with these advantages, a tax on nonliquid assets also presents important difficulties. A recurrent asset tax can encounter resistance when it requires payment from an owner who has realized no increase in net wealth, either through property appreciation or income. Property appreciation itself can present other problems. In times of rising market values, taxpayers' assessments may increase without any corresponding change in the income from which they pay the tax. The need to sell an asset in order to pay tax on it is problematic in any circumstance, and never more so than in the case of a residence. In theory, the tax rate can drop as property values rise, leaving actual tax bills and total collections unchanged. Revenue pressure often delays

---

1. In 1990, the property tax provided more than 50 percent of total local tax revenues in all states except Alabama and Louisiana. Advisory Commission on Intergovernmental Relations (ACIR), *Significant Features of Fiscal Federalism 1992* (1992), vol. 2, table 102.

2. See *Quill Corp. v. North Dakota*, 112 S.Ct. 1904, 119 L.Ed.2d, 91 (1992).

3. For criticism of efforts by Philadelphia and New York to enforce nonresident income taxation, see G. Henderson, "All Aboard the Tax Express!" *State Tax Notes* 93 (January 28, 1993): 18–25. ("[W]hile our competitors in the European common market are working to reduce the barriers to commerce within their common market, we seem to be moving in the opposite direction.")

or inhibits rate reductions, however, particularly when value increases are not distributed uniformly across all taxable properties. If only certain portions of a jurisdiction experience sharp price inflation, it may not be possible to reduce tax rates across all sectors in order to prevent a rapid rise in tax bills for the neighborhoods or property types undergoing unusual increases in value.

A disparity between cash income and property value can cause special problems for retired and elderly taxpayers, farmers owning land on the urban fringe, and homeowners in times of rapid housing inflation. The introduction of many tax limitation measures in the mid-1970s, for example, coincided with a near doubling in the market value of single-family homes from 1976 to 1981.[4] The political difficulties these cases present are obvious, for they affect groups that are among the most influential in the electorate. They also raise a question as to the role of financial intermediaries, such as banks. How should the availability of loans secured by increased property value affect the problem of liquidity? Few elderly taxpayers have taken advantage of statutory provisions allowing their unpaid property taxes to accrue as long-term, low-interest loans secured by their property. This suggests that political resistance to asset taxation stems as much from reluctance to diminish the net value to the owner and his or her heirs as it does from the problem of liquidity itself.

Because the advantages of the property tax are so closely tied to local government autonomy, it is not surprising that nearly all its revenue accrues to cities, counties, school districts, townships, and special districts (see table 1 for percentage of revenue derived from the property tax). In 1990 more than 96 percent of all property tax collections in the United States supported these local government units,[5] a dramatic change from earlier times. At the turn of the century, before widespread adoption of sales and income taxes, property taxes represented nearly half of all state revenue.[6] The portion of *state* tax revenue derived from the property tax has since fallen to less than 2 percent.[7] At the same time the property tax share of local tax revenue only dropped from 88.6 percent in 1902 to 74.5 percent in 1990.[8] The property tax contributed at least 66 percent of local tax collections in every region of the country in 1990; in New England, the figure was 98 percent (table 2).[9]

---

4. A. Manvel, "House Prices and Property Taxation," *Tax Notes,* July 9, 1984, p. 212.

5. ACIR, *Significant Features of Fiscal Federalism 1992* (1992), vol. 2, table 64.

6. G. Fisher, "Property Taxation and Local Government: Four Hypotheses," *Property Tax Journal* 8 (1989): 113, 119–20. See generally, U.S. Bureau of the Census, *Historical Statistics of the United States from Colonial Times to 1970* (1976), pp. 1086–1135.

7. ACIR, *Significant Features of Fiscal Federalism 1992* (1992) vol. 2, table 65.

8. *Ibid.,* table 102; ACIR, *Significant Features of Fiscal Federalism 1991* (1991), vol. 2, table 81.

9. ACIR, *Significant Features of Fiscal Federalism 1992* (1992), vol. 2, table 102.

Table 1
Percentage of Tax Revenue
Derived from the Property Tax, 1957–1990

Level of government	1957 (percent)	1990 (percent)
State and local governments	44.6	31.0
State governments	3.3	1.9
Local governments	86.7	74.5
Cities	72.7	50.9
Counties	93.7	73.3
School districts	98.6	97.5
Townships	93.6	92.4
Special districts	100.0	70.0

Source: ACIR, *Significant Features of Fiscal Federalism 1992* (1992), vol. 2, table 65.

Table 2
The Property Tax in Local Government Finance, 1990

	Percentage of local government general revenue	Percentage of local government tax revenue
United States average	29.2	74.5
New England	49.0	98.0
Mideast	31.7	66.7
Great Lakes	35.2	81.1
Plains States	31.4	82.9
Southeast	23.4	70.2
Southwest	32.0	78.7
Rocky Mountain States	30.7	76.4
Far West	20.8	70.0
Selected states		
New Hampshire	71.1	99.3
Connecticut	56.2	98.5
New Jersey	50.8	98.1
Oregon	42.3	89.5
Michigan	40.6	92.6
Iowa	36.4	95.9
Colorado	30.7	68.7
New York	29.5	61.0
Georgia	25.2	69.2
California	19.7	69.1
Washington	18.1	59.7
Louisiana	15.7	43.4
New Mexico	11.9	56.1

Source: ACIR, *Significant Features of Fiscal Federalism 1992* (1992), vol. 2, tables 92 and 102.

The distinctly local character of the property tax is also due to constitutional limitations on federal taxation of property. Article I, section 9[4] of the United States Constitution states: "No Capitation, or other direct, Tax shall be laid, unless in Proportion to the Census or Enumeration herein before directed to be taken." The federal income tax is exempted from this apportionment requirement by the Sixteenth Amendment, and the federal estate tax has been held to constitute an excise on the privilege of transmitting property, rather than a direct tax on the property itself.[10]

Real Property, Personal Property, Tangibles, and Intangibles: From a General Property Tax to a Real Property Tax

The evolution of the property tax from a state tax to a local tax was accompanied by its equally significant transformation from a general tax on real, personal, tangible, and intangible property to a tax largely limited to real property alone. Land and buildings form the major part of the property tax base today, together with only selected items of personal property, such as certain equipment, inventories, and automobiles. The 1987 Census of Governments found that locally assessed personal property constituted only 9.8 percent of the property tax base in 1986, down from 17.2 percent thirty years earlier.[11] This shift reflected the changing American economy of the nineteenth century. In colonial times tangible property served as an index of ability to pay, the base for a "faculty" tax imposed "upon every man according to his estate, and with consideration to all his other abilities whatsoever."[12] This was no longer the case in an industrialized economy.

These classifications are rooted in Anglo-American property law, which distinguishes real (or immovable) property, basically land and buildings, from personal (or movable) property,[13] with personalty further divided between

---

10. In *New York Trust Co. v. Eisner,* 256 U.S. 345 (1921), Justice Holmes rejected the argument that the estate tax constituted a direct tax. In a characteristically peremptory manner, he stated that he was guided "not by an attempt to make some scientific distinction, which would be at least difficult, but on an interpretation of language by its traditional use—on the practical and historical ground that this kind of tax always has been regarded as the antithesis of a direct tax . . . . Upon this point a page of history is worth a volume of logic." *Id.* at 349. Note that customs receipts, which in some respects resembled nonrecurrent ad valorem property tax revenue, were by far the most important source of federal government tax funds until the Civil War.

11. 1987 Census of Governments, *Taxable Property Values* (1987), vol. 2, table B. See also S. Gold, "How the Taxation of Business Property Varies among the States," *Assessment Digest* 9 (1987):14; A. Manvel, *Paying for Civilized Society* (1986), chapter 3.

12. J. Jensen, *Property Taxation in the United States* (1931), p. 27 (quoting the 1634 Massachusetts property tax statute).

13. "Material things, regarded as the objects of legal rights, belong to either one of two classes, that is, they are either (1) land, or things so annexed to land as to be considered

tangible and intangible property. Tangible personal property includes such items as equipment, machinery, and household effects. Intangible property may be considered in two categories: those intangibles that are valuable in themselves, such as patents, trademarks, and copyrights, and those representing rights in other property, such as stocks, bonds, and bank accounts, and currency itself, which represents a claim against the government that issues it (table 3). The distinction between representative and nonrepresentative intangibles has important implications concerning double taxation when tangibles and intangibles are both included in the tax base.[14] A potential dual burden must be recognized when a tax reaches both tangible property and the intangible rights in it. This is the case, for example, when a property tax on the full value of a residence is accompanied by an intangible tax on a mortgage on the same property held by a bank.[15]

Table 3
Types of Real Property and Personal Property

Real Property	Personal Property

• Land
• Buildings
• Fixtures—personal property that is attached to real estate and becomes a part of it. For example, an elevator may be personal property before installation, and real property after it is incorporated into a building.
	• Tangible property, such as
	  - Machinery and equipment
	  - Inventory
	  - Household goods (e.g., jewelry)
	  - Automobiles
	  - Artwork
	
	• Intangible property, such as
	  - Going-concern value; Goodwill
	  - Licenses; Franchises
	  - Representative property, such as
	    Stocks Bonds
	    Bank accounts Currency
	    Commercial paper Notes

---

a part thereof, or (2) articles of a movable character, not annexed to land . . . . This classification of the objects of rights, based as it is on an essential difference in their character, was recognized in Roman law and in systems derived therefrom; but in English law it attained a peculiar importance . . . ." H. Tiffany, from B. Jones (ed.), *The Law of Real Property*, 3d ed. (1939), vol. 1, §1.

14. Jens Jensen was one of the first writers to examine this distinction, suggesting that a tax base limited to tangible property and nonrepresentative intangibles would avoid double taxation. "Wealth consists of material things plus such incorporeal rights as do not diminish the rights of others in material things." J. Jensen, *Property Taxation in the United States* (1931), p. 49.

15. Cases on this point were dealt with in the early annotation, "Taxation in the Same State of Real Property and Debt Secured by Mortgage or Other Lien Thereon as Double Taxation," *American Law Report* 122 (1939): 742.

A more precise legal formulation equates *all* property with intangible rights, some relating to physical objects and others to intangibles. The legal philosopher Wesley Hohfeld recognized that the word "property" is used in common speech "to indicate the physical object to which various legal rights, privileges, etc. relate; then again—with far greater discrimination and accuracy—the word is used to denote the legal interest (or aggregate of legal relations) appertaining to such physical objects."[16]   James Bonbright, a professor of finance at Columbia University, wrote in his classic 1937 treatise *The Valuation of Property:*

> Because the law of early capitalism concerned itself so largely with rights of full, undivided ownership, and because these rights attached mainly to specific, tangible objects, like land or chattels, the property rights in these objects were closely identified with the objects themselves . . . . A court, no less than a layman, will sometimes refer to a tract of land or a shipment of wheat as property, and will sometimes refer to the interests of people in this land or this shipment as property.[17]

By the post–Civil War period real property and readily identifiable farming equipment were no longer the primary forms of personal wealth in the United States. Yet state and local officials were ill-equipped to assess a comprehensive tax on such items as corporate securities and bank accounts, which could easily be concealed or moved to another jurisdiction. A tax that in form covered all types of property but in fact was limited to real estate and certain specific forms of personal property greatly favored those taxpayers whose major assets took intangible form. The economist Edwin Seligman surveyed tax studies issued from 1872 to 1897 and found that "[e]very annual report of the state comptrollers and assessors complains bitterly that the assessment of personalty is nothing but an incentive to perjury."[18]   Such an assessment was labelled "a tax upon ignorance and honesty," "corrupting and demoralizing," "a premium on perjury and a penalty on integrity," "a school of perjury, imposing unjust burdens on the man who is scrupulously honest." He quoted an 1897 New Jersey report: "[I]t is now literally true that the only ones who pay honest taxes on personal property are the estates of decedents, widows, and orphans, idiots and lunatics."

Seligman concluded, "[T]he general property tax as actually administered is beyond all doubt one of the worst taxes known in the civilized world . . . . It is the cause of such crying injustice that its alteration or its abolition must

---

16. W. Hohfeld, "Some Fundamental Legal Conceptions as Applied in Judicial Reasoning," *Yale Law Journal* 23 (1913): 16, 21.

17. J. Bonbright, *The Valuation of Property* (1937), vol. 1, pp. 100–101.

18. E.R.A. Seligman, *Essays in Taxation*, 10th ed. (1931), pp. 27–28 [citations omitted].

become the battle cry of every statesman and reformer."[19]   The results of efforts such as his can be seen in the current exemption of most individual personal property and intangibles.

The crusade in which Seligman participated so eloquently was ultimately successful, and the property tax in the United States has become overwhelmingly a tax on real estate. Moreover, to the extent that personal property is taxed, specific exemptions for inventories, machinery, and manufacturing equipment are widely available.[20]   This simplifies tax administration, for personal property, unlike land and buildings, may have a tax situs in more than one jurisdiction over the course of a year.[21] For example, a 1989 Oregon case dealing with a property tax on aircraft held that the tax could be apportioned according to the time the aircraft spent in flight over the state, even without landing there.[22]

Direct and Indirect Taxation of Intangibles

Taxes on intangibles as such now exist in only a minority of states.[23] Despite this, the valuation and taxation of intangibles raise urgent legal issues in many jurisdictions, primarily when assessed valuation of real property is increased by intangible factors, such as going-concern value. The valuation of many

---

19. *Ibid.*, p. 62.

20. Commerce Clearing House, *1990 State Tax Guide*, paragraphs 20–150 (business inventories completely exempt from tax in thirty-three states). See also S. Gold, "How the Taxation of Business Property Varies among the States," *Assessment Digest* 9 (1987): 14.

21. See *Japan Line, Ltd. v. County of Los Angeles*, 441 U.S. 434 (1979) (dealing with application of the commerce clause to the taxation of foreign-owned cargo shipping containers).

22. *Alaska Airlines, Inc. v. Department of Revenue*, 307 Or. 406, 769 P.2d 193 (1989), *cert. denied*, 493 U.S. 1019 (1990). Under this approach, a nonstop flight from Seattle to Los Angeles would serve to increase the apportionment factor, and therefore the total property tax, assessed in Oregon. The Oregon Supreme Court observed, "As might be expected, overflights involved little contact with ground facilities, and the State of Oregon did not provide regular services to overflights." However, because the aircraft was found to be part of a unit with a taxable situs in the state, and the apportionment formula was found to be fair, the tax was upheld.

23. A major 1990 study found "only 22 states or their subdivisions levy any tax on intangibles, *per se.*" J. Bowman, G. Hoffer, and M. Pratt, "Current Patterns and Trends in State and Local Intangibles Taxation," *National Tax Journal* 43 (1990): 439, 441. The policy advantages and drawbacks of intangibles taxation as such were debated in a set of *National Tax Journal* articles in 1965 and 1966: J. Blackburn, "Intangibles Taxes: A Neglected Revenue Source for States," *National Tax Journal* 18 (1965): 214; and J. Aronson, "Intangibles Taxes: A Wisely Neglected Revenue Source for States," *National Tax Journal* 19 (1966): 814.

types of property reflects both tangible and intangible elements, not readily separated, and therefore intangible property may be taxed indirectly through its enhancement of the value of tangible property for assessment purposes. In addition, many railroads and utilities are subject to "unit valuation" by which state officials assign a systemwide value to be allocated among local jurisdictions. This often includes a going-concern element over and above the value of tangible real estate and personal property.[24]

The most common forms of intangible property subject to direct taxation are equities and bonds, but other specific intangibles are taxed in various states. For example, Georgia, Kentucky, and West Virginia impose a property tax on patents, copyrights, licenses, and franchise agreements.[25] Washington taxes software as an intangible, and Florida taxes private leaseholds on government property as intangibles.[26] The taxation of computer software illustrates the manner in which valuation of tangible property can serve to bring intangible values into the tax base. Most states classify noncustomized software as tangible property for tax purposes.[27] The valuation of custom-written software, however, presents a difficult question; Does valuation at anything more than the price of the tangible materials constitute the taxation of intangible property?[28] When this question is answered no, a state has achieved the same result through its tangible property tax that Washington has achieved through the taxation of intangible property.

Such disputes far predated the development of commercial software. In *Michael Todd Co. v. County of Los Angeles*,[29] the same question arose with

24. See A. Woolery, *Valuation of Railroad and Utility Property* (n.d.).

25. J. Bowman, G. Hoffer, and M. Pratt, "Current Patterns and Trends in State and Local Intangibles Taxation," *National Tax Journal* 43 (1990):439, 443; ACIR, *Significant Features of Fiscal Federalism 1991* (1991), vol. 1, table 45.

26. J. Bowman, G. Hoffer, and M. Pratt, "Current Patterns and Trends in State and Local Intangibles Taxation," *National Tax Journal* 43 (1990): 445-46.

27. "States universally have held that 'canned' software and hardware are subject to sales tax. Only sixteen states have found custom software to be subject to sales tax." M. Friedman and L. Taylor, "State and Local Taxation of Software," *Computer Lawyer* 7 (1990): 20, at n. 4. Disputes as to whether software constitutes tangible or intangible property arise with respect to sales tax statutes because those generally apply only upon the transfer of tangible property.

28. E.g., *Touche Ross & Co. v. State Board of Equalization*, 203 Cal. App. 3d 1057, 250 Cal. Rptr. 408 (1988) (software held to be tangible); *Northeast DataCom v. City of Wallingford*, 212 Conn. 639, 563 A.2d 688 (1989) (software intangible, except for the physical medium); *District of Columbia v. Universal Computer Associates, Inc.*, 465 F.2d 615 (D.C. Cir. 1972) (software an intangible, upon similar facts); *Comptroller of the Treasury v. Equitable Trust Co.*, 296 Md. 459, 464 A.2d 248 (1983) (software tangible, upon similar facts).

29. 57 Cal.2d 684, 371 P.2d 340, 21 Cal. Rptr. 604 (1962).

regard to valuation of the copyrighted film negatives of the motion picture *Around the World in Eighty Days*. The studio argued that they should be valued only on the basis of their physical material and taxed at a nominal sum. The county sought to value them on the basis of the copyrighted information that they contained—a completed film production.[30] The California Supreme Court upheld a valuation of over $1.5 million, although the stipulated value of the negatives without the copyright was $1,000.[31] This led to 1968 legislation in California limiting the taxation of motion pictures to the value of their tangible materials.[32]

Although intangible property is often easier to conceal from assessment than real estate, when assessed it may sometimes be more readily assigned a market value. This disparity between the process of estimating a value for real estate and for financial assets was another factor contributing to the demise of the general property tax. In *Von Ruden v. Miller*,[33] a 1982 Kansas case upholding a tax on intangible property, the court explained the historical background to the 1924 state constitutional amendment exempting intangibles from the uniformity otherwise required in property taxation:

> Prior to the amendment all property in the state, except that exempted by statute or the constitution, was required to be uniformly assessed at its fair market value in money and equally taxed within its taxing district. There was only one class of property for tax purposes. The assessing was accomplished by township trustees and county clerks. They were untrained and tended to view fair market value as the lowest possible value they could get by with, particularly since the taxpayer was often a neighbor and the assessor had similar property. Intangibles

---

30. Walt Disney Studios took the opposite position when it successfully sought an investment tax credit (ITC) for its master negatives, a federal income tax benefit available only for tangible property:

In *Walt Disney Productions v. United States* [327 F. Supp. 189 (C.D. Cal. 1971), *modified*, 480 F.2d 66 (9th Cir. 1973), *cert. denied*, 415 U.S. 934 (1974)], the taxpayer, a producer of motion pictures, claimed that certain of its motion picture "master" negatives came within the statutory provisions describing section 38 property and therefore were eligible for the ITC. The negatives, it claimed, were standardized articles of tangible business capital used to produce the taxpayer's products, motion picture prints. Accordingly, the taxpayer had capitalized all the costs it had incurred in creating the master negatives—such as costs of labor, editing and film developing—into the value of the motion picture master negative. It sought to claim the aggregate basis in its motion picture negatives as an investment in "tangible personal property."

J. Pavluk, "Computer Software and Tax Policy," *Columbia Law Review* 84 (1984): 1992, at 2004–5 [citations omitted].

31. See generally K. Ehrman and S. Flavin, *Taxing California Property*, 3d ed. (1988), §4:04.

32. Calif. Rev. & Tax. Code, §988. The *Michael Todd* case is discussed in Note, "Indirect Taxation of Motion Picture Copyright," *Stanford Law Review* 15 (1963): 372.

33. 231 Kan. 1, 642 P.2d 91 (1982).

presented a troublesome problem because money and evidence of debt had a stated value thus presenting no opportunity to lower values to the ridiculous levels placed on tangible property. The only remaining method to satisfy the constitutional mandate of uniform and equal [valuation] was to assess tangibles at comparable values to the stated values of intangibles. Even though the increased assessed valuation would in theory lower levies accordingly, this solution was unacceptable to property owners. They did not trust local authorities to put this theory into practice.[34]

As in the case of personal property generally, this concern led to a separate classification of intangibles, removing them from the uniform property tax. The court in *Von Ruden* noted that because "intangibles are transitory and easy to hide, the tax was the subject of wholesale evasion . . . . [A] 1955 Citizens Advisory Commission Study found Kansas residents owned $691,000,000 in common stocks while the assessed value of both stocks and bonds in Kansas that year was only $39,000,000." Gradually a tax on the income from intangibles, such as cash and securities, came to replace a property tax on the intangibles themselves.

When the valuation of property for tax purposes includes any element of good will or going-concern value, these intangibles are brought within the tax base. In the simplest case, the distinction between property value and business value is clear. The rental value of a commercial site, not the business income of the enterprise occupying it, provides an index of property value. In numerous situations, however, the delineation of property value is nowhere near so clear-cut. A business renting premises under a percentage lease pays rent based on enterprise income. Whenever property has a particular utility to a business or enterprise, its value will reflect that utility and, indirectly, intangible business values as well. This problem arises in every form of taxation that prescribes differential treatment for tangible and intangible property. The federal income tax law, for example, permits no depreciation or amortization deductions for property without an ascertainable useful life, such as business goodwill.[35] This means that the purchase of an ongoing business requires allocation of the payment for income tax purposes, not only between depreciable buildings and nondepreciable land, but also between depreciable assets and goodwill.

Goodwill, such as reputation or consumer loyalty, is just one of a number of intangible assets that may be included in the purchase price for a business. Others include going-concern value, or the benefit of an established business

---

34. *Id.* at 95.

35. U.S. Treasury Reg. §1.167(a)-3 states, "An intangible asset, the useful life of which is not limited, is not subject to the allowance for depreciation . . . . No deduction for depreciation is allowable with respect to good will."

operation, and public or private licenses or franchises necessary or beneficial to conduct of the business. Even if it is agreed that the licenses or franchises have value in themselves over and above the value of the tangible business property, a question still remains: does assessment of specialized tangible property at its value to an owner with a license or franchise indirectly incorporate those intangible elements into the tax base?

In the California Supreme Court case of *Roehm v. County of Orange*,[36] the extremely influential jurist Roger Traynor[37] set a compromise pattern whereby intangible property excluded from the tax base could still influence the valuation of other taxable property. In that case, a liquor license was held to be intangible property, not subject to tax, but the court acknowledged that a rise in the valuation of taxable property as a result of issuance of the license would be permissible. This approach has been followed in many later California decisions.[38]

Although the exemption of much personal property from direct taxation was an important reform, it further removed the property tax from a general tax on wealth. A true wealth tax would measure the value of all assets, not just real property. It would also consider the net value of a taxpayer's assets and liabilities, reducing total asset value to reflect obligations such as mortgage indebtedness. Owners of houses of identical value may differ in the value of their other assets, such as stocks, bonds, bank accounts, and other types of personal property. Homes of identical market value do not even indicate equivalent housing wealth if one is owned outright and the other is subject to a substantial mortgage. The real property tax in this country is imposed on gross value, with no offset for debt, so these two homeowners could face equivalent tax bills. The link between taxable value and ability to pay has diminished correspondingly since colonial times.

Note on Cable Television Networks and Property Taxation

The increasing economic importance of cable television property has raised many questions concerning the taxation of personal and intangible property. One recurring problem involves the characterization of "house drops," the components connecting individual residences to the main cables. If these are considered personal property belonging to the cable television companies they

---

36. 32 Cal.2d 280, 196 P.2d 550 (1948).

37. See, e.g., A. Kragen, "Chief Justice Traynor and the Law of Taxation," *Hastings Law Journal* 35 (1984): 801.

38. E.g., *Simplicity Pattern Co. v. State Board of Equalization*, 27 Cal. 3d 900, 615 P.2d 555, 167 Cal. Rptr. 366 (1980); *Michael Todd Co. v. County of Los Angeles*, 57 Cal. 2d 684, 371 P.2d 340, 21 Cal. Rptr. 604 (1962); *ITT World Communications, Inc. v. County of Santa Clara*, 101 Cal. App. 3d 246, 162 Cal. Rptr. 186 (1980).

may be taxed as business property. However, if they are considered "fixtures" that have become incorporated into the residential real property itself they can only be taxed through an increase in the value of the homeowner's property.[39]

Cable television cases also illustrate the difficulty of separating the value of tangible property from the value of intangible business assets such as goodwill. This problem often arises when business property is valued by reference to the income that a purchaser could expect from it, because that income is generally the joint product of tangible and intangible factors. In response to growing litigation on this point, legislation was enacted in California in 1988 stating that intangible assets or rights in a cable television system were not subject to property taxation, but that the system's right to use public property "may be assessed and valued by assuming the presence of intangible assets or rights necessary to put the cable television possessory interest to beneficial or productive use in an operating cable television system."[40]

The difficulty of applying such a standard was illustrated in a case the following year[41] in which the Post-Newsweek cable television network charged that an increase in its assessment from $5.5 million to $16.1 million reflected the inclusion of the value of its franchise in the assessment of its right to use public property. The assessor contended that the network's ability to charge a fee for cable access and to make a profit from its franchise were inseparable from the value of its possessory interest. Although the franchises were themselves exempt, the court found it permissible for the assessor to take into consideration "the presence of the intangible assets necessary to put the possessory interest to beneficial or productive use."

---

39. In a representative dispute, the Michigan Supreme Court, after reviewing other cases in this area, held in *Continental Cablevision of Michigan, Inc. v. City of Roseville*, 425 N.W.2d 53, 430 Mich. 727 (1988), that house drops remain personal property taxable to the cable company. Other cases on this point include *Metrovision of Prince George's County, Inc. v. State Department of Assessments and Taxation*, 92 Md. App. 194, 607 A.2d 110 (1992), and *Tele-Vue Systems, Inc. v. County of Contra Costa*, 25 Cal. App. 3d 340, 101 Cal. Rptr. 789 (1972) (portions of cable systems incorporated into realty owned by subscribers were improperly assessed to the cable system operators). A similar question is dealt with in the context of fire and security alarm systems in *Morse Signal Devices of California, Inc. v. County of Los Angeles*, 161 Cal. App. 3d 570, 207 Cal. Rptr. 742 (1984), which found the systems taxable to the installer. For a general review of these and other questions relating to state and local property, sales, and income taxation of cable television systems, see J. Gibbs, *State and Local Taxation Issues in Cable Television* (Practicing Law Institute No. G4-3845, 1990).

40. Calif. Rev. & Tax. Code, §107.7(d).

41. *County of Stanislaus v. County of Stanislaus Assessment Appeals Board*, 213 Cal. App. 3d 1445, 262 Cal. Rptr. 439 (1989).

Assessing and Collecting the Tax

The annual cycle of property taxation commonly begins with the assessors' computation of the total value of taxable property within the city, town, or other taxing jurisdiction. The tax rate for the year is then set at a level designed to raise the amount required by the jurisdiction's budget, subject to state legislative and constitutional limitations on rates and considering funds available through fees, charges, nonproperty taxes, and intergovernmental grants. The property tax is sometimes termed a "residual" tax when its rate is determined by the revenue needed after accounting for other sources of local income. In the *Von Ruden* case discussed above, the court described the process in this way:

> [A]d valorem tax levies are controlled by the program they fund. They are set by calculating the taxing unit's assessed valuation, adopting a budget, crediting carryover funds and state funds, then dividing the adjusted budgeted amount into the assessed valuation. The resulting quotient is the levy. This process is subject to the legislatively imposed limitation of budget and levies.[42]

The tax rate is frequently expressed in mills. A mill is one-tenth of a percent, or one one-thousandth. For example, a tax rate of 11.5 mills per dollar of assessed value would produce a tax of $11.50 on each $1,000 of assessed value. This is equivalent to a tax rate of 1.15 percent, which was approximately the nationwide average for single-family homes in 1987.[43]

Local property taxes are administered by elected or appointed assessors subject to varying degrees of oversight by state agencies. The assessment of specific classes of property may be the responsibility of state officials, even if the resulting tax revenue accrues to local governments. These classes often include railroad and public utility property assessed on a single statewide basis and apportioned among local jurisdictions; they may also include industrial sites, manufacturing plants, and mineral property.[44] The total values of state- and locally assessed property in the United States in 1986 are compared in table 4.

Assessors in the United States frequently do not bring any specialized academic background in property valuation and tax administration to their positions. Initial training, certification, and continuing education courses are offered by professional organizations such as the International Association of

---

42. 642 P.2d at 99–100.

43. ACIR, *Significant Features of Fiscal Federalism 1990* (1990), vol. 1, table 34 (data on FHA-insured single-family homes).

44. For example, in the *Alaska Airlines* case discussed above at note 22, the Oregon Department of Revenue, and not a local assessor, was responsible for valuation and apportionment of the airline property, and was therefore a party to that case.

Table 4
Assessed Value of Property Subject to Local Taxation in 1986
After Deduction of Exemptions

	Assessed value (millions of dollars)	Percentage
Locally assessed property:		
Real property	3,910,658	84.7
Personal property	466,253	10.1
State assessed property	242,816	5.3
Total	4,619,724	100.0

Source: 1987 Census of Goverments, vol. 2, table 3. Sum of components differs from total due to rounding.

Assessing Officers and by many state revenue agencies.[45] Requirements for training and certification vary widely among the states, as does the level of technical proficiency necessary to administer a property tax system. A thinly populated, homogeneous residential area might be served adequately by a local citizen willing to assume the position of town assessor. A major urban center requires staff and computer capacity sufficient to keep track of taxpayer identification, property records, sales and lease transactions, building costs and resale price levels, changes in property use, new construction, renovation, property loss, and eligibility for exemptions.

The most challenging aspect of assessment, assigning a value to each taxable parcel, has been revolutionized in recent decades by the development of computerized methods for predicting market values. Computer-assisted mass appraisal (CAMA) compares the characteristics of recently sold properties with those of properties that have not changed hands in order to estimate the market value of properties in this second group. The availability of data on large numbers of comparable properties permits the correlation of characteristics such as location, size, design, and type of construction with sale price. This allows a market value based on these features to be projected for other properties that have not been sold. These methods do not necessarily require a large, permanent assessment staff. State revenue departments sometimes provide computer support to small jurisdictions, and a number of commercial firms offer CAMA services on a contract basis.

---

45. J. Malme, *Assessment Administration Practices in the U.S. and Canada* (Chicago: International Association of Assessing Officers [IAAO], 1992, updated periodically), provides a comprehensive summary of current approaches to tax administration issues of this type. Section 12 lists assessor training and certification programs by state and province.

It has occasionally been suggested that appointed assessors, insulated from political pressure, may value property more accurately than those who are elected. Although there is some supporting evidence for this hypothesis from New York State, where there has been a long-term shift from election to appointment of town assessors, other empirical studies have found no difference in the accuracy of assessments on this basis,[46] perhaps because appointment by elected officials is itself not divorced from political pressure.[47]

Fractional Valuation and Classification

The amount of tax any given property owner must pay is the product of the assessed property value and the tax rate. There are several basic patterns that link these two elements of the assessment process. The law may call for a single uniform rate of tax levied on the full market value of the property. Alternately, it may prescribe a single uniform rate of tax on some specified fraction of full market value. For example, North Dakota statutes define the assessed value of taxable property as 50 percent of its full and true value, and taxable value as a percentage (9 percent for residential property, and 10 percent for other property) of assessed value.[48] In such a case the effective tax rate, or percentage of full market value represented by the tax, would be a corresponding percentage of the stated or nominal rate. Finally, the law may in either case call for a nonuniform system of taxation, with the effective tax rates differing according to property category, such as residential, commercial, or industrial. Such classification may be achieved either through varying the fraction of full value on which the assessment is made, or through varying the tax rates according to category, or both.

Beyond these patterns of legal and explicit classification there exist many varieties of extralegal classification, both deliberate and inadvertent, that vary the tax burden across property categories through inaccuracies in valuation. A failure to revalue property periodically will produce distortions in assessment as values rise in prosperous areas and fall in declining neighborhoods. If properties are revalued only when sales are recorded at the registry of deeds, parcels that once sold for similar amounts will continue to bear equivalent tax burdens as their market values later diverge. This illustrates the difference between the nominal tax rate, the rate prescribed by law, and the effective tax

---

46. D. Gaskell, "More Towns Joining Trend toward Appointed Assessors," in New York State Board of Equalization and Assessment, *The Survey*, March-April 1988, p. 1; J. Bowman and J. Mikesell, "Assessment Uniformity: The Standard and Its Attainment," *Property Tax Journal* 9 (1990): 219.

47. For a comprehensive introduction to issues of property tax administration, see the compilation by the IAAO, *Property Appraisal and Assessment Administration* (1990).

48. J. Malme, *Assessment Administration Practices in the U.S. and Canada* (1992), section 2, "Definition of Assessable Value."

rate, the actual percentage of true market value represented by the tax bill. In this example, property owners who have suffered a loss in value will bear a heavier effective tax rate than the owners of appreciating property because their tax bills will constitute a higher percentage of their property's market value, even though the nominal tax rate is the same in each case.[49]

This pattern may not be the result of simple inadvertence. Owners of property in prosperous neighborhoods may be more aware of property values and more likely to challenge an overassessment than other taxpayers. Moreover, the desire to benefit politically powerful groups has long motivated the relative over- and underassessment of entire classes of property. In the past this resulted in specific instances of overassessment of property owned by nonresidents in vacation areas, underassessment of farm property, overassessment of business property, and underassessment of single-family residential property nearly everywhere.

In this way the valuation of property for tax purposes actually becomes a part of the rate-setting process. A tax system with a single, uniform nominal rate for all property can in fact impose many different effective rates if different parcels are assessed at varying percentages of full market value. If all assessments were at the same percentage of full value, each taxpayer would face the same effective rate, even though this might differ from the nominal rate. If, however, the values assigned to different properties represent different percentages of full market value, the taxpayers whose valuations reflect a lower percentage of full value will pay tax at a lower effective rate than will others whose properties are assessed on a higher fraction of full value.

This is why *relative* overassessment can be critical to the distribution of the tax burden. A taxpayer whose property is valued at half of its full market price will be unlikely to protest this mistake. But if in fact most property in the jurisdiction is valued at one-quarter of its full market price, that taxpayer is bearing a disproportionate share of the total burden. When entire categories of property are subject to systematic under- and overvaluation, as in the examples above, the tax system has been "classified," even if no legal enactment has prescribed different tax rates for different types of properties.

Courts have in the past sometimes hesitated to overturn fractional assessment systems, reasoning that taxation on a uniform percentage of

---

49. A 1980 study by the New York University Graduate School of Public Administration found that 1979 assessment ratios (assessed value as a percentage of full market value) for residential property alone in New York City varied from 22.3 percent of market value for single-family houses to 68.3 percent for newer elevator buildings. Effective tax rates, actual tax bills as a percentage of full market value, ranged from 2.15 percent for one- and two-family houses to 5.19 percent for other housing to 5.55 percent for nonresidential property. Graduate School of Public Administration, New York University, *Real Property Tax Policy for New York City* (1980), I-11, I-14.

market value can in practice achieve the same results as full-value assessment, although with a higher nominal tax rate.[50] However, the assumption that all fractional assessments represent the same fraction of market value is almost never realistic. Moreover, failure to list a full-value figure on the tax bill inhibits challenges to incorrect assessments. A taxpayer who knows that the assessed value he sees represents only a small part of his property's market value is rarely inclined to challenge the assessment. If, however, as described above, that assessment represents a higher percentage of full market value than assessments of other property in the jurisdiction, the taxpayer is overassessed. Yet in order to prove that this situation exists, the taxpayer must determine the average level of assessment in the jurisdiction. This could be a formidable task where the average level is the composite of many unrelated instances of varying degrees of underassessment. The expense and difficulty of proving jurisdictionwide assessment levels has been an important impediment to taxpayer challenges in the past.[51]

Legal attacks on such practices have been increasingly successful in recent years, aided by legislative and administrative moves toward full-value assessment. However, it has not been uncommon for legal efforts overturning illegal tax classification of property to be followed by countermeasures to amend state tax statutes to permit such classification, explicitly imposing lower rates on favored classes such as single-family residential property. In response to a legal decision which would have required uniform full-value assessment,[52] the New York legislature in 1981 prohibited New York City from raising assessments on one-, two-, and three-family houses by more than 6 percent a year. As a result, the rapid housing inflation of the 1980s left the disparity between the effective tax on favored and disfavored properties more dramatic than ever. A 1990 study by the New York State comptroller echoed the New York University findings of a decade earlier, detailing "a distressing lack of uniformity within every property class and within almost every neighborhood in the city . . . . [T]he less valuable the property, the more it is taxed in relation to its market value."[53]

---

50. For a thorough examination of these developments, see the three-part article by Robert Beebe and Richard Sinnott, "In the Wake of Hellerstein: Whither New York?" in *Albany Law Review* 43 (1979): 203–93, 411–86, 777–860.

51. For example, in *Pierre Pellaton Apartments v. Board of Assessors*, 43 N.Y.2d 769, 372 N.E.2d 801, 401 N.Y.S.2d 1013 (1977), taxpayers who prevailed on the merits in challenging relative overassessment then sought statutory recovery of their costs. They requested reimbursement of $484,000, including $281,000 for expert testimony on appraisal and statistics, and were awarded $435,000.

52. *Hellerstein v. Assessor of Islip*, 37 N.Y.2d 1, 332 N.E.2d 279, 371 N.Y.S.2d 388 (1975). This case is discussed in Chapter 7, below.

53. A. Finder and R. Levine, "When Wealthy Pay Less Tax than the Other Homeown-

A study by Jerome F. Heavey[54] demonstrated how interjurisdictional assessment disparities can replicate these intrajurisdictional problems. He examined thirty-five Pennsylvania school districts whose boundaries included at least one city and one or more other local government units. For example, the Weston Area School District included the City of Weston, Wilson Township, Nether Township, and Bucks Borough. As a separate taxing jurisdiction, the school district imposed its own property tax, but like all of the other units it used values computed by the county assessor. Although the law required uniform assessment levels throughout the county, there was widespread relative overassessment in the core cities and underassessment in the outlying areas. Like most states, Pennsylvania established an agency to sample and compare assessment levels in different localities. When state aid to localities depends in part on the local tax capacity, this equalization process is necessary to prevent assessment inaccuracies from distorting the distribution of funds.[55] Heavey used equalization board data to conclude that in fourteen of the thirty-five districts studied the excess taxes collected from the cities equalled or exceeded 10 percent of the taxes collected by the cities for their own use. Five cities' annual school tax "overpayment" exceeded 20 percent of their own tax revenue, and in one case it exceeded 30 percent.

This example demonstrates one additional reason for the historical assessment of property at less than full market value. If all property within a taxing jurisdiction were assessed at the *same* percentage of full value, fractional assessment would have no necessary effect on tax liabilities. Nominal tax rates would rise, but effective rates, measured as a percentage of full market value, would remain unchanged. Prior discussion has focused on the incentives for nonuniform fractional assessment as a means of favoring one class of property over another. But even uniform fractional assessment provides an advantage

---

ers," *New York Times*, May 29, 1990, A1, p. B6. This study found that in 1988 and 1989 the average assessment error in the city was 43 percent for one-family houses. On a house valued at $200,000, the owner should have paid $1,153 in property taxes, but with a 43 percent assessment error, there was an equal chance that the owner paid taxes as high as $1,649 or as low as $657. The average error was even worse for other types of properties. In 1988 and 1989 the annual tax on a walk-up apartment building worth $300,000 could have been as little as $982 or as much as $6,100. *Id.*

54. J. Heavey, "Patterns of Property Tax Exploitation Produced by Infrequent Assessments," *American Journal of Economics & Sociology* 42 (1983): 441.

55. Equalization data can sometimes be used by taxpayers seeking to prove assessment levels in a jurisdiction; because the data are not compiled for this purpose, legislation has occasionally restricted their admissibility in such cases. See, for example, *Colt Industries, Inc. v. Finance Administrator*, 54 N.Y.2d 533, 430 N.E.2d 1290, 446 N.Y.S.2d 237 (1982), *appeal dismissed*, 459 U.S. 983 (1982); *Slewett & Farber v. Board of Assessors*, 80 A.D.2d 186, 438 N.Y.S.2d 544 (1981), *modified*, 54 N.Y.2d 547, 430 N.E.2d 1294, 446 N.Y.S.2d 241 (1982).

if the valuations are to be used by another level of government, such as a school district, to impose a tax on several jurisdictions, or if state aid is to be distributed according to a formula based on local property values. Either of these situations can give rise to competitive underassessment.

One common benchmark for inequality in assessment is the coefficient of dispersion. This measures the amount by which assessments vary from the common level, that deviation expressed as a percentage of the common level. For example, consider a community where assessments are generally set at 30 percent of market value. A taxpayer whose property is valued at 45 percent of market value will not receive a tax bill that is 15 percent too high. Rather, that bill will be 50 percent higher than the correct amount. If the prevailing assessment ratio is 60 percent, assessment at 75 percent of market value will produce a bill that is 25 percent higher than it would be if all assessments within the jurisdiction were uniform. Note that these examples deal only with inaccuracies in the valuation process and assume that the correct tax rate is applied in each case. The coefficient of dispersion measures the proportionate error in the ultimate tax by calculating the variation or "dispersion" of assessments from the prevailing rate as a percentage of that rate. The 1980 New York study cited above described a coefficient of dispersion of 20 percent as "a barely adequate assessment performance" for property subject to frequent sales, such as single-family housing, and found less than one-half of one percent of all housing in New York City to be in a class with a coefficient under this level.[56]

An explicit, legal system of tax classification differs significantly from one due to assessor bias or inaccuracy in valuation. Consider, for example, a statute calling for two rates of tax, one rate for residential property and a second, higher rate for all other property, with both rates imposed on a full market value base. Given accurate valuations, this system produces uniform tax burdens on all properties in a given class. By contrast, a system in which property values are updated only when a parcel is sold yields an array of effective tax rates—in theory, potentially as many tax rates as parcels in the jurisdiction, each rate determined by the relationship of the individual property's current market value to its previous sale price.

Property Tax Relief Measures

In addition to a full exemption for various classes of religious, educational and charitable, and governmental[57] property, most states offer an array of partial

---

56. New York University Graduate School of Public Administration, *Real Property Tax Policy for New York City* (1980), I-17, discussed above at note 49.

57. The federal government and its instrumentalities are immune from state and local taxation under the Supremacy Clause of the U.S. Constitution, Art. VI, §2, rather than

exemptions and tax reductions to benefit taxpayers deemed needy, worthy, or politically powerful, such as widows, veterans, and homeowners. All states offer tax reduction programs for qualifying farmland whose value in agricultural use is less than its market value for development. Two of the most important other tax relief measures are "circuit breakers" and homestead exemptions. Circuit breakers limit property taxes to a designated percentage of income; as their name implies, they are designed to protect against a tax overload. They generally are administered and financed by the state through an income tax credit, although some function as independent programs. As in the case of other income tax credits, special efforts are required to reach potential recipients who do not file income tax returns. The specific details of these programs vary widely among the states. Among the thirty-two states with circuit-breaker programs in effect in 1991, the average benefit to homeowners ranged from $55.06 in Hawaii to $593.45 in Maryland.[58]

"Homestead" exemptions or credits are the most common form of residential property tax relief, used in some form by forty-four states in 1991.[59] These reduce the tax on qualifying residential property, either by exempting a portion of its value or by extending a credit against the tax. Homestead exemptions may be limited to property owned by certain groups of taxpayers, such as low-income, elderly, or disabled homeowners, or they may apply to all owner-occupied residences. Some states provide tax relief to renters as well, such as an income tax deduction. Although the revenue loss from circuit-breaker programs is generally borne by state governments, in the case of homestead allowances it usually falls on localities. The cost of homestead relief programs in 1991 was estimated at $451 million in Illinois, $1.7 billion in Florida, and $3.3 billion in California.[60]

Tax benefits limited to specific groups sometimes face constitutional objections. A 1974 decision by the Supreme Court found no equal protection[61] violation in a Florida statute allowing a $500 property tax exemption to widows, but not to widowers.[62] Some exemptions are available only to state

---

exempted by any provision of state law. This doctrine was first enunciated in *McCulloch v. Maryland*, 17 U.S. 316 (1819), which overturned a Maryland tax on notes issued by the Bank of the United States.

58. ACIR, *Significant Features of Fiscal Federalism 1992* (1992), vol. 1, table 41. See also R. Ebel and J. Ortbal, "Direct Residential Property Tax Relief," *Intergovernmental Perspective*, Spring 1989, p. 9.

59. ACIR, *Significant Features of Fiscal Federalism 1992* (1992), vol. 1, table 40.

60. ACIR, *Significant Features of Fiscal Federalism 1992* (1992), vol. 1, table 42.

61. U.S. Constitution, Amend. XIV, §1, provides that no state shall "deny to any person within its jurisdiction the equal protection of the laws."

62. *Kahn v. Shevin*, 416 U.S. 351 (1974).

residents, and are denied to nonresidents owning vacation property in the state. Provisions of this type have been upheld against attack under the equal protection clause and the privileges and immunities[63] clause of the United States Constitution.[64] By contrast, the Supreme Court held in 1985 that a New Mexico property tax exemption limited to Vietnam veterans who resided in the state before May 8, 1976, violated the federal equal protection clause, failing to meet even the minimal standard of rational relationship to a legitimate state purpose.[65] The court held that a state "may not favor established residents over new residents based on the view that the State may take care of 'its own' . . . . Newcomers, by establishing bona fide residence in the State, become the State's 'own' and may not be discriminated against . . . ."[66]

Tax relief measures must also satisfy the provisions found in nearly all state constitutions requiring uniformity in property taxation. In a typical dispute the Idaho Supreme Court considered a homeowners' exemption passed by initiative in 1982 exempting the lesser of the first $50,000 or 50 percent of the value of an owner-occupied residence. To maintain revenue, property tax rates rose by approximately one-third between 1982 and 1983, resulting in a significant increase in the tax burden on other properties. Owners of rental property in Bonneville County challenged this exemption as a violation of the state constitution's requirement that "every person or corporation shall pay a tax in proportion to the value of his, her, or its property," and that "[a]ll taxes shall be uniform on the same class of subjects within the territorial limits of the authority levying the tax." The decline in total taxable value caused by the exemption resulted in a rise in tax rates. The

---

63. U.S. Constitution, Art. IV, §2, cl. 1, provides, "The Citizens of each State shall be entitled to all the Privileges and Immunities of Citizens in the several States." This "does not preclude disparity of treatment in the many situations where there are perfectly valid independent reasons for it . . . . [But] it does bar discrimination against citizens of other States where there is no substantial reason for the discrimination beyond the mere fact that they are citizens of other States." *Toomer v. Witsell,* 334 U.S. 385, 396 (1948) (striking down South Carolina license fee for shrimp boats of $2,500 for nonresidents and $25 for residents). The privileges and immunities of national, as opposed to state, citizenship are protected by the Fourteenth Amendment, §1: "No State shall make or enforce any law which shall abridge the privileges or immunities of citizens of the United States . . . . " However, the Supreme Court has interpreted this so narrowly as to render it nearly irrelevant to state and local taxation. See, e.g., *Colgate v. Harvey,* 296 U.S. 404 (1935) (the only case to strike down a state enactment under this section; overturned a state income tax limited to dividends and interest earned outside the state); *Madden v. Kentucky,* 309 U.S. 83 (1940) (overruling *Colgate v. Harvey*).

64. *Rubin v. Glaser,* 83 N.J. 299, 416 A.2d 382 (1980), *appeal dismissed,* 449 U.S. 977 (1980); *Baker v. Matheson,* 607 P.2d 233 (Utah 1979).

65. *Hooper v. Bernalillo County Assessor,* 472 U.S. 612 (1985).

66. *Id.* at 613.

effect of the increased homeowners' exemption was illustrated by the example in table 5, considering two properties of equivalent market value.

Table 5
Effect of Homeowners Exemption

	Assessed value	Tax liability	
		1982	1983
Owner-occupied property	$100,000	$1,453	$1,085
Other property	$100,000	$1,615	$2,170

The Idaho Supreme Court found this result sanctioned by the state constitution's allowance for such exemptions from taxation "as shall seem necessary and just," rejecting the argument that this provision permitted only complete exemptions and not partial exemptions equivalent to disparate tax rates.[67]

The exemption of property used for religious purposes raises important first amendment questions as to the ability of a state to question the legitimacy of any given religious sect. For example, a 1981 Minnesota case[68] rejected both a religious exemption and a homestead exemption for the residence of a family whose eleven members formed the complete original congregation of the Ideal Life Church. Seven neighbors were added later. The Ideal Life Church had no doctrine, no belief in a supreme being, and no religious ceremonies except a monthly dinner.

That family had obtained a charter for fifty dollars from the Universal Life Church, an organization that figured in a more serious tax-avoidance scheme in New York state. More than 200 of the 236 full-time resident taxpayers in the town of Hardenburgh in upstate Ulster County, including the town assessor, claimed a religious property tax exemption after obtaining Universal Life Church charters by mail. This left the property tax burden almost entirely on vacation property owned by nonresidents. After eight years of litigation, the exemptions were overturned because the property was owned by individu-

---

67. *Simmons v. Idaho State Tax Commission*, 111 Idaho 343, 723 P.2d 887, 892-893 (1986). For a comprehensive review of all state constitutional provisions on uniformity in property taxation, see W. Newhouse, *Constitutional Uniformity and Equality in State Taxation*, 2d ed. (1984).

68. *Ideal Life Church of Lake Elmo v. County of Washington*, 304 N.W.2d 308 (Minn. 1981).

als and not held in trust for members of a church. The New York Court of Appeals found this requirement a reasonable regulation and not an interference with or discrimination against any religious practice or belief.[69]

The New York State Division of Equalization and Assessment's annual comprehensive survey of exempt property in that state found that approximately 26 percent of the market value of all real property in the state was exempt from taxation in 1990. In ten of the state's sixty-two cities at least half the total property value was exempt; the figure for New York City was 31 percent.[70] Studies of this sort are not common, but in their absence there is no way to measure the cumulative economic impact of exemption measures.[71]

Exempt organizations owning large amounts of property sometimes make voluntary payments in lieu of taxes to offset the cost of public services provided to them. Harvard University has described itself as the first nonprofit institution to make such payments, having begun this practice in 1929. Its 1989 payments to the city of Cambridge totalled slightly under $1 million, compared with taxes and fees on its nonexempt properties of $4.5 million. Yale University began in-lieu payments to the city of New Haven in 1990 with an agreement to pay $1.16 million for fire services, an amount approximately equivalent to 6 percent of the city's annual fire department

---

69. *Town of Hardenburgh v. State of New York*, 52 N.Y.2d 536, 421 N.E.2d 795, 439 N.Y.S.2d 303 (1981), *appeal dismissed*, 454 U.S. 958 (1981). The actual legitimacy of the religious charters was never litigated. The political problem of exemptions was greatly diminished by the transfer of 5,000 acres of parkland from exempt organizations to the state, which pays local property tax on it. "Tax Rebellion," *New York Times*, March 13, 1983, p. 49. For other cases on the tax status of nontraditional religions, see *Holy Spirit Association for the Unification of World Christianity v. Tax Commission*, 55 N.Y.2d 512, 450 N.Y.S.2d 292, 435 N.E.2d 662 (1982) (finding the Reverend Moon's Unification Church to be a religious rather than a political organization) and *Foundation of Human Understanding v. Department of Revenue*, 301 Or. 254, 722 P.2d 1 (1986).

70. New York State Board of Equalization and Assessment, Exemptions from Real Property Taxation in New York State (1992). New York state law requires assessors to furnish a comprehensive annual listing of exempt property, and the state board to publish an annual summary of exemptions. N.Y. Real Property Tax Law, §496. The New York exemption is analyzed in depth in P. Swords, *Charitable Real Property Tax Exemptions in New York State* (1981).

71. The 1987 Census of Governments provides estimates of the value excluded from the tax base by total exemptions in eighteen states, and by partial exemptions in thirty states, but notes that "it is unlikely that assessors devote more than minimal appraisal resources to valuing excluded property (since no tax revenue stems from the activity) . . . ." 1987 Census of Governments, *Taxable Property Values* (1987), vol. 2, tables J–K, at XX. A review of the background of the tax exemption for charitable property and a state-by-state summary of provisions relating to it may be found in H. Wellford and J. Gallagher, *Unfair Competition? The Challenge to Charitable Tax Exemption* (1988).

budget.[72] The federal government also sometimes provides voluntary payments in lieu of taxes to local jurisdictions.[73]

An exemption from property taxes generally does not carry an equivalent exemption from special assessments, which are imposed to cover the cost of public improvements, such as sidewalks or street lighting. Special assessments are often allocated among the benefited properties according to a physical measure, such as street frontage, rather than valuation. The distinction between a property tax and a special assessment has been considered in many cases.[74]

Multiuse facilities owned by charitable or educational institutions are sometimes found to be partially exempt and partially taxable. For example, the public cafeteria or gymnasium in a YMCA could be treated as equivalent to a commercial restaurant or health club rather than as part of an exempt institution. Space for doctors' offices on hospital premises or in adjacent office buildings owned by the hospital has long been subject to disputes of this sort.[75]

---

72. J. Barron, "Yale Will Pay $2.6 Million to New Haven," *New York Times,* April 3, 1990, p. B1. In these situations university officials generally stress the voluntary nature of the payments and the services provided to the community by the university, such as maintenance of public roads on campus, while local officials point to the unreimbursed services received by the exempt institution and the reduction in the local tax base through exemptions. For example, this article reported that the University of Scranton makes in-lieu payments of $120,000 annually to the city and county for fire services. It quoted the university president as saying, "It's voluntary . . . . I think it's appropriate for us to do it, even though ultimately this has to come from tuition . . . . We run a very close budget." The Scranton fire department superintendent replied, "I believe they should pay at least a million."

73. See generally ACIR, *Payments in Lieu of Taxes on Federal Real Property* (1981), which found, "there is no guiding principle regarding the extent to which the federal government as a property owner should contribute to the financial support of state and local governments."

74. For example, *Zelinger v. City and County of Denver,* 724 P.2d 1356 (Colo. 1986), considered a charge for storm drainage facilities in the county of Denver. The charge rose with a parcel's ratio of "impervious" land, developed and therefore no longer absorbing rainfall, to "pervious" land. The court held that this charge was not a tax, and therefore need not comply with the uniformity provisions of the Colorado constitution. It was found to be a special assessment rather than a tax because it was directed only against users of the public improvement and all revenue raised by it was devoted to the maintenance, operation, or development of the improvement.

75. *Little Falls Hospital v. Board of Assessors,* 348 N.Y.S.2d 856, 75 Misc.2d 731 (1973) found rental space for private medical practices taxable, as any office building would be. The lower court in *Genesee Hospital, Inc. v. Wagner,* 76 Misc.2d 281, 350 N.Y.S.2d 582 (1973), rev'd, 47 A.D.2d 37, 364 N.Y.S.2d 934 (1975), aff'd, 39 N.Y.2d 863, 352 N.E.2d 133, 386 N.Y.S.2d 216 (1976), took the opposite position, finding the doctors' office building to further the hospital's exempt purpose by making its Rochester location more attractive to doctors. The opinion stressed the bad weather and high taxes

Taxation of partial interests in exempt property is the rule rather than the exception when an exempt organization leases its property for commercial use. Even when the underlying full ownership interest cannot be taxed, the leasehold may be taxed, and may in fact be assigned a value equivalent to the full value of the property. This situation has arisen frequently with respect to federal government property leased to defense contractors. Although the federal interest is immune from state and local tax, the Supreme Court has held that a tax on the nonexempt use could be equivalent to the value of the property itself. The court found "no essential difference so far as constitutional tax immunity is concerned between taxing a person for using property he possesses and taxing him for possessing property he uses when in both instances he uses the property for his own private ends."[76] Where such a tax is imposed, the taxing jurisdiction has no ability to seize the underlying federal property as a means of enforcing payment of the tax on the leasehold. Nor may leased federal property be taxed if property leased from state or local governments is exempt.[77]

A different issue arises in evaluating the desirability of tax reductions designed to promote construction and economic development. New York City has had a long and controversial history of granting abatements and partial exemptions for this purpose. In its fiscal crisis of the 1970s the city obtained state approval for exemptions of up to 95 percent of the first year's taxes due on new construction, a provision that benefited the AT&T, IBM, and Philip Morris, Inc. headquarters, among other major projects. This caused an outcry in 1987 when AT&T, which had received $42 million in tax reductions, announced plans to move its staff to New Jersey. The *New York Times* reported that even after AT&T agreed to limit these transfers, "questions remained about whether the city should have gotten AT&T and some of the other beneficiaries of the tax break program to put job-related commitments on paper in the first place." Moreover, there was no means of ascertaining how much construction would have taken place absent these incentives. "The less a company needed something," said John Mollenkopf,

---

suffered by residents of upstate New York, but was nonetheless reversed on appeal. *Barnes Hospital v. Leggett,* 589 S.W.2d 241 (Mo. 1979), abandoned Missouri's all-or-nothing approach to the exemption, ordering an allocation of taxable value to the portions of a doctors' office building not used solely for nonprofit purposes. A dissenting opinion argued that such an allocation was impractical, pointing to difficulties in imposing a lien for unpaid taxes on only a part of a building. This approach also raises many difficulties encountered in the valuation and assessment of taxes on partial interests generally.

76. *City of Detroit v. Murray Corp.,* 355 U.S. 489, at 493 (1958).

77. *U.S. v. City of Manassas,* 830 F.2d 530 (4th Cir. 1987), *aff'd,* 485 U.S. 1017 (1988).

a representative of the City Planning Commissioner, "the more likely they were to have high-priced talent arguing that they should get it."[78]

The Economics of the Property Tax: Incidence Analysis

Any evaluation of the political, legal, and administrative aspects of the property tax is complicated by the fact that many questions concerning its economic effects remain unresolved. In particular, an active debate in recent years over the impact or incidence of the tax has attempted to clarify which parties actually bear its ultimate economic burden, a critical factor in considering the fairness, political merit, distributional consequences, or incentive effects of any tax measure.

Because the supply of land is fixed, it has long been accepted that a tax on bare land cannot be shifted forward from the landowner to the tenants. If the pretax rent was set at its most profitable level, the landowner is in theory powerless to recoup the tax through rent increases. This reasoning provided the impetus for the "single tax" movement of the nineteenth century. The populist reformer Henry George argued in his 1879 work *Progress and Poverty* that a confiscatory tax on bare land value could replace all other forms of taxation without affecting economic production. Moreover, he considered a confiscatory tax just, as rising land values were the results of social growth rather than the landowner's own efforts. A number of varied jurisdictions, including Jamaica, districts in Australia and New Zealand, and the city of Pittsburgh, have experimented with variations on a site value tax, or tax on bare land value, including "graded" taxes that fall more heavily on land than on buildings.

Traditionally, a tax on buildings was analyzed differently from a tax on land, because the supply of buildings, unlike that of land, can be increased through new construction or decreased through a failure to maintain existing improvements. Therefore, in the long term the supply of building capital will respond to a tax by reducing the building stock, resulting in less construction and higher prices. Because any number of productive investments will compete for capital, this line of reasoning assumed that the burden of the property tax would be borne by users of property rather than suppliers of capital. In the case of business property, the potential for shifting the tax to suppliers or customers left the ultimate incidence uncertain. In the case of residential property, where this possibility did not exist, it was assumed that the long-run incidence of the tax was on the homeowner or renter. Studies of housing consumption have differed as to whether expenditures on housing

---

78. S. Verhovek, "Builders Got Tax Breaks, but What Did the City Receive?" *New York Times*, May 24, 1987, p. E6.

remain proportional to income or form a lower percentage of income as income rises. The widespread belief that the percentage of income devoted to housing falls as income rises has supported the popular view that the residential property tax is regressive.

These assumptions concerning the incidence of a tax on building value have been questioned in the past two decades. The newer analysis has considered the property tax to consist of two elements: a basic rate equivalent to the tax common to all forms of wealth or capital, and the additional tax that would bring the rate to the actual amount paid by real property in a given jurisdiction. That second element could be in the form of a subsidy where actual property taxes were below the hypothetical common tax rate on capital. A tax on all wealth or capital would have incidence effects similar to those of a tax on bare land. To the extent the supply of capital was fixed, owners of capital would bear the economic burden of the tax. Under this approach only the second, variable tax could be avoided by withdrawing building stock from high-tax areas. The first component would remain in place whatever form the owner's investment might take. From this perspective, the uniform portion of the property tax may be viewed as part of a nationwide tax on capital. Because capital ownership generally increases with income, to this extent the property tax would be progressive. The second element of the tax, which varies with the local rate, would be a selective tax on certain forms of capital, and therefore appropriately analyzed under the older view of property taxes.

These two approaches are not mutually exclusive. In some circumstances, a change in the property tax should clearly be analyzed as a local, selective measure. This would be the case if a specific jurisdiction were contemplating a change in its tax base or rate. On the other hand, nationwide property tax changes would be appropriate for consideration under the newer view of property taxes as in part a uniform tax on capital. Recent efforts to abolish residential property taxes in Ireland and Great Britain illustrate the type of dramatic legislative changes that require a broader economic perspective than was traditionally applied to this tax.

A further complication in determining the incidence of the property tax concerns the process of "capitalization," by which the imposition of a tax on durable property in fixed supply—such as land—reduces its price. A buyer comparing the purchase of real property and an alternative investment, identical in every other respect but not subject to the property tax, would judge the taxable realty to be worth less than the nontaxable investment, the reduction being equivalent to the present value of the annual real estate taxes. This suggests that the economic burden of a capitalized tax is borne by the owner holding the taxable asset at the time the tax was first imposed, because the tax did not reduce the price that owner paid but will reduce the price he receives in the future.

Consider the implications of yet another perspective on the property tax, one that views it as the equivalent of a fee for local services. This position has gained much attention in recent years, particularly because many services typically provided by local government lend themselves more readily to this analysis than do such federal functions as national defense and foreign relations. The Treasury Department study initiating the 1986 Tax Reform Act went so far as to contend that both state and local taxes are no more than "the cost paid by citizens for public services provided by State and local governments, such as public schools, roads, and police and fire protection," equating these with personal consumption expenditures.[79] To the extent a property tax may be considered a charge for local government services it would not properly be analyzed as a "tax" at all. Questions of incidence and market distortion that are critical to understanding the economic operation of a tax on goods or services are largely inapplicable to an analysis of the price of those goods or services themselves.[80]

The simplifications involved in all aspects of this description are evident. The relationships among income, wealth, and property ownership are not well understood and differ according to the period over which they are measured. Taxes on capital generally are far from uniform, and the extent to which the property tax can be analyzed as consisting in part of such a uniform tax is uncertain. Neither the supply of capital nor even the supply of land is fixed in the long run for any specific jurisdiction. A city may annex neighboring land; farmland in one locality may become an office park or residential complex serving another urban center; even the physical supply of land may be increased through reclamation operations. It is important to

---

79. *Treasury Report on Tax Simplification and Reform*, U.S. Treasury Department, Report to the President, November 27, 1984, Ch. 5, §IV(B)(1) ("To the extent that state and local taxes merely reflect the benefits of services provided to taxpayers, there is no more reason for a Federal subsidy for spending by state and local governments than for private spending.")

80. "If consumers choose residential locations based on the property tax and service package offered by the local government and if some mechanism arises to maintain the equilibrium, consumers who desire the same fiscal package are grouped together. The property tax is the 'price' for consuming local services, with all consumers paying the costs that their consumption imposes on the government. In that case, it does not make sense to separately discuss the incidence of the tax separate from the provision of public services because the tax simply reflects the demand for services." R. Fisher, *State and Local Public Finance* (1988), p. 156. "If consumers treat the local property tax as a price for public services, then this price should not distort the housing market any more than the price of eggs should distort the housing market." B. Hamilton, "Property Taxes and the Tiebout Hypothesis: Some Empirical Evidence," in E. Mills and W. Oates (eds.), *Fiscal Zoning and Land Use Controls, the Economic Issues* (1975), p. 13, quoted in H. Rosen, *Public Finance*, 1st ed. (1985), p. 488.

recognize that many aspects of the economic impact of the property tax are not resolved, and that common generalizations as to its regressive nature may in fact not be supported by economic theory.[81]

---

81. These issues are discussed in detail in "Property Tax: Economic Analysis and Effects," in R. Fisher, *State and Local Public Finance* (1988), chapter 8, and treated more generally in many introductory public finance texts, including R. Musgrave and P. Musgrave, *Public Finance in Theory and Practice*, 5th ed. (1989); H. Rosen, *Public Finance*, 3d ed. (1992); and C. Shoup, *Public Finance* (1969), chapter 15. The basic technical articles in this area are C. Tiebout, "A Pure Theory of Local Expenditures," *Journal of Political Economy* 64 (1956): 416; P. Mieszkowski, "On the Theory of Tax Incidence," *Journal of Political Economy* 75 (June 1967): 250; P. Mieszkowski, "The Property Tax: An Excise Tax or a Profits Tax?" *Journal of Public Economics* (April 1972): 73; P. Mieszkowski and G. Zodrow, "Taxation and the Tiebout Model: The Differential Effects of Head Taxes, Taxes on Land Rents, and Property Taxes," *Journal of Economic Literature* 27 (September 1989): 1098. A less technical work, accessible to the noneconomist, on the distinction between the "old" and "new" views of property tax incidence is H. Aaron, *Who Pays the Property Tax: A New View* (Brookings Institution, 1975).

2 VALUATION OF PROPERTY FOR TAX PURPOSES

Introduction

This chapter deals with the basic principles of valuation for tax purposes, particularly the relationship of the three methods of valuation based on cost, income, and comparable sales. Ideally, in a competitive market, these three measures might be expected to converge. The cost of producing a new structure sets an upper bound to the price buyers would bid for an existing one, and bids are calculated by reference to the income expected from the property. Perfectly competitive markets are rare, however, especially in the case of real property, where each parcel is, at least in location, unique. Mathematical precision is further undermined by the array of assumptions required for each approach, assumptions about such matters as interest rates, depreciation, obsolescence, and the adjustments to sales prices of comparables necessary to account for differences in the properties. Parties who find it worthwhile to carry their disputes to the point of a fully argued and reported appellate decision generally have a good deal at stake, which means that the courts are faced with alternative approaches to assessment, or even to the same valuation method, whose results do not converge at all.

The cases in this chapter illustrate several different judicial responses to the problem of correlating divergent valuation results. In the *G.R.F.* case, the New York Court of Appeals expressed some impatience with any attempt at correlation, declaring, "Pragmatism . . . requires adjustment when the economic realities prevent placing the properties in neat logical valuation boxes." The Oregon Supreme Court, in the *Medical Building Land* case, undertook a more studied and methodical approach, but candidly referred to this as "the somewhat mystical process appraisers refer to as 'correlation.'" In the *Dotson* case, the alternative valuation approaches presented to the Georgia Court of Appeals actually represented incompatible assumptions as to what constituted the property subject to tax. This demonstrates the limits of "correlation," and also provides the setting for the agricultural-use cases considered in the following chapter.

Methods of Valuing Property

The property tax is usually computed on an ad valorem basis as a percentage of the fair market value of the land and buildings subject to tax. Simply assigning an accurate fair market value to all taxable property in a jurisdiction annually is a formidable task. Moreover, the very meaning of fair market value can be ambiguous when property is of a type not frequently bought and sold. Major industrial plants, utility property, and buildings designed for the needs of specific owners often fall into this category. Disputes as to the proper method of measuring the market value of such properties may affect hundreds of millions of dollars of a jurisdiction's tax base. Even property without unusual physical features may raise questions as to how legal restrictions, such as zoning, rent control, or lease agreements, should affect the calculation of market value. In such cases a seemingly technical choice among valuation methods in effect determines the base of the property tax.

The three primary methods of valuing property are usually termed the cost, income, and comparable sales (or "market") approaches. The cost approach estimates market value on the basis of a property's cost of construction, reduced to reflect obsolescence and physical depreciation. The income approach computes market price by estimating the present value of the future stream of net rental income a purchaser could expect to realize from an investment in the property. Finally, the comparable sales approach estimates value by adjusting the purchase price of similar properties to account for differences in size, location, construction, and date of sale; it may also examine the results of a recent arm's-length sale of the property at issue itself. It is somewhat misleading to call the comparable sales approach the "market" approach, because all three approaches are designed to estimate current market value.

In *Northerly Centre Corp. v. County of Ramsey,* 311 Minn. 335, 248 N.W.2d 923, 925 n. 2 (1976), the Supreme Court of Minnesota described these "three recognized approaches to valuation of real property" in this way:

> Under the "cost approach," one determines the cost of constructing the building and subtracts an amount for depreciation to determine the building's present value and then adds the value of the underlying land. Under the "income approach," one determines the income that the property should reasonably be expected to generate, subtracts the expenses that should reasonably be incurred, and capitalizes this net "economic" income at a rate of capitalization which investors would reasonably expect to obtain. Under the "market data approach," one surveys the market to determine if there have been a sufficient number of recent voluntary sales of similar property to provide dependable information as to the selling rate of "comparable property."

In *Rebelwood, Ltd. v. Hinds County,* 544 So.2d 1356, nn. 5–7 (Miss. 1989) the Supreme Court of Mississippi analyzed a number of treatises and legal opinions and offered the following summary of the three approaches to value:

> The cost approach involves a determination of the "current" cost of reproducing property less loss in value from deterioration and functional and economic

obsolescence—accrual depreciation. There are five basic steps involved in this approach:

1. The estimate of the *land value* as if vacant,

2. The estimate of the current *cost of reproducing or replacing* the existing improvements,

3. The estimate of accrued depreciation from all causes,

4. Deduction of accrued depreciation estimate to arrive at indicated value of improvements,

5. The addition of the land value to the indicated value of the improvements to develop indicated property value.

The market data approach involves an analysis of actual arm's length sales of property similar to the subject property. An application of this approach involves five basic steps:

1. [Seek] out similar properties for which pertinent sales, listings, offerings, and/or rental data are available.

2. [Ascertain] the nature of the conditions of sale, including the price, terms, motivating forces, and its bona fide nature.

3. [Analyze] each of the comparable properties' important attributes with the corresponding ones of the property being appraised, under the general divisions of time, location and other characteristics, including physical and economic.

4. [Consider] the dissimilarities in the characteristics disclosed in Step 3, in terms of their probable effect on the sale price.

5. [Formulate] in the light of the comparisons thus made, an opinion of the relative value of the subject property as a whole, or, where appropriate, by applicable units, compared with each of the similar properties.

The income or earnings approach determines value by reference to the property's income-producing capacity under *typical* management . . . . In a commercial rental context, the four steps basically followed are:

1. Obtain the rent schedules and the percentage of occupancy for the subject property and for comparable properties for the current year and for several past years. This information provides gross rental data and the trend in rentals and occupancy. This data is then compared and adjusted to an effective estimate of gross income which the subject property may reasonably be expected to produce.

2. Obtain expense data, such as taxes, insurance and operating costs being paid by the subject property and by comparable properties. The trend in these expenses is also significant.

3. Estimate the remaining economic life of the building to establish the probable duration of its income, or, alternately, estimate the suitable period of ownership before resale.

4. Select the appropriate capitalization method and the applicable technique and appropriate rate for processing the net income.

In a perfectly functioning competitive market, with no single buyer or seller able to influence sale price, market value could reflect the factors measured by each of these three valuation methods. The cost of building a replacement structure would act as a ceiling to the price any seller could achieve, and buyers would bid an amount reflecting income yielded by alternate investments.

The reality of property valuation is far more complex. The unique location of any parcel of land and inevitable variations among any set of buildings prevent even closely similar structures from serving as perfect substitutes for one another. Moreover, buildings that are truly unusual, such as industrial assembly plants or manufacturing structures designed for a specific purpose, may lack comparable sales altogether. Income data for a commercial structure will often reflect a combined return on business carried on there together with a return to the property itself. Therefore, use of such data for purposes of real property taxation will require estimation of that portion of the income due to the real property alone. Property which is rented may be subject to complex lease provisions and divisions of financial responsibility between the landlord and tenants, leaving the nominal rental figure only a starting point for calculating the return to real property.

There are also practical difficulties in applying these approaches. For example, many items of business income data are proprietary information that the owner will not divulge under ordinary circumstances. Use of the cost approach for older structures presents special difficulties, requiring an estimate of depreciation due to outmoded design and neighborhood deterioration, as well as to physical decay. These factors may be impossible to estimate in the absence of income data.

Notes on Valuation

1. If the market value of property has been diminished through the owner's neglect, should that action be "rewarded" with a lower assessment? *Inmar Associates, Inc. v. Borough of Carlstadt*, 214 N.J. Super. 256, 518 A.2d 1110 (1986), *aff'd in part and rev'd in part*, 112 N.J. 593, 549 A.2d 38 (1988), considered the site of a former industrial solvent recovery plant that had been operated by a tenant, Inmar Associates. The plant had been shut by the New Jersey Department of Environmental Protection, which took custody of the property and imposed a lien on Inmar's assets to pay for the cost of removing toxic wastes from the site. On the assessment date there could be found on the land, in the words of the New Jersey Tax Court, "approximately 60 storage tanks and tank wagons containing various substances, including, but not limited to, oils, sludge, crude thinner, methanol/water, solvents and paint residues." These cases considered what effect, if any, the presence of toxic waste required by law to be

removed before sale should have upon a calculation of the property's market value. The appellate division found a reduction for this factor contrary to the legislative intent to discourage pollution:

> Basically, where police power is involved, government action is undertaken for the public good. Where the situation involves privately created contamination, remedial action is required because the private party intentionally or unintentionally disregarded the public good. It would indeed be incongruous for the Legislature to enact strict liability provisions for cleanup of hazardous wastes as it has done and at the same time intend that a polluter's tax assessment may be reduced because of the contamination. That would tend to encourage rather than discourage polluting which would be contrary to the legislatively formulated public policy of protecting the environment against toxic pollution. We do not perceive any legislative intent to permit an owner-created exemption to taxation based upon contamination by an owner or its tenant. Polluters can hardly complain of lowered fair market values to a hypothetical buyer because of contamination, which is caused by the business activities of the landowner or its commercial tenant. In the present cases it was the contamination and not the cleanup legislation which lowered the land values in the eyes of hypothetical buyers.[1]

The New Jersey Supreme Court disagreed, finding the constitutional mandate for uniformity in valuation and the legislative provision for assessment at "true value" to require consideration of the effect of these costs upon market value. "We would be no more able to alter that standard to effectuate environmental policy than is the Legislature able to alter that standard to effectuate economic policy." 549 A.2d at 41.

The *Inmar* case raises many questions that illustrate the conceptual as well as computational problems encountered in the valuation process:

(1) The New Jersey Supreme Court stated that the contaminated property had a "distinct 'value in use' to the owner so long as the owner continued to operate the facility," even if state law would not permit a sale in this contaminated condition. If this is so, should the "value in use" be considered a "market value" for tax purposes?

(2) If the removal of contamination is required by law before any sale, should the fair market value for tax purposes be based on a hypothetical sale price increased by the cost of this expensive procedure, as a capital improvement?

(3) Does a tax reflecting a lower market value for contaminated property "reward" the taxpayer? Does a tax reflecting a higher market value for a well-designed and maintained structure "penalize" its owner?

---

1. 518 A.2d at 1115.

2. The problem of separating the value of real property from the value of any business associated with it has been a long-standing challenge to property taxation. Only the income yielded by the property, the net rental value, reflects the value of the real property as opposed to the value of licenses, franchises, business good will, and commercial operations that are not subject to the property tax. In *Susquehanna Power Co. v. State Tax Commission,* 283 U.S. 291 (1931), a hydroelectric power company argued that the lands flooded by its dam derived their value from the company's authority (from the Federal Power Commission) to produce electric power. Therefore, it argued that a 1919 assessment of the submerged lands at over two million dollars constituted in effect a taxation of that license. The Supreme Court rejected this position:

> [T]he distinction has long been taken between a privilege or franchise granted by the Government to a private corporation in order to effect some governmental purpose, and the property employed by the grantee in the exercise of the privilege, but for private business advantage.
>
> . . . .
>
> No basis is laid in the present record for assailing the tax on constitutional grounds, either because the Commission has placed a higher value on appellant's lands than on others having a similar location and use, or because it has directly taxed appellant's license. The contention urged is that the lands are assessed at a higher value than they were before they were submerged, and higher than farm uplands in the neighborhood, and that since their use as a part of appellant's power project is rendered possible only by the federal license and by the water in the river, the assessment at the higher value, in effect, involves a forbidden tax on the license, and taxation of appellant for the value of the waters of a navigable stream.
>
> Accepting, as we must on this record, the valuation of the Commission as neither excessive nor discriminatory, we can perceive no basis, either legal or economic, for relieving appellant from the burden of the tax by attempting the segregation of a part of that value and attributing it to independent legal interests, not subject to taxation, because those interests have a favorable influence on the value of the property.
>
> An important element in the value of the land is the use to which it may be put. That may vary with its location and its relationship to the property . . . .
>
> A large part of the value of property in civilized communities has been built up by its inter-related uses; but it is a value ultimately reflected in earning capacity and the price at which the property may be sold, and hence is an element to which weight may appropriately be given in determining its taxable value. It has never been thought that the taxation of such property at its enhanced value is in effect taxation of its owner for the property of others.[2]

---

2. 283 U.S. at 294–96.

Do you find the Supreme Court's reasoning persuasive? Should "market value" be calculated at the amount for which this submerged property could be sold to a buyer with a Federal Power Commission license to use it for hydroelectric power generation, or to a buyer without such a license? Does this situation pose the same distinction between "market value" and "value in use" as that discussed with regard to the *Inmar* case above?

G.R.F., INC. V. BOARD OF ASSESSORS
41 N.Y.2d 512, 362 N.E.2d 597, 393 N.Y.S.2d 965
Court of Appeals of New York, 1977

BREITEL, Chief Judge.

In a tax certiorari proceeding, petitioner G.R.F., Inc., owner of Gimbel's department store in the Roosevelt Field Regional Shopping Center, seeks a reduction in the assessment of the land and building owned by it. Supreme Court granted the reduction, in part; the Appellate Division affirmed; and the Nassau County Board of Assessors appeals.

There should be an affirmance. The trial court, in reducing the assessments, rejected both the value arrived at by petitioner, using exclusively a capitalization of income approach, and the value urged by the Board of Assessors, using a computation based only on reproduction cost less depreciation. For the reasons to be discussed, the rejection of each theory of valuation as an exclusive basis was not error, and the adaptation of both on economic analysis was appropriate.

The Gimbel's store was built in 1962. The owner and developer of Roosevelt Field, in return for Gimbel's agreement to construct and operate a department store in the shopping center, conveyed the necessary land to Gimbel's. The owner-developer had previously done the excavation and foundation work and now agreed to contribute $1,320,139.48 toward the building construction. As part of the arrangement the developer guaranteed Gimbel's minimum gross annual sales of $14,000,000 and agreed to pay Gimbel's 3% of the deficit. Gimbel's agreed to pay parking and tunnel fees of ½% of the excess of sales over $14,000,000. Most of the remainder of the vast shopping center consists of retail stores rented by Roosevelt Field to individual merchants. At issue are the tax assessments only of the Gimbel's property for the period of 1963 to 1972.

Capitalization of income generally provides an acceptable and, in the absence of market data, a preferred method of valuing rental property [citations omitted]. Where, however, a building is held for the owner's own use, and especially where the building bears the owner's name, income capitalization may not adequately reflect the property's total value (*Matter of Seagram & Sons v. Tax Comm.,* 18 A.D.2d 109, 112, 116, 238 N.Y.S.2d 228, 231, 235, affd., 14 N.Y.2d 314, 318, 251 N.Y.S.2d 460, 462, 200 N.E.2d 447, 448; *Matter of Pepsi-Cola Co. v. Tax Comm.,* 19 A.D.2d 56, 61, 240 N.Y.S.2d 770, 777 *supra*). Thus, without equating Gimbel's situation with the one existing in the Seagram case, Gimbel's presence in Roosevelt Field, a large and prestigious shopping center, may have value apart from the income that use of the subject property would bring.

At the same time, an assessment based exclusively on reproduction cost less depreciation would seriously overvalue the subject property. The cost approach, which, among other things, ignores entirely factors like functional obsolescence, is useful principally, apart from specialties, to set a ceiling on valuation.

Construction of the Gimbel's store would not have been justified, economically, on the basis of the expected return from the Gimbel's store alone. Instead the improvements were justified in part by Gimbel's status as a "flagship" store, drawing shoppers to the remainder of the shopping center. The developer, eager to increase the rental value of the smaller stores, subsidized the construction of Gimbel's and for the same reason would have charged a lower rental to a "flagship" store if the property had been rented, as is usually the case.

Thus, to the extent that a flagship store is an attraction to the satellite tenants, part of the cost of construction may reflect not value to the flagship store, but value to the remainder of the typical shopping center. That value, in turn, is reflected in the increased rental value of the shopping center property other than the flagship store, and, presumably, in the tax assessment of the whole shopping center property. On this view, it would be inequitable to assess the Gimbel's property on the basis of reproduction cost less depreciation. The problem, obviously, arises in this case because of the separate ownership of the flagship store from that of the satellite rented stores.

Presented only with these incompatible theories of valuation, flawed if either be used exclusively, the trial court reached an adjustment by treating each basis as a factor in a balancing analysis. On the record made at trial, the trial court was entitled to select one of the theories of valuation as primary, here the reproduction cost theory, but to adjust it by recognizing the influence of the income capitalization computation. Hence, the balancing adjustment was not error.

Logic and economic analysis suggest the incongruity of combining what are on their face incompatible theories of valuation, and such combinations should be avoided where possible. Pragmatism, however, requires adjustment when the economic realities prevent placing the properties in neat logical valuation boxes. These pragmatic considerations are present in this case, and in that respect the affirmed findings of fact are demonstrably sound. Thus, an adjustment, derived it is true, from an incompatible theory of valuation, if rationally and discriminately applied, is in the exceptional case acceptable, because the adjustment, properly factored, comes closest to establishing the true market value, the ultimate basis, if determinable, for assessment.

The exceptional case arises, in large measure, when no one of the accepted but alternative (and therefore to some extent incompatible) theories of valuation will account for the divers economic purposes served by a single property. Not to be confused with a major adjustment of the kind involved in this case are adjustments for "special features" in a building otherwise capable of valuation on any single theory or method. Nor should it be said that all of the legitimate exceptions have been considered in this analysis, as for example where an inefficient enterpriser is involved; but it can be said that before there are adjustments based on what are otherwise incompatible theories of valuation, the discovery and use of the exception must be demonstrated to be legitimate in economic theory.

Accordingly, the order of the Appellate Division should be affirmed, with costs.

JASEN, GABRIELLI, JONES, WACHTLER, FUCHSBERG and COOKE, JJ., concur.

Notes and Questions

1. The court notes that "Gimbel's presence in Roosevelt Field, a large and prestigious shopping center, may have value apart from the income that use of the subject property would bring." If that presence does not enhance the income realized by the owner, to whom does it have value?

2. Similarly, the opinion states that a valuation based on income may be too low when "a building is held for the owner's own use, and especially where the building bears the owner's name." What benefit does the owner receive from this use of its name? Is it a property value? Can it be sold to future purchasers of the real property?

3. This opinion also states that the cost of constructing this "flagship" store could only be justified by its role in "drawing shoppers to the remainder of the shopping center." How would this enhanced business affect the value of the other stores? How should it affect the valuation of the "flagship" store?

4. Does the opinion succeed in convincing you that this is a case where "economic realities prevent placing the properties in neat logical valuation boxes"? Does the court view its own solution as illogical?

5. What income should be used in computing the value of the store under the income approach? Is it appropriate to use the sales income realized by the department store in valuing its real property? How could the income attributable to the property alone be computed?

6. The *G.R.F.* opinion states, "The cost approach, which, among other things, ignores entirely factors like functional obsolescence, is useful principally, apart from specialties, to set a ceiling on valuation." Need the cost approach ignore obsolescence and other forms of depreciation? Can you explain why the cost approach would generally set a ceiling on valuation? New York courts have defined a "specialty" as "a structure which is *uniquely* adapted to the business conducted upon it or use made of it *and* cannot be converted to other uses without the expenditure of substantial sums of money." *Great Atlantic & Pacific Tea Co. [A & P] v. Kiernan*, 42 N.Y.2d 236, 397 N.Y.S.2d 718, 366 N.E.2d 808 (1977) [emphasis in the original]. Why would the valuation of "specialties" (or special-purpose properties) be an exception to the general New York rule that the cost approach sets a ceiling to value? Would you consider the Gimbel's department store at Roosevelt Field a "specialty"? The *A & P* case, and the *Seagram* case mentioned by the court in *G.R.F.*, are reprinted in chapter 5 of this book.

7. The *Boston Globe* reported that the developer of the Atrium shopping mall in Newton, Massachusetts, "began discussions with possible anchor stores,

including Nordstrom, but he discovered that they wanted a minimum of 100,000 square feet—half the mall—and they wanted it for free. That would mean the other specialty tenants would have to supply all the income for the owner."[3] How should a rent-free arrangement affect the value of the property leased to an anchor tenant? In the *G.R.F.* case, why do you think Gimbel's agreed to construct its own building while other merchants in the shopping center leased their stores?

MEDICAL BUILDING LAND CO. v. DEPARTMENT OF REVENUE
283 Or. 69, 582 P.2d 416
Oregon Supreme Court, 1978

Before HOLMAN, P. J., BRYSON and LENT, JJ., and THORNTON, J. Pro Tem. LENT, Justice.

Defendant-Department of Revenue (Department) appeals from a decree of the Tax Court reducing the assessed valuation of plaintiffs' property, a medical office building in Multnomah County, from $3,368,660 to $2,625,000. The sole issue is the determination of the true cash value of the subject property on the assessment date, January 1, 1975.

Our review is de novo on the record. ORS 305.445; ORS 19.125(3). Aside from conflicting opinion testimony on the ultimate issue, the facts of this case are uncontradicted. The building in question was constructed between 1972 and 1974 across the street from Good Samaritan Hospital in the city of Portland. It is a modern concrete structure of seven levels, with brick veneer exterior. The lower three levels are designed for garage parking (the first two being below ground level), and the upper four levels are designed for and occupied by medical offices, except space on the lowest office level used for a pharmacy, cafeteria and branch bank. Two elevators give access to each floor, and an enclosed bridge or "skywalk" connects the subject building with Good Samaritan Hospital.

The building has a gross floor area of approximately 150,000 square feet, of which approximately 70,000 square feet is garage space and approximately 80,000 is office space. Of the latter area, approximately 63,000 square feet is rentable. As of the assessment date, the building was 99% complete and 80% occupied. The Multnomah County Tax Assessor determined the true cash value of the subject property to be $3,368,660, of which $3,200,000 was attributed to the building and $168,660 to the land.

Plaintiffs' appeal of this determination to the Department was denied, and plaintiffs filed suit in the Tax Court seeking to set aside this denial and to establish the true cash value of the subject property at $2,625,000. The Department answered, denying plaintiffs' allegations that its determination of the true cash value of the subject property was erroneous and alleging the true cash value of the subject property to be $4,110,000. The parties stipulated at trial that the true cash value of the land upon which the subject building was built was $210,000, which value is not at issue here. At trial before the Tax

---

3. David Mehegan, "The Atrium Blues," *Boston Globe,* December 26, 1989, p. 44.

Court, each side put on a single witness, both being characterized by the Tax Court as "able, experienced men, clearly qualified as an expert." Each gave his opinion as to the true cash value of the subject property as of the assessment date. Each referred to the three standard approaches used in determining true cash value: the market data approach, the income approach, and the cost approach.

Plaintiffs' witness reviewed eight comparable sales and arrived at a market data estimate of a range of $2,726,000 to $2,968,000. His income approach, based on gross income and expense data from comparable medical office buildings, yielded an estimate of $2,625,000. His cost estimate was $3,500,000.

The Department's witness considered both the market data and income approaches but opined that insufficient data was available to support an estimate for either. Defendant's cost approach yielded an estimate of $4,110,000. Plaintiffs' witness correlated[2] his three approaches by choosing the estimate based on the income approach as his final estimate of the true cash value of the subject property on January 1, 1975.

---

2. The process of correlation has been defined and explained as follows:

"The term 'correlation' implies a reciprocal relation and interdependence of functions—that is, an orderly connection of related elements. In the appraisal process, under the three-approach concept of value, correlation refers to the problem of bringing into focus the varying estimates of value arrived at by two or all of the three approaches—the Market Approach, the Income Approach, and the Cost Approach. The appraiser makes a thorough study of all pertinent information gathered by him, and analyzes and weighs the strongest and most applicable data under each approach. The final conclusion as to value is based on the approach which is supported by the most convincing data, that is, the *primary* approach. The accuracy of this estimate is checked by the results reached under the other approaches used, the *secondary* approaches.

" . . . .

"In every appraisal, a vast amount of data must be sifted, analyzed, and related to the subject property before a final estimate of value can be made. The purpose of correlation is to boil down this information and to choose the basic and fundamental facts that give the greatest support to an estimate arrived at by a particular approach.

"In applying any approach to value, the appraiser makes certain assumptions based on observation and sound reasoning. Each approach rests to some extent upon *opinion* evidence. The task of the appraiser in correlation is to seek out the approach that is supported by a preponderance of *factual* evidence. An approach that lacks support of a quantity of important factual data rests to a greater degree on opinion evidence. All available data for each approach must be processed, even if it may seem that an approach is relatively weak and less supportable than other approaches. The process of relating, weighing, and analyzing the data must go on within the development of each estimate of value.

"Value can never be calculated by adding up the several estimates arrived at in processing various approaches and taking an average of these estimates. Averages do not lead to a sound conclusion as to value; if an error was committed in estimating under any one of the approaches, it would merely be carried forward in a final estimate by average." Sarles, Correlation, Analysis, and Conclusion as to Value, in *Encyclopedia of Real Estate Appraising* (E. Friedman, ed., 1968), 120–121. [Hereinafter *Encyclopedia.*] [Emphasis in original.]

He concluded that the cost approach did not reflect true market conditions existing on the assessment date and acknowledged that the comparable sales used to support the market data approach were "not as comparable as [he] would have liked." The Department's witness, of necessity, relied exclusively on his cost approach estimate.

The Tax Court, having considered the conflicting opinion evidence, determined that the true cash value of the subject property on the assessment data was $2,625,000, as plaintiffs proposed.[3] The Department's appeal involves two separate questions whose answers will resolve the ultimate issue of the true cash value of the subject property on the assessment date: (1) What are the proper estimates yielded by each approach, and (2) What is the proper correlation of the three approaches to yield the true cash value of the subject property?

The only point of conflict on the first issue involved the cost approach. The Department's witness arrived at his figure by applying a construction cost per square foot from the Marshall Valuation Service to the gross area of the subject building for a total of $3,959,589. That figure was then multiplied by the 99% completion rate as of January 1, 1975, to yield a total reproduction cost of $3,919,993 (rounded to $3,900,000). The efficacy of this figure was indicated by a cross-check to the actual cost of construction as reported by the plaintiffs—$4,020,000. Including land value of $210,000, the Department's witness' cost estimate was $4,110,000.

Plaintiffs' witness' cost approach methodology was similar. The construction cost per square foot figure was based only in part on Marshall Valuation Service cost data and in part on actual cost experience from other buildings. The total cost estimate given by him for the subject building was $3,760,520. From this amount, he deducted $392,050 for "incurable functional depreciation"[4] for the construction cost of the brick veneer, excess parking space and the skywalk to Good Samaritan Hospital. Defendant objects to these

---

3. Inherent in the exercise of our function is the question of the weight to be accorded to the findings of the Tax Court upon our de novo review. As with other such cases, factual findings based on conflicting evidence *where the issue of the credibility of witnesses is involved* are entitled to "great weight." *Jeddeloh v. Department of Revenue,* 282 Or. 291, 294, 518 P.2d 233 (1978); *Reynolds Metals v. Dept. of Rev.,* 258 Or. 116, 119, 477 P.2d 888, 258 Or. 128, 481 P.2d 352 (1971). In a case such as the present one, "credibility," in its commonly understood meaning, is not at issue. *Cf. Buschke v. Dyck,* 197 Or. 144, 150, 251 P.2d 873 (1953). However, deference in matters of credibility is based on two interrelated theories—one, the opportunity of the trial court to observe the demeanor of the witnesses and, two, the experience of the trial judge in evaluating and drawing conclusions from his observations. The latter aspect may be equally relevant to a case such as the present one, where an experienced tax judge evaluates and draws conclusions from evidence in a specialized field of inquiry where specialized knowledge and expertise is necessarily involved. In such a case, the tax court's findings may be entitled to some weight in our de novo consideration of the evidence in the record. Since there is no precedent for this deference, however, and the issue was not fully briefed in the present case, we have given no such weight to the tax court's findings in the present case.

4. Plaintiffs' witness explained this deduction in his Appraisal Report as follows: "Our allowance for incurable functional depreciation reflects the cost of those items that exceed the standards of the market and for which the market is not willing to recognize a rental increment." Functional depreciation includes losses in value brought about by (1) over-adequacy, (2) inadequacy, (3) inefficiency, and (4) out-of-date equipment. It

deductions, and we agree. We find each of the items listed added an increment of value to the subject building reasonably commensurate with its cost.

Plaintiffs' witness explains the variance from actual cost by characterizing actual cost as "on the high side" due to a negotiated, rather than bid, contract and several work stoppages. We, therefore, must determine which estimate under the cost approach was more accurate. While the difference is not overwhelming considering the acknowledged imprecision of the appraiser's art, we find that plaintiffs' estimate, based as it is on standardized data tempered by data from actual cost experience from other buildings, forms a better basis for fixing value. We find, then, that the cost approach yields a value for the subject building of $3,760,520 (rounded to $3,800,000). To this figure must be added $210,000 for the land, for a total of $4,010,000.

Defendant asserts that there was insufficient data to support any opinion as to the value of the subject building according to the market data or income approaches. Plaintiffs offered an opinion of value pursuant to each approach. We find that plaintiffs' estimates were supported by sufficient data, both in quality and quantity, to justify the making of an estimate.[7] Since defendant offered no counter-estimates under these two approaches, we accept those of the plaintiff as offered. Thus, we find the estimates of value pursuant to each of the approaches as follows:

Cost approach—$4,010,000
Market data approach—$2,726,000 to $2,968,000
Income approach—$2,625,000

Now we embark on the somewhat mystical process appraisers refer to as "correlation."[8] From the three estimates above we must come up with a single figure for the true cash value of the subject property. Defendant argues that the cost figure alone reflects the true cash value, while plaintiffs argue (and the Tax Court agreed) that the income figure alone is the proper measure. Before we begin our search for true cash value, it is necessary to define exactly what it is we are looking for.

ORS 308.232 provides that "[a]ll real or personal property within each county shall be assessed at 100 percent of its true cash value." "True cash value," in turn, is defined by ORS 308.205 as follows:

"True cash value of all property, real and personal, means market value as of the assessment date. True cash value in all cases shall be determined by methods and procedures in accordance with rules and regulations promulgated by the

---

is "incurable" if it cannot be accounted for by an estimate of "cost to cure." See Anderson, Appraisal of Residential Property in *Encyclopedia* 168, *supra* note 2.

7. Even if a particular approach is "relatively weak and less supportable than other approaches," the approach should be used unless no data is available at all. See Sarles, *supra* note 2.

The Code of Ethics of the American Institute of Real Estate Appraisers, § 10.213, states: "It is unethical for an appraiser to issue an appraisal report giving his opinion of value based solely upon the cost approach unless his reasons and justification are clearly and explicitly set forth in the appraisal report."

We cite this only to indicate the strong feeling within the profession that *all* available data be used to process each of the three approaches. *But see* Department of Revenue Regulation 150-308.205(A)(2) quoted in the text, *infra*.

8. See *supra* note 2.

Department of Revenue. With respect to property which has no immediate market value, its true cash value shall be the amount of money that would justly compensate the owner for loss of the property."

Department of Revenue Regulation 150-308.205(A)(1)(a) provides:

"Market value as a basis for true cash value shall be taken to mean the highest price in terms of money which a property will bring if exposed for sale in the open market, allowing a period of time typical for the particular type of property involved and under conditions where both parties to the transaction are under no undue compulsion to sell or buy and are able, willing and reasonably well-informed."

In addition, paragraph two of this Regulation provides:

"Real property shall be valued through the market data approach, cost approach and income approach. Any one of the three approaches to value, or all of them, or a combination of approaches, may finally be used by the appraiser in making an estimate of market value, depending upon the circumstances."

Thus, it is clear that it is market value that we are seeking. As to the approaches which are employed to ascertain this elusive value, much has been said about their relative efficacy.[10] Little, however, is to be gained from these abstract characterizations, since the efficacy of each approach depends, of necessity, on the facts and circumstances of each case, as recognized by the department regulation quoted above.

The Department's correlation in favor of the cost approach appeared to be based as much on the process of elimination as upon the merits of that approach. The Department felt no comparable sales existed to justify the market data approach and that, as a rule of law, without three to five years of actual historical net income experience of the subject building itself, no income approach could be used. Both contentions are erroneous. Plaintiffs acknowledge that the eight sales it uses as "comparables" were less than ideal because of differences in age, size, physical condition and location. Plaintiff's use of his market data estimate, however, was limited to corroboration of the estimates yielded by the other approaches. We agree that the comparables were not such as to justify the market data estimate as true cash value of the subject property but that its use as corroboration of the value yielded by the income approach was correct.

The Department is also incorrect in asserting that the income approach may be used *only* where there is substantial historical data (income and expense) available from the subject property to support it. For this proposition, defendant relies on *Shields v. Department of Revenue,* 266 Or. 461, 464-466, 513 P.2d 784 (1973), where this court, in adopting language from the Tax Court's opinion, *Shields et al. v. Department of Revenue,* 5 OTR 160, 164-166 (1972), stated that the income approach urged by the

---

10. It is said, for example, that ordinarily the market data approach, guided as it is by actual buyers and sellers of comparable property in the market, is the best guide to market value. Some would say it is the only valid approach. It is also said that the income approach is the most effective approach in determining the value of investment properties, and is the "chief approach" to value for large office buildings. Finally, it is generally agreed that the cost approach is the least reflective of market value and is used only as a check of the estimates obtained from the other approaches and usually as an upper limit of market value. This is especially true for large office buildings. [Citations omitted.]

Department in that case was "grossly premature." The Tax Court in *Shields* expressly distinguished that case from *Multnomah County v. Department of Revenue*, 4 OTR 383 (1971), the case primarily relied on by plaintiffs here. *Shields* concerned a regional shopping center, characterized by the Tax Court as "unique," where economic rental data from comparables were not available, while *Multnomah County* concerned a newly constructed apartment complex, where comparables were available. The building in the present case is more similar to the apartment building in *Multnomah County*, where "comparables" in the form of other medical office buildings in the geographic area are available.

From these comparables, plaintiffs developed a fair market rental value of $8.25 per square foot of rental space per annum (62,895 square feet) on the assessment date, yielding $518,884 gross rent at 100% occupancy. At the projected 95% occupancy rate, plaintiffs would realize $492,839 as "effective gross rent." To this figure plaintiffs added income realized from the separate rental of parking spaces to yield a total of $511,899 effective gross income. Projected operating expenses, based again on a study of comparables, totaled $187,162 for a net operating income of $324,737. Plaintiffs then capitalized this net annual income at a 9.5% capitalization rate (increased by 2.865% to reflect the 1975–76 real estate tax rate of $28.65 per thousand) to arrive at their estimate for the true cash value under the income approach of $2,625,000. The Department challenges plaintiffs' use of this approach. We find it to be a valid approach worthy of this court's reliance.

The Department contends that it is the cost approach which deserves our exclusive attention. The dispute is not over the estimate yielded by this approach but over its reliability. Plaintiffs have pointed out several cogent factors which explain the disparity between the cost estimate and what plaintiffs claim is the market value on the assessment date. The market value, according to plaintiffs, was lower than the costs figure, because (1) the market for medical office space is highly localized, with doctors preferring to locate close to the hospitals on whose staffs they serve, (2) the demand for medical office space in the area had fallen sharply with the relocation of St. Vincent's Hospital, formerly located approximately four blocks from the subject property and having 200 to 250 doctors on staff, and (3) the supply of medical office space expanded sharply with the completion of Flanders Medical Building, approximately five blocks from the subject property on or about the assessment date.[11] While these reasons do not completely invalidate the cost approach in this case, they are sufficient to relegate it to its recognized role of supplying an upward limit to the market value.

Thus, plaintiffs' correlation of the three approaches which concluded that the income approach provided the most satisfactory estimate of true cash value of the subject property on the assessment date was amply justified. The decree of the Tax Court is affirmed.

---

11. Plaintiffs' analysis is supported by generally accepted appraisal theory. *See, e.g.,* Johnson [Johnson, Cost Approach to Value, *Encyclopedia of Real Estate Appraising*], 67, *supra* note 2:

"An estimate obtained by the Cost Approach may not reflect entirely the prevailing economic or market conditions. The cost of an improvement cannot be recovered in the market *if there is no need for the improvement,* if the property is not put to its highest and best use, if the structure is an overimprovement or of poor design, or *if rentals are reduced due to economic conditions.* " (emphasis added [by the court.])

THORNTON, Justice Pro Tem., dissenting.

Contrary to the majority, I am of the firm opinion that the "cost of construction approach" is the only proper method for fixing the true cash value of this newly constructed medical office building. After weighing the arguments of both sides, I am compelled to agree with the Department of Revenue's argument that the "cost of construction" is the only accurate and practical measure of the valuation at this time, given the fact that this building has just been constructed and was only partially occupied by tenants. Both the "income approach" and the "comparable sales approach" are plainly speculative here.

The so-called "income approach," which is the method urged by the building owners and accepted by the Oregon Tax Court, in my view is not proper under the facts presented here. I say this mainly because there is at present no earnings history of this building to go on. The "earnings history" apparently relied upon by the Oregon Tax Court was subsequent to the assessment date, January 1, 1975, and therefore was probably not admissible evidence. After the plaintiffs' building has an earnings history of at least a year, it would then be appropriate to reexamine the issue of valuation, and in doing so to consider the "income approach," but not until then, and certainly not to the exclusion of all other factors. *See, Shields v. Dept. of Rev.,* 266 Or. 461, 513 P.2d 784 (1973).

For the above reasons I respectfully dissent.

Note on the "Correlation" of Valuation Methods

The opinion in this case was unusually candid in acknowledging the "somewhat mystical" process by which three divergent valuation figures for the cost, income, and comparable sales approaches are expected to yield a single numerical result. It is more helpful to consider the entire process a calculation of market value that draws upon information concerning comparable sales, income, and reproduction cost. Because the purpose of the calculation is to estimate market value, a recent sale price of the property itself or of a similar property in a neighboring location is usually considered more reliable evidence than the results of the other two, more indirect methods. However, recent sales figures are frequently unavailable, particularly in the case of commercial or industrial properties that are unique or unusual. Rental income can be the most important indicator of sale value in the case of business property purchased as an investment, and the cost of construction can serve as both an index of value and a ceiling to the results obtained by the other methods, on the theory that no purchaser would pay more for property than it would cost to reproduce or replace.

Because each of these methods is designed to approximate market value, the income and cost approaches, as well as the comparable sales approach, must build on market data. The calculation of market value from net income depends on the capitalization or discount rates, as the amount of money bid for a given income stream depends on the rate of return demanded by investors. These rates can be derived from market observation by comparing the amounts paid for other properties or forms of investment with their net yield. Moreover, market data will provide a standard for determining whether the income actually derived from the property under review is in fact the amount that could be realized at its highest and best use. Similarly, cost figures must be adjusted in response to market data to reflect the effects of physical deterioration, functional obsolescence, or an inappropriate location. For example, an extremely expensive home constructed in an industrial area might have a market value of only a fraction of its construction cost. This reduction in value would be accounted for under the cost approach as a kind of obsolescence, similar to physical depreciation.

Questions

1. How can an assessor judge the likelihood that a building's vacancy rate will change in the future? How would this judgment affect the choice of valuation method?

2. Which of the factors offered by the plaintiff to explain the disparity between construction cost and the claimed market value could have been foreseen at the time the building was planned?

3. What earnings are relevant to an "earnings history" for property valuation purposes? Would the earnings of the tenants' medical practices affect the building's value? A building may be constructed by one company that in turn leases it to another, the ultimate tenants being sublessees. What income stream is relevant to the valuation of the property in this case: the rents received by the lessor or the rents received by the sublessor from the ultimate tenants?

DOTSON V. HENRY COUNTY BOARD OF TAX ASSESSORS
155 Ga. App. 557, 271 S.E.2d 691
Court of Appeals of Georgia, 1980

DEEN, Chief Judge.

This case involves an appeal from the assessment of real estate taxes for the year 1979 on the appellant's 266 acre farm, a part of which was open meadow land used to graze dairy cattle, a part woods, a part flood plain, and a part on which the farmhouse was located. The main contentions are that the appraisal methods did not comply with Code sec. 92-5702, that the taxes assessed are confiscatory in nature, and that the finding violates uniformity and equality in the assessment of rural property.

The appellant and her husband have lived on and run the acreage as a dairy farm for the past 20 years, during which time ad valorem taxes have increased from $200 to $4,300. The farm has expenses of approximately $5,000 per year for dairy feed, fertilizer and veterinary services, and constitutes the family's sole income except for Social Security and a small pension. It is uncontroverted that taxes assessed cannot be paid without selling off timber or otherwise going into capital. The owner therefore appealed the valuation of $1,425 per acre to the Board of Equalization, which lowered it to an average of $1,220.77. This ruling was appealed to the Henry County Superior Court and by that judge lowered to $1,088 per acre. From the latter assessment the case comes to this court.

In arriving at valuation, the assessors considered five "comparable" sales, one in the neighborhood of $2,200 per acre, and another witness, an appraiser, testified that he based his valuation on five such sales, four of which were speculative and the other one for a private airport.

The plaintiff's witnesses, who zeroed in on the value of the land for its existing uses of timber and grazing land, placed values of between $200 and $700 per acre. A careful reading of all the testimony, as well as the brief of the appellee, make clear that the underlying disagreement here is the extent to which, in an area believed to be shifting from traditional agricultural to speculative subdivision and commercial uses, "highest and best use" shall take precedence over "existing use" in the determination of value. Counsel states: "Appellee submits that Appellant's view of 'value' is based on something other than Ga. Code Ann. sec. 92-5702, which clearly defines 'value' in terms of an exchange, not in terms of present use." We disagree with this conclusion, based on an analysis of the statute itself and on the latest decision of the Supreme Court on this subject, *Chilivis v. Backus*, 236 Ga. 88, 222 S.E.2d 371 (1976).

The prime duty of this court is to construe the intent of the Legislature in the wording of the statute. The last amendment, while substituting "fair market value" for "cash sale" specifically retained the classic definition of market value in terms of willing buyer/ willing seller arm's length transactions, as modified by three specific criteria to be used in determining this value (zoning, existing use, and deed restrictions) plus a catchall phrase allowing the use of "any other factors deemed pertinent." It is significant that while under this fourth criterion highest and best use may be considered, the Legislature did not base market value on highest and best use, nor did it list highest and best use as a specific criterion. An honest evaluation of the state of real property sales in the present economy of this country fosters the conclusion that in an area such as that described in rural Henry County in the 1970's a basing of fair market value primarily on sales for developmental purposes (as the testimony shows was done in the instant case) will in 100 percent of the cases yield a figure having no relation to that obtained by a willing seller/ willing buyer contract for the purpose of continuing the existing agricultural or dairy use of the property. In such an economy, basing market value for tax purposes on acreage intended for income from agriculture on the basis of prior speculative acreage sales has two disadvantages: first, the speculative use indubitably ballooned the value at the time of that sale, and secondly, if subdivision and commercial expansion did not follow rapidly on sales, the remaining land would not in fact bring an equivalent price in the open market. "Highest and best use" is thus itself a much more speculative assigned value than existing use. Large tracts of acreage in Henry County, under the evidence here, are not worth more than $200 to $700 for agricultural purposes—in fact one of the defendant's witnesses said he knew of no sales for purely agricultural purposes; yet, this part of the county is admittedly rural and in general the existing uses are agricultural uses. It is true that one of the assessors stated that they took these facts into consideration and in fact assigned values somewhat lower than what they would expect the land to bring on a speculative sale, but the point is that the existing use is agricultural and the assigned value is at least twice the estimated appraisal value for use as woods or dairy farming. In considering existing use, where the use is income producing, it would appear that the income capitalization method used by one of the plaintiff's expert witnesses should at least be considered under Ga. Code 92-5702(4), (now Ga. Code sec. 91A-1001(b)(B)(iv)), this being a standard method of arriving at value.

It might further be pertinent to point out that the subdivision (a) (knowledgeable buyer/willing seller definition of market value) cannot be determined until *after* subdivision (c) (existing use, etc.) has been used as a yardstick. It follows that where the assessed value is based primarily on sales of other property, and all the so-called comparable sales are for speculative or development purposes (with the exception of one which was intended for use as a private airport) the formula has not been properly applied. In *Cobb County Bd. of Tax Assessors v. Sibley*, 244 Ga. 404, 405, 260 S.E.2d 313, 315 (1979), where "the trial judge found . . . that the value was determined by the sale price of other vacant lands purchased for development; that the assessors relied upon the property's highest and best use; that the sales relied upon did not accurately reflect the value of other vacant land because such sales were often for special purposes such as schools or parks, or speculative development" (in other words, where existing use did not function as a bona fide yardstick in determining value) the trial court properly remanded the case for reconsideration.

The trial court here correctly held that the assessors erred in considering foreclosure sales as comparable sales, and held that they erroneously over-valued a restricted use flood plain which comprised a significant portion of the land being appraised.   The court erred, however, in approving a valuation which tilted market value in favor of an assumed "highest and best use" to appear from future speculation and development, rather than first determining the criteria for zoning, existing use, and deed restrictions, if any, at which time other pertinent factors may be considered. *Chilivis v. Backus*, 236 Ga. 88, 222 S.E.2d 371, *supra*, was written before the Legislature substituted "fair market value" for "cash price" in subsection (a) of Code sec. 92-5702; the specific criteria were, however, a part of the statute at that time and the court held that "highest and best use" is a factor only if it would reflect the amount that would be realized from a cash sale of the property; that valuation will not be confined to actual use alone, and that all criteria added by the General Assembly (see Ga.L.1975, p. 96) are to be considered.

Judgment affirmed in part and reversed in part with direction that the case be remanded for reconsideration to the Henry County Board of Tax Assessors.

BIRDSONG and SOGNIER, JJ., concur.

Questions

1. The Georgia Code, sec. 48-5-2(1), defines "fair market value" as "the amount a knowledgeable buyer would pay for the property and a willing seller would accept for the property at an arm's length, bona fide sale." The criterion of "highest and best use" is sometimes considered implicit in any determination of market value according to a willing buyer–willing seller standard in the absence of an explicit statutory exception, such as a provision valuing agricultural land according to its farming income. The court in *Dotson* takes a different view when it describes highest and best use as one element that may enter the valuation process under the "catchall phrase allowing the use of 'any other factors deemed pertinent.'" In a case such as *Dotson*, how is a court or an assessor to choose between the sale price for farming purposes and the sale price for development in determining

"fair market value"? If, as the assessor argued, there were comparable sales of $2,200 an acre, would Dotson be a willing seller at $200 to $700 an acre?

2. The opinion states, "It is uncontroverted that taxes assessed cannot be paid without selling off timber or otherwise going into capital." How should this affect a determination of market value?

3. If all owners of property similar to the Dotson farm offered their land for sale, could they expect to receive $2,200 an acre? How does this affect the value of their property? Publicly traded securities with published daily price quotes are considered among the easiest forms of property to value. Could each shareholder expect to receive the listed price if all owners of shares in the corporation were to offer their stock for sale at the same time? Valuation studies sometimes discount the income from rental or sales of property to reflect the time it takes for the market to "absorb" new units. See, for example, *Golder v. Department of Revenue*, 123 Ariz. 260, 599 P.2d 216 (1979); *Genola Ventures-Shrewsbury v. Borough of Shrewsbury*, 2 N.J. Tax 541 (1981); *Cherokee Water Co. v. Gregg County Appraisal District*, 773 S.W.2d 949 (Tex. Ct. App. 1989), *aff'd*, 34 Tex. Sup.J. 239, 801 S.W.2d 872 (1990). The Department of Housing and Urban Development also publishes data on various absorption rates, such as the length of time required to rent apartments in newly constructed buildings. *Mathias v. Department of Revenue*, 11 Or. Tax 347 (1990), *aff'd*, 312 Or. 50, 817 P.2d 272 (1991), considered the effect of Or. Rev. Stat. §308.205(3), which required that properties consisting of four or more lots within one subdivision "be valued under a method which recognizes the time period over which those lots must be sold in order to realize current market prices for those lots." The Tax Court found this provision a violation of the state's constitutional requirement of uniformity:

> The statute directs disparate taxation of properties which are not different. Their physical characteristics and uses may be virtually identical. In fact, even the owners may be identical. A taxpayer may own four lots in one subdivision, the values of which are reduced, and three lots in another subdivision, the values of which are not reduced.

4. The *Dotson* opinion criticizes a valuation based on sales for nonagricultural development, pointing out that this "will in 100 percent of the cases yield a figure having no relation to that obtained by a willing seller/willing buyer contract for the purpose of continuing the existing agricultural or dairy use of the property." Is this an appropriate criticism of the valuation process? Is it a criticism of a tax based on market value?

5. The definition of "fair market value" quoted by the court from sections 92-5702 and later 91A-1001 of the Georgia Code are now contained in section 48-5-2(1)(B), which provides:

The tax assessor shall consider the following criteria in determining the fair market value of real property:

(i)   Existing zoning of property;
(ii) Existing use of property;
(iii) Existing covenants or restrictions in deed dedicating the property to a particular use; and
(iv) Any other factors deemed pertinent in arriving at fair market value.

What does it mean to "consider" existing use in valuing property when, as in *Dotson,* property may have one value at its current use and another, radically different, value at its most profitable use? Is the ability to sell the property to a developer in the future part of its current "use"? Is this current value the reason that the Dotsons would not be willing sellers of their land at $200 an acre?

It is not unusual for a statute to direct that assessment be based on "consideration" of factors such as these. The Florida statute dealing with "Just Valuation," stat. 193.011, requires the property appraiser to "take into consideration the following factors": (1) the present cash value of the property; (2) its highest and best use and present use, (3) location, (4) size, (5) cost and replacement value of any improvements, (6) condition), (7) income, and (8) net proceeds of sale. Are factors (2) through (8) subsumed under "the present cash value"?

6. Political opposition to the property tax has centered largely on the unpopularity of a tax based on market value. In 1982 Alan Hevesi, the deputy majority leader of the New York State Assembly, wrote in the New York newspaper *Newsday*:

> Can market value ever be fair? Not when it is the sole basis of assessments. Use of market value alone means that if my house has the same selling potential as yours, say a market value of $90,000, then we should both pay the same taxes on that property. That would be true even if I were a 42-year-old corporation president with a salary of $160,000 per year (not including dividends, stock options and the like) while you were an 84-year-old retiree living on $365 per month from Social Security. It would be true even though I purchased my home last year for $89,500 while you bought your house 45 years ago for $8,000 when it was the only homestead in a large undeveloped tract. The fact that I really intend to sell my house in a year or so (since my purchase was a speculative investment) while you intended solely to raise your children and die in your home is never considered.[4]

---

4. A. Hevesi, "100% Market Value as Assessment Basis for Homes Is Unfair," *Newsday,* January 29, 1982. Mr. Hevesi was elected New York City comptroller in 1993. During the campaign, the *New York Times* characterized him as having "one of the Legislature's most agile minds and one of its most gilt-edged tongues." K. Sack, "Hevesi's Primary Jump-Starts His Career," *New York Times,* September 19, 1993, p. 48.

To some extent, the inequalities Mr. Hevesi points out here argue against overreliance on any one form of taxation. Do they establish that a tax based on property value is inherently unfair? The example of neighboring homes purchased at different times for widely different values illustrates how elusive concerns as to "fairness" can become. The quoted passage seems to suggest that the taxpayer purchasing a home for $89,500 should pay a higher tax than the neighbor who purchased a comparable property for $8,000. Many young families coping with inflated mortgage payments would dispute that their neighbors who purchased homes for a fraction of current market values should for that reason pay property tax based on 1940 prices. Should the tax system provide an incentive for older homeowners to remain in large houses? This issue poses a difficult choice between, on the one hand, using scarce resources to subsidize homeowners, and, on the other hand, having older persons forced by reason of tax burdens to relinquish their family homes. As Henry Aaron has written, "While economists tend to argue that this predicament is a signal that the taxpayer is over-housed, legislators have been loath to agree that the aged, the sick, or the temporarily unemployed should be compelled to move because they live in 'more' house than their current incomes justify."[5] One creative solution to this dilemma has been the establishment of programs to defer property taxes for older homeowners, allowing the unpaid amount, together with interest, to accumulate as a debt secured by the property until it changes ownership through sale or inheritance. Interestingly, few eligible taxpayers have chosen to participate in such programs, preferring to avoid encumbering their property with tax obligations.

7. What would be the advantages and disadvantages of a property tax not based on current sale value? Consider these alternatives: (a) a percentage of original acquisition cost; (b) a flat fee per household; (c) a tax on annual gross rental value rather than capital value, and (d) a tax measured by the physical characteristics of the property, such as length, or front footage, land area, or building size. Physical characteristics of this type are frequently used to allocate the cost of specific local improvements, such as sidewalks, not funded by general tax revenue. The property tax system instituted by California's Proposition 13 is largely based on acquisition value for properties that have changed ownership since 1975, with no more than a 2 percent annual inflation adjustment. The British system of property taxes, or "rates," was long based on rental value rather than capital value, although property taxes on residential property, or "domestic rates," are now based on a modified capital value.

---

5. H. Aaron, *Who Pays the Property Tax?* at 94 (1975).

3 VALUATION FOR CURRENT USE OR SPECIAL USES

Introduction

Valuation for tax purposes generally rests on "highest and best use"—the most profitable use that is legally, physically, and financially feasible. However, in some situations statutory or constitutional provisions provide an alternative basis for assessment. Each of the fifty states has some provision for assessment of bona fide agricultural property at its value for farming purposes rather than the "fair market value" that would otherwise control its assessed value. Some states simply tax qualifying land on its value for agricultural purposes, with no penalty imposed or repayment required in the event of a later change in use. Other states defer the additional taxes that would be imposed if assessment were on full market value, requiring payment of that additional amount for some period, with interest, upon a later change in use. In other states participating property owners enter into a contractual agreement to retain the property in agricultural use for a specified period. Similar provisions often apply to open-space property, forest- or timberland, recreational property, or environmentally sensitive property.

In a tax system based purely on market value at highest and best use, the current use of the property would not affect the valuation of the land itself. Of course, valuation at a use inconsistent with the present use might require a calculation of the cost of changing or replacing existing structures, which would in turn reduce the price a prospective purchaser would bid for the property. The combined valuation of the land and buildings as reduced by this obsolescence would show the effect of a current uneconomic use, but the land itself would have a value reflecting its highest and best use.

This approach conflicts with efforts to maintain assessments on farmland at their agricultural level, even when land in the urban fringe is ready for development and would command a market value far above the price that agricultural use alone would justify. At the same time, public opinion is firmly opposed to land speculation, the withholding of property from productive use in hopes of realizing gain from later price increases. This means that the preferential tax provisions permitting agricultural land an exception to the general rule of market-value assessment generally seek to limit their scope to "bona fide" agricultural uses. This chapter examines some of the difficulties faced by that effort.

Such difficulties stem from two sources. First, courts with sympathetic inclinations toward farmers (and, perhaps, toward real estate developers) may interpret restrictions of this type so narrowly as to render them ineffective. More fundamentally, there is a conceptual difficulty in clearly distinguishing "bona fide agricultural use" from speculation, for frequently the two are one and the same. Farmers may legitimately expect the increasing value of their land to supplement the savings realized from agricultural income as a store of wealth available for retirement, investment, or transmission to the next generation. The familiar adage that farmers "live poor and die rich" expresses a widely held expectation that sale of land for nonagricultural purposes may be one reward of a lifetime of farming. In such a case the farmer would not accept the current use valuation as payment for the property, even if the buyer were intending to continue cultivation.

The first set of cases in this chapter trace judicial interpretations of a Florida statute designed to limit this preferential treatment to land used for "bona fide agricultural purposes." The statute itself sets out a number of methods by which the legislature sought to distinguish "bona fide" from other agricultural uses. A number of factors, such as size of the parcel and period of cultivation, may be "considered" in this determination. Some situations, such as rezoning to a nonagricultural use at the owner's request, mandate a loss of agricultural classification. A sale at a price at least three times the agricultural assessment gives rise to a rebuttable presumption of nonagricultural status. That is, absent evidence to the contrary, such a purchase price would be enough to disqualify the land from agricultural assessment, but evidence of special circumstances may be introduced to rebut the presumption.

The Florida cases that follow this statute demonstrate that ample room for judicial interpretation exists even in a legislative scheme as detailed and specific as this. To the extent the judicial determinations appear at odds with the intent of the statute, a question arises as to whether more careful drafting could have prevented such an outcome, or whether the concept of "current use," and particularly bona fide current use, is inherently imprecise and not amenable to clear tests and predictable outcomes.

The second section of this chapter attempts to explore this issue by considering other cases seeking to distinguish current use from highest and best use. The first case in this section, *Lanier v. Walt Disney World Co.*, dealt with undeveloped land within the grounds of Disney World. The determination that the vacant land was in fact being put to use as a "psychological mind conditioner" is more than a comic illustration of a sympathetic tribunal's acceptance of an imaginative argument. In fact, it touches on a central problem in the preferential taxation of agricultural land: the need to distinguish productive use from speculative use. The fact that farmers or other users can legitimately be speculators—and, as the Florida cases demonstrate, speculators may continue "bona fide" agricultural use pending development—means that preferential assessment provisions may actually encourage speculation and urban "sprawl" by reducing the cost of withholding land ripe for development from the market. To the extent this is so, it undermines attempts to distinguish genuine agricultural land use from the speculative withholding of land from the market until the price rises to a sufficiently high level.

The final two cases illustrate other questions concerning current use value. The *Burnsville* case demonstrates that an unrestricted search for "use value" could potentially lead to assessments above market value, and that imaginative arguments are not restricted to taxpayers alone. Finally, the *Federated Department Stores* case raises an issue of consistency in the assessment of property that might not be used in its most productive individual capacity but which supports (in this case, as a parking area) a lucrative "highest and best" use of another parcel. Taken together, all the cases in this chapter are intended to suggest the range of puzzling and subtle issues raised by all considerations of "use" in assessment.

Preferential Assessment of Agricultural Property

The Florida statute reproduced below takes the simplest approach to preferential assessment of agricultural property, allowing preferential assessment with no contractual restrictions and no penalties for a change in use. The cases that follow demonstrate the difficulty of interpreting and applying a provision designed to limit this benefit to land in "bona fide" agricultural use.

FLORIDA STATUTES
Title XIV. Taxation and Finance
Chapter 193. Assessments
Part II. Special Classes of Property

193.461. Agricultural lands; classification and assessment

(1) The property appraiser shall, on an annual basis, classify for assessment purposes all lands within the county as either agricultural or nonagricultural.

(2) Any landowner whose land is denied agricultural classification by the property appraiser may appeal to the value adjustment board. The property appraiser shall notify the landowner in writing of the denial of agricultural classification on or before July 1 of the year for which the application was filed. The notification shall advise the landowner of his right to appeal to the value adjustment board and of the filing deadline. The board may also review all lands classified by the property appraiser upon its own motion. The property appraiser shall have available at his office a list by ownership of all applications received showing the acreage, the full valuation under sec. 193.011, the valuation of the land under the provisions of this section, and whether or not the classification requested was granted.

(3) (a) No lands shall be classified as agricultural lands unless a return is filed on or before March 1 of each year. The property appraiser, before so classifying such lands, may require the taxpayer or his representative to furnish the property appraiser such information as may reasonably be required to establish that such lands were actually used for a bona fide agricultural purpose. Failure to make timely application by March 1 shall constitute a waiver for 1 year of the privilege herein granted for agricultural assessment. The owner of land that was classified agricultural in the previous year and whose ownership or use has not changed may reapply on a short form as provided by the department. The lessee of property may make original application or reapply using the short form if the lease, or an affidavit executed by the owner, provides that the lessee is empowered to make application for the agricultural classification on behalf of the owner and a copy of the lease or affidavit accompanies the application. A county may, at the request of the property appraiser and by a majority vote of its governing body, waive the requirement that an annual application or statement be made for classification of property within the county after an initial application is made and the classification granted.

(b) Subject to the restrictions set out in this section, only lands which are used primarily for bona fide agricultural purposes shall be classified agricultural. "Bona fide agricultural purposes" means good faith commercial agricultural use of the land. In determining whether the use of the land for agricultural purposes is bona fide, the following factors may be taken into consideration:

1. The length of time the land has been so utilized;
2. Whether the use has been continuous;
3. The purchase price paid;
4. Size, as it relates to specific agricultural use;
5. Whether an indicated effort has been made to care sufficiently and adequately for the land in accordance with accepted commercial agricultural practices, including, without limitation, fertilizing, liming, tilling, mowing, reforesting, and other accepted agricultural practices;
6. Whether such land is under lease and, if so, the effective length, terms, and conditions of the lease; and
7. Such other factors as may from time to time become applicable.

(c) The maintenance of a dwelling on part of the lands used for agricultural purposes shall not in itself preclude an agricultural classification.

(4)(a) The property appraiser shall reclassify the following lands as nonagricultural:

1. Land diverted from an agricultural to a nonagricultural use.
2. Land no longer being utilized for agricultural purposes.
3. Land that has been zoned to a nonagricultural use at the request of the owner subsequent to the enactment of this law.

(b) The board of county commissioners may also reclassify lands classified as agricultural to nonagricultural when there is contiguous urban or metropolitan development and the board of county commissioners finds that the continued use of such lands for agricultural purposes will act as a deterrent to the timely and orderly expansion of the community.

(c) Sale of land for a purchase price which is three or more times the agricultural assessment placed on the land shall create a presumption that such land is not used primarily for bona fide agricultural purposes. Upon a showing of special circumstances by the landowner demonstrating that the land is to be continued in bona fide agriculture, this presumption may be rebutted.

(5) For the purpose of this section, "agricultural purposes" includes, but is not limited to, horticulture; floriculture; viticulture; forestry; dairy; livestock; poultry; bee; pisciculture, when the land is used principally for the production of tropical fish; aquaculture; sod farming; and all forms of farm products and farm production.

(6) (a) In years in which proper application for agricultural assessment has been made and granted pursuant to this section, the assessment of land shall be based solely on its agricultural use. The property appraiser shall consider the following use factors only:

1. The quantity and size of the property;
2. The condition of the property;
3. The present market value of the property as agricultural land;
4. The income produced by the property;
5. The productivity of land in its present use;
6. The economic merchantability of the agricultural product; and
7. Such other agricultural factors as may from time to time become applicable.

(b) In years in which proper application for agricultural assessment has not been made, the land shall be assessed under the provisions of sec. 193.011.

RODEN v. K & K LAND MANAGEMENT, INC.
368 So.2d 588
Supreme Court of Florida, 1978

BOYD, Justice.

The decision of the District Court of Appeal in this cause, *Straughn v. K & K Land Management, Inc.*, 347 So.2d 724 (Fla. 2d Dist. Ct. App. 1977), conflicts with the decision in *First National Bank of Hollywood v. Markham*, 342 So.2d 1016 (Fla. 4th Dist. Ct. App. 1977). We have jurisdiction of the petition for certiorari. Article V, Section 3(b)(3), Florida Constitution.

The issue in conflict is whether more than just agricultural use is required to establish for purpose of tax assessment that land may be classified agricultural and be entitled, therefore, to preferential tax treatment. In *Straughn v. Tuck*, 354 So.2d 368 (Fla. 1978), we reviewed the constitutionality of Section 193.461(3), Florida Statutes. The statute mandates that to gain "agricultural" classification land must be "actually used for a bona fide agricultural purpose," Section 193.461(3)(a), which means "good faith commercial agricultural use of the land." Section 193.461(3)(b). In the course of the opinion upholding the statute the following was stated, at 370: "'use' is still the guidepost in classifying land, although other specifically enumerated factors relative to use may also be considered. Agricultural use is now and has always been the test." We adhere to this view. As we intimated in *Tuck* the factors listed in subsection (b) of Section 193.461(3) are to be considered in making the determination of good faith agricultural use but none is determinative. We disapprove of *Markham* to the extent it conflicts with *Tuck*. This resolves the conflict between *Markham* and this case, too.

A problem not present in *Markham* and *Tuck* is present in this case. Sale of land for a purchase price three or more times greater than its agricultural assessment creates a presumption that the land is not used for good faith agricultural purposes. Section 193.461(3), Florida Statutes. The presumption may be overcome "[u]pon a showing of special circumstances by the landowner demonstrating that the land is to be continued in bona fide agriculture." In this case the District Court upheld the trial court's determination that there existed special circumstances sufficient to rebut the presumption. As the Department of Revenue has done before, it stresses that commercial success is a necessary circumstance for rebuttal. We reject this notion. As we stated in *Straughn v. K & K Land Management*, 326 So.2d 421 (Fla.1976), "special circumstances" may be drawn from the factors for consideration in the classification process listed in Section 193.461(3)(b). The presence of all or any one factor in particular is not necessary for the presumption's rebuttal.

In this case K & K Land Management purchased approximately 350 acres of producing citrus grove for six times the agricultural assessment. Twenty-five of the acres were developed into an amusement park, but the remainder of the grove was continued to be used for citrus production. The issue was whether the presumption of nonagricultural use in Section 193.461(4)(c) was overcome as to the acreage continued for citrus production. On the record before us, we cannot say the trial court found incorrectly that the presumption had been rebutted and that respondent was entitled to agricultural classification. The decision of the District Court is affirmed. *First National Bank of Hollywood v. Markham*, 342 So.2d 1016 (Fla. 4th Dist. Ct. App. 1977), is disapproved. It is so ordered.

ENGLAND, C. J., and SUNDBERG and HATCHETT, JJ., concur.
ALDERMAN, J., concurs in result only.

ORDER PER CURIAM.

The motion of petitioner Florida Department of Revenue for rehearing or clarification is denied.

It is so ordered.

ADKINS, BOYD, OVERTON and HATCHETT, JJ., concur.
ALDERMAN, J., dissents with an opinion, with which ENGLAND, C. J., and SUNDBERG, J., concur.

ALDERMAN, Justice, dissenting.

Because I believed that the twenty-five acres of highway frontage developed into an amusement park must have had a much higher value than the remaining 325 acres of citrus grove property, I concurred in result only in this Court's opinion filed July 20, 1978, which allowed the taxpayer the benefit of an agricultural classification on its grove land. I reasoned that the purchase price of the grove land could not be determined by simply dividing the total number of acres purchased into the overall purchase price to get an average price per acre, and I assumed that the actual price for the grove land was less than the average price per acre of all the land purchased by K & K. During oral argument on petitioner's motion for rehearing, however, it became clear to me that the record contains no evidence to contradict the property appraiser's conclusion that K & K paid a uniform price per acre for all the land it purchased. Assuming then that K & K paid six times the agricultural assessed value for the grove land, I find that section 193.461(4)(c), Florida Statutes (1973), creates a presumption that "such land is not used primarily for bona fide agricultural purposes." This presumption may be rebutted "[u]pon a showing of special circumstances by the landowner demonstrating that the land is to be continued in bona fide agriculture . . . ." Section 193.461(4)(c). "Bona fide agricultural purposes" means "good faith commercial agricultural use of the land." Section 193.461(3)(b).

Special circumstances, sufficient to overcome the statutory presumption, must be more than a showing that an existing agricultural use of the land is continued. *Markham v. Nationwide Development Co.*, 349 So.2d 220 (Fla. 4th Dist. Ct. App. 1977). In the present case, K & K failed to contradict the property appraiser's finding that it paid six times the agricultural assessed value of the grove land, and it has not shown any special circumstances, consistent with good faith commercial agricultural use of this land, that would justify paying such an inflated price. Certainly, its continued use of the land as a grove could not be considered a good faith commercial agricultural use when there is no reasonable expectation of meeting investment costs and realizing a reasonable profit. This does not mean that K & K cannot continue to use the land as a grove, thereby generating some income to reduce the costs of its speculative investment. Rather, it means that K & K cannot use the Green Belt Law, which was intended as a shield to protect bona fide farmers, to avoid its fair share of ad valorem taxes, thereby forcing the other taxpayers of the county to subsidize its speculative investment. Upon rehearing, I would quash the decision of the district court and reverse the trial court.

ENGLAND, C. J., and SUNDBERG, J., concur.

Notes and Questions

1. The court found that the sale price of the 350 acres was six times the agricultural assessment, with twenty-five of the acres then developed as an amusement park. In order to avoid the presumption of nonagricultural use, the price allocated to the remaining 325 acres could not exceed three times their agricultural assessment. If the total price of $(350 \times 6) = 2,100$ times the agricultural assessment per acre were allocated so the 325 acres commanded no more than three times their agricultural assessment (a total of 975 times the agricultural assessment per acre), the remaining allocation to the twenty-five amusement park acres would be $2,100 - 975 = 1,125$ times the agricultural assessment per acre. That means that each of the twenty-five acres would have sold at a minimum of forty-five times its agricultural assessment, while the neighboring acres sold at three times their agricultural assessment. What evidence would you require in order to accept this allocation?

2. Note, however, that payment of an amount in excess of three times the agricultural assessment only creates a presumption of nonagricultural use under Florida law. What evidence would you require in order to rebut this presumption? Do you agree with the dissent that "continued use of the land as a grove could not be considered a good faith commercial agricultural use when there is no reasonable expectation of meeting investment

costs and realizing a reasonable profit"? How does the allocation of purchase price discussed in the previous question affect the calculation of "investment costs"?

HARBOR VENTURES, INC. V. HUTCHES
366 So.2d 1173
Supreme Court of Florida, 1979

HATCHETT, Justice.

We are asked to determine whether section 193.461(4)(a)3., Florida Statutes (1973), is unconstitutional because it sets up an irrebuttable presumption that land rezoned non-agricultural at the request of its owners will not be used for a bona fide agricultural purpose. Exercising jurisdiction under article V, section 3(b)(1), Florida Constitution, we decline to address the constitutional question and find the statute inapplicable to the facts of this case because the zoning change was from one non-agricultural use to another non-agricultural use.

In 1973, appellants, Harbor Ventures, Inc. and others, owned land in the unincorporated area of Manatee County. The land was zoned R-1AA (non-agricultural). Agricultural use of land in a non-agriculturally zoned district is permitted by an exception granted by the County Commissioners of Manatee County. The appellants' property was classified and assessed as agricultural in 1973. On December 18, 1973, the land was rezoned at the request of its owner to a use classification of planned unit development (PUD) (non-agricultural). In a timely manner and in accordance with all existing laws, appellants sought agricultural classification and assessment for 1974. The request was denied by the appellees, the Property Appraiser for Manatee County and other county officials. After exhausting administrative remedies, appellants instituted this action in the circuit court seeking declaratory relief.

The facts in this case are undisputed. As of January 1, 1974, the land which is the subject of this suit was being used in the same manner as it was being used on January 1, 1973. The sole reason for the denial of agricultural classification and assessment was the rezoning of the land at the request of its owners. Because of the denial of the agricultural classification and assessment, appellants' land was assessed at a higher value than adjacent land devoted to the same use.

Appellants attack section 193.461(4)(a)3., Florida Statutes (1973), alleging that it denies equal protection of the laws as guaranteed by the fourteenth amendment to the Constitution of the United States and article I, section 2 of the Florida Constitution. The trial judge upheld the constitutionality of the statute.

We must initially determine whether section 193.461(4)(a)3, Florida Statutes (1973), applies where land is rezoned from one non-agricultural use to another non-agricultural use. If the statute applies, we must address the constitutional question.

Article VII, section 4(a) of the Florida Constitution provides:

Section 4. Taxation; assessments—By general law regulations shall be prescribed which shall secure a just valuation of all property for ad valorem taxation, provided: (a) Agricultural land or land used exclusively for non-commercial recreational purposes *may be classified by general law and assessed solely on the basis of character or use.* [Emphasis added.]

In interpreting these provisions, we have held that the policy of the Greenbelt law and its 1972 amendments is to promote agricultural use of land.

Section 193.461(4)(a)3., Florida Statutes (1973), provides:

> The assessor shall reclassify the following lands as nonagricultural: . . . 3. Land that has been zoned to a nonagricultural use at the request of the owner subsequent to the enactment of this law . . . .

Considering the stated purpose of the Greenbelt law and our adherence to the actual use test, we find that the legislature intended to limit application of this statute to those cases where land is rezoned from an agricultural use to a non-agricultural use at the owner's request. Such an interpretation provides an incentive for agricultural lands to remain devoted to agricultural production by discouraging speculative rezoning. Such speculative rezoning must have been viewed by the legislature as a first step toward non-agricultural use. The legislature could not have intended to deny the benefits of the Greenbelt law where a clear bona fide commercial agricultural use was being made of land that was rezoned from one non-agricultural use to another non-agricultural use.

We believe this interpretation is in compliance with our duty to construe tax statutes in favor of taxpayers where an ambiguity may exist.

We hold that section 193.461(4)(a)3. applies only to those situations where land zoned agricultural is changed to a non-agricultural zoning at the request of its owner. In light of this disposition, we need not reach the constitutional issue.

Accordingly, the trial court is reversed and the case remanded to that court for further action consistent with this opinion.

It is so ordered.

ENGLAND, C. J., and ADKINS, OVERTON, SUNDBERG and ALDERMAN, JJ., concur.

BOYD, J., dissents with an opinion.

BOYD, Justice, dissenting.

It seems to me that the majority opinion in effect rewrites section 193.461(4)(a)(3), Florida Statutes (1973), in order to avoid the constitutional issue. The statutory words are clear, however, and the strained construction utilized by the majority is beyond this Court's power. I would meet directly the constitutional challenge.

To reach the result obtained by the majority it is necessary to construe the legislative intent to require reclassification only when the zoning change is from agricultural to non-agricultural. This conflicts with the clear language of the statute. The law provides for reclassification when zoning is changed, at the request of the owner, *to* a non-agricultural use and it makes no reference to the type of zoning *from which* the change is made. The majority is correct in stating that this Court has in the past held that actual use should be the basic test in interpreting the provisions of the greenbelt law. In *Straughn v. K & K Land Management, Inc.*, 326 So.2d 421 (Fla. 1976), the issue was whether the rebuttable presumption established by Section 193.461(4)(c), Florida Statutes (1973) was reasonable in view of the policy objectives of the statute.

It should be noted, however, that the statutory provision at issue here is not a legislative presumption. It is a clear legislative directive to the property appraisers of the state. If the greenbelt law and the decisions interpreting it have established actual use of land as the general test for entitlement to the agricultural assessment, then clearly section 193.461(4)(a)(3) constitutes a legislatively-mandated exception to that test. For the enactment directs that the preferential tax treatment be denied upon the happening of an event, regardless of actual use. The question before us, then, is whether this statutory exception denies due process or the equal protection of the laws.

The Constitution mandates that all property is to be assessed for ad valorem taxation at a "just valuation." Art. VII, sec. 4, Florida Constitution. This Court has declared that these words mean assessment at fair market value. *Walter v. Schuler*, 176 So.2d 81 (Fla. 1965). So, there is a general mandate for all property to be assessed for ad valorem tax purposes at the amount a purchaser willing but not obliged to buy, would pay to a seller willing but not obliged to sell. The Constitution authorizes a more favorable treatment for agricultural land, Art. VII, sec. 4(a), Florida Constitution, but the constitutional language is permissive only, so that the assessment of agricultural land is a policy matter. *Straughn v. Tuck*, 354 So.2d 368 (Fla.1978).

We have said that the "reduced taxation for farmland is based on a legislative determination that agriculture cannot reasonably be expected to withstand the tax burden of the highest and best use to which such land might be put." *Straughn v. K & K Management, Inc.*, above, at 424. Viewed differently, the lower assessment for agricultural land is an indirect subsidy to agriculture. Agriculture is one of the leading industries of our state, and the precious commodities it produces bring high prices in the marketplace. Nevertheless, the Legislature in its wisdom has determined to promote agriculture by partially insulating it from the pressures of encroaching and competing land uses and the increases in market value associated with a rapidly developing state and region.

The legislative policy of giving preferential tax treatment to agricultural lands does not create any right in the owner to receive the preferential treatment. Its denial does not violate any personal or property right. *Rainey v. Nelson*, 257 So.2d 538 (Fla. 1972). Therefore the issue is whether the legislative enactment and the classification it establishes are rationally related to some permissible state objective.

As the majority opinion recognizes, "speculative rezoning must have been viewed by the Legislature as a first step toward non-agricultural use." It is just as reasonable, however, to view a change of zoning from one non-agricultural classification to planned unit development as the precursor to a change in actual use as it is to so view a change from agricultural zoning to non-agricultural zoning. Administrative convenience in the task assigned to the property appraisers of the state is served by the enactment. The legislative directive is rationally related to the purposes of the greenbelt law.

The fact that the statutory provision sets up a classification under which some lands actually being used for agriculture will receive the favorable assessment while others will not does not violate equal protection. If we can conceive of any basis of justification for the classification made, we must hold that equal protection is not violated. In establishing classifications, in which no fundamental rights or suspect classes are involved, and especially in economic matters, the Legislature need not draw lines with mathematical precision.

For the foregoing reasons, I respectfully dissent. I would hold that section 193.461(4)(a)(3) is applicable to this case and is constitutional. The judgment of the circuit court, upholding the reclassification of appellant's land, should be affirmed.

Question

The dissent acknowledges that under its approach "some lands actually being used for agriculture will receive the favorable assessment while others will not." Is this distinction inherent in a legislative enactment designed to benefit "good faith commercial agricultural use"? If so, could the legislation have been drafted to provide any greater assistance to courts facing cases such as this?

FISHER V. SCHOOLEY
371 So.2d 496
District Court of Appeal of Florida, 1979

OTT, Judge.

The lower court entered a final judgment denying appellant/plaintiff landowner's requested agricultural classification. We reverse.

Appellant purchased the subject property in 1971 for $500,000. At that time the property was classified as agricultural. The purchase price was more than three times the agricultural assessment placed on the land. Appellant acquired the property as trustee under a trust agreement for a limited partnership in the business of developing real estate. The intent behind the purchase was to develop the land as a commercial property or resell it for such purposes. Accordingly, prior to closing and as a condition of the purchase, the zoning of the subject property was changed from agricultural to commercial.[1] This rezoning was at the appellant's request and expense.

In 1974, (the tax year in question) the tract was leased to Wendell Crosby, a farmer, who raised various vegetable crops thereon. For the previous seven years, Mr. Crosby had leased the same property for exactly the same purpose, i.e., to raise vegetables. Prior to 1971, he had leased the property in question from the prior owners; then, after the sale, from appellant under essentially identical year-to-year written leases. The property was agriculturally assessed in each of the prior years through 1973. Crosby's farming activities were the subject of some testimony. In essence, Crosby testified that the entire 100 acre tract was under irrigation and cultivation, that he cultivated and sold various crops and that his farming activities were for a profit making purpose; that he farmed only the appellant's property except for an additional 40 acres he leased near the end of his operation on appellant's property. His testimony suggests that fewer improvements (such as in the irrigation system and barn) were made than might have been desirable. Moreover, Crosby's testimony was mostly general; he was unable to provide specific figures as to his costs, his yield per acre for each crop, the exact market price secured for

---

1. This opinion does not deal with a zoning change from a nonagricultural use to another nonagricultural use. In *Harbor Ventures, Inc. v. Hutches*, 366 So.2d 1173 (Fla.1979, reh. denied March 22, 1979) the supreme court held that "the legislature intended to limit application of (sec. 193.461(4)(a)(3)) to those cases where land is rezoned from an agricultural use to a non-agricultural use at the owner's request." The supreme court declined to address the issue whether this statutory section was unconstitutional. Section 193.461(4)(a)(3) provides:

"(4)(a) The property appraiser shall reclassify the following lands as nonagricultural:
(3) Land that has been zoned to a non-agricultural use at the request of the owner *subsequent to the enactment of this law* .... " (Emphasis supplied.)

Since the zoning change in the instant case from agricultural to nonagricultural use was accomplished in 1971, this later statute does not apply.

a certain crop or the gross or net profit per acre, etc. He indicated he had such records and tax returns but had not been advised he should bring them to court.

Upon acquiring the property, appellant undertook preliminary action looking to future commercial development of the land. The primary goal was to use all or part of the land for a shopping center. Accordingly, appellant secured a land planner to conduct a market study showing traffic and population patterns. Appellant then attempted to attract two or more "prime" tenants, i.e., a supermarket or drug store, which he would use as a basis to apply for bank financing. Although appellant received a tentative commitment from one supermarket, further commitments for the requisite financing were not forthcoming. Thus, development remained only a hope or future expectancy. There was absolutely no *non*agricultural commercial activity on the land. In other words, the developer had every intention to devote the property to nonagricultural use. However, the property continued to be devoted exclusively to agricultural purposes until commercial development became feasible.

For the years 1975 and 1976 the property was leased to a corporate agricultural operation.

Appellant/plaintiff timely filed an application for agricultural classification of his land under the Florida Green Belt Law for the year 1974.[2] The tax assessor (today referred to as the property appraiser) denied appellant's application. On appeal, the Lee County Board of Tax Adjustment reversed the tax assessor and granted the requested agricultural classification. However, the Florida Department of Revenue reversed and the tax assessor's denial was reinstated. Appellant then brought this action in the circuit court below.

At trial the tax assessor gave the following reasons for such denial:

(1) The purchase price paid.
(2) The landowner had future plans for development of the land as a shopping center site, thus the agricultural use was an interim use until the land was ready for development.
(3) The land use zoning was changed from agricultural to commercial.
(4) The area in which appellant's lands are located was changing from an agricultural area to a commercial use area.
(5) The owner (appellant) was not a farmer.
(6) There was no reasonable expectation that the continued agricultural activities would return a reasonable rate of return on the landowner's investment in the land.

The lower court made, inter alia, the following findings of fact:

15. The owner, since he purchased the property, has not made bona fide agricultural use of the land.
16. The evidence is insufficient to overcome the Property Appraiser's determination, which is supported by a presumption of correctness, that the various tenants who used the property under lease did not make a good faith commercial agricultural use of the land.
17. The actual use of the land by the various tenants was for agricultural purposes.

---

2. It was stipulated that the lawsuit would be concerned only with the year 1974 and that the court's decision would be binding on all parties for the subsequent tax years 1975 and 1976.

18. Even if the tenants made a good faith commercial agricultural use of the land, that use does not inure to the benefit of the owner . . . because of the purchase price paid, the terms of the lease and the other factors testified to by the Defendant Property Appraiser.

The evidence conclusively establishes a "good faith commercial agricultural use of the land" pursuant to sec. 193.461, Fla. Stat. (Supp.1978). That statute provides in pertinent part:

(3)(a) [The taxpayer must establish] [T]hat said lands were actually used for a bona fide agricultural purpose.
(b) Subject to the restrictions set out in this section, only lands which are used primarily for bona fide agricultural purposes shall be classified agricultural. "Bona fide agricultural purposes" means good faith commercial agricultural use of the land. In determining whether the use of the land for agricultural purposes is bona fide, the following factors may be taken into consideration:
1. The length of time the land has been so utilized;
2. Whether the use has been continuous;
3. The purchase price paid;
4. Size, as it relates to specific agricultural use;
5. Whether an indicated effort has been made to care sufficiently and adequately for the land in accordance with accepted commercial agricultural practices, including, without limitation, fertilizing, liming, tilling, mowing, reforesting, and other accepted agricultural practices;
6. Whether such land is under lease and, if so, the effect of length, terms, and conditions of the lease; and
7. Such other factors as may from time to time become applicable.

There is little, if any, question that only #3 above (purchase price paid) is not fully satisfied under the evidence of this case. The price paid derives further import from subsection (4)(c) of the applicable statute, which provides: "Sale of land for a purchase price which is three or more times the agricultural assessment placed on the land shall create a presumption that such land is not used primarily for bona fide agricultural purposes. Upon a showing of special circumstances by the landowner demonstrating that the land is to be continued in bona fide agriculture, this presumption may be rebutted."
In *Straughn v. K & K Land Management, Inc.*, 326 So.2d 421 (Fla. 1976), Justice Sundberg illustrated the interplay between sections (3)(b) and (4)(c). He stated:

"Purchase price paid" is set forth . . . as one of seven criteria to be considered by tax assessors in making their determination as to whether property qualifies as agricultural for purposes of the lower tax assessment. Presumably evidence tending to confirm the agricultural nature of assessable land, i.e, "special circumstances," should conform to the other six statutory considerations if the presumption established by Section 193.461(4)(c), Florida Statutes, is to be overcome."

326 So.2d at 423. Later, Justice Sundberg stated:

"The phrase 'special circumstances,' indicating what must be shown in order to overcome the statutory presumption at issue, should be read *in pari materia* with

Section 193.461(3)(b), Florida Statutes, and the seven criteria for determination of taxable status enumerated therein."

Id. at 423.

In *Roden v. K & K Land Management, Inc.*, 368 So.2d 588, No.51, 954 (Fla. 1978), the supreme court stated the following with reference to the "special circumstances" sufficient to rebut the presumption:

> As the Department of Revenue has done before, it stresses that commercial success is a necessary circumstance for rebuttal (of the presumption). We reject this notion. As we stated in *Straughn v. K & K Land Management*, 326 So.2d 421 (Fla. 1976), "special circumstances" may be drawn from the factors for consideration in the classification process listed in sec. 193.461(3)(b). The presence of all or any one factor in particular is not necessary for the presumption's rebuttal.

368 So.2d at 589.

In *Walden v. Tuten*, 347 So.2d 129 (Fla. 2d Dist. Ct. App. 1977) this court stated:

> [P]rofit motive is a relevant consideration in determining whether a given agricultural use is in fact a bona fide "commercial" agricultural use. Such a motive would certainly be one of the "other factors as may . . . become applicable" within the contemplation of subsection (7) of the aforequoted factors listed under subsection (3)(b) of sec. 193.461, supra.

347 So.2d at 131.

Implicit in the tax assessor's reasons for denying the agricultural classification and explicit in the lower court's findings is the notion that there did not exist a "good faith commercial agricultural use of the land." In the words of the tax assessor:

> (5) The owner [appellant] was not a farmer.
> (6) There was no reasonable expectation that the continued agricultural activities would return a reasonable rate of return on the landowner's investment in the land.

The lower court stated:

> (18) Even if the tenants made a good faith commercial agricultural use of the land, that use does not inure to the benefit of the owner . . . because of the purchase price paid, the term of the lease and the other factors testified to by the Defendant Property Appraiser.

Both the tax assessor and the lower court have misconstrued the statutory requirement that land must be used for "bona fide agricultural purposes," i.e., a "good faith commercial agricultural use." It is not required that the owner be a farmer or that there be a profit realized on the owner's overall investment.

As we pointed out above, the supreme court in *Roden* stated that commercial success was not a necessary circumstance for rebuttal of the statutory presumption.

In addition, the supreme court stated in *Straughn v. Tuck*, 354 So.2d 368, 370–71 (Fla. 1978):

> "Commercial agricultural use" simply adds another factor, i.e., profit or profit motive, which may be considered by the tax assessor in determining whether or

not a claimed agricultural use is bona fide. It does not , . . . limit agricultural classification to commercially profitable agricultural operations.

Also, in this court's opinion in *Straughn v. K & K Land Management, Inc.*, 347 So.2d 724 (Fla. 2d Dist. Ct. App. 1977) (styled *Roden v. K & K Land Management, Inc.* in the supreme court) this court stated the following with reference to "profit motive":

> The "profit motive" we spoke of in *Tuten* doesn't necessarily mean that a profit need immediately be sought on the total investment, i.e., the purchase price for an entire tract of land. The purchase price may well have contemplated that the land is to be held for speculation or for a future nonagricultural use, but the statute obviously permits this so long as the land, . . . is nevertheless presently put to a bona fide commercial agricultural use. Moreover, a potential profit to be made solely from the claimed commercial agricultural use may indeed only sustain such agricultural use itself or, perhaps, it may simply help carry the lands or reduce the investment until such time as the full speculative profits on the purchase price can be realized; but that doesn't mean that such agricultural use should be any less a legislatively encouraged agricultural use.

347 So.2d at 726.

In light of the above authority, we hold that the statutory requirement for "bona fide agricultural purposes" and a "good faith commercial agricultural use of the land" were satisfied in the instant case. As the supreme court pointed out in *Roden*:

> "'[U]se' is still the guidepost in classifying land, although other specifically enumerated factors relative to use may also be considered. Agricultural use is now and has always been the test. We adhere to this view."

368 So.2d at 589, citing *Straughn v. Tuck*, 354 So.2d at 370.

REVERSED and REMANDED.
HOBSON, Acting C. J., and SCHEB, J., concur.

Question

This opinion touches on a central issue when it quotes the Florida supreme court in *Straughn v. Tuck*: "'Commercial agricultural use' simply adds another factor, i.e., profit or profit motive, which may be considered by the tax assessor in determining whether or not a claimed agricultural use is bona fide. It does not . . . limit agricultural classification to commercially profitable agricultural operations." Is *Fisher v. Schooley* consistent with the logic of this quotation? Is this quotation consistent with a statute that defines "bona fide agricultural purposes" as "good faith commercial agricultural use of the land"? Would a contrary decision in *Fisher v. Schooley* necessarily imply that only profitable agricultural operations could qualify for preferential tax treatment under Section 193.461?

MARKHAM V. FOGG
458 So. 2d 1122
Supreme Court of Florida, 1984

JUDGES: Adkins, Overton, Alderman, McDonald and Ehrlich, JJ., concur. Boyd, C.J., dissents.

OPINION: PER CURIAM.

We review the opinion of the Fourth District Court of Appeal in *Fogg v. Broward County*, 397 So.2d 944 (Fla. 4th Dist. Ct. App. 1981), which directly conflicts with *Lauderdale v. Blake*, 351 So.2d 742 (Fla. 3d Dist. Ct. App. 1977), on the same point of law. We have jurisdiction, article V, section 3(b)(3), Florida Constitution. We quash the decision of the district court.

This is an agricultural classification case pertaining to the classification under section 193.461, Florida Statutes (1973) of certain lands in Broward County for the years 1974 and 1975. Particularly, the litigation concerns the "Fogg Parcel" of 270 acres. Prior to 1974, the parcel was classified as agricultural land and taxed as such. On January 1, 1974, the Tax Assessor reclassified the property as nonagricultural and reassessed it. The landowners brought actions for declaratory judgment and injunctive relief to have their property classified and taxed as agricultural for 1974 and 1975. The trial court denied the relief sought and upheld the nonagricultural classification. The trial court found that the case was primarily controlled by section 193.461(4)(c) because there was a sale of land at a price more than three times the agricultural assessment and because the landowners had not provided sufficient evidence to rebut the presumption. In addition, the trial court found that the land had been rezoned to a nonagricultural use at the request of the owner as per section 193.461(4)(a)3. Finally, the trial court applied the criteria set forth in section 193.461(3)(b) and found that the landowners had not shown that the land was primarily being used for bona fide agricultural purposes.

. . . .

The district court reversed. It held that section 193.461(4)(c) applied only to completed sales of realty and that the landowners, while having numerous contracts to sell the land, had not in fact sold the land. The court also held that the rezoning from agricultural to planned unit development did in fact occur but that such did not require the land to be reclassified as nonagricultural since agricultural use continued on the property pending its actual use as a development. Finally, the district court held that the evidence failed to support the trial court's finding that the land in question was not being used primarily for bona fide agricultural purposes.

The petitioners raise three issues on this appeal. First, they contend that the district court erred when it rejected the application of section 193.461(4)(c) to this case. That section, the "three times rule," creates a rebuttable presumption that the sale of land for a purchase price which is three or more times the agricultural assessment placed on the land shows that the land is not being used for bona fide agricultural purposes. The district court was correct in noting that the statutory language applies only to a completed sale and not mere contracts to sell. In the instant case, there was no completed sale.

The next point raised by petitioners concerns the issue left undecided by this court in *Harbor Ventures, Inc. v. Hutches*, 366 So.2d 1173 (Fla. 1979). There, the constitutionality of section 193.461(4)(a)3 was brought up but because of the particular facts of that case the constitutional question was not addressed. Since the facts of the case sub judice squarely fall within the purview of that section, we must reach that issue now. It is incontrovertible that the section has been triggered because abundant evidence appears in the record to support the conclusion that the property was in fact rezoned even though the landowners argue that no rezoning has taken place. This was the conclusion of the trial court with which the district court concurred.

We have in the instant case land that has been rezoned to a nonagricultural use at the request of the owner subsequent to the enactment of the 1972 law. The statute specifically mandates that "[t]he assessor shall reclassify" land that has been rezoned to a nonagricultural use at the request of the owner. The language is mandatory and "is a clear legislative directive to the property appraisers of the state." 366 So.2d at 1175 (Boyd, J., dissenting). Unlike the above-mentioned section 193.461(4)(c) which allows the landowner to present evidence in opposition to the appraiser's reclassification, section 193.461(4)(a)3 is in the form of a mandatory presumption. We have stated that the test to determine the constitutionality of a mandatory presumption is three-fold:

> [c]onstitutionality . . . under the Due Process Clause must be measured by determining (1) whether the concern of the legislature was reasonably aroused by the possibility of an abuse which it legitimately desired to avoid; (2) whether there was a reasonable basis for a conclusion that the statute would protect against its occurrence; and (3) whether the expense and other difficulties of individual determinations justify the inherent imprecision of a conclusive presumption.

Bass v. General Development Corp., 374 So.2d 479, 484 (Fla. 1979). See also *Gallie v. Wainwright*, 362 So.2d 936 (Fla. 1978).

Concerning the first prong of this test, it is apparent that the legislature's concern was reasonably aroused by the possibility of land developers taking advantage of the agricultural classification provisions to minimize their holding costs prior to development. As to the second prong, the legislature could have concluded that since rezoning to a nonagricultural use was an obvious and necessary prerequisite to development, the statute in question would protect against the abuse of this special tax classification. As stated in *Harbor Ventures*, "Such an interpretation provides an incentive for agricultural lands to remain devoted to agricultural production by discouraging speculative rezoning." 366 So.2d at 1174. Quite clearly, the statute proscribes speculative rezoning and hence is rationally related to the overall greenbelt purpose.

Moreover, this reasoning is not inconsistent with the view expressed in *Bass* where the related section 193.461(4)(a)4 was declared unconstitutional. That section was found to be infirm because there was no rational connection between the greenbelt purpose and that section's mandatory reclassification upon the occurrence of recording of a subdivision plat. We held then that the filing of a subdivision plat has little to do with the use of property. As related to that section, use was the standard against which to measure reasonableness. With the instant section, however, use is not the standard. Our Constitution does not mandate a use standard; instead, article VII, section 4(a), only says that "Agricultural land or land used exclusively for non-commercial recreational purposes may be classified by general law and assessed solely on the basis of character or use." Our cases have held that in implementing that provision "the legislature has generally chosen to classify land on the basis of use rather than an implication that article VII, section 4(a) of our Constitution requires that result." *Bass* at 482. Of note is the case of *Rainey v. Nelson*, 257 So.2d 538 (Fla. 1972), wherein we sustained a related legislative enactment that classified land as nonagricultural according to criteria completely unrelated to the actual use of the taxpayer's property. Or, as noted in *Harbor Ventures*, "If the greenbelt law and the decisions interpreting it have established actual use of land as the general test for entitlement to the agricultural assessment, then clearly section 193.461(4)(a)3 constitutes a legislatively-mandated exception to that test." 366 So.2d at 1175 (Boyd, J., dissenting). Therefore, the instant section is rationally related to the legislative purpose and hence is proper.

As to the final prong of the test, the landowner has no right of rebuttal to the mandatory reclassification of the subject property. This is not fatal, however, because the instant statute can be read in pari materia with section 193.461(3)(b). After property has been reclassified under subsection (4)(a)3 as nonagricultural, the landowner is not precluded from presenting evidence under subsection (3)(b) to show that his property is indeed being used primarily for bona fide agricultural purposes. That latter subsection lists several factors that may be shown by the landowner and if sufficient, the property would then be classified agricultural. The procedure, in essence, would be the same as if subsection (4)(a)3 itself were rebuttable. For this reason, it clearly satisfies the third prong of the due process test.

Basically, this procedure is what the trial judge employed in the proceedings below. That judge determined that the landowners had not shown sufficient evidence to prove that the land in question was being used primarily for bona fide agricultural purposes for the years 1974 and 1975. As long as there is competent, substantial evidence to buttress this finding, an appeals court should not substitute its judgment for that of the trier of fact. Since the issue of whether the land was primarily being used for agricultural purposes is one of fact, the trial court's finding is clothed with a presumption of correctness. Since the evidence was conflicting, we find that there was ample credible evidence adduced at the trial to sustain the trial judge's findings. The district court was hence in error in overruling the trial court on this point.

The last issue merits but little discussion. Argument is made that the statute violates equal protection. However, the test under equal protection was highlighted in *In re Estate of Greenberg*, 390 So.2d 40 (Fla. 1980):

> The rational basis or minimum scrutiny test generally employed in equal protection analysis requires only that a statute bear some reasonable relationship to a legitimate state purpose. That the statute may result incidentally in some inequality or that it is not drawn with mathematical precision will not result in its invalidity. Rather, the statutory classification to be held unconstitutionally violative of the equal protection clause under this test must cause different treatments so disparate as relates to the difference in classification so as to be wholly arbitrary.

390 So.2d at 42.

This Court has already recognized in *Harbor Ventures* that the legislature could have concluded the statute was rationally related to the legitimate state goal of minimizing and discouraging speculative rezoning. *Harbor Ventures*, 366 So.2d at 1174. The treatment afforded the instant landowners are not so disparate from others as to be wholly arbitrary.

We hold, therefore, that section 193.461(4)(a)3, applying to a situation where land zoned agricultural is changed to a nonagricultural zoning at the request of its owner, is constitutional and was proper as applied to the facts of this case. Accordingly, we quash the decision of the district court and instruct it to enter an order affirming the final judgment of the trial court.

It is so ordered.

ADKINS, OVERTON, ALDERMAN, MCDONALD and EHRLICH, JJ., Concur.

BOYD, C.J., Dissents.

Notes and Questions

1. Given the earlier cases in this series, why do you think Justice Boyd dissented in *Markham v. Fogg?*

2. In the case that follows, *Robbins v. Yusem,* note the reduction in the amount of the preliminary assessment that followed agricultural classification. This may help explain some of the volume of appeals on this issue in Florida.

ROBBINS V. YUSEM
559 So. 2d 1185, *appeal denied,* 569 So.2d 1292 (1990)
District Court of Appeal of Florida, 1990

JUDGES: Schwartz, C.J., Jorgenson, and Cope, JJ.

JORGENSON, J.

Opinion: The Dade County Property Appraiser (Property Appraiser) appeals an order dismissing with prejudice his complaint to reinstate a nonagricultural classification and tax assessment on a parcel of real property. For the following reasons, we reverse.

Melvyn R. Yusem, Trustee (taxpayer), is the legal titleholder of record of a parcel of real property zoned IU-C (Industrial District, Conditional) under the Dade County Zoning Code. Although the land was zoned for industrial use, the property was actually used for the commercial farming of yucca and calabaza. The property had not been used for farming in 1983, 1984, or 1985. In 1987, the Property Appraiser denied the taxpayer's application for an agricultural classification on the grounds that the agricultural use was illegal under the zoning code and thus could not be considered a "good faith" use of the property within the meaning of the Greenbelt Law, section 193.461, Florida Statutes (1987). The taxpayer appealed to the Property Appraisal Adjustment Board of Dade County (PAAB). A special master heard the petition and recommended agricultural classification. The PAAB adopted the special master's recommendation and reduced the property's preliminary assessment from $1,900,584 to $8,730. The Property Appraiser then filed an action in the circuit court seeking reinstatement of the preliminary assessment and denial of the agricultural classification. The taxpayer moved to dismiss the action for failure to state a claim, arguing that present agricultural use of the property is the dispositive factor in classifying the land for ad valorem taxation. The trial court granted the motion and entered a final order dismissing the complaint with prejudice. The Property Appraiser appeals; we reverse.

The issue presented by this appeal is whether the actual commercial agricultural use of property in violation of Dade County zoning ordinances can be considered a "good faith" agricultural use entitled to preferential tax treatment under section 193.461, Florida Statutes (the Greenbelt Law). The question is one of appellate first impression.

Agricultural classification or "exemption" for property tax purposes is governed by section 193.461, Florida Statutes (1987).

. . . .

In applying the "good faith" requirement, Florida courts have consistently construed "good faith" to mean "real, actual and of a genuine nature as opposed to a sham or deception." Agricultural use alone does not entitle a taxpayer to an agricultural exemption. *See Markham v. Fogg,* 458 So. 2d 1122 (Fla. 1984) (land used primarily for grazing cattle did not qualify for "good faith" agricultural classification); *Champion Realty Corp. v. Burgess,* 541 So. 2d 615, 618 (Fla. 1st Dist. Ct. App.) (even if the "sole act of cutting down trees . . . was the most significant physical activity on the land," no agricultural classification would be granted where the Property Appraiser and the court found that such use was not "bona fide"), *rev. denied,* 549 So. 2d 1013 (Fla. 1989). The Property Appraiser concluded, and we agree, that, if the "good faith" requirement excludes from agricultural classification *sham* physical agricultural use, it must also exclude from agricultural classification *unlawful* physical agricultural use.[2]

The taxpayer's agricultural use of the property was unlawful under the Dade County, Florida Code @33-268, which reads: "No land . . . in an IU-C district shall be used or permitted to be used . . . (except as a legal nonconforming building or use), except for one or more of the uses hereinafter enumerated . . . ." Commercial agricultural use is not one of the many enumerated permitted uses and is thus an unlawful use.

The legislative history of the Greenbelt Law supports the Property Appraiser's denial of an agricultural classification. The legislative intent of the Greenbelt Law is to conserve, protect, and encourage the development and improvement of agricultural lands suffering from the urban pressure of expanding metropolitan development. See preambles to chapters 59-226 and 72-181, Laws of Florida. The property in question was not agricultural land threatened by urban development but urban land classified exclusively for industrial development. There was no previously existing agricultural use to conserve or protect.

We must strictly interpret the agricultural exemption statute. "While doubtful language in taxing statutes should be resolved in favor of the taxpayer, the reverse is applicable in the construction of exceptions and exemptions from taxation." *United States Gypsum Co. v. Green,* 110 So. 2d 409, 413 (Fla. 1959). This court, affirming a summary judgment denying a taxpayer favorable tax treatment, stated: "[I]n order for a taxpayer to receive a benefit different in kind from other taxpayers, it is necessary for him to strictly comply with all conditions which would be necessary to entitle him to the special treatment." *Jar Corp. v. Culbertson,* 246 So. 2d 144, 145 (Fla. 3d Dist. Ct. App.), *cert. denied,* 246 So. 2d 690 (Fla. 1971).

Where, as here, the use of the property for commercial agriculture was prohibited by law and therefore was not in "good faith" as required by the Greenbelt Law, the Property Appraiser's denial of agricultural classification was proper.[4] Contrary to the taxpayer's argument, our decision will not create an unconstitutional irrebuttable presumption. At the outset, a finding that commercial agricultural use is not bona fide because it is prohibited under the zoning laws may be overcome by a showing that the use is a legal nonconforming use. Once the Property Appraiser determines, however, that the use is prohibited and is not a legal nonconforming use, the use, as a matter of law, is not bona fide and is not in good faith. That conclusion is a rule of substantive law, not an evidentiary presumption. *See* Ehrhardt, *Florida Evidence* §301.3 (2d ed. 1984) ("Although some rules of law are called conclusive presumptions from time to time, they are

---

2.   *See, e.g., Bower v. Edwards County Appraisal Dist.,* 752 S.W. 2d 629 (Tex.App. 1988) (taxpayer could not claim agricultural exemption for land used for raising deer and the vegetation which they ate where deer were wild and state law prohibited private ownership of wild deer).

4.   The County's failure thus far actively to enforce its zoning code does not transform the prohibited use into a permitted use.

not properly included in a codification of the law of evidence since they are rules of substantive law in the particular area in which they exist.").

Moreover, there is an eminently rational basis for the rule of law that we announce today. The determination of the Property Appraiser is reasonably related to legitimate legislative aims, while the order of dismissal entered by the trial court grants the taxpayer a substantial tax reduction based on an illegal use of land. No statute, judicial decision, or principle of equity permits us to sanction an illegal act by conferring upon the taxpayer substantial tax relief at the expense of other taxpayers. Accordingly, we conclude that, as a matter of law, agricultural use of property in violation of applicable zoning regulations cannot be considered "good faith" commercial agricultural use of the land entitling its owner to an agricultural exemption. The Property Appraiser's complaint therefore stated a cause of action.

Reversed and remanded for further proceedings consistent with this opinion.

Notes and Questions

1. Maryland introduced the first program for use-value assessment of agricultural and recreational land in 1956; by 1982 some variation on this approach had been enacted in every state, sometimes after amendment of the state constitutional provisions requiring uniformity in taxation. Proponents see these measures as a means of avoiding development pressure from escalating property taxes; critics see them as a subsidy to developers and speculators holding land for future construction. The economist Henry Aaron wrote, "In the absence of evidence supporting artificial deferral, special farmland exemptions are inequitable and should be repealed. They specifically reduce taxes for owners of a rapidly appreciating asset and, hence, rapidly growing wealth."[1] Among the points to consider in evaluating such programs are (1) the ability of farmers to borrow against the value of their property in order to pay taxes; (2) the desirability of preserving farmland in the urban fringe, and its effect on community development; (3) the criteria for distinguishing between "speculators" and farmers holding land but willing to sell it upon a high enough offer; (4) the importance of property taxes to a family's decision to continue farming or to sell their land; and (5) fairness to the other property owners in the jurisdiction whose taxes are higher as a result of these preferences.

2. What advice would you offer a legislator seeking to restrict the benefit of agricultural use valuation in Florida? Should preferential assessment be available for land temporarily held vacant in preparation for future development? What minimum amount of agricultural activity would qualify as an agricultural "use"? Can a requirement of "bona fide" agricultural use be meaningful?[2] Problems of this type arise frequently in

---

1. H. Aaron, *Who Pays the Property Tax?* (1975).

2. See B. Currier, "An Analysis of Differential Taxation as a Method of Maintaining Agricultural and Open Space Land Uses," *University of Florida Law Review* 30(1978):821.

the classification of various types of open space, forestland, quarries, and meadows. In *Barrett v. Borough of Frenchtown*, 6 N.J. Tax 558 (1984), the New Jersey Tax Court held that the taxpayer's five-acre lot was not sufficiently "devoted to" honey production to qualify for a reduction in its assessment as agricultural land. Judge Conley wrote:

> I conclude from the testimony that plaintiff's land is in a relatively wild state, not having been cultivated for any purpose. I find that the bees from the hives on plaintiff's property gather some nectar from that property; however, to a much greater extent they gather it from a wider area, up to as far as three miles away in all directions from the property. Finally, I conclude that the bees would produce just as much honey of the same type if they did not forage at all on plaintiff's land. The essence of this conclusion is that the contribution of plaintiff's land to the production of honey is de minimus.

3. With the 1965 California Land Conservation Act, or Williamson Act, California pioneered the approach of making open-space or agricultural use assessment contingent on agreements between property owners and local governments restricting development for a given period. Of course, property tax limitations and rate reductions correspondingly diminish the incentive offered by current-use valuation.[3]

4. Having pioneered open-space preferential assessment, Maryland again made news in this area when the United States Supreme Court in 1989 denied a petition to review the state's revocation of an open-space agreement with a golf club not open to women. That agreement had limited the valuation of the Burning Tree golf club's property to its value as open space in exchange for the club's agreement not to develop the property. After the fifty-year agreement was signed in 1981, the state revoked its benefits because the club did not accept women as members. Burning Tree, President Eisenhower's home course, has long been famous as a favorite club for members of government and the diplomatic corps. Former Attorney General Benjamin Civiletti represented the club in its challenge to the state's revocation of these tax benefits, worth an estimated $300,000 annually. This challenge invoked state law, the first amendment right to freedom of association, and the contract clause of the federal constitution. *State v. Burning Tree Club, Inc.*, 315 Md. 254, 554 A.2d 366 (1989), *cert. denied*, 493 U.S. 816 (1989).

---

3. See "Proposition 13: A Mandate to Reevaluate the Williamson Act," *Southern California Law Review* 54(1980):93; K. Ehrman and S. Flavin, *Taxing California Property*, 3d ed. (1988), chapter 25.

5. Florida is by no means unique in allowing great latitude in the classification of land for agricultural preferences. Robert Glennon has offered the following commentary on the Arizona system of agricultural assessment:

> Arizona has a tax scheme affectionately dubbed "rent-a-cow" by county assessors and state revenue officials. Trying to protect agricultural interests, the Arizona legislature mandated that agricultural and grazing land be assessed solely by an income approach to value (annual net cash rental), not by market value. Land used for agricultural purposes, even if adjacent to urban areas and a prime target for development, qualifies for this benefit. In a recent Pima County, Arizona case, the Assessor took the position that, when a developer purchased the land for investment, the land no longer qualified as agricultural land. The developer candidly testified that the purchase was for investment and that he had taken initial steps toward developing it. The developer, however, leased grazing rights to a neighboring rancher for five to seven head of cattle for $250 a year. The Arizona Court of Appeals held that the developer was entitled to have the land assessed as agricultural, notwithstanding the owner's intention to develop, and that the paltry annual rental did not provide a reasonable rate of return on the investment. The upshot was that land purchased for $4,500,000 was assessed at $3455. The differential between the assessed and actual value is approximately 1300 times. The beneficiary of this loophole, according to the Pima County Assessor, is "any developer who is big enough to have his own legal staff."[4]

6. S. Ceglowski has recently commented on the potential application of current-use assessment to land subject to conservation easements.[5]

"Current Use" and "Highest and Best Use"

LANIER v. WALT DISNEY WORLD CO.
316 So.2d 59
Florida District Court of Appeal, 1975

WALDEN, Judge.
We adopt the appealed final judgment, prepared by the Honorable Roger A. Barker, Circuit Judge of the Circuit Court in and for the Ninth Judicial Circuit, as the official opinion of this court:

---

4. R. Glennon, "Taxation and Equal Protection," *George Washington Law Review* 58(1990):261, 305. [citations omitted]. The case Professor Glennon refers to is *Stewart Title & Trust v. Pima County*, 156 Ariz. 236, 751 P.2d 552 (Ariz. Ct. App. 1987).

5. S. Ceglowski, "Note: Changing Vermont's Current Use Appraisal Program to Provide Property Tax Incentives for Conservation Easements," *Vermont Law Review* 17(1992):165.

"WALT DISNEY WORLD CO., a corporation, and MADEIRA LAND COM-
PANY, INC., a corporation, Plaintiffs, vs. WADE H. LANIER, JR., as Tax Assessor of
Osceola County, Florida; MURRAY A. BRONSON, as Tax Collector of Osceola
County, Florida; and J. ED STRAUGHN, as Executive Director of the Department of
Revenue, State of Florida Defendants.

"FINAL JUDGMENT
"This is a suit attacking the 1972 ad valorem valuation of Plaintiffs' properties located
in Osceola County. It is alleged the Assessor failed to comply with the essential
requirements of F.S. 193.011 in arriving at 'just value' as provided by Article VII, Section
4, of the Florida Constitution.

"Upon a consideration of the evidence the Court finds:

"It has jurisdiction of the subject matter and of the parties.

"In the early 1960's WALT DISNEY PRODUCTIONS, acting through the named
Plaintiffs herein as subsidiary corporations, acquired approximately 27,000 acres of
contiguous lands located in Orange and Osceola Counties; approximately 10,300 acres
of which are in Osceola County.

"A master plan for the development of the 27,000 acre unit of property was prepared
by WALT DISNEY PRODUCTIONS. It was anticipated that the 27,000 acre unit of
property was to be developed over at least a 15-year period into a unique, total, planned
environment consisting of closely interrelated recreational, industrial, residential and
transportational complexes. Specifically, the plan contemplated the development and
construction of an entertainment and recreational complex which included a theme park
similar in concept to Disneyland in California, five hotels, each of which was to be
developed pursuant to an individual theme, and other tourist facilities including a
unique transportational complex; an industrial park which would be a laboratory for the
development and public exposure to new products, services and facilities. The plan
anticipated the use of the most modern techniques and methods of construction and the
development of a totally unique project.

"The development of the land in accordance with the plan was commenced in 1968
and has continued to the present date. The theme park has been constructed, two hotels
have been completed, and other tourist facilities, including the first phase of the
transportational complex, have been completed. All of the development so far has been
in Orange County with the exception of an entrance road which connects the theme park
with U.S Route 192 in Osceola County. The vast majority of the Osceola County
acreage consists of undeveloped swamp and pine-woods flatlands. There are a few area[s]
of improved pasture land and canals with water control devices.

"The theme park, known as DISNEY WORLD, opened its doors during October,
1971. During its first year of operations there were approximately 10,700,000 paid
admissions. All these millions of visitors were funneled into the theme park via U.S.
Route 192 from several major arterial highways.

"The evidence further revealed clearly and unequivocally that as of January 1, 1972,
the 10,300 acres located in Osceola County were being used and the immediate expected
use was for the following purposes:

(1) A buffer to commercial development on U.S. Route 192.
(2) A vast water storage area of several thousand acres for flood control and
      conservation purposes in maintaining . . . environment and ecological condi-
      tions and features in their natural state.
(3) As a psychological mind conditioner for the millions of visitors to the theme park.

"The Disney imagineers are of the opinion that as a visitor approaches the theme park our God-given wild, undeveloped swamps and piney flatwoods are conducive in establishing a proper frame of mind by one to enter into and thoroughly enjoy a delightful fantasy-land of make-believe for children as well as grown-ups.

"Ever since the announcement of the plans for Disney World Osceola County, as well as all the other counties of Central Florida, have experienced an influx of land speculators and developers. Again it is 'boom time' in Central Florida with all its attendant growth problems and tax problems. This is nothing new for this state. If we are to avoid the 'bust' which so often follows the 'land boom' our tax assessors must strictly adhere to the tax laws in every respect insofar as humanly possible.

"The evidence further reveals that upon the building of U.S. Route 192 from its interchange with the Sunshine Parkway on the east and U.S. Route 27 on the west land speculation became quite prevalent along U.S. Route 192. Small plots of land sold for as much as $150,000 per acre or more. The county zoning for all the lands adjacent to the Disney tract was zoned agricultural. However, it appears that upon the actual development of the land for a tourist-oriented use the zoning for that particular parcel was changed accordingly by the Osceola County authorities, leaving the adjacent undeveloped parcels with the agricultural classification.

"The evidence further reveals the history of the assessed value of the Disney lands, to-wit:

YEAR	VALUATION
1967	$526,655
1968	$1,106,730
1969	$1,106,730
1970	$2,280,112
1971	$2,324,202
1972	$15,172,850

"The art of appraising the fair market value of real estate is not an exact science. For this reason our Legislature has laid down certain factors in F.S. 193.011 for the assessor to follow in arriving at 'just value' or 'fair market value.' Our Supreme Court and Appellate Courts in their recent pronouncements concerning F.S. 193.011 have clearly indicated that the assessor must consider each of the factors set forth in the law, and if he fails to do so his assessed values must be set aside when proper allegations and proof of such facts are presented to the Court.[1]

"Plaintiffs allege the assessor failed to consider two of the factors, namely,

(1) the highest and best use to which the property can be expected to be put in the immediate future and the present use of the property.

(2) the quantity or size of the property.

---

1. The proper text for measuring the validity of a tax assessor's action is set out in *Powell v. Kelly* (Fla.), 223 So.2d 305:

While the assessor is accorded a range of discretion in determining valuations for the purpose of taxation *when the officer proceeds in accordance with and substantially complies with the requirements of law designated to ascertain such values,* yet, if the steps required to be taken in valuation are not in fact and in good faith actually taken, and the valuations are shown to be essentially unjust or unequal abstractly or relatively, the assessment is invalid.

"After carefully reviewing the evidence on these two grounds the Court finds the assessor made fundamental error in assessing the property lying adjacent to and a depth of 200 feet deep from U.S. Route 192 and along the entrance road leading into the theme park.

"The Court further finds Plaintiffs have failed to demonstrate fundamental error on the part of the assessor in assessing the remaining property on an acreage basis at the rates applied by the assessor.[2]

"F.S. 193.011 provides:

> 193.011 *Factors to consider in deriving just valuation.*—In arriving at just valuation as required under #4, Art. VII of the state constitution, the tax assessor shall take into consideration the following factors:
>
> (1) The present cash value of the property;
> (2) The highest and best to which the property can be expected to be put in the immediate future and the present use of the property;
> (3) The location of said property;
> (4) The quantity or size of said property;
> (5) The cost of said property and the present replacement value of any improvements thereon;
> (6) The condition of said property;
> (7) The income from said property; and
> (8) The net proceeds of the sale of the property, as received by the seller, after deduction of all of the usual and reasonable fees and costs of the sale, including the costs and expenses of financing.

"In discussing the factors as set forth in F.S. 193.011 the assessor was of the opinion that he was not obliged under the law to give each factor equal weight. THE COURT AGREES WITH THIS INTERPRETATION PROVIDED EACH FACTOR IS FIRST CAREFULLY CONSIDERED AND SUCH WEIGHT IS GIVEN TO A FACTOR AS THE FACTS JUSTIFY. [Emphasis supplied.]

"In this age of rapid population growth which in turn creates a greater diversity in the use of land we are becoming more aware of the value of long range planning for land uses. In assessing real estate at its 'just value' the Assessor must consider the highest and best use to which the property can be expected to be put in the *immediate* future and the *present* use of the property. This in turn is directly influenced by the zoning, if any, that affects the property as of January 1st of the taxable year.

" *The 'Use' factor set forth in F.S. 193.011 is entitled to great weight in the assessment process of each parcel of land. If the assessor fails to comply with literally applying this factor to each of his assessments, then he departs from the essential requirement of the law by indulging in speculation.*[3] [Emphasis supplied.]

---

2. As constitutional officers, the actions of tax assessors are clothed with a presumption of correctness. To overcome this presumption appropriate allegations and proofs excluding every reasonable hypothesis of legal assessment are necessary. *Powell v. Kelly* (Fla.), 223 So.2d 305. *Folsom v. Bank of Greenwood* (97 Fla. 426), 120 So. 317. *District School Board of Lee County v. Askew* (Fla.), 278 So.2d 272.

3. The statutory guidepost for the "use" factor set forth above in F.S. 193.011 has been construed by the Florida Supreme in *Lanier v. Overstreet* (Fla.), 175 So.2d 521, 524, and

"In the matter sub judice the Disney land and the other properties along U.S. Route 192 were all zoned agricultural as of January 1, 1972, except those properties where development had been commenced or completed.

"As to those vacant lands outside of the Disney property and fronting U.S. Route 192, it is clear and unequivocal that much of the lands, although zoned agricultural, were being used on the speculators' market as a commodity in land titles with no physical use of the land itself. An assessment based upon such use in arriving at 'just value' is a fair one under our State Constitution. On the other hand, the bona fide physical uses of the Disney land fronting on the U.S. Route 192 and the entrance road were entirely different from the so-called comparable properties on U.S. Route 192 highway used by the assessor in assessing the Disney property. The uses by the Plaintiffs' of their properties fronting U.S. Route 192, on January 2, 1972, were consistent with the highest and best use to which the property could be expected to be put in the immediate future. The uses of the Disney highway frontage were essentially the same as all the rest of the Disney property in Osceola County. The uses were consistent with the zoning in effect as of January 1, 1972.

"IT IS THEREUPON ORDERED AND ADJUDGED the 1972 assessed values of Plaintiffs' land lying adjacent to U.S. Route 192 and the entrance road leading into the theme park assessed by the assessor on a front footage basis be, and the same are hereby set aside and held for naught.

"IT IS FURTHER ORDERED the assessor shall forthwith reassess the lands next above described in accordance with this Opinion and report the reassessed values to the Plaintiffs and this Court within thirty days from the date of His Order unless for good cause shown further time is needed by the assessor.

"IT IS FURTHER ORDERED AND ADJUDGED the 1972 assessments on a acreage basis of the remainder of Plaintiffs' land are valid. The temporary injunction heretofore entered by this Court concerning the lands upon which the Court finds to be validly assessed be, and the same is hereby dissolved, and the collection of the 1972 taxes thereon may proceed.

"The costs, including the Court Reporter's costs, are assessed against Osceola County.

"The Court reserves jurisdiction of the subject matter and of the parties to enter such other Orders as may seem meet and just.

"ORDERED at Kissimmee, Osceola County, Florida, this April 18th, 1974.

/s/ Roger A. Barker CIRCUIT JUDGE

Affirmed.

OWEN, C.J., and CROSS, J., concur.

---

later re-affirmed by the 1st District Court of Appeal in *Williams v. Simpson*, 209 So.2d (262) 263 as follows:

By authorizing tax assessors to consider, as one of the factors in arriving at a just valuation of property, the use to which the property "can be *expected* to be put in the *immediate* future" (emphasis added) the Legislature has . . . prohibited tax assessors from considering potential uses to which the property is reasonably susceptible and to which it might possibly be put in some future tax year or, even, during the current tax year. To be considered, the use must be *expected* not merely potential or a reasonably susceptible type of use; it must be expected *immediately*, not at some vague uncertain time in the future . . . .

Notes and Questions

1. What is a "psychological mind conditioner"?

2. What was the "current use" of the property at issue in *Lanier?* How, if at all, could the taxpayer's position on that issue be refuted?

3. Consider the opinion's discussion of the meaning of "highest and best use." In *Board of Assessment Appeals v. Colorado Arlberg Club*, 762 P.2d 146 (Colo. 1988), the Supreme Court of Colorado wrote at pp. 151–53:

> The next question before this court is whether the court of appeals was correct to conclude that the Board could not consider reasonable future use of the Club's property to determine its present fair market value. We have explained that market value is "what a willing buyer would pay a willing seller under normal economic conditions". . . . Our definition is consistent with the basic definition of market value used by appraisers:
>
>> The most probable price in cash, terms equivalent to cash, or in other precisely revealed terms, for which the appraised property will sell in a competitive market under all conditions requisite to fair sale, with the buyer and seller each acting prudently, knowledgeably, and for self-interest, and assuming that neither is under undue duress.
>
> American Institute of Real Estate Appraisers, *The Appraisal of Real Estate* 33 (8th ed. 1983); *see also* Comment, *The Road to Uniformity in Real Estate Taxation: Valuation and Appeal*, 124 U. Pa.L.Rev. 1418, 1430 (1976) (market value is defined as the price reached "in a fair, arm's length transaction between willing parties") (footnote omitted).
>
> As the court of appeals acknowledged, we have ruled that reasonable future use is relevant to market value in several eminent domain cases . . . . However, the court of appeals reasoned that because the "assessor can periodically reassess the tax on a property, based on changes in the property's use, on new improvements, or on changes in present market value . . . equity dictates that the principles of the law of eminent domain not be transferred to tax assessment situations." *Colorado Arlberg Club*, 719 P.2d at 373. For several reasons, we disagree.
>
> First, the one-time nature of an eminent domain payment has nothing to do with our rule that reasonable future use must be considered in calculating just compensation for a government taking. Instead, reasonable future use is considered because it is relevant to the property's present market value. *See Board of County Comm'rs v. Vail Assocs.*, 171 Colo. 381, 388, 468 P.2d 842, 845 (1970) ("It is fundamental that evidence of the highest and best use to which the property may reasonably be applied in the future by [people] of ordinary prudence and judgment is admissible to assist the commission or jury in arriving at the present cash market value of the property being taken."). For example, a tract of undeveloped land with potential for development has a higher present fair market value than the same size tract of undeveloped land with no such potential, i.e., even in its

undeveloped state, a willing buyer and a willing seller would agree on a higher price for it.

Given this rationale, it becomes clear that the fact that periodic reassessments and reassessments based on certain "unusual conditions" pursuant to sec. 39-1-104(11)(b)(I), 16B C.R.S. (1983 Supp.), are permitted in tax cases is irrelevant to the concept or calculation of a property's present fair market value for tax assessment purposes. Because the distinction relied on by the court of appeals provides no basis for analysis, and because the legislature has never indicated that it intended the words "market approach" or "market value" to be given any special meaning for tax purposes, our common law interpretation applies . . . .

A second reason for considering reasonable future use is that it is one element of the technical meaning of market value. It is a well-established rule of statutory construction that "[w]ords and phrases that have acquired a technical or particular meaning, whether by legislative definition or otherwise, shall be construed accordingly." §2-4-101, 1B C.R.S. (1980). *See generally* 2A N. Singer, *supra*, §47.29 (in absence of contrary evidence, "technical terms or terms of art used in a statute are presumed to have their technical meaning").

"In the market, the current value of a property is not based on historical prices or cost of creation; it is based on what market participants perceive to be the future benefits of acquisition." American Institute of Real Estate Appraisers, *supra*, at 21; *see also* Comment, *supra*, 124 U.Pa.L.Rev. at 1431–32 (comparable sales method to determining market value involves "taking into consideration all uses to which the property is adapted and *might be applied*") (footnote omitted and emphasis added). Accordingly, a property's "highest and best use," which is "[t]he use, from among reasonably probable and legal alternative uses, found to be physically possible, appropriately supported, financially feasible, that results in highest land value," is a "crucial determinant of value in the market." American Institute of Real Estate Appraisers, *supra*, at 28, 243. Further, the Board clearly considered the property's future use to be relevant to its present market value and "[t]he construction of statutes by administrative officials charged with their enforcement should be given deference by a reviewing court." *Hewlett-Packard Co. v. State, Dep't of Revenue*, 749 P.2d 400, 406 (Colo. 1988).

Finally, while we recognize that some courts have been reluctant to allow consideration of future uses in tax assessments, many of the cases on which the Club relies involved assessments based on future uses that were speculative or impossible. *See, e.g. People ex rel. Empire Mortgage Co. v. Cantor*, 197 A.D. 437, 189 N.Y.S. 646 (1921) (reliance on fanciful "prophetic vision" of development was "even more absurd" in tax case than in eminent domain case); *Finch v. Grays Harbor County*, 121 Wash. 486, 209 P. 833 (1922) (when cost of clearing land would exceed its value, much of the land could never be drained, and there was no demand for use on which assessor relied, "valuation was grossly excessive").

Other cases cited by the parties prohibit valuing undeveloped property as if it had been improved. *See, e.g., City of Newark v. West Milford Township, Passaic County,* 9 N.J. 295, 88 A.2d 211, 215 (1952) (value must be based on "actual condition in which the owner holds it" and assessor cannot ignore lack of public utility service or value land as though it already were subdivided); *Allied Stores, Inc. v. Finance Adm'r,* 76 A.D.2d 835, 428 N.Y.S.2d 316 (1980) (not permissible to determine that property's actual use was no longer viable and to value it as though it had been used more profitably). As explained in Part V below, these limitations apply to both eminent domain and tax cases in Colorado, and do not preclude consideration of reasonable future uses.

. . . .

Other states with statutes more similar to ours, requiring only that the assessment be based on the property's full and fair value, have recognized that "the normal uses to which potential purchasers could put [the property] must be considered" because that is part of the property's market value. *Pacific Mut. Life Ins. Co. v. County of Orange,* 187 Cal.App. 3d 1141, 1148, 232 Cal.Rptr. 233, 236 (1985); *see also Wild Goose Country Club v. Butte County,* 60 Cal.App. 339, 212 P. 711, 712 (1922) (in valuing property for tax purposes, "[t]he question is, not what its value is for a particular purpose, but its value in view of all the purposes to which it is naturally adapted."); *Division of Tax Appeals v. Township of Ewing,* 72 N.J.Super. 238, 178 A.2d 229, 231 (1962) ("assessor must consider the possibility of sale to a buyer who intends a different use, unless such possibility is so remote as to have no real bearing upon current value"). N.J.Stat.Ann. section 54:4–23 (West 1986) provides that the assessor shall "determine the full and fair value" based on the price which the property "would sell for at a fair and bona fide sale." That definition is similar to our definition of market value, and we agree with the distinction stated by the New Jersey Superior Court:

> An assessor who values a farm as though actually subdivided into the building lots of a residential development, when in fact that has not yet occurred, would be in error; but he would also err if he refuses to consider that a developer would pay a higher price for the farm than another farmer.

Division of Tax Appeals v. Township of Ewing, 178 A.2d at 232.

To summarize, the reasonable future use of real property is an element of its fair market value under its technical definition as well as its common law interpretation in Colorado and elsewhere. Because there is no indication that the legislature intended to reject or distinguish those definitions here, we conclude that reasonable future use is relevant to a property's current market value for tax assessment purposes. The court of appeals' contrary holding was erroneous.

What is the proper role of "highest and best use" in determining value for nontax purposes, such as (1) income taxation, (2) eminent-domain awards, (3) insurance settlements, and (4) evaluation of security for bank loans?

Should "fair market value" have a different meaning in these contexts than it does for tax purposes?

4. The *Lanier* property lies within the Reedy Creek Improvement District, a forty-three–square mile area including Disney World. All but twenty-five acres, less than 1 percent of the total area, are owned by the Disney Corporation. Florida legislation in 1967 provided that the powers of the district supervisors were to be

> exclusive of any law now or hereafter enacted provided for land use regulation, zoning or building codes by the State of Florida or any agency or authority of the State, and the provisions of any such law shall not be applicable within the territorial limits of the District. Laws 1967, c. 67-764, §23.[6]

In 1988, *Business Week* described Reedy Creek as

> a developer's dream. It levies taxes, sets building codes, and maintains roads. It has its own fire fighters and paramedics. It even has the authority, so far unused, to build an airport or a nuclear power plant. And Disney, whose title to 98 percent of the land gives it 98 percent of the vote in elections for board of supervisors and bond issues, can finance improvements with low-cost, tax-free Reedy Creek bonds.[7]

Are the taxes at issue in the *Lanier* case imposed by the Reedy Creek Improvement District or by another level of government?

5. A 1993 article in *The Orlando Sentinel* provided interesting background on the original acquisition price of the Disney World property:

> Working under a strict cloak of secrecy, real estate agents who didn't know the identity of their client began making offers to landowners in southwest Orange and northwest Osceola counties in April 1964—shortly after Walt Disney chose the site for his new theme park.

> Careful not to let property owners know the extent of their land-buying appetites, the agents quietly negotiated one deal after another—sometimes lining up contracts to buy huge tracts for little more than $100 an acre.

> Walt Disney Productions attorney Paul Helliwell had set up dummy corporations—with such names as Latin American Development and Management Corp. and Reedy Creek Ranch Corp.—in Miami to act as purchasers of the land. To make the deals, Helliwell worked through Roy Hawkins, a Miami real estate consultant.

---

6. See R. Martin, Jr., "Disney World: A Kingdom unto Itself," *Stetson Law Review* 9(1979):46.

7. G. DeGeorge, "A Sweet Deal for Disney Is Souring Its Neighbors," *Business Week*, August 8, 1988, p. 48.

Hawkins contacted Nelson Boice, president of Florida Ranch Lands Inc., an Orlando realty firm, and "expressed a casual interest in a 'super-sized' parcel of land," according to a November 1965 news account.

Swearing their office staff to secrecy, the Realtors began assembling information from Orange and Osceola county tax rolls on the ownership of land in the area in which the "mystery industry" was interested.

. . . .

The first purchases, recorded on May 3, 1965, included one for 8,380 acres of swamp and brush from state Sen. Ira Bronson at a price of $107 an acre. The deal had been made seven months earlier.

. . . .

Within three weeks of recording the Bronson transaction, Florida Ranch Lands had wrapped up deals with 47 owners. Eventually, Boice and his associates negotiated agreements with 51 owners to buy some 27,400 acres for more than $5 million—an average price of $182 per acre.[8]

What effect, if any, should these purchase prices have on the assessment of the Disney property?

6. The court notes that the zoning for the Disney tract was changed "upon the actual development of the land for a tourist-oriented use." Given that the agricultural zoning was not changed before actual development, what weight should be given to the current zoning restrictions? Should Disney control over the Reedy Creek Improvement District affect the weight given to zoning restrictions?

7. The court's reference to Disney "imagineers" uses a long-standing Disney term, although the company always capitalizes that designation. The division of the Walt Disney Company responsible for the design and development of Disney theme parks, originally named WED Enterprises, was later titled "Walt Disney Imagineering." The 1992 Walt Disney Company annual report states, "Walt Disney Imagineering celebrated its 40th anniversary, and Imagineers rose to the occasion with some of the most remarkable accomplishments in the division's magical history."

VILLAGE OF BURNSVILLE v. COMMISSIONER OF TAXATION
295 Minn. 504, 202 N.W.2d 653
Supreme Court of Minnesota, 1972

PER CURIAM.

---

8. Mark Andrews, "Disney Assembled Cast of Buyers to Amass Land Stage for Kingdom," *Orlando Sentinel,* May 30, 1993, p. K2. [One of a series of articles discussing the book *Vinyl Leaves: Walt Disney World and America,* by Stephen Fjellman (1992).]

Relator, Village of Burnsville, by writ of certiorari, challenges the Minnesota Tax Court's finding of the fair market value of a 1,420-acre tract of land owned by respondent-taxpayer, Northern States Power Company. The assessment of taxes is as of January 2, 1968. Taxpayer, a public service corporation engaged in the business of generating and distributing electric energy to the general public, has its Black Dog Generating Plant located on a portion of the tract, but the value of the plant structures and improvements is not involved in these tax proceedings.

Taxpayer's land is located in the bottomlands of the Minnesota River, generally bounded on the north by the river, on the south by tracks of the Chicago & North Western Railway Company, on the east by Cedar Avenue, and on the west by Interstate Highway No. 35W. Approximately 560 acres of the land consist of Black Dog Lake, a long, narrow slough with an average normal depth of about 2 feet, the plant structures and improvements are on 52 acres, and the remaining acreage is unimproved, raw land.

The tract is zoned for heavy industrial uses, but its utility for such purposes is limited by its low elevation and poor soil conditions. Because of its low elevation and proximity to the river, the entire tract is subject to periodic flooding and was flooded seven times in the period 1951 to 1969. To mitigate the hazard to the plant structures, those areas were raised from 10 to 20 feet with fill material. The worst of the floods occurred in 1965, when the river elevation rose 15.35 feet above flood stage, flooding the land to depths of 14 feet. Continuous pumping was necessary to maintain the plant's substation in operation, and the only access to the plant was by boat.

The soil and subsoil throughout the tract consist of soft, silty materials that will not support the weight of substantial structures without the use of pilings to depths of from 40 to 55 feet. Construction of the 500-foot by 500-foot powerhouse, the largest structure, required the driving of more than 5,000 pilings, and another 2,000 or more pilings were required in the construction of the smaller outlying structures.

Location of the tract on the Minnesota River does have two favorable aspects. The first is that the river, the channel of which was dredged and straightened by the Army Corps of Engineers, is utilized by barges for the economical transport of coal and other bulk materials used by taxpayer. The second is that proximity to the river permits the economical use of larger quantities of water in taxpayer's power generating processes. Black Dog Lake is connected to the Minnesota River by an improved natural outlet at one end and by an artificial inlet at the other end, upon which control gates were constructed by taxpayer. Water is introduced from the river into the plant. The intake water is used in the process of condensing steam from the steam turbine generators and the heated water is discharged into the slough for cooling before return to the river. This use of the slough permits taxpayer to comply with state thermal pollution control standards during prescribed warm months of the year without any necessity for constructing cooling towers.

The assessor for the village of Burnsville placed a market value on the entire tract of land, exclusive of the stated structures and improvements, of $2,525,000, to which he added a so-called 'use increment' of $3,965,000 (later reduced by him to $1,343,000) because of taxpayer's use of Black Dog Lake for cooling water in lieu of constructing cooling towers.[1] Taxpayer, on the other hand, contended that the fair market value of the land was not more than $710,000.

---

1. Prior to the January 2, 1968, assessment, the assessor had treated the 560 acres of Black Dog Lake as valueless wasteland. The tract was valued at $963,840 in the prior 1966 assessment.

The commissioner of taxation, by order, thereafter determined that the market value of the land was $2,525,000, eliminating the village assessor's added value for use increment. Upon appeal from that order by both the village and the taxpayer, the Tax Court found the fair market value of the land to be $1,420,000.

The essence of relator's argument is that the expert witnesses for respondent-taxpayer on the issue of market value of the land did not consider taxpayer's use of Black Dog Lake for cooling purposes as an increment to the value of the land so that their appraisals and the findings of the Tax Court failed, in the words of Minn.St. 273.12, 'to consider and give due weight to every element and factor affecting the market value thereof.' This intrinsic value, they contend, is a factor mandated by *Schleiff v. County of Freeborn,* 231 Minn. 389, 394, 43 N.W.2d 265, 268 (1950).[2]

This claim must be examined in the context of what these appraisers affirmatively did consider in reaching their opinions as to value. Weighing the location and character of the land, they concluded that it was not suited for industrial development and that the highest and best use was for park and recreation purposes, or like flood plain applications. The 16,000 acres of industrial land in the Twin City metropolitan area, according to the testimony, represent a 50-year supply, with a comparatively negligible demand for river bottomlands as industrial sites for reasons of economic feasibility of development and use. Based upon recent sales of lands they considered comparable bottomlands on navigable parts of the same river, ranging from $277 to $973 an acre, they variously estimated the per acre value of taxpayer's land at $225 (Marzitelli), $400 (Moffet), and $475 (Dolan). The Tax Court, however, found the per acre value to be $1,000.

Valuation of taxpayer's land by these appraisers did not include a factor of use increment or intrinsic worth for the water cooling uses of Black Dog Lake. The statutory test of 'market value,' Minn.St. 272.03, subd. 8, is the 'usual selling price' at the place where the property is located.

. . . .

The Tax Court itself, moreover, did not wholly ignore relator's claimed use increment value. It had before it not only the testimony of taxpayer's expert witnesses but, in addition, the testimony of expert witnesses for relator who did assign a higher value to the lake because of its use for cooling purposes, and it made a finding of value substantially more than stated in the opinions of taxpayer's expert witnesses. The court said:

> . . . If we were to add a 'use increment' to the value of this property then we would have to add a similar 'use increment' to all property in the State of Minnesota, which could be used for cooling purposes.[6] The fact that the lake has such capabilities is an item of value but the Village and its assessor have placed entirely too much emphasis on that factor. Therefore, even if the use as a cooling device

---

2. Relator's assessor had, as noted earlier in the text, placed a separate value in terms of an unproved cost of constructing a cooling tower for taxpayer's generating processes. Seemingly retreating from that untenable position, relator on oral argument in this court stated: 'We don't claim that there should be any specific amount of money added to the value of this lake because it is used for a cooling tower. We only claim that the fact that it is used or usable for a cooling tower is one of the considerations that a real estate expert should take into consideration in determining the value of this land.'

6. Witness Dolan testified to the obvious fact that actual or potential "Black Dog Lakes" exist in the bottomlands "all the way up and down the river."

represents the highest and most profitable use of Black Dog Lake, the market value of the Black Dog tract is affected only to the extent that demand for this use would increase the usual selling price of the land.

It thereafter concluded:

. . . As we view the evidence of those sales that were comparable, and based on all other evidence of value, we find that the evidence will not support a finding of value in excess of $1000 per acre.

Our review of the independent findings of fact by the Tax Court is addressed to whether this specialized tribunal proceeded in conformity to law and whether the evidence reasonably supports its determination of value. We accordingly affirm.

. . . .

Affirmed and remanded.

Notes and Questions

1. The *Burnsville* case illustrates another side to the question of "value in use." In the case of agricultural property in the urban fringe, "use value" denoted the present value of expected future farming income, or the price that would be paid for the property if it were restricted to agricultural use in the future. This figure was well below the "market value" that would be paid if the property could be developed for residential, commercial, or office use. In *Burnsville*, property with a negligible market value—due "to the obvious fact that actual or potential 'Black Dog Lakes' exist in the bottomlands 'all the way up and down the river'"—could nonetheless be assigned a "use increment" of nearly four million dollars because of its importance to a particular owner. The farmer would not be a willing seller at the agricultural-use value. Would the Northern States Power Company be a willing buyer of Black Dog Lake at $3.9 million? Could the logic of the original assessment in *Burnsville* be used to raise current-use agricultural assessments above the full market value of the property for development?

2. What should the result be in a case such as this if there is only one Black Dog Lake, and no substitutes? Would the perhaps negligible price originally paid by the power company influence your answer? Could the assessor make the argument in the current case that, given the presence of an electrical generating plant at this location, there in fact is no practical substitute for the Northern States Power Company?

3. Consider the distinction between the market value of property and its value to the owner, as measured by the payment that would be necessary to compensate for its loss. What would these two measures be in the case of (a) a corporation owning a custom-designed machine uniquely suited for

its manufacturing processes; (b) a farmer owning land in the urban fringe; (c) the Northern States Power Company owning Black Dog Lake; (d) a taxpayer owning a family home or heirloom of great sentimental value? Should an owner be permitted to insure property for a sum above its market value? Should that higher sum govern its assessment for property tax purposes?

4. Can you distinguish the "use value increment" originally added to the assessment in this case from valuation at "highest and best use"?

FEDERATED DEPARTMENT STORES, INC. v. BOARD OF TAX REVIEW
162 Conn. 77, 291 A.2d 715
Supreme Court of Connecticut, 1971

RYAN, Associate Justice.

. . . .

In cases number 3224, 3225 and 3226, concerning the valuation of the three parking lots for the purpose of tax assessments, the referee concluded that the assessors' valuation and assessments were correct and that the plaintiff had failed to sustain its burden of proof.

The plaintiff assigns error in the overruling by the referee of the following claims of law: (1) Land having extensive frontage and extensive corner exposure, but which is limited by economic necessity to use as a parking facility in connection with a department store property, cannot be given any extra value for the frontage or for the corner influence, and should be valued and assessed as an inside lot, not as a lot having any street frontage. (2) Where a building obtains a taxable value as a department store, because it is the dominant tenement, other parcels kept as servient tenements for a limited use such as parking facilities only must be assessed as to value in accordance with their servient use, and not in accordance with the use to which they might be put as independent properties not subject to an economic easement.

The referee found the following facts: In connection with the operation of Bloomingdale's Department Store in Stamford, Federated owns and operates three adjacent free parking areas for customers of the store. The major distinction between the parking lot valuations given by the plaintiff's expert and by the defendant's expert involved the issue whether there should be a 50 percent functional depreciation factor applied on the basis of Federated's contention that (1) the parking areas are essential to maintain the market valuation of the department store property and that (2) the servient restricted use of these parking lot areas severely depreciates their otherwise normal value for commercial availability. The three parcels of land are zoned for commercial-general business and are in the principal commercial area of Stamford. The highest and best use of these three parcels of land would be for commercial buildings. Their actual use is for parking lots restricted to customers of the department store. The fair market value of the Washington Avenue lot A was arrived at by the assessor using the comparable market sales data. This was accomplished by applying a valuation on a square foot basis and then converting it to a front foot price using a front foot base value for a lot depth of 100 feet and an additional sum for depth beyond 100 feet, computed on a mathematical ratio, and then applying an additional sum for corner influence. In arriving at the fair market value of the Winthrop parking lot, lots 6, 7 and 8, located at Broad Street and Winthrop Place, the assessor used the same approach as he used on the Washington Avenue lot A but without any corner influence. In arriving at the fair market value of the Franklin parking lot, lots 1 and 2, at the northeast corner of Broad and Franklin Streets, the assessor used the same comparable market sales data approach and arrived at a basic front-foot figure for land on Broad Street, then added a figure based on a formula to compensate for the difference in the frontage and rear area and then added a depth factor and a corner influence factor. The referee sustained the action of the assessor in all three cases and concluded that the plaintiff was not entitled to relief.

. . . .

In these cases, the finding by the referee that the highest and best use for each of the parking lots would be for commercial buildings has not been attacked by the plaintiff. A taxpayer who chooses to use his land in a manner which is not consistent with its highest and best use should not be rewarded with a lower assessment, the effect of which is to increase the tax burden on others. The process of evaluation for tax purposes is, at best, one of approximation and the conclusion of the referee is a matter of opinion based on his own knowledge and experience as well as on the facts and the expert opinions in evidence. National Folding Box Co. v. New Haven, 146 Conn. 578, 586, 153 A.2d 420.

In urging the adoption by this court of a functional depreciation factor in the valuation of the parking lots, on the ground that the parking areas are essential to the market valuation of the department store property, and that the servient restricted use of these parking areas severely depreciates their otherwise normal value for commercial availability, the plaintiff cites cases from other jurisdictions. No case, however, has been cited by the plaintiff wherein the functional depreciation factor has been applied in a factual situation similar to that of the present case.

The plaintiff contends also that this court has subscribed to a rule that property should be valued according to the practical influences on its use and not according to the fair market value predicated on the highest and best use, citing Brothers, Inc. v. Ansonia Redevelopment Agency, 158 Conn. 37, 43, 255 A.2d 836, 840. Through inadvertence only a portion of the pertinent sentence has been recited in the plaintiff's brief. The complete sentence reads as follows: "'The usual measure . . . is in general, the fair market value of the property, in the determination of which it is proper to consider the use which is being made of the property *if, in truth, that use of the property enhances the value of it.*' [Emphasis added.] Housing Authority of City of Bridgeport v. Lustig, 139 Conn. 73, 76, 90 A.2d 169." Ibid.

There is no error in cases Nos. 3224, 3225, 3226; there is error in case No. 3227, the judgment is set aside and a new trial is ordered.

In this opinion the other judges concurred.

Notes and Questions

1. Do you expect that the market value of the Stamford Bloomingdale's would be unaffected by the loss of a parking lot if that space were used for commercial building? If the parking lot is to be valued as if it were available for development, should Federated Department Stores demand a corresponding reduction in the value assigned to Bloomingdale's for tax purposes?

2. In *Burnsville*, the assessor initially added $3.9 million to the valuation of a lake that had previously been treated as "valueless wasteland," reasoning that its special utility to the owner should justify this "use increment." In *Federated Department Stores*, the assessor considered the highest and best use of a lot to be for commercial building, ignoring the special utility it provided to the department store as a parking facility. In your opinion, what would be the best method of dealing with these disputes in a consistent manner?

4 SPECIAL PROBLEMS IN THE COMPARABLE SALES APPROACH

Introduction

This chapter deals with three special issues regarding the measurement of "fair market value" through use of comparable sales benchmarks. The first concerns the meaning of this term in times of widespread economic depression, when market prices have fallen below the level associated with long-term "intrinsic" value. This situation raises a question as to what is meant by "fair" market value for various purposes, such as taxation, foreclosure proceedings, and compensation in eminent domain cases. The same question also arises, with appropriate reversal of roles, in times of rapidly rising prices.

The second issue concerns the comparability of physically similar or identical units that are held in different forms of legal ownership, such as condominiums, cooperatives, time-share units, and rental apartments. Conversion of an apartment building into such units can produce a dramatic increase in their aggregate market price. There can be equally dramatic differences in the market price for rental buildings themselves if some are subject to rent control and others are not. Different sales figures for comparable "bricks and mortar" raise contentious debate as to whether an assessment based on the higher prices taxes intangible values.

Finally, this chapter considers a set of cases dealing with the valuation of property that may have potential for conversion to a more lucrative use. These cases illustrate the implications of concerns as to the meaning of "highest and best use" for the comparable sales approach. Sales can only be considered "comparable" if the use contemplated by the purchasers is also economically appropriate for the property under review. The *Hackensack* cases demonstrate the difficulty of determining that comparability as a hypothetical matter when actual market transactions have not yet tested the feasibility of such a change in use.

"Fair Market Value" in a Depressed Market

The agricultural assessment cases discussed in chapter 3 illustrate some of the problems raised when market-value figures are considered too high to use as a basis for taxation. During the Great Depression of the 1930s, "fair market value" presented difficulties of a different type. At that time many homeowners unable to meet their mortgage payments saw their houses sold in foreclosure for extremely low prices and found themselves liable for the "deficiency," the amount outstanding after the proceeds were applied against the mortgage debt. *Heiman v. Bishop*, 272 N.Y. 83, 4 N.E.2d 944 (1936), considered the effect of §1083-a of the Civil Practice Act, the New York legislature's response to this situation. The New York Court of Appeals explained the legislation in this way:

> The section provides in effect that a deficiency judgment may not be entered in cases where "the fair and reasonable market value of the mortgaged premises" as of the date of sale equalled or exceeded the amount due and unpaid on the mortgage; and, in cases where no market value existed at that time, that the court shall fix such value at "such nearest earlier date as there shall have been any market value thereof." In any event, the court is required to determine the market value of the premises either at the date of the sale or at such earlier date.[1]

That meant that the amount realized at a foreclosure sale was not necessarily the amount to offset the mortgage debt. If the "fair and reasonable market value" was deemed to exceed the debt, there would be no deficiency judgment; if the court determined that there was *no* "market value" on the date of sale, the last market value that was deemed to exist would be treated as the amount realized.

This attempt to substitute a more acceptable measure for "fair market value" encountered the same problems of subjectivity and uncertainty encountered in the cases dealing with current use value. "Fair" market value is generally interpreted as referring to the fairness of the sale procedure, such as sufficient time for advertising, lack of duress, and standard terms of sale. If "fairness" instead refers to the resulting value figure, an entirely different inquiry is required as to what constitutes a fair or just price. The court in *Heiman* faced this problem, for the referee had determined that no fair market value existed between 1930 and the foreclosure sale in 1935. This judgment could not be attacked directly in the absence of clear criteria for "fair market value," but the court saw the risk of corresponding unfairness toward mortgage lenders:

> In the depressed condition of the market for real property, the old standard of market value has become utterly useless. The new and unusual conditions necessarily required a new standard for determining value, otherwise the section would have the effect of depriving mortgagees of deficiency judgments in practically all cases. That certainly could not have been the intent of the Legislature. The court below adopted the old standard. The learned referee during the hearing and in his report repeatedly stated that there was no fair and reasonable market value of the premises on the date of sale in June, 1935, or between that date and 1930, which he fixes as the "nearest earlier date" when there existed a market value of the premises. At the hearing, he stated "the

---

1. 272 N.Y. at 86.

question to be decided in cases of this kind is not the value of the property; the question to be decided is 'what is the fair and reasonable market value' and for that purpose a market must exist . . . . [W]hat is the fair and reasonable market value has several times been determined prior to this emergency legislation. It must be an open market."

We think that the learned official referee adopted a view too narrow and strict, and contrary to the spirit and purpose of the statute. In carrying out the directions contained in the statute, the court should receive evidence of all elements that can in reason affect the value of the premises together with the opinion of experts upon the subject.

. . . .

In a proceeding under section 1083-a, the court should receive evidence of the age and construction of the buildings on the premises, the rent received therefor, assessed value, location, condition of repair, the sale price of property of a similar nature in the neighborhood, conditions in the neighborhood which affect the value of property therein, accessibility, and of all other elements which may be fairly considered as affecting the market value of real property in a given neighborhood. With such evidence before it, the trial court, in the exercise of its best judgment, should determine the market value of the premises in the existing circumstances.[2]

Judicial opinions and commentary from the 1930s and 1940s give dramatic evidence of the collapse of real estate prices in the depression. A 1942 New York decision noted:

In 1939 and 1940 the market for real estate was severely demoralized. Over a period of approximately three and one-half years before the relator purchased his property on Windemere Road, the East Side Savings Bank alone sold about 840 parcels of property which it had acquired in the City of Rochester, and the Alliance Realty Corporation from 1937 to 1941 sold on the average about 725 parcels of property a year, representing an average annual volume of over $2,000,000. In 1939 about 135 of the 225 residences in Browncroft were owned by banks and by other loaning institutions. There is evidence that it was the policy of the East Side Savings Bank to liquidate the properties which it had acquired for the amount of its investment in them and that this policy depressed still further the prices of properties in Browncroft already lowered by the economic stringency confronting many property owners. Frequently prices on these properties were reduced three, four or even five times until they were sold, and from 1931 through 1934, with the surplus supply of these properties, all prices fell abruptly.[3]

Similarly, a 1933 article commented on real estate foreclosures in Cook County, Illinois:

---

2. *Ibid.* at 87–88.

3. *People ex rel. Buck v. Rapp*, 36 N.Y.S.2d 790, 794 (1942), *aff'd*, 266 A.D. 709, 41 N.Y.S.2d 185 (1943), *appeal denied*, 266 A.D. 821, 42 N.Y.S.2d 576 (1943).

The seriousness of the world-wide depression in its effect upon Cook County real estate can be realized best after a glimpse at some figures. The number of foreclosure suits commenced in the Circuit and Superior Courts of Cook County for the respective years was as follows:

1926—1,435;
1927—2,157;
1928—3,148;
1929—3,852;
1930—5,818;
1931—10,075;
1932—15,332.

. . . As of January 1, 1933, more than $1,300,000,000 worth of Cook County real estate was in mortgage foreclosure receivership. That figure exceeds the total value of all the real estate in the states of Nevada, New Mexico and Vermont combined.[4]

Enactments such as the New York provision considered in *Heiman v. Bishop* were a common legislative response to the wave of foreclosures accompanying this fall in market values. In the landmark case of *Home Building & Loan Association v. Blaisdell,* 290 U.S. 398 (1934), the Supreme Court upheld a Minnesota foreclosure moratorium against constitutional attack. This permitted state courts to extend the mortgagor's period for redemption beyond that specified in the loan contract.

Although nearly all other such provisions have now expired, the New York legislation at issue in *Heiman* continues in effect as Real Property Actions and Proceedings Law §1371(2). An attempt to invoke this in more recent times failed in *Farmers National Bank v. Tulloch,* 55 A.D.2d 773, 389 N.Y.S.2d 494 (1976). There, the owner of a gasoline service station argued that depressed prices for service station property as a result of the 1973–74 oil embargo brought the foreclosure of his station within the terms of §1371(2). The court disagreed:

Undoubtedly there was an energy crisis in 1974 when the sale took place. However, while the gasoline station business may have been depressed, it is clear that section 1371 of the Real Property Actions and Proceedings Law has reference only to the fair and reasonable market value of the mortgaged premises, and not the fair and reasonable value of the business conducted on the premises. Moreover, even though the value of the gas station property may have been depressed at the time of the foreclosure sale, it should not affect the mortgagee's right to a deficiency judgment. It is only when the mortgaged premises are shown to have no fair and reasonable market value at the time of the sale, taking into

---

4. H. Carey, "Mortgage Foreclosures in Cook County," *American Bar Association Journal* 19(1933):275.

consideration all elements which may fairly affect value, that resort may be had to the nearest earlier date when there was a market value.[5]

This theoretical line between fair values that are depressed and depressed values that are not "fair and reasonable" can be elusive. During the depression, Professor James Bonbright wrote:

> A friendly critic warns the author to stress more clearly the disagreement among appraisers as to whether the term "value," even when used without any qualifying adjective or adjunct, imports the idea of a *normal* or an *intrinsic* value. In this treatise we ourselves answer this question in the negative. That is to say, we make no distinction between money value and price, preferring to follow those economists who define market price as market value measured in terms of money. To us an abnormal, or evanescent, or extortionate, or dangerously low market price represents just as true a current *value* as does a normal, or permanent, or fair, or reasonably high market price.
>
> . . . .
>
> During the pending business depression, concepts of normal value, often undistinguished from concepts of intrinsic value, have been stressed as never before in various fields of litigation, by parties who have insisted that property should not be valued at the prevailing low market prices . . . . In some cases the courts have been influenced by these arguments to the point of finding or sanctioning appraised values materially in excess of current market prices. Sometimes they have stated that prevailing prices do not represent "fair market values"; at other times they have stated or implied that, even if they do measure "fair *market* value," some different type of value is required by the exigencies of the case.
>
> But other courts have held that prices prevailing even during a prolonged depression like the present one, nevertheless represent "market value" or "value" in law. One of the reasons for a reluctance to depart from the verdict of the market place, is the very forcible one that no long-run or "normal" value can be intelligently estimated. It is well enough to say that the prices at which New York City real estate has changed hands during the past year are no indication of "true value," in the sense of such a price as will prevail when the depression is a matter of history. But who can say what these post-depression prices will be? Cautious economists refuse to venture an answer, except perhaps as a mere guess; and if they should attempt an answer, they would be in violent disagreement.[6]

Notes and Questions

1. How should the *Heiman* case have been decided if there were no legislation similar to §1083-a in effect, and the only relevant statute called for assessment at "fair market value"?

---

5. 55 A.D. at 774.

6. J. Bonbright, *The Valuation of Property* (1937), vol. 1, at p. 29 n. #23, pp. 33–34.

2. In *Farmers National Bank* the court stated that the legislation concerning "fair and reasonable value" referred "only to the fair and reasonable market value of the mortgaged premises, and not the fair and reasonable value of the business conducted on the premises." Is it possible for the gasoline station business to be depressed without affecting the value of gasoline station property?

3. In *Underwood Typewriter Co. v. City of Hartford*, 99 Conn. 329, 122 A. 91 (1923) (cited by the Connecticut court in the *Federated Department Stores* case reprinted in chapter 3), assessment of a typewriter plant at $2,432,700 had been lowered by a court to $1,700,000 on the grounds that this lower figure represented its actual sale value. The Connecticut Supreme Court held this to be in error, finding that the absence of willing buyers for the property meant that there could be no "market value" as such. "In fact, at that time there was no market for this property and it did not have a value which was a fair market value within the proper and approved meaning of the term." Because the legislature was deemed not to have intended that the property escape taxation altogether, "true and actual value" was to be substituted as the base of the tax. Thus, the fact that "there was no market for the property, and it did not have a value which was the fair market value in the proper and approved meaning of the term" resulted in a higher assessment on the plant. The *Underwood Typewriter* case did not deal with a business depression, but the same logic led in the 1930s to what Bonbright termed "an almost universal refusal of the courts to insist on those drastic reductions in assessment that would be called for by the test of current market prices." He continued:

> This point would not be so serious, were it possible for communities to raise the *rates* of taxation so as to compensate for the reductions in the assessments. But constitutional and statute law, passed largely through the influence of the real-estate interests, has built up impediments to this solution by imposing restrictions of debt limits to a certain percentage of assessed values, and by fixing limits upon the rates of taxation. In view of this situation, the frequent remark that the absolute amounts of assessments do not matter, and that only *relative* assessments are of any concern, is quite beside the point. During a depression, therefore, assessors and judges must conspire in a gigantic legal lie about property values—a lie which is concealed by all sorts of loose talk about the stability of real values as contrasted with the collapse of mere market prices.[7]

4. The depression-era cases make clear the numerous transfers of ownership that accompanied the economic collapse of the 1930s and subsequent mortgage foreclosures. In fact, "wholesale" transactions of this type were

---

7. J. Bonbright, *The Valuation of Property* (1937), vol. 1, pp. 470–71.

faulted for driving prices down even further. For example, a 1940 mortgage deficiency case stated:

> The expert Stern in his testimony brought out the known fact that several of the Savings Banks have been "dumping" dozens of properties on the market in the Williamsburgh section in the last few years, for a nominal consideration, selling them to speculators from one to seventy parcels at a time; that this type of transaction has so affected realty values that there has been no fair market as contemplated by the so-called Deficiency Judgment Law, Civil Practice Act, sec. 1083 et seq.[8]

Given that large numbers of transactions accompanied the original depression that gave rise to §1083, how would you analyze the New York court's later position in *Tulloch* that the successor statute could be invoked only when there existed "no fair and reasonable market value," as opposed to a "depressed" value alone?

5. How should an insurance contract calling for payment of a building's "fair market value" be interpreted if this structure is destroyed by fire during an economic depression? How should the fact of an economic depression affect the calculation of an award for the taking of property under eminent domain?

6. Reconsider the *Dotson* case in the context of an economic depression. Was *Dotson* an attempt to base the tax on "normal" values rather than speculative prices? Would its reasoning support taxes based on "normal" prices in a falling market? Recall also the court's concern in *Lanier* to avoid the "boom and bust" cycle typical of Florida real estate development. How would a court go about calculating "normal" value in such a situation? Would substitution of "normal" value for market value in the case of Walt Disney World property in Orlando in 1975 have provided a superior indicator of the taxpayer's economic position?

7. If "value to the owner" is calculated as the amount necessary to compensate for the loss of property, what would be the effect of a general business depression on this measure, considering both the cost of purchasing a comparable replacement and the cost of constructing a new building?

8. For a contrasting example of a valuation dispute arising from an "overheated" real estate market, see *City and County of Honolulu v. Steiner*, 73 Haw. 449, 834 P.2d 1302 (1992). One aspect of that case involved the taxpayer's contention that sales to Japanese investors should not be considered "comparable" for tax assessment purposes:

---

8. *Home Title Ins. Co. v. Alrose Realty Corp.*, 23 N.Y.S.2d 724 (1940), *aff'd*, 260 A.D. 878, 23 N.Y.S.2d 726 (1940).

Steiner [the taxpayer] argued in the tax court that sales to Japanese investors were not "comparable" without adjustment, thus such sales should have been disregarded or discounted in calculating the benchmark value and the fair market value of Steiner's property. Steiner's experts opined that Japanese investors were paying more than fair market value because they had special influences, motivations and conditions and they were armed with "tremendous financial wallop." The experts testified that, at the time of the alleged "above market" sales, the dollar to yen ratio was high, Japan real estate prices were high, and low interest rates were available in Japan. Thus, they argued, Japanese buyers were paying much higher prices than were "economically justified" by any measure of value.

Although wealthy Japanese investors in Hawaii property may be a modern phenomenon, Steiner's theory is not. Bonbright's 1937 treatise on the appraisal of property discusses a similar theory that property should be valued at its "intrinsic value" or "justified price" rather than its fair market value. J. Bonbright, 1 Valuation of Property 24–29 (1937). Intrinsic value differs from fair market value "in that it represents, not what the property could presently be sold for, but what, in the appraiser's judgment, the property would sell for, were the market composed of (a) intelligent individuals who (b) were interested in buying and selling the property only by reference to its investment merits." *Id.* at 27.

The intrinsic value theory mirrors Steiner's argument that sales to Japanese buyers are not economically justified, thus the court should adjust the sales data to reflect what would be a property's intrinsic value or justified price.

Bonbright states that one reason why courts have "wisely hesitated" to embrace the concept of intrinsic value is that "it would be extremely difficult to estimate." *Id.* at 28–29.

"If [tax assessors or tax courts] were compelled to find the intrinsic value . . . for tax purposes, the administration of the law would become almost hopeless. Endless controversies would arise between taxpayers and assessors, many of which would be carried into the courts. Faulty as is market price as an index of value, it supplies a relatively objective and easily administered basis of valuation that no other method can supply." *Id.* at 29.

We agree with this analysis and will not inject uncertainty into Hawaii's property tax assessments by subscribing to Steiner's theory. We further note that Steiner's theory invites a sale-by-sale analysis of the "justified price;" we find this to be repugnant to the concept of "using appropriate systematic methods suitable for mass valuation." See ROH [Revised Ordinances of Honolulu] @8-7.1(a). Thus, we reject Steiner's argument that sales to Japanese buyers do not reflect the fair market value of the properties sold to them.

In particular, we reject Steiner's argument that the 1987 sale of the parcel next to the Steiner property should be discounted because the buyer was a Japanese citizen and thus he paid more than fair market value. "Market value . . . is no more than the value in money of any property for which that property would sell on the open market by a willing seller to a willing buyer." *In re Puna Sugar Co., Ltd.*, 56 Haw. 621, 624, 547 P.2d 2, 4 (1976). The property next door was listed on the open market for 95 days at $3,000,000 and sold for $2,750,000; and there is no evidence suggesting other than an arms-length transaction between a willing buyer and a willing seller. Furthermore, although the buyer was Japanese, he has owned and lived in a Kahala beach condominium since 1979 and is the owner of a local business, the Pearl City Tavern. Even if we agreed with Steiner's "above-market" theory, which we do not, nationality alone would be insufficient to establish that this transaction was tainted by the "Japan factor."

Condominiums, Cooperatives, and Time-Share Units

The market approach to valuation begins by identifying recent sales prices of properties comparable to the one being valued. The unique nature of each parcel of real property, at the very least with regard to location, requires adjustments for any significant differences between the property being valued and the property considered comparable.

Obvious physical differences among properties are often the least problematic factors in this adjustment. Mass appraisals drawing on large numbers of sales can correlate differences in price with location, age, and specific building features, such as number of rooms and type of construction. Such adjustments can also be made in the valuation of a single parcel. The identification of intangible differences, such as the form of ownership and legal restrictions on the use of property, can be far more complex, and many legal issues concerning the effect of such intangible factors on valuation for tax purposes are currently unresolved.

Changes in a property's form of ownership can affect its sale price even without any corresponding alteration of its physical condition. The most dramatic example of this phenomenon in recent years has been the conversion of apartment property into cooperatives or condominiums sold individually at prices whose sum exceeds the amount the entire building would command from a single buyer. Similarly, time-share vacation property in which multiple purchasers each have the right to a fixed period of occupancy annually may be physically identical to condominiums sold as individual units for much lower prices. Questions of "comparability" affect income capitalization as well as sales analysis, for the rental income that a prospective purchaser could expect would depend on the use to be made of the property.

Cooperatives and condominiums are similar in many respects. Each permits an individual owner to occupy a specific unit and to use specified common areas. The sale of a condominium conveys an interest in real property, whereas the sale of a cooperative conveys an interest in personal property, stock in the corporation holding title to the building. That stock carries with it a proprietary lease for the occupancy of a specific unit. Each unit of a condominium is subject to a separate assessment and property tax; but the entire cooperative building is assessed and taxed as a whole.[9] Condominium ownership in the United States was encouraged by 1961 legislation permitting Federal Housing Administration mortgage insurance on "a one-family unit in a multifamily structure." This was conditioned on separate assessments for each unit, so that no one owner's default could threaten another owner's unit.[10]   Cooperative ownership had earlier taken root in the New York metropolitan area as a result of the housing shortage facing that city after the First World War, and the great majority of cooperative housing units in the United States are still located in New York City and the neighboring New Jersey communities.[11] Owners of these units are a politically powerful force in New York City, with an estimated 480,000 cooperative units and 80,000 condominiums.[12]

Although many states have special statutory provisions to deal with the taxation of unit ownership arrangements, none compares to New York in the number and complexity of such enactments. In 1982 New York City proposed to change its method of assessing cooperative apartment buildings. Required by law to set assessments at a level equivalent to similar rental apartment units, the city planned to compare cooperatives with new apartment buildings that were not subject to rent control or rent stabilization. Note that (1) the cooperative units were not being compared with other cooperatives, but with rental apartments, and (2) the rents that tenant-owners of cooperative units pay are not subject to rent control. The city's deputy mayor said, "The question is, which rental buildings are comparable? Do you choose buildings that have a lot of rent-control and rent-stabilized apartments, where the rental income and the value are artificially low? Or do you choose buildings where the rents more accurately reflect the market?"[13]

---

9. On condominium and cooperative ownership generally, see P. Rohan and M. Reskin, *Condominium Law and Practice* (1965 and supplements).

10. For a comprehensive overview of early developments in this area, see C. Berger, "Condominium: Shelter on a Statutory Foundation," *Columbia Law Review* 63(1963):987.

11. Note, "Examining Cooperative Conversion: An Analysis of Recent New York Legislation," *Fordham Urban Law Journal* 11(1983):1089.

12. S. Kennedy, "Making the Choice: A Co-op or a Condo," *New York Times,* September 6, 1992, §10, p. 1.

13. M. Goodwin, "City Revises Method of Assessing Co-ops, Raising Their Taxes," *New York Times,* January 22, 1982, p. A1.

Although local officials expected this change to increase annual tax revenue by $10–$20 million, the city reversed its position and dropped this proposal within five days,[14] after a state senator representing the city's Upper East Side charged that this represented a "breach of faith" and the assemblyman representing the Upper West Side characterized it as "a complete double cross."[15] The assistant majority leader of the state assembly wrote to the *New York Times*, "Bricks and mortar are not worth more simply because a building goes co-op."[16] The *Times* in turn speculated that owners of rent-controlled apartment buildings could now "bring suit to reduce their assessed valuation on the grounds they are worth less than unregulated cooperatives."[17]

New York regulation of condominium and cooperative assessments is even more complex than this episode indicates. The 1964 Condominium Act contained a provision, now §339-y of the state's Real Property Law, limiting the aggregate assessed values of all associated units, together with the common areas, to no more than their total value as a single parcel. Legislation in 1981 required that condominium or cooperative assessment not exceed the assessment on that property were it not in condominium or cooperative ownership.[18] The New York State Board of Equalization and Assessment estimated that these restrictions reduced condominium assessments by as much as 40 percent, "meaning residential condominium units pay significantly lower taxes than single-family homes of equal value." Application of these restrictions, however, was later curtailed in jurisdictions adopting a 1981 classification scheme designed to limit the share of the tax burden borne by residential property.[19]

---

14. M. Goodwin, "New Tax Policy Covering Co-ops Dropped by City," *New York Times*, January 27, 1982, p. B1.

15. M. Goodwin, "City Revises Method of Assessing Co-ops, Raising Their Taxes," *New York Times*, January 22, 1982, p. A1.

16. R. Gottfried, "How Much Is a Co-op Worth?" (letter), *New York Times*, February 13, 1982, p. 24.

17. "A Realty Tax with Soft Spots" (editorial), *New York Times*, February 8, 1982, p. A18.

18. New York Real Property Tax Law §§581(1)(a), 581(2).

19. Among the provisions of New York Law are limits on condominium assessments, favorable "homestead" classification for specified residential property, a limitation on condominium "homesteads" not converted from conventional ownership, and an option for varying these last provisions by the seven municipalities that adopted a dual tax rate before 1983. See, for example, *Verga v. Town of Clarkstown*, 137 A.D.2d 809, 525 N.Y.S.2d 272 (1988), *appeal dismissed*, 72 N.Y.2d 1042, 531 N.E.2d 660, 534 N.Y.S.2d 940 (1988), which held that disparities in the methods of assessment chosen by different towns within a single county or other larger taxing unit were unconstitutional as a violation of equal protection.

Florida taxation of time-share units poses an interesting contrast to the exceptionally favorable treatment of cooperatives and condominiums in New York. Of course, far from being a potent political force, owners of time-share interests are generally neither residents nor voters in the jurisdiction where the units are located.

In *Spanish River Resort Corp. v. Walker*, 526 So.2d 677 (Fla. 1988), the Florida Supreme Court approved a lower court's holding that tax could properly be assessed on the value of each "week" in a time-sharing unit, not limited by the comparable value of a physically similar condominium unit that had not been converted to time-sharing interests. In that case, the assessment on the value of individual "weeks" resulted in valuations of time-sharing condominiums that were ten times as high as the valuations of physically similar units retained as single units. The lower court had pointed out that time-share units were transferred by standard warranty deeds, with title insurance available. Sales brochures for the units stated, "The person who buys at Spanish River Resort is an owner with deed, and full rights of ownership. You may lend your property, sell it, rent it, or give it away during the weeks you own it. Or you can keep it forever." 497 So.2d 1299, 1302 (Fla. Dist. Ct. App. 1986). It is interesting that the time-share owners also attacked use of their purchase price as evidence of fair market value, citing "excessive costs of sale" that reached 55 percent of the amount paid, and arguing that they would "never be able to recoup the original purchase price," inflated as it was by the developer's marketing costs. The court noted that "the promotional material did not advise the potential buyers of this dismal forecast," but found no error in relying upon the purchase price as evidence of market value. "That the developers overcharged the purchasers does not make the latter unwilling buyers and most certainly does not cause the developers to be unwilling sellers."

In *Oyster Pointe Resort Condominium Association, Inc. v. Nolte*, 524 So.2d 415, 418 (Fla. 1988), the Florida Supreme Court reached a similar result when taxpayers alleged that the costs of sale amounted to 75–80 percent of the purchase price of their property. Florida law required the appraiser to take into consideration "reasonable fees and costs of sale" in determining taxable value, Fla. Stat. 193.011(8), but the state supreme court found this to include "only those fees and costs typically associated with the closing of the sale of real property such as reasonable attorney's fees, broker's commissions, appraisal fees, documentary stamp costs, survey costs and title insurance costs."[20]

---

20. See generally the annotation, "Sale Price of Real Property as Evidence in Determining Value for Tax Assessment Purposes," *American Law Reports* 3d series 89 (1979 and annual supplements):1126.

Notes and Questions

1. Is it true that "bricks and mortar are not worth more simply because a building goes co-op"? Should such changes in market price affect a tax based on real property values? If a well-maintained building remains physically unchanged over time, should its tax assessment change to reflect such elements as neighborhood decline or revival?

2. Is the form of ownership a "use" of property, to be treated in the same way as other questions of highest and best use?

3. If valuation of a cooperative building is based on the sale price of its stock, has the tax become one improperly imposed on personal property? Conversely, if the sole asset of the cooperative corporation is the real estate in which its shareholders live, does the sale price of its stock indicate the market value of this real estate? In *200 Country Club Associates v. Board of Assessors*, 83 A.D.2d 637, 441 N.Y.S.2d 705, 708 (1981), the New York Appellate Division found there to be

   > sufficient nexus between the selling prices of the shares of a co-operative apartment complex and the value of that improved real estate to make the selling price competent and relevant on the issue of value, subject to adjustment and discount.

   The New York law requiring that condominium or cooperative property be assessed "at a sum not exceeding the assessment which would be placed upon such parcel were the parcel not owned or leased by a cooperative corporation or on a condominium basis" was the legislative response. Does this represent an application of the "fair market value" standard or a circumvention of it?

4. A 1981 New Jersey case concerned a taxpayer's challenge to an assessment based on the sale of stock in the cooperative corporation holding title to the building being taxed. The taxpayer charged that "such approach values the manner in which the real property is utilized rather than its market value and that a true gauge of its market value would be to compare it with a like structure in which the tenants pay rent to the owner. . . ." *Southbridge Park, Inc. v. Fort Lee*, 4 N.J. Tax 30, 33 (1981), *aff'd*, 6 N.J. Tax 351 (App. Div. 1984). How would you respond?

5. In valuing nonrental property, how would you determine whether to base the value on the sale price of a physically similar unit subject to rent control or the sale price of a unit that could be leased at market value?

6. Consider the administrative implications of changes from single ownership of an apartment building to individual ownership of condominium units, and from individual ownership of condominium units to ownership

of time-share "weeks" in those units. In *Day v. High Point Condominium Resorts, Ltd.*, 521 So.2d 1064 (Fla. 1988), the Florida Supreme Court upheld the constitutionality of a statute designating the managing entity of a time-share development as the taxpayer, in the capacity of agent for the titleholders, and permitting a single assessment on the value of the combined time-share units in each development. The court found this approach reasonable, pointing out that conversion of a 200-unit condominium building to week-long time shares could result in the addition of 10,000 new taxpayers, many of them not resident in the jurisdiction or even in the state.

7. Conversely, consider the burden placed on a taxpayer seeking to challenge the assessment of a condominium or cooperative on grounds that the valuation reflects the value of this conversion where state law prohibits such an increase. Must the taxpayer prove what the value of the entire building as an apartment complex would be in the postconversion year? See *Nugent v. Waldmiller*, 73 A.D.2d 1033, 425 N.Y.S.2d 396 (1980).

8. What assistance would the earlier cases dealing with value in depressed markets offer for the assessment of time-share property if the taxpayers' pessimistic predictions with regard to resale values turned out to be accurate?

9. For further information on condominium and cooperative conversion, see "Cooperative Housing, Homeowner Association and Timesharing Interests" and "Real Estate Taxation of Condominiums," Chapters 9 and 10 of P. Rohan, "Real Estate Tax Appeals."[21] The best source for detailed continuing coverage of New York property tax legislation is the bimonthly newsletter of the New York State Division of Equalization and Assessment, *The Survey*. A 1985 law review note[22] proved influential in the Florida cases discussed above. Cases on both areas are collected in an annotation.[23]

---

21. On New York, also see "The New York Assessment Anomaly: Valuation Following Condominium Conversion," *Columbia Business Law Review* (1987):733, and "Examining Cooperative Conversion: An Analysis of Recent New York Legislation," *Fordham Urban Law Journal* 11(1983):1089.

22. "Ad Valorem Taxation of Time-Share Properties: Should Time-Share Estates Be Separately Assessed and Taxed?" *University of Florida Law Review* 37(1985):421.

23. W. Shipley, "Real-Estate Taxation of Condominiums," *American Law Reports* 3d series 71(1976 and annual updates):952.

Alternate Uses, Hypothetical Uses, and "Highest and Best Use"

HACKENSACK WATER COMPANY V. BOROUGH OF OLD TAPPAN
77 N.J. 208, 390 A.2d 122
Supreme Court of New Jersey, 1978

The opinion of the court was delivered by SCHREIBER, J.

This case presents a difficult problem in real property tax valuation involving the assessment under *N.J.S.A.* 54:30A-52 of land beneath a reservoir created and owned by the Hackensack Water Company, a private water public utility. The municipal taxing authority is the Borough of Old Tappan.

I

The background of this controversy is as follows. In the late 1950s, the taxpayer, Hackensack Water Company, purchased 940.805 acres of natural basin property along the Hackensack River in the Borough of Old Tappan. The Company excavated the land and built a dam across the river, creating a reservoir which it called Lake Tappan. The river bed is now located generally in the middle of the reservoir. Part of the reservoir (about 20%) extends into the Township of River Vale, which is adjacent to Old Tappan. The bed of the Hackensack River marks the boundary between the Borough and the Township.

Of the 940.805 acres located in Old Tappan, 424.151 are dry upland, and the remaining 516.654 are submerged under as much as twenty feet of water. The bulk of the land now under water was swamp land before it was excavated and flooded. The 424 upland acres are undeveloped and, according to the taxpayer's testimony, are necessary to maintain the integrity of the reservoir. The dam, built at a cost of several million dollars, is the only structure on the Old Tappan tract.

This litigation began in 1970, when the Company appealed the Borough's 1970 property tax assessment of the Old Tappan tract to the Bergen County Board of Taxation. The County Board reduced the assessment of $7,118,900 to $3,869,175. The lowered assessment was based on a valuation of the upland acreage at $6500 per acre and of the underwater property at $2500 per acre. The Borough acquiesced in the reduction and assessed the property at the lower amount for the 1971, 1972 and 1973 tax years. The Company, however, appealed the 1970, 1971, 1972 and 1973 County Board determinations to the Division of Tax Appeals. The four appeals were tried together before the Division.

The Company's appeal was limited to the objection that its underwater property had been overvalued. The Division reduced the County Board's assessment from $3,869,175 to $2,835,875. The reduction was based solely on the finding that the 516 underwater acres had a nominal value of $500 per acre. Upon the Borough's appeal, the Appellate Division in an unreported decision adopted the reasoning of the Division of Tax Appeals and affirmed. We granted certification.

II

The Hackensack Water Company is a privately owned public utility which furnishes water to approximately 800,000 customers in Bergen and Hudson Counties. It is subject to comprehensive regulation by the Board of Public Utility Commissioners. The

Company could not, for example, sell the Lake Tappan reservoir without Board approval. *N.J.S.A.* 48:3-7. As a water public utility the Company is subject to "a complete scheme and method" for taxation for public utilities, *N.J.S.A.* 54:30A-49 et seq., under which it pays a percentage of its gross receipts to the State, some of which are then distributed to municipalities in which the Company has its facilities. Under the statutory format all real estate must "be assessed and taxed at local rates in the manner provided by law for the taxation of similar property owned by other corporations or individuals . . . ." *N.J.S.A.* 54:30A-52.

Real estate is defined as "land and buildings, but it does not include . . . reservoirs (except that the lands upon which dams and reservoirs are situated are real estate) . . . ." *N.J.S.A.* 54:30A-50(b). The problem here, then, is to evaluate the land beneath the reservoir according to the criteria established generally for assessment of real property. The statutory test calls for an assessment of the land at its "full and fair value . . . at such price as . . . [the property] would sell for at a fair and bona fide sale by private contract . . . ." *N.J.S.A.* 54:4-23. A fair sale encompasses a transaction between "a buyer willing but not obliged to buy, and a seller willing but not obliged to sell." *Greenwich Tp. v. Gloucester Cty. Bd. of Taxation,* 47 N.J. 95, 99, 219 A.2d 507, 508 (1966). In applying that test it is appropriate to consider the highest and best use of the property.

The parties assumed the highest and best use of the land was for residential development and presented proofs designed to demonstrate value on that basis. However, it was shown that conversion of this reservoir bottom into a tract amenable to suburban living would require a number of costly engineering maneuvers: a dam would have to be dismantled and the water captured by it drained away without flooding the surrounding countryside; millions of cubic yards of landfill would then have to be dumped into the resulting basin to create land suitable for building and high enough to withstand flooding; and the Hackensack River, now stopped up by the dam, would have to be rechanneled, a feat that would cost, according to one expert's estimate, around $5,000,000. The evidence showed that the conversion expense would far exceed the fair market value of residential property in the area. Since property owners cannot be charged with the cost of restructuring their property (property should be valued in the actual condition in which the owner holds it), the Division's finding that financially it was not feasible to develop the property for residential use was fully supportable in the record.

However, the Division ignored basic precepts when it assumed that residential use was the sole guidepost for valuation and that the taxpayer would have been compelled to give its property away for residential purposes. Underlying the settled rule that remote uses are irrelevant is the more basic principle that property valuation should have some relationship to reality, and the reality of the matter is that the land is useful as a reservoir. Therefore, it would have been proper to consider the actual highest and best use of the land, namely as a reservoir in conjunction with the operation of a utility water system. The ultimate inquiry remains what is the fair market value of the land?

Various methods have been used to ascertain the price which parties would freely fix in the market place. One standard technique is to examine comparable sales. Another is to capitalize income derived from the property. These approaches are not compatible with the unique problem posed here.

In the case of public utilities, in situations in which it is not feasible to evaluate land by utilizing the standard criteria, other factors must be considered.

 . . . .

 . . . Nothing in the record indicates that the land under the reservoir could be used for any purpose other than a reservoir, the highest and best use of the property. The land was adapted to a single use and its value depends upon continuance of that use. That is the only element shown to have created value in this land.[3]

Consideration of the contribution of this land to the Company's earnings, therefore, becomes relevant. As a public utility, its rates have been fixed by the Board of Public Utility Commissioners. In making that determination the Board has consistently included in rate base the "original cost"[4] of the reservoir land. In other proceedings the Board has also approved the use of original cost for rate making purposes. It is true that rate base is but one factor in determining revenues and much may be lost in the translation of the value of that base by comparison with the market value of the owner's equity. See Samuels, "On the Effect of Regulation on Value," 25 *National Tax Journal* 311, 315 (1972). However, it is probable that a prospective purchaser, public or private, of the system would in computing value include an amount at least equal to the original cost of the land beneath the reservoir.[5] The original cost at least bears some relationship to the value of the reservoir land and it is appropriate to rely upon it in the absence of any other evidence.[6] Cf. *Troy Hills Village v. Parsippany Troy Hills Tp. Council,* 68 N.J. 604, 622-623, 350 A.2d 34 (1975) (rent control case indicating that public utility precedents are of limited usefulness in determining market value and that meaning of the term "value" must be derived from the purpose for which valuation is being made). We hasten to add that it would have been proper to consider, even under the unusual circumstances of this case, other factors such as the trending of costs incurred in acquiring the land and in preparing for its use as a reservoir. Here the only relevant evidence was that of an expert, a member of a public utility consulting firm, who testified that the original cost of the reservoir land per the Company's books was approximately $670 per acre. Accordingly, the assessed value should be $670 per acre.

As so modified the judgments are affirmed.

For affirmance as modified: Chief Justice HUGHES and Justices MOUNTAIN, CLIFFORD and SCHREIBER - 4.

For reversal: Justices SULLIVAN, PASHMAN and HANDLER - 3.

HANDLER, J., dissenting.

Although I share the frustration of the majority in determining the fair market value of the underwater property of the Hackensack Water Company based upon the record

---

3. We do not intend here to disturb the principle that valuation of land for economically feasible uses other than its actual use is appropriate.

4. Original cost is the cost of the property to the first person who devoted the property to utility service. For a general criticism of the use of net original cost, see D. Eiteman, "Approaches to Utility Valuation for Ad Valorem Taxation," 71 *Pub. Util. Fortnightly* 19 (May 23, 1963).

5. "Original cost" should probably include the associated costs incurred in placing the land in position for its use as a reservoir.

6. An analogy may be found in eminent domain proceedings when property because of its unusual character has no market value in the traditional sense and there must be resort to other methods. 4 Nichols, Eminent Domain, sec. 12.32 (3d ed. 1971). See *Penn. Gas & Water Co. v. Penn. Turnpike Comm'n,* 428 Penn. 74, 236 A.2d 112 (1967) (land held for reservoir purposes compensated for in condemnation case on basis of cost to replace rather than fair market value because there existed no market for such utility property).

in this case, I would not, to the obvious detriment of the remaining taxpayers of the Borough of Old Tappan, ascribe as the true value of the reservoir land its remote original cost which has no relevance whatsoever to current market value. In doing precisely this, the majority fosters regressive and unsound valuation practices in the field of Ad valorem taxation. I dissent.

. . . .

Both parties in this litigation shared the assumption that the highest and best use of the land was for residential development. The persuasive proofs disclosed, however, that the cost of preparing the reservoir land for such use would be truly prohibitive, that it would far exceed the fair market value of residential property in the area. The majority, therefore, soundly accepts the Division's finding that it was not financially feasible to develop this property for residential use, a finding fully supported by the record.

The Division of Tax Appeals believed, however, that the only use which it could consider in the assessment of the reservoir property was its hypothetical residential use, even though that use was fiscally totally unfeasible. Confronted by this apparent dilemma, its resolution was completely unsatisfactory: it simply assigned a nominal value, $500 per acre, to the underwater reservoir land.

Although the majority recognizes that the decision of the Division is flawed, it does not improve much upon the resolution or result. The Court's reasoning process is two-fold. It determines that for tax purposes the highest and best use of this land is as a reservoir. It observes, fairly enough, that "the reality of the matter is that the land is useful as a reservoir." It then transmutes this simple usefulness into "the actual highest and best use of the land, namely as a reservoir in conjunction with the operation of a utility water system." The majority concludes that conventional valuation precepts are inapplicable to such reservoir property and assigns a value to the land virtually as nominal and arbitrary as that employed by the Division, namely, its original historical cost of $670 per acre.

. . . .

Even if the reservoir land is considered specialty property,[1] the usual theory employed to value such property is reproduction cost less depreciation and obsolescence. As is true of cases valuing nonspecialty property, original cost is a factor in determining true value where it reflects present value and it is ostensibly fair to apply such cost as one indicator of value.

The majority does not bother itself with such distinctions. It reasons that the land constituting the base of the reservoir may be considered at its pure original cost because "[t]he land was adapted to a single use and its value depends upon continuance of that use." It goes on to state "[t]hat [the continued use of the reservoir] is the only element shown to have created value in this land" and that historical cost "becomes relevant" because the land contributes to the Company's earnings and the Company's rates are fixed by the Board of Public Utility Commissioners which consistently includes the land at its original cost in the rate base.

From the standpoint of sound *ad valorem* tax valuation practices, nothing could be further from the truth. In instances where such original cost may be said to be "relevant"

---

1. A specialty is "a structure which is *uniquely* adapted to the business conducted upon it or use made of it *and* cannot be converted to other uses without the expenditure of substantial sums of money" (citations omitted). *Great Atlantic & Pacific Tea Co. v. Kiernan*, 42 N.Y.2d 236, 240, 397 N.Y.S.2d 718, 721, 366 N.E.2d 808, 811 (Ct.App.1977) (emphasis in original).

for purposes of ad valorem valuation of utility property, it is never accepted uncritically and without consideration of other pertinent factors. The majority recognizes this when it states "that it would have been proper to consider, even under the unusual circumstances of this case, other factors such as the trending of costs incurred in acquiring the land and in preparing for its use as a reservoir." However, inexplicably it fails to follow this approach in its application of original costs as the measure of current market value.

. . . .

[I]n this case the Court uses the original purchase price of $670 per acre because there is no other satisfactory evidence of the fair market value of this land. I cannot acquiesce in this passive, wrong and purely expedient result. It is grossly unjust to the municipality and its taxpayers to tilt the tax burden so sharply away from the utility. This counters the statutory design of requiring that all relevant factors be brought to bear upon the valuation of utility property to the end that neither the utility taxpayer nor other municipal taxpayers are visited with the unbalanced consequences of the valuation of the utility's property which is unrealistically high or low.

I would remand this matter to the Division of Tax Appeals for a redetermination of the fair market value of the underwater reservoir acreage. The parties should be instructed to marshall additional evidence bearing upon the market value of the land. To the extent there is expert evidence introduced with respect to historical acquisition cost, such evidence must include factors to show that such costs can be related meaningfully to *present* market value.

. . . .

For these reasons, I dissent. Justice SULLIVAN and Justice PASHMAN join in this dissent.

HACKENSACK WATER COMPANY V. BOROUGH OF HAWORTH

178 N.J. Super. 251, 2 N.J. Tax 303, 428 A.2d 934, *cert. denied,* 87 N.J. 378,
434 A.2d 1063 (1981)
Superior Court of New Jersey, Appellate Division, 1981

The opinion of the court was delivered by POLOW, J. A. D.

On this appeal we are called upon to establish the appropriate technique for assessing real property under *N.J.S.A.* 54:30A-52, including not only underwater land in a reservoir as was dealt with in *Hackensack Water Co. v. Old Tappan,* 77 N.J. 208, 390 A.2d 122 (1978), but also the marginal land surrounding the reservoir and substantial upland "buffer" acreage used for the pumping and filtration plant and otherwise unimproved. Plaintiff is a private utility which provides water for approximately 800,000 customers in Bergen and Hudson counties. Among others, it owns and operates the Oradell Reservoir, a portion of which is located within defendant Borough of Haworth. The company appeals from the final determination of the Tax Court fixing the value of its land at $2,179,481 for 1972 and 1973, and at $2,090,834 for 1974, 1975 and 1976.

Plaintiff started to acquire land for the Oradell Reservoir in 1914 and bought additional real estate over the next 40 years. Although the Oradell Reservoir spreads over seven different municipalities, the portion which lies within Haworth includes 251.73 acres of land under water, 47.30 acres of marginal marshy land surrounding the submerged property and 135.45 upland acres on 40 acres of which the pumping station and water filtration plant are located. This is one of three reservoirs operated by the company in northern New Jersey providing water to about 60 communities. All of the company's land located within defendant municipality is zoned for residential use.

The Tax Court judge concluded that "the highest and best use of these lands is for residential lake community purposes." Reasoning that the high, wooded and well-drained upland area consisting of 135.45 acres had a value one-third greater than other comparable lots because of its strategic location overlooking the "lake," his term for the reservoir, and adjacent to a golf course, he placed a per acre value of $12,500 on that portion of the land. The $12,500 per acre value was applied to the 40 acres within the upland area upon which the company maintains its pumping and filtration facilities because the judge found that to be the unit price which would have to be paid to acquire that parcel now.

The underwater and marginal lands were evaluated at $1,330 an acre by the Tax Court judge. He arrived at that figure by apportioning what he conceived to be the increase in the value of the uplands because of the existence of the "lake," and dividing that total increase by the number of acres under water and in marginal lands.

A water utility's real estate must "be assessed and taxed at local rates in the manner provided by law for the taxation of similar property owned by other corporations or individuals . . . ." *N.J.S.A.* 54:30A-52. The underwater lands constitute real estate for tax purposes. *N.J.S.A.* 54:30A-50(b). Hence, all of the land of the company under and around the reservoir must be assessed at its "full and fair value . . . at such price as . . . it would sell for at a fair and bona fide sale by private contract . . . ." *N.J.S.A.* 54:4-23.

However, in dealing with reservoir property it is "proper to consider the actual highest and best use of the land, namely as a reservoir in conjunction with the operation of a utility water system." *Hackensack Water Co. v. Old Tappan, supra,* 77 *N.J.* at 214, 390 A.2d 122 (footnote omitted). Reservoir lands should be assessed in a manner which has "some relationship to reality." *Ibid.* "It is the fitness and availability of property for particular uses which should be given consideration in arriving at its taxable value . . . ." *In re East Orange Appeal,* 80 *N.J.Super.* 219, 231, 193 A.2d 377 (App.Div.1963), *certif. den.* 41 *N.J.* 200, 195 A.2d 468 (1963). Although the possibility of sale for different uses must be considered as a general rule, it is not applicable where "such possibility is so remote as to have no real bearing upon current value." *Tax Appeals Div. v. Ewing Tp.,* 72 *N.J.Super.* 238, 243, 178 A.2d 229 (App.Div. 1962). Where different uses are remote, they are irrelevant. *Hackensack Water Co. v. Old Tappan, supra.*

The Tax Court concluded that use of the upland property as a residential lake community is not remote. That conclusion was apparently based upon the statement that "the property need not be restructured," as was the problem with the underwater property with which the court was concerned in *Old Tappan.* Therefore, presumably, this land could be used for residential purposes in its present condition without "restructuring." But such use may be considered in assessing for tax purposes only if it is not too remote and only if it has some relationship to reality. *Ibid.*

Hence, we cannot accept the Tax Court's application of remoteness and feasibility on this record. "In this case of public utilities, in situations in which it is not feasible to evaluate land by utilizing the standard criteria, other factors must be considered." *Id.* 77 *N.J.* at 215, 390 A.2d 122. Whether the use of the uplands for residential purposes reflects a reasonable expectation in the foreseeable future is a question of fact not considered by the trial judge but essential to a determination of this issue. As a utility, the company may not sell its land without approval of the Board of Public Utility

Commissioners (BPU). *N.J.S.A.* 48:3-7. For example, no proofs were offered nor were findings directed to whether it is necessary to maintain the uplands in their natural state or to keep a buffer zone of any particular size to protect the quality of the company's water utility operations. Nor was any evidence received or consideration given to whether the BPU would permit sale of any of that property for private residential purposes. If the entire acreage must be preserved for water utility purposes, residential use may well be too remote and unfeasible to be utilized as the standard for evaluation of the land value. In such event, the only evaluation which would fairly relate to reality is its use "in conjunction with the operation of a utility water system." *Hackensack Water Co. v. Old Tappan, supra,* 77 *N.J.* at 214, 390 A.2d 122 (footnote omitted). See *In re East Orange Appeal, supra.*

We conclude that the Tax Court judge's determination that "the highest and best use of these lands is for residential lake community purposes" and that such residential use is not remote but bears "a sound relationship to reality," is not supported by substantial credible evidence in the record as a whole. The Oradell Reservoir is not merely a "lake" but is the terminal reservoir for the water supply system which serves 800,000 people in 60 municipalities. The record indicates that there is "no other water supply . . . in terms of quantity or in terms of low cost" equal to that of this company in the vicinity. One of the experts produced by the borough acknowledged that since there was no other water supply in Bergen County this system would continue to be used for the "foreseeable future." If the uplands should be determined to be an integral and essential part of that system, its use for residential purposes would be remote and thus irrelevant. On remand, the parties must be given the opportunity to produce additional evidence regarding "feasibility" and "remoteness" of potential residential uses in the upland acreage.

. . . .

The judgment of the Tax Court is vacated and the matter remanded with the following instructions to the Tax Court:

(1) That it take such additional evidence as may be offered to determine whether the uplands may be used for residential purposes in the foreseeable future;

(2) That it value the various portions of the Oradell Reservoir property within the Borough of Oradell based upon whether or not it must be retained for water utility purposes; all property which must be so retained must be assessed at its actual highest and best use as a reservoir in conjunction with the operation of a utility water system; such portion, if any, which, based upon the proofs to be submitted, is not necessary to be retained for water utility purposes, should then be assessed as appropriate for the highest and best use to which it may be put;

(3) That it consider such additional expert testimony as offered as to value of water utility lands and the trended costs incurred in acquiring all reservoir property located in the borough and in preparing it for its use for that purpose, in computing the value of the land for tax purposes;

(4) That it may consider all evidence previously submitted, as well as such additional evidence on all issues as is received, and

(5) That the Tax Court reconsider the company's motion to amend its appeals for the years 1975 and 1976 to allege discrimination in light of the fact that the company's petitions to the county board for those years did include such charges.

We do not retain jurisdiction.

Questions

1. Can a use, such as conversion to residential property, be considered "highest and best" if the costs of conversion exceed the postconversion market value of the land? What does "highest and best use" mean in this situation?

2. Given the New Jersey requirement that water supply property be taxed in the same manner as the land of private persons, what should be the effect of the taxpayer's status as a regulated utility, and the resulting limitations on its ability to sell its property? The *New York Times* reported in 1987 that the Hackensack Water Company received regulatory approval to sell 900 acres of land surrounding its reservoirs. The watershed land was first transferred to the company's real estate subsidiary, Rivervale Realty, and then to developers planning to construct housing and office space. Twenty-three acres in Rockland County were sold to Rivervale in 1985 for $304,000, and resold two months later to a housing developer for $1.8 million. Six hundred acres in Bergen County were transferred to Rivervale in 1984 at an appraised value of $10.7 million, or $16,000 an acre; one and one-half acres were then resold for $540,000.

   The appraised value was the average of the values submitted by an appraiser hired by the company and one hired by the State Board of Public Utilities. On the basis of that average value the company was ordered to pay each of its 164,000 customers $18 in 1985 as their share of the land's value, after deduction of taxes and the costs of the sale. Although regulators considered this a "full and final settlement" of customer claims to the land, the state's Public Service Commission announced plans to review the appraisal at the time of the company's next request for a rate increase.

   The company's development plans in Bergen County centered on the land near Lake Tappan and on the Oradell Reservoir. "The utility wants to build 900,000 square feet of offices and 160 condominium town houses on 170 acres of woods on the bank of the Oradell. It also wants to subdivide 43 acres on Lake Tappan for 34 homes next to a development of homes valued at $500,000 and up."[24] Does this later history lead you to question (1) the reliability of original cost figures as an index of current value; (2) the arm's-length nature of an exchange between a company and its subsidiary; (3) the difficulty of obtaining regulatory approval for a sale of property in appropriate instances; or (4) the wisdom of the common practice of splitting the difference between the valuation figures submitted by oppos-

---

24. R. Hanley, "Utility Selling Watershed Land for Large Profits," *New York Times,* August 5, 1987, p. B1.

ing parties? A detailed, adversarial examination of the sale by Hackensack Water Company appeared in 1991 in the *Village Voice*.[25]

---

25. R. Hennelly, "Water Gate: How the Hackensack Water Company Tricked Its Customers by Selling the Watershed down the River," *Village Voice*, November 19, 1991, p. 24.

5 SPECIAL PROBLEMS IN THE COST APPROACH

Introduction

Attempting to value a building through a measure of its construction cost, adjusted for depreciation and obsolescence, combines tangible and verifiable elements with the most imprecise and contentious aspects of valuation. The physical nature of a structure, including wear and tear, may be the subject of an engineering evaluation, but translation of these results into monetary terms is a matter of appraisal judgment. Once other forms of loss in value, such as economic and functional obsolescence, are introduced to the calculation, an enormous gulf may separate even the value estimates of experts who agree on the initial cost figure.

The first section of this chapter deals specifically with the problem of functional obsolescence through consideration of the *Reynolds Metals* case and its aftermath. In the second section, the *Onondaga* case presents another aspect of the debate over functional obsolescence, this time in the context of public utility property. The *Public Service Company of New Hampshire* case and the notes that follow deal with the more general problem of reconciling valuation for property tax purposes with valuation for rate-setting purposes when the regulated return allowed to a public utility is based on initial or "book" value rather than current market value.

The third section considers the problem of "specialty" property, property with a particular value to its current owner not reflected in its value to the market generally. In some cases this situation has led courts, for assessment purposes, to substitute a cost-based value, approximating value to the owner, for the lower market value. The 1927 case concerning assessment of the New York Stock Exchange set forth these issues clearly, and the later cases in this section demonstrate that they have never been completely resolved.

The fourth section deals with one variation on the specialty category: the "prestige" classification for buildings whose value to their owners stems from architectural merit and from the business value of association with a corporate name. The *Seagram* cases concerning the Mies van der Rohe landmark on Park Avenue illustrates the difficulties encountered in appraising such structures.

The final section of this chapter attempts to place this technical material in a broader perspective by considering the assessment history of the General Motors plant in Tarrytown, New York. The extreme difficulty of valuing an aging and highly specialized industrial plant eventually led the company, state, and town to agree to substitute payments (in lieu of taxes) not based on valuation figures at all. This agreement led to taxpayer resentment and constricted local budgets; the benefits of such attempts to retain jobs through tax concessions were the subject of considerable public debate when General Motors announced plans to shut the plant despite this agreement.

Although this narrative involves many larger issues, including tax competition, industrial policy, and intrastate fiscal relations, the initial crisis was due to the problem of calculating functional obsolescence. The lack of a market for such a specialized plant, together with the infeasibility of valuing it by reference to the income of General Motors, required a cost-based valuation. The difficulties and uncertainties of valuing a century-old plant under the cost approach led in turn to years of nearly arbitrary tax valuations. Encouraged by the success of similar cases in Michigan, counsel for General Motors planned to attack its assessments as insufficiently reflective of functional obsolescence, while the prospect of losing such a case and issuing refunds and interest to its largest taxpayer led the local jurisdictions to negotiate the out-of-court settlement discussed here.

The cost approach, with all its difficulties, may be reserved as a check on the upper bounds of valuation in the case of large subdivisions where comparable houses are bought and sold on a regular basis, or in the case on income-producing property that can be valued on the basis of its rents. The problems presented by cost-based valuation are of great public and legal significance because properties such as large manufacturing and assembly plants that are not suitable for either the sales comparison or income approaches may, like the General Motors site in Tarrytown, be the largest individual contributors to their local tax jurisdictions.

Problems of Functional Obsolescence

REYNOLDS METALS COMPANY V. DEPARTMENT OF REVENUE
258 Or. 116, 481 P.2d 352
Supreme Court of Oregon, 1971

DENECKE, Justice.

This appeal presents this court with a task of extreme perplexity,—fixing the true cash value of the plaintiff's aluminum reduction plant at Troutdale, Oregon. The county assessor fixed the value for 1968-1969 ad valorem tax purposes at $18,000,000. The taxpayer contends its value is $9,924,432. The Tax Court found the value to be $12,358,717. 3 OTR 470 (1970). Both the taxpayer and the Department of Revenue appeal.

The function of the plant is to reduce a raw material, alumina, to aluminum by an electrolytic process. The plant now produces 100,000 tons of aluminum yearly. The facility was completed in 1942 and taken over by Reynolds in 1946. Prior to the present appraisal, the last appraisal for property tax purposes was in 1961 when an independent appraisal company appraised it in the amount of $18,770,500 for the predecessor agency of the Department. The assessor placed a value on it at that time of $18,440,000. Subsequent to 1961, the assessed values were reduced each year but apparently took into consideration any capital improvements made during any tax year. The assessed valuation for 1967 was $12,610,936.

ORS [Oregon Revised Statutes] 308.234 requires a reappraisal at least every six years. In 1967 the office of the Multnomah County Assessor, with the assistance of the defendant Department of Revenue, reappraised the facility. The reappraisal was performed by a physical inspection of the buildings, machinery, and equipment, securing information from the taxpayer, securing information from persons dealing or familiar with machinery and equipment of the type used by Reynolds, and a study of the literature on the subject.

Reynolds sought independent appraisals and engaged the services of two appraisal firms represented by Mr. Vaughan and Mr. Nichols who made appraisals in the same general manner as the assessor. Mr. Vaughan determined the true cash value to be $9,858,000 and Mr. Nichols—$10,280,000.

The Tax Court refused to accept the assessor's appraisal for reasons enunciated in its opinion and for reasons not enunciated, did not accept the appraisals of Messrs. Vaughan or Nichols. The Tax Court's only statement of its determination of true cash value was in its opinion, as follows:

> In determining the true cash value of the plant for 1967 the Multnomah County Department of Revenue reduced the prior year's valuation of $12,852,107 by approximately 2 percent. Applying this same percentage to the 1967 value of $12,610,936 results in valuation of $12,358,717, which the court finds to be the true cash value of the subject property as of January 1, 1968.

We hear appeals de novo from the Tax Court. ORS 305.445. We ordinarily give great weight to the Tax Court's findings. In this case, however, we are of the opinion that with three current appraisals, the preferable method of fixing value is making use of the best of these appraisals or portions thereof. When the legislature established a policy of requiring reappraisal every six years, it recognized the deficiencies in attempting to determine value by applying factors to out-of-date appraisals. The record does contain the assessed values for each year after the appraisal of 1961. These show a downward trend, but there is no explanation in the record for the basis of the yearly valuation. A reduction of 2 percent in valuation from 1966 to 1967 might have been too large or too small. We reluctantly conclude that we are obliged to go into the details of the three appraisals and on the basis of these appraisals make a determination of true cash value.

The first decision to be made by the appraisers was which of the three traditional approaches to valuation would be used. The market or sale approach could not be used because there were no comparable sales. The income approach also could not be used as the income from this plant was not available. This left the cost or summation approach as the only feasible method and this is what the assessor, the department and Reynolds agree is a correct basic approach.

The cost approach determines the value of improvements by estimating the reproduction or by estimating the replacement cost and subtracting the estimated decrease in value due to depreciation and obsolescence.[2] The appraisers and the assessor were in

---

2. Obsolescence can be treated as a part of depreciation. In the instant case all treated it as separate.

agreement on a reproduction or a replacement cost of approximately $50,000,000. The testimony was that reproduction cost is the cost of duplicating the plant as it stands, whereas replacement cost is the cost of constructing a substitute, and if the technology has improved, the substitute will be modernized by incorporating the technological improvements.

The Department, before the Tax Court and in this court, argued that the assessor's $50,000,000 reproduction cost is too low, that replacement cost, not reproduction cost, is the correct starting point and replacement cost in this instance is $70,000,000. This figure was based upon the testimony of an employee of the Department who had done some investigation but had made no appraisal. The Tax Court rejected this contention and so do we.

. . . .

In addition to a decrease in value due to age and use of the property another factor decreases the value and this is at the heart of the entire controversy. This factor is the functional or technological obsolescence of the plant and equipment. Mr. Nichols' report states: "Due to technological advances as represented in the modern replacement plant previously described, functional obsolescence exists due to the excessive costs of continuing operation of the Troutdale plant as presently constituted." Stated another way, if the Troutdale plant were completely reproduced at a cost of $50,000,000, it would not have a value of $50,000,000 to a buyer because its operating costs would be higher per ton than new plants which have incorporated the new technological changes.[3]

All agree functional obsolescence has occurred and has decreased the value; however, the three evaluators substantially disagree upon the amount of the decrease. Nichols found a decrease of $15,220,000, Vaughan of $6,243,250 and the assessor of $2,115,000. All agree that the best measure of functional obsolescence is the excessive costs of operating the old plant. The appraisers engaged by Reynolds estimated substantially higher excess costs than did the assessor. The best method of determining how excessive the costs are would be by comparing the operating costs of the old plant and a new plant. Grant and Norton, *Depreciation*, ch. 13, p. 268 (1955); 1 Bonbright, *Valuation of Property*, examples in ch. 10, p. 177 (1937). Reynolds had such information but it refused to reveal it and apparently neither the Department nor the assessor sought to obtain this information by legal compulsion. The Troutdale plant manager based his refusal upon the advantage the statement of such costs would be to Reynolds' competitors. This is plausible; nevertheless, it places Reynolds at a disadvantage in sustaining its burden of proof on this aspect of the valuation.

Both appraisers estimated that the Troutdale plant had about $2,500,000 per year in excess labor costs. The assessor estimated $2,150,000. Excess labor cost was the only excess cost used by the assessor, whereas both the appraisers estimated additional yearly excess costs in the approximate amount of $2,200,000. Both appraisers computed total yearly excess costs to be in the amount of $4,700,000.

---

3. Functional or technological obsolescence should be distinguished from economic obsolescence. "Economic obsolescence is the result of forces outside of the building itself . . . ." *Encyclopedia of Real Estate Appraising*, Johnson, "Cost Approach to Value," 37, 50 (1959). *Georgia-Pacific Corp. v. Tax Comm.*, 237 Or. 143, 390 P.2d 337 (1964), considered the functional obsolescence of a lumber manufacturing plant. *Oregon Portland Cement Co. v. Tax Comm.*, 230 Or. 389, 369 P.2d 765 (1962), involved a claim of economic obsolescence.

The difference in the procedures followed by the appraisers and the assessor in using these excess costs to determine true cash value is of particular significance.

Mr. Vaughan evaluated the effect of these excess costs from the point of view of a prospective purchaser who would be willing to purchase Troutdale at true cash value. He reasoned that a prospective purchaser would have to consider, in addition to the total excess operating costs of Troutdale, the reduced depreciation costs of an old plant as compared to a new, modern one. A new plant, estimated to cost $50,000,000, would have $2,500,000 additional depreciation a year than the present old plant. Or, stated differently, the value of a new plant would lessen in value $2,500,000 per year because of depreciation.[4] This annual depreciation would be a cost of operating a new plant and must be offset against the excess operating costs of Troutdale. For this reason Vaughan deducted the yearly "depreciation requirement" of a new plant, $2,500,000, from the excess costs that would be incurred if the Troutdale plant were purchased. The remainder, $2,200,000, is the yearly net excess costs the purchaser would have to pay if it should buy the Troutdale plant. Vaughan reduced this amount still further in order to allow for the effect of federal income tax on that money which would be saved by a modern plant that eliminated the net excess operating costs. Using the federal corporate rate of 50 per cent (federal taxes would take 50 per cent of the additional profits realized if the purchaser did not have $2,200,000 in excess costs) Vaughan concluded that the annual net reduction in profits after taxes due to functional obsolescence is only $1,100,000.[5]

This $1,100,000 represents a yearly loss of profits. To determine the total decrease in value of plant and equipment that this loss would occasion the appraiser has to first estimate the remaining life of the facilities, which he determined to be 10 years. Therefore, this yearly loss would be incurred annually for 10 years. He also estimated that if the sum represented by these lost profits had not been lost such sum would have yielded a 12 per cent annual return. He then reduced this 10-year loss to its present value. This was computed to be $6,243,250, which represented the decrease in value because of functional obsolescence.

Nichols followed the same procedure with two major exceptions. Nichols did not deduct from gross excess operating costs which would be incurred if one purchased the Troutdale plant the larger depreciation requirement which would be incurred if the would-be purchaser instead built a modern plant. No explanation was given for this omission. Nichols used an expected rate of return on investment of 9 per cent as compared to 12 per cent by Vaughan. This increased the present worth of the obsolescence deduction by $2,000,000. Because of these two differences, Nichols' obsolescence deduction was $15,220,000 rather than $6,243,250, as found by Vaughan.

The assessor's procedure in determining the decrease in value because of obsolescence substantially varied from the procedures used by either of the other appraisers. As stated, the assessor's estimate of annual excess costs was $2,150,000 as he only recognized excess labor as incurring excess costs. He then reduced this amount by 50 per cent to allow for the effect of federal income tax; this left a sum of $1,075,000. The assessor estimated the remaining life of the facility to be 23 years, as compared to 10 by the two appraisers, and the return on investment to be 8 per cent as compared to 9 per cent and 12 per cent

---

4. Depreciation must be considered as an expense or as a decrease in value of the asset and not as a desirable deduction from income for tax purposes.

5. This overlooks the state corporate tax; however, with all appraisals using some very general estimates we do not believe it necessary to attain complete precision.

by the two appraisers. On this basis he multiplied $1,075,000 by the present worth factor and arrived at a sum of $11,100,000.[6]

The assessor did not, however, deduct the $11,000,000 as the decrease in value due to obsolescence. Instead, he deducted $9,000,000 from the $11,100,000, leaving $2,100,000, which latter figure was deducted for obsolescence. Neither the assessor's representative nor the Department witnesses were able to clearly express why this $9,000,000 was deducted from the capitalized decrease in value caused by obsolescence or how the $9,000,000 was determined. The Department made the $9,000,000 estimate but the Department witnesses were unable to be specific about its ingredients and one characterized the estimate: "It was strictly an estimate and it is probably a pretty broad one." The assessor's representative stated: "The $9,000,000 was an estimate of what it would cost to have better craneways, better handling of materials—."

The representative testified the reason for the $9,000,000 deduction was: "The $9,000,000 deduction represents the excess—the extra amount of money that would have had to have been spent in the original design and construction of this plant to realize these savings."

A supervisor from the Department testified:

> "There's nothing to generate the $11,000,000 from. I can't take one old plant and compare another old plant to it and say $11,000,000 of excess operating costs. I have to take the replacement cost if I'm going to develop this difference. I will take the $11,000,000 off the replacement cost but I can't take it off reproduction cost. So we tried to make this adjustment by saying that the amount of mechanization and other improvements necessary in this old plant to effect this savings would be $9,000,000."

Counsel for Reynolds referred to deducting the $9,000,000 as increasing the market value because of obsolescence, an obvious incongruity, and argued that this was the crux of the case. The Tax Court also was unable to follow the assessor's reason for deducting the $9,000,000.

We have had the benefit of refinement in counsel's thinking since the decision of the Tax Court. The briefs and oral argument reflect this refinement. With this advantage and from extensive study of the transcript and exhibits we are of the opinion that we have some comprehension of the reasoning the assessor used when he deducted $9,000,000 from $11,000,000. We believe he was attempting to accomplish the same result that Vaughan was when he deducted $2,500,000 per year as the additional depreciation requirement of a modernized plant, from the Troutdale plant's excess operating costs. The assessor, the Department and Vaughan believed a prospective purchaser, when deciding whether to buy the old plant or build a modern one, would take into consideration that a new one would cost much more and this additional cost in some way would at least partially offset the savings of excess costs that would be obtained by building a modern plant. This belief appears reasonable.

We are of the opinion, however, that the calculations of Vaughan in computing the net decrease in value because of obsolescence are more acceptable than those of the

---

6. The present worth of the decreased value computed by the assessor is substantially larger than that computed by Vaughan despite the excess costs estimated by the assessor were less than those estimated by Vaughan. This occurred because the assessor used a longer life expectancy for the facility and a lower rate of return on investment. The longer the life and the lower the rate of return, the more the present worth will be.

assessor and Department. None of the Department witnesses were able to testify with any certainty to the detailed makeup of the $9,000,000 deducted. Vaughan in his report went into detail describing how he arrived at his estimate of $2,500,000. While this figure was only an estimate, the witness nonetheless appeared to have followed standard factors and procedures. In addition, the assessor did not take into account the cost of modernization in making a reduction for federal income tax; rather, he only reduced the excess costs. Vaughan, on the other hand, did not take the tax consequences into account until he had offset excess costs by the cost of modernizing, that is, the deduction for increased depreciation. This procedure appears to us to be more realistic.

For these reasons we conclude that the decrease in value for obsolescence of $6,243,250 as determined by Vaughan is the most acceptable. On this basis we compute the true cash value of the Troutdale facility to be:

Reproduction Cost		$49,587,451.
Less depreciation	$29,500,000.	
Less obsolescence	$6,243,250.	
	$35,743,250.	
		$35,743,250.
True cash value		$13,844,201.

Modified.

Notes on Functional Obsolescence

The problem of calculating functional obsolescence demonstrates some of the difficulties the cost approach presents for property that has not been recently constructed. Physical, functional, and economic depreciation can require enormous deductions against construction cost. At the same time, their effect on property value can be verified only through sales data, or indirectly through the higher operating costs the property incurs by comparison with a modern substitute. In this respect the cost approach relies on market and income data to gauge depreciation. Alfred A. Ring wrote, "Fortunately for the professional appraiser, estimating accrued depreciation directly is usually of secondary importance. In fact, depreciation cannot accurately be determined until value is known."[1]   Bonbright was similarly pessimistic as to the accuracy of depreciation measures based on projected income:

> In the light of what has been said, the *ideal* method of estimating depreciation would be a direct forecast of the differences, year by year, between the income of the enterprise with the old asset and the income of the same enterprise with the new asset. This forecast would require the inclusion of future asset replacements among the outlays, contrary to the accounting concept of income. In practice, however, it is usually hopeless to attempt such forecasts directly. The appraiser is therefore compelled to resort, partly to guesswork (usually misnamed "judgment"), and partly to mathematical formulas which make some plausible

1. A. Ring and J. Boykin, *The Valuation of Real Estate,* 3d ed. (1986), p. 246.

assumptions as to the discrepancies between the income streams derivable from the two comparable assets.[2]

The court in *Reynolds* recognized that the

best method of determining how excessive the costs are would be by comparing the operating costs of the old plant and a new plant . . . . Reynolds had such information but it refused to reveal it and apparently neither the Department nor the assessor sought to obtain this information by legal compulsion.

However, without income data there is no way to verify that design or layout deficiencies actually reduce market value. It is always possible that a different structure, perhaps with greater automation and more sophisticated facilities, could reduce staffing and equipment needs. But it is not sufficient to subtract these "excess" costs from the value of the present plant. The hypothetical state-of-the-art plant may carry higher utility costs, suffer from more frequent malfunctions, require more specialized technical staff, or in other ways incur greater expenses than the present plant. Moreover, the extra cost of constructing the hypothetical plant may outweigh the operating savings. The only way to determine whether the hypothetical plant is a better investment is to compare overall construction and operating costs.

It is critical to distinguish "reproduction" cost, or the cost of constructing an exact new copy, from "replacement" cost, or the cost of constructing a substitute that performs the same function, even if with a different design. If replacement with a more modern substitute costs less than reproduction of the current plant, clearly no purchaser will offer more for the existing building than its replacement cost, reduced to reflect physical depreciation. A replacement may be more expensive to construct but offer savings in operating expenses which, capitalized over the life of the plant, still make it the least costly alternative. If the cost of replacement, adjusted for the increase or decrease in operating costs, exceeds the cost of reproduction, no functional obsolescence has been shown—even if technological advances reduce staffing requirements. Recall in this regard the testimony of the department of revenue's representative in *Reynolds*: "There's nothing to generate the $11,000,000 from. I can't take one old plant and compare another old plant to it and say $11,000,000 of excess operating costs. I have to take the replacement cost if I'm going to develop this difference."

The *Reynolds* opinion demonstrates the importance of a clear explanation of such comparisons. When the department of revenue sought to reduce the estimated $11 million savings from modern equipment by its $9 million cost, the court noted,

---

2. J. Bonbright, *The Valuation of Property* (1937), vol. 1, pp. 190–91.

Neither the assessor's representative nor the Department witnesses were able to clearly express why this $9,000,000 was deducted from the capitalized decrease in value caused by obsolescence or how the $9,000,000 was determined . . . . Counsel for Reynolds referred to deducting the $9,000,000 as increasing the market value because of obsolescence, an obvious incongruity, and argued that this was the crux of the case.

Later, with "the benefit of refinement in counsel's thinking since the decision of the Tax Court," the *Reynolds* court understood that

[t]he assessor, the Department and Vaughan believed a prospective purchaser, when deciding whether to buy the old plant or build a modern one, would take into consideration that a new one would cost much more and this additional cost in some way would at least partially offset the savings of excess costs that would be obtained by building a modern plant. This belief appears reasonable.

But the absence of a comprehensive explanation for the derivation of these figures led the court to reject them in favor of the taxpayer's evidence.

A purchaser formulating a bid for an existing plant will take into account both its net income and the cost of constructing a modern replacement plant that serves the same function. Consider the four examples in table 1.

Table 1
Relation of Construction Costs and Operating Costs

	Higher operating costs for reproduction plant	Higher operating costs for replacement plant
Higher reproduction costs	(1) $10M to reproduce $5M to replace Excess operating costs of $1M	(2) $10M to reproduce $5M to replace *Lower* operating costs of $1M
Higher replacement costs	(3) $5M to reproduce $10M to replace Excess operating costs of $1M	(4) $5M to reproduce $10M to replace *Lower* operating costs of $1M

In situation 1, the existing plant incurs higher operating costs than the most efficient functional substitute. The construction costs of reproducing the existing plant in its current design (less physical depreciation) are also higher than the construction costs of a more efficient replacement. In this example, the future stream of these excess costs over the life of the plant, discounted to present value, equals $1 million. Therefore, by purchasing this plant as it exists, a buyer obtains the capacity of a plant that could be built at a cost of $5 million. However, the buyer will also incur $1 million in cap-italized excess costs over the life of the plant. Taken together, these considerations would lead to an initial bid of $4 million for the plant. Here, the fair market value equals the replacement costs minus the excess operating costs.

In situation 2, the cost of reproducing the existing plant (less physical depreciation) is again higher than the construction cost of a modern substitute. In this case, however, the operating costs of the plant are *lower* by an amount that, discounted to present value, equals $1 million. Therefore a prospective purchaser would understand that this plant offers the same operating capacity as a plant costing $5 million to construct, but is worth an additional $1 million in forgone costs. This would lead to an initial bid of $6 million. Here, the fair market value again equals the replacement cost minus the excess operating costs; but unlike those in situation 1, the excess operating costs are negative, because the existing plant is less expensive to operate than its modern substitute.

Situation 3 considers a plant whose reproduction is less costly than replacement with a modern substitute, although the substitute would save total operating costs with a present value of $1 million. By definition, the replacement is not the most efficient substitute in this case because, even with an offset for the operating savings, its total cost exceeds the cost of reproduction. No functional obsolescence has been demonstrated. Note that this conclusion depends on income data for verification.

Finally, in situation 4 replacement would be out of the question. Again, functional obsolescence is absent. Replacement with a modern substitute would incur both higher construction costs and higher operating costs than reproduction of the existing plant.

Notes and Questions

1. Was the Oregon court successful in calculating a deduction for functional obsolescence without reference to income data? After *Reynolds*, a 1981 Oregon enactment provided that owners of industrial plants may exclude the income approach from assessment only if they relinquish claims to functional and economic obsolescence. Or. Rev. Stat. §308.411(2). Otherwise, the owner must make available "all information requested by the assessor or department needed to determine the real market value for the plant." Or. Rev. Stat. §308.411(4). A New York City ordinance requiring owners of certain income-producing properties to furnish income and expense statements to the Commissioner of Finance for tax assessment purposes was held constitutional in *41 Kew Gardens Road Associates v. Tyburski*, 70 N.Y.2d 325, 514 N.E.2d 1114, 520 N.Y.S.2d 544 (1987).

2. A building that is inappropriate to its site, such as an expensive residence in an industrial area, will also generally suffer nonphysical depreciation reducing its market value below its cost of construction. An investment too lavish for its surroundings or purpose is sometimes termed an "over–improvement." The converse situation, an "underimprovement," was at issue in *Trump-Equitable Fifth Avenue Co. v. Gliedman,* 87 A.D.2d 12, 450 N.Y.S.2d 321 (1982), *rev'd,* 57 N.Y.2d 588, 443 N.E.2d 940, 457 N.Y.S.2d 466 (1982), which denied a tax abatement for Trump Tower in New York City. The abatement was available to buildings that replaced structures on underutilized land. The taxpayers argued that the Bonwit Teller department store formerly on that site was not of the maximum height allowable, and therefore Trump Tower had replaced a "functionally obsolete" building. The appellate division considered that this interpretation would classify most sites in Manhattan as underutilized, producing "a universal tax exemption, hardly consonant with the statutory purpose." This decision was reversed by the court of appeals, which after remand and another reversal held that the commissioner of housing preservation and development had exceeded the terms of the governing statute by requiring "substantial" underutilization for replacement construction to be eligible for this exemption. *Trump-Equitable Fifth Avenue Co. v. Gliedman,* 62 N.Y.2d 539, 467 N.E.2d 510, 478 N.Y.S.2d 846 (1984). Recall this debate when reading the appellate division opinion in the *Seagram* case later in this chapter. There, Judge Breitel's concurring opinion states, "Worth discarding, although urged, is the argument that because a building does not occupy all of the assembled land, there is an inadequate improvement. This does not follow. The improvement is inadequate to the land only if that is not a sound economic way to construct a building."

3. What benefits and drawbacks do you perceive to the Oregon system of permitting a trial de novo, "anew upon the record," by the state's highest court? *Publishers Paper Co. v. Department of Revenue,* 270 Or. 737, 530 P.2d 88 (1974), calculated the functional obsolescence of a lumber mill built in the 1920s. Its interesting design defect was originally considered a benefit: it was "built astraddle Johnson Creek to allow waste material to be carried away by the stream," a practice now "unacceptable on both ecological and economic grounds." The Oregon Supreme Court engaged in a detailed examination of the fifty excess staff positions claimed by the taxpayer to be due to this layout deficiency, and also considered numerous items of similarly contested equipment, including straddle carriers, fork lift trucks, log tractors, and yard cranes. Yet the court took pains to deny any wider implications to these findings:

> This holding does not constitute the rule that the methods used to determine functional obsolescence in this case are necessary or appropriate

in all cases as a matter of law . . . . We hold, merely, that on the record before us the plaintiff is entitled to an adjustment in the amount stated above.

In a later case, *Bend Millwork Co. v. Department of Revenue*, 285 Or. 577, 592 P.2d 986, 992 n.8 (1979), Judge Lent commented: "This writer has often wondered why this court in this kind of case spends so much time in sifting *in writing* the evidence . . . . I suppose we do it to show that indeed we have carefully considered the evidence." Again, a detailed twenty-page examination of staffing and equipment needs concluded with the admonition, "As in *Publishers*, the methodology used here to determine the value of the property should not necessarily be held the standard in assessments of other property." Would it have been within the court's power in these cases to rule as a general matter that no claims for functional obsolescence would be entertained in the absence of income data? By 1985 the Oregon court had "determined to forego those extensive discussions of the evidence in this kind of case." *Reynolds Metals Co. v. Department of Revenue*, 299 Or. 592, 705 P.2d 712, 715 (1985), *modified*, 300 Or. 250, 709 P.2d 710 (1985).

4. Bonbright challenged the usual distinction between physical depreciation, or wear and tear, and functional obsolescence in this way:

> [T]he popular distinction between "physical" and "functional" depreciation is a false antithesis. *Any* depreciation of a physical asset, so far as it need be considered by an appraiser, is at once physical and functional. Consider two dynamos, the one of which is depreciated because its commutator has worn out and its insulation has become defective, whereas the other is depreciated because a more efficiently designed substitute is now on the market. Ordinarily the former depreciation would be called "physical" or "structural," whereas the latter would be called "functional." Clearly, however, the obsolescence is no less physical than the wear and tear; for a difference in design is certainly physical or structural in nature. Moreover, the wear and tear has a functional significance; otherwise it would be of no concern to an appraiser.[3]

The concept of obsolescence does offer a means of explaining a loss in value not attributable to defects revealed through visual measurement or inspection. The inherent problem of verifying the amount of obsolescence is compounded when a lack of market data prevents direct observation of the effects of obsolescence on sale price. If buildings suffering from a specific type of obsolescence were regularly bought and sold, their market value would not need to be calculated by the cost method. The absence of market data prevents a direct sales approach to the valuation of specialized property constructed for the needs of a particular owner.

---

3. *Ibid.*, p. 185.

The Cost Approach and Public Utility Property

***

ONONDAGA COUNTY WATER DISTRICT V. BOARD OF ASSESSORS
39 N.Y.2d 601, 385 N.Y.S.2d 13, 350 N.E.2d 390
New York Court of Appeals, 1976

***

BREITEL, Chief Judge.

Petitioner water district brought four separate proceedings to review the 1969 real property tax assessments by respondent towns on its water pipeline facilities located within the respective towns in Oswego County (Real Property Tax Law, art. 7). The parties stipulated that the determination made for 1969 would be binding for the 1970 and 1971 assessments.

Special Term denied the petitions and confirmed the assessments. The Appellate Division reversed and remanded for a determination of the amount of "functional depreciation" to be deducted from cost in arriving at the value of the facilities.

On remand, Supreme Court dismissed the petitions, finding that no functional depreciation had been proved. The Appellate Division reversed and granted the petitions, allowing a 50% deduction for functional depreciation. Respondents appeal.

The issue is whether the owner of specialty property, planned and constructed with a capacity for service in excess of present needs but in reasonable anticipation of future needs, is entitled to a deduction for "functional depreciation."

There should be a reversal. "Functional depreciation," commonly referred to as "obsolescence," may also connote a capacity of the property for service in excess of reasonably anticipated needs. This type of functional depreciation, termed "superfluity," is properly deductible from cost as a factor diminishing the value of the property. Where, however, as in this case, the excess capacity for production was planned and constructed in reasonable anticipation of future needs, that is, with deferred utility, there is no functional depreciation. This is because the excess capacity does not diminish the value of the property but instead constitutes a real element of value. Thus, it was error to allow a deduction for functional depreciation in this case.

The Onondaga County Water District was organized pursuant to article 5-A of the County Law as a nonprofit agency to develop from Lake Ontario a source of public water supply for Onondaga County, and eventually for parts of Oswego County.

The water system was completed in June, 1967, when it began operation. Water is taken from Lake Ontario at the City of Oswego and passed through a treatment plant in the Town of Oswego. The water is then pumped through a pipeline, crossing portions of the Towns of Oswego, Volney, Minetto and Schroeppel, to a terminal in Clay, Onondaga County, from which it is then distributed to facilities in Onondaga County.

On May 1, 1969, the taxable status date, the water system was operating at about 25% capacity. Deliberately planned and constructed to meet the future needs of Onondaga County and parts of Oswego County, the system has an estimated useful life of 40 years. By 1969, its use had steadily increased since starting operations two years before, and its use is still increasing.

The boards of assessors of the four Oswego County towns assessed the property at full value, based upon the actual cost of construction. Reproduction cost was not used, apparently because of the newness of the facilities.

While accepting original cost for assessment purposes, the water district nevertheless contends that, since the system was operating at only 25% capacity, the remaining 75%

of capacity represents an "overbuilding," thus entitling it to a 75% deduction for "functional depreciation."

All real property must be assessed at "full value." Where property is regarded as a "specialty," that is, property designed for "unique" purposes and for which there is no market, the proper method of valuation is ordinarily reproduction cost less depreciation.

While the parties agree that, apparently because of the newness of the facilities, actual construction cost is the convenient method of valuation, the controversy centers around the propriety of allowing a deduction for "functional depreciation."

Functional depreciation has been defined as "obsolescence" or as "the loss of operating efficiency" (see, e.g., 1 Bonbright, *Valuation of Property*, at pp. 187–188; 2 Orgel, *Valuation Under Eminent Domain*, sections 211, 213, at pp. 97–98, 105–106). More sophisticated analysis has recognized various subclasses, based upon causal distinctions, of the class "functional depreciation." Thus, for example, the writers have distinguished among "physical obsolescence," the out of datedness of an asset; "inadequacy," the failure of the asset to meet present or projected needs; and "superfluity," "duplication of facilities," or "overbuilding," the opposite of "inadequacy," where the capacity of the asset exceeds reasonable anticipated demands.

The common thread running through each subclass of functional depreciation is that each is an "undesirable feature," an "adverse influence," or a "deterioration;" in short, a disutility diminishing in some way the value of the property. Thus, true "superfluity" is present where there is "duplication of facilities or overbuilding . . . where the capacity of the existing plant is beyond the reasonable limit of possible demand" (2 Orgel, *Valuation Under Eminent Domain*, at p. 107). Put another way, functional obsolescence in the form of superfluity occurs when there is a capacity for service in excess of reasonably anticipated needs and thus is functionally useless, now and in the future.

But there was no superfluity or improvident overbuilding in this instance, but deliberate and wise construction in reasonable anticipation of future needs. As such, it is perverse to regard such deferred utility as an "adverse influence" on, or "deterioration" of the property rather than as a real element of the value of the property because of future utility. Thus, as Special Term properly concluded, there should be no deduction from construction cost on account of "functional depreciation," which is denominative of disutility rather than deferred utility.

As a matter of economic analysis, the builders of the water system invested what it was worth to them to build a system useful now and useful in the future. A gold mine is no less a gold mine because its exploitation is by choice or necessity deferred to a future time. In so investing its capital the water district acted as a thrifty, and perhaps wise, planner. Thus, it should be assumed that it invested as much as it did, recognizing (discounting) the fact that the presently excess capital investment would not yield a return until the future. It is not unlike the investor who purchases an asset knowing that its yield will issue only in the future. In so doing, he will pay no more for the asset than he would for a capitalized deferred income. Consequently, in this case, the original cost of construction was, by concession, the best expression of the value of this specialty property in 1969.

In effect what the water district is claiming is an exemption from taxes for its thrifty advance planning. Whether this is desirable is a matter of legislative policy in which the encouragement to advance planning is balanced against the possible burden without benefit to the municipalities through which the pipelines run. Notably, it is not foreign to legislative policy to provide by statute for tax exemption for water system aqueducts. What is certain is that it would be a distortion of the judicial function to provide that exemption by fiat to the effect that what is valuable is not valuable because the return in value from the investment is deferred from the present to the future, when in truth an asset with future benefit deferred is valuable indeed. Nor is it appropriate to discount for deferral of utility just because either market value or voluntary investment of capital will take into account the deferral of utility.

Accordingly, the orders of the Appellate Division should be reversed, with costs, and the original judgments of Special Term confirming the assessments should be reinstated.

JASEN, GABRIELLI, JONES, WACHTLER, FUCHSBERG and COOKE, JJ., concur. Orders reversed, etc.

Question

Can a special-purpose structure built for its current owner and fulfilling its intended purpose ever suffer functional obsolescence? This question often arises in the valuation of lavish corporate headquarters and other buildings when the owners argue that the actual price they would realize if the structure were offered for sale would not equal the cost of construction. In *CPC Int'l, Inc. v. Borough of Englewood Cliffs*, 193 N.J. Super. 261, 473 A.2d 548 (App. Div. 1984), *cert. denied*, 97 N.J. 578, 483 A.2d 124 (1984), the court held that

> no allowance will be made for the special purpose character of the building or for overbuilt features where the original owner erected the building for his own needs, remains in possession, and continues to enjoy the improvements which it installed and for which the allowance is claimed.

What situations might contradict this general rule? A concurring justice in that case added,

> A wealthy financier is reputed to have remarked that if you must be concerned about the cost of upkeep, you should not buy a yacht. Similarly, corporate officials who must worry about a large tax assessment should not construct a place of splendor and magnificence.

See also *WCI-Westinghouse, Inc. v. Edison Township*, 7 N.J. Tax 610 (1985), *aff'd*, 9 N.J. Tax 86 (App. Div. 1986); *Pacific Mutual Life Insurance Co. v. County of Orange*, 187 Cal.App.3d 1141, 232 Cal.Rptr. 233 (1985).

PUBLIC SERVICE COMPANY OF NEW HAMPSHIRE V. NEW HAMPTON
101 N.H. 142, 136 A.2d 591
Supreme Court of New Hampshire, 1957

Petition, for abatement of taxes under RSA [Revised Statutes Annotated] 76:16 brought by Public Service Company of New Hampshire against the town of New Hampton because of the refusal of the selectmen of the town to abate any portion of the taxes assessed against the plaintiff for the year 1955. Trial by the Court after a view, resulting in a denial of the petition.

As of April 1, 1955, all the plaintiff's property in the defendant town was appraised at $1,218,899. On the basis of that appraisal and on the basis of a tax rate of $45.30 per thousand, a tax of $54,881.25 was assessed. The plaintiff complied with all statutory formalities required in order to perfect an appeal to the Superior Court under N.H.Rev.Stat.Ann. 76:17.

The plaintiff's property in New Hampton consists of: (1) a portion of the so-called Ayers Island hydro-electric generating plant; (2) transmission facilities; (3) distribution facilities; and (4) general plant.

The parties stipulated without prejudice to any other issue in the case that the full and true market value of all the plaintiff's property in New Hampton, with the exception of the portion of the Ayers Island hydro-electric generating plant located there, is its net book cost of $462,995. They further stipulated that on the average all property in New Hampton taxable by the town, other than the plaintiff's was assessed in 1955 at fifty-one per cent of its full and true value. The principal issue of fact tried by the Court was the full and true, or market value, as of April 1, 1955 of that portion of the Ayers Island generating plant located in New Hampton. The Court found that the fair value of all the plaintiff's property in New Hampton as of April 1, 1955 was $2,400,000 which, multiplied by the agreed proportional figure of fifty-one percent, would justify an assessment of $1,224,000. The Court therefore dismissed the petition.

The property about which the dispute centers consists of a concrete dam originally built in 1924 and raised in 1931 extending across the Pemigewasset River from its west or right bank in the Town of Bristol to the east or left bank in the defendant town. The plaintiff company owns in fee the bed and banks of the river where the plant is located and also land or flowage rights coextensive with the lands flowed by the water impounded by the dam. The line between the towns of New Hampton and Bristol is half-way between the banks of the river. The generating plant housed in a brick structure at the east end of the dam is in New Hampton. The generating facilities consist of three generators, each driven by a water wheel and each having a rated capacity of 2,800 kilowatts. The plant is one of many hydro-electric generating plants owned by the plaintiff which are all interconnected by a transmission system and operated in conjunction with each other to furnish electricity for customers. Other facts appear in the opinion. Transferred by Wescott, J.

OPINION.

BLANDIN, Justice.

The plaintiff's position in broad outline is, first, there was "no competent evidence to support a finding of a market value of the Ayers Island plant . . . in excess of its net book cost," and, second, "That the Trial Court, in reaching its decision applied incorrect principles of law, made findings and rulings contrary to and unsupported by the evidence, and otherwise erred . . ."

At the outset it must be said that unusual problems are inherent in utility cases such as this. An obstacle to a rational and plain exposition is that due to factors hereinafter discussed, truly satisfactory standards for testing value do not exist. Again, in rate base disputes the interest of the utility is to show the value of its property at the maximum while that of the rate payers is to establish the lowest possible value. In tax cases the situation is exactly reversed. It is the public, represented by the assessors, which seeks to include the last dollar of worth in the assessment, while the company is avidly eager to have the value of its property considered in the most modest light. Generally there are readily available to both parties experts, the disparity of whose estimates increases the difficulty of reaching a fair conclusion.

On the question of value in the present case the plaintiff's evidence was that the property is electric utility property, having its highest value as such, that it is subject to regulation by the Public Utilities Commission of the State, and in the past its rate base and that of similar utilities has been based on net book cost, or original cost less depreciation. From this the plaintiff argues that the tax value of its plant cannot exceed its rate base or net book cost, both as a matter of law and fact.

The defendant disagrees with this conclusion and produced evidence on valuation consisting of reproduction cost figures less depreciation, a figure based on the cost of an equivalent steam-generating capacity, and a valuation based on the capitalized earning power of the Ayers Island plant. The Court, in its findings and rulings, stated that in reaching its conclusion it considered the rate base, the original cost less depreciation, the factor of regulation, the dependable capacity of the plant at low water, the value of this capacity "based on the annual cost of alternative steam power capacity," the return upon investment, and the cost of construction of a new plant. It ruled that "fair market value for purposes of taxation involves valuation in a free market," and having weighed all the above factors, made a finding that the market value of the plaintiff's taxable property in New Hampton was $2,400,000 which, multiplied by the agreed figure of fifty-one percent, that being the proportion of full value at which other property in New Hampton was assessed, would justify an assessment of $1,224,000. The actual assessment being $1,218,899, the Court dismissed the petition.

To resolve the dispute as to whether there was competent evidence to support the verdict it is necessary first to examine the applicable law. N.H. Rev. Stat. Ann. 75:1 lays down the rule for appraisal of taxable property as follows: "The selectmen shall appraise all taxable property at its full and true value in money as they would appraise the same in payment of a just debt due from a solvent debtor, and shall receive and consider all evidence that may be submitted to them relative to the value of property the value of which cannot be determined by personal examination.". . . Such value is the market value, or the price which the property will bring in a fair market, after fair and reasonable efforts have been made to find the purchaser who will give the highest price for it." The principle laid down here has never been questioned in this state and is recognized elsewhere.

The establishment of market value as a test for taxation purposes presupposes a market. In instances such as this where only a part of an integrated system is involved, the difficulty, if not the impossibility of finding an actual customer, especially where, as here, the owner has a lawful monopoly in the surrounding area, is obvious. Yet it is plain that to hold there is no market value in such instances would mean that valuable property would entirely escape its just share of the burden of taxation. Such a policy would make neither good law nor good sense. Courts recognizing this have acted accordingly and have considered all factors calculated to influence an assumed buyer and seller in a free market. In so considering, it must, as previously stated, be remembered that the property is and may be used as an integral part of an entire system and that its value may be enhanced for this very reason. In all the circumstances here it is obvious that ordinary standards may not furnish an adequate guide to determine value.

Since indisputably the property has its greatest value as an electric public utility the purchaser may be assumed to be such. The plaintiff excepted to the granting of requests that it could be considered as a potential customer. However, it appears under the law that the price an electric utility, including the plaintiff itself or a buyer in its position, would pay to an assumed third person may be considered. *Arlington Mills v. Town of Salem*, 83 N.H. 148, 140 A. 163. See also *Boston Gas Co. v. Assessors of Boston*, 137 N.E.2d 481, where the Court sanctioned evidence of the value for a sale and lease back to the present owner and others in its class. The evidence of the worth of the property to an electric public utility purchaser including the plaintiff was properly received, and the plaintiff's exceptions are overruled.

The plaintiff claims that evidence of reproduction cost was incompetent. . . . [W]e believe testimony as to the economic value of the plant based upon the cost of providing equivalent steam-generated capacity was properly admitted. If one is contemplating buying an article, the cost of purchasing it as against building a new one is a natural consideration affecting the price. The authorities support the competency of such evidence. The plaintiff's objection to this evidence was based upon the proposition that it indicates only the worth to the owner and as such is incompetent. *Trustees of the Phillips-Exeter Academy v. Exeter*, 94 N.H. 473, 33 A.2d 665; *Sisters of Mercy v. Town of Hooksett*, 93 N.H. 301, 42 A.2d 222. However, the principle established in the *Exeter* case and approved in the *Hooksett* opinion is that although worth to the owner alone which could not be transferred to a purchaser may not be considered, transmissible value is material. In the present instance, the Court weighed with other factors the worth to the owner which could be transferred to others. Since, as previously pointed out, the owner may be considered a hypothetical buyer, it is apparent the price he would have to pay for building a new equivalent plant would influence his judgment in the purchase of this one. Furthermore, the defendant's expert testified he did not base his calculations solely on value to the owner but also on his knowledge of costs generally. He considered the "cost of moderately-sized fuel plants of recent design in the northeastern part of the United States," and tested the figures of the plaintiff against other companies. Applying this method of valuation which he testified without contradiction was "one of the most common methods" of evaluating a hydro-electric plant, and which indeed the plaintiff's evidence to a degree confirmed, the witness, assuming "a dependable capacity" of 7,000 kilowatts, at times of lowest stream flow, operating on a peak of 7½ hours duration, which the Court found to be the plant's most valuable potential use, arrived at a valuation of the property of $3,133,900.

The plaintiff also objects because the defendant's expert failed to take into account depreciation in this connection. It must be remembered that the Court's valuation for tax purposes was well under the findable valuation based on the testimony of the expert. When it is considered, among other factors, that the life of the Ayers Island dam was fixed by the plaintiff itself at one hundred and fifty years, it would appear that in reaching its final conclusion the Court, as stated in its findings, made substantial allowance for such depreciation.

The defendant also relied upon a valuation based upon evidence as to the earning power of the Ayers Island plant. That such a factor is an element to be considered, though not necessarily controlling, in assessing tax values is well established. The fact that there may have been discrepancies in the testimony of the defendant's expert and that his method of evaluation was not approved by the plaintiff, although it produced no expert to refute it, went to the weight of the evidence, but not its admissibility. The calculations of this expert show that the value of the plant based on its earning power amounts to $3,336,644. This result was reached by capitalizing at 5.65% the net return on the investment, computed by the witness to be $188,511. Thus, accepting this testimony as the Court could if it wished, the actual earnings show a value for the hydro plant well above that claimed by the defendant. Furthermore, the resulting capitalized value would be about $80,000 more if depreciation were taken on depreciable plant only, instead of on the whole plant including land and rights, as was done for the sake of simplicity.

It is argued that this computation is fallacious, because a hydro plant could not earn this much unless backed up by an adequate steam plant. However, each type of generation is dependent on the other, and each has its period of lesser dependability when the other assists it. In the spring the hydro plants carry the base load while the steam plants carry the peaks, the steam plants utilizing this period to be successively taken out of service for their annual 30-day overhauls. In the fall the steam plants carry the base load, while, due to lower water, the hydro plants carry the peaks. Thus each source complements the other, and each needs the other. It could also be found that in a balanced, integrated utility system, assuming average water conditions, an efficient hydro plant is a higher-than-average earner. This is due among other reasons to the fact that it consumes no fuel and that it could be found that this particular plant had better than average water conditions which enhance its value.

The defendant argued that under the law applied to the findings of fact the Court's decision that the taxable value of the plaintiff's property was $2,400,000 was supported by competent evidence and was well within the bounds of reason. However, the plaintiff attacks this conclusion vigorously, partly on the basis that the fair market value *cannot* exceed the net book cost of $1,102,908 since the Company's net earning power as regulated by the commission is based upon this figure and the plaintiff asserts that no one would pay more for the property than the amount on which he would be able to earn a return. There is force in this argument and to determine its ultimate validity it is necessary to further examine certain decisive factors.

At the outset it is conceded by the plaintiff and established by the authorities that the value of the plant for tax purposes and the value for rate making purposes need not be the same. However, the company attempts to avoid the consequences of this principle by arguing that in this state "earnings are limited to a particular type of rate base," so that the rate base value marks the ceiling of the fair market value as fixed by the commission and hence limits the tax value of its plant. The Court ruled, however, that under the laws governing the transfers of utility property the commission might not lawfully disapprove the sale of the property "at a fair and reasonable price, even though that price exceeds net book cost."

The applicable statute [N.H. Rev. Stat. Ann. 374:30] so far as material provides that "Any public utility may transfer . . . its franchise, works or system, or any part of such . . . , when the commission shall find that it will be for the public good . . . ." The plaintiff agrees that the Public Utilities Commission is not bound as a matter of law to disapprove a sale at a price in excess of net book cost but says that our Court would sustain it if it did so. It further asserts the Court's ruling is erroneous on other grounds. One is that the *Grafton* case, 78 N.H. 330, 334, 100 A. 668, which supports the Court's conclusion, has been overruled. We do not find that this case as applied to the transfer of utility assets has ever been overruled. The conclusion that the seller of property is entitled to a fair and reasonable price, whether a utility or a private individual, is still the law here. See also *Grafton County Electric Light & Power Co. v. State,* 77 N.H. 490, 93 A. 1028. Although through its power over the issuance of securities the commission may indirectly control the selling price, it cannot reduce it below "a fair valuation." *Grafton County Electric Light & Power Co. v. State,* 78 N.H. 330, 100 A. 668. Since this is so, the transfer price is entitled to consideration in fixing a reasonable and fair return.

That the commission recognizes this is shown by its system of uniform classification of accounts for electric utilities which became effective January 1, 1935, and so far as material here remains unchanged. In adopting this new system the commission referred to the *Grafton* case, 77 N.H. 490, 497, 93 A. 1028, and recognized that the transfer price might exceed net book cost. *Re Uniform Classification of Accounts for Electric Utilities,* 16 N.H.P.U.C. 282, 291–292. To cover this situation a separate account No. 304, "Fixed Capital Adjustment" was set up, the purpose of which was therein stated to be as follows: "This account shall be debited (or credited) with the amount if any, by which the price paid, under authority granted by . . . this commission, for operating property acquired since January 1, 1935, from a predecessor public utility differs from the book value thereof." When the plaintiff came under this account some years later (22 N.H.P.U.C. 124) it recorded nearly $1,000,000 in Account No. 304 representing the difference between prices *paid* by it for utility property and the *net book cost* of this property when first devoted to public use. It appears that this item has ordinarily been allowed in establishing the rate base of a utility. The record therefore supports the ruling of the Court that a sale at a fair price even though it exceeded net book cost would be permitted if "for the public good" (N.H. Rev. Stat. Ann. 374:30) and rates of the utility fixed accordingly. Although no cases in this jurisdiction covering this point have been brought to our attention, other jurisdictions seem in accord with this view. *New York Edison Co. v. Maltbie,* 271 N.Y. 103, 2 N.E.2d 277; *American Telephone & Telegraph Co. v. United States,* 299 U.S. 232, 57 S.Ct. 170, 81 L.Ed. 142.

In connection with the plaintiff's insistence that net book cost and the value for tax purposes must be the same, it seems that, among other considerations, changing price levels would render such a method impractical and unfair. The inequities of holding rigidly to the formula of net book cost for tax purposes can well be illustrated by assuming two approximately equivalent plants in the same town, the first built in an era of high costs, such as the present, and the second built in a low-cost era such as we encountered in the '30s and may well experience in the future. Applying the net book cost theory in the event of construction during depressed prices, the town would be entitled to a higher tax value on the older plant than on the newer one, though the latter was performing the same function, was equally well constructed, and contained newer and less worn equipment. Also, the valuation for rate base purposes represents the composite value of the utility system as a whole with some high cost and some low cost, some efficient, some less efficient, plants. An individual plant such as the one at New Hampton might have more intrinsic or market value than another in the system but this is not necessarily reflected in its rate base value because of the date of acquisition or the circumstances under which it was acquired. The selectmen could properly take this into account in making their assessment. It is obvious, too, that any one would pay more than rate base value for a needed plant if current reproduction cost made it a good buy, and the selectmen were entitled to consider this.

A further reason why taxation value should not be fixed at net book cost is because a regulatory body such as the Public Utilities Commission should have no difficulty in accommodating itself to the valuation principles of the taxing authority. Since property taxes are a proper operating expense, any erosion of the return of the utility may be compensated for by an increase in rate. The taxing authority, on the other hand, is not free to adjust the rate of taxation in order to bring about equitable results among taxable properties.

. . . .

In summary, it appears to us that it may be justly said of the conclusions of the selectmen of the defendant town, as of "many honest and sensible judgments" that "They express an intuition of experience which outruns analysis and sums up many unnamed and tangled impressions,—impressions which may lie beneath consciousness without losing their worth. The board was created for the purpose of using its judgment and its knowledge." Holmes, J., in *Chicago, B. & Q. Ry. Co. v. Babcock,* 204 U.S. 585, 598, 27 S.Ct. 326, 329, 51 L.Ed. 636. We believe here that the Board of Selectmen did use its knowledge and judgment and that the result reached was within the bounds of reason. The record discloses that the Superior Court committed no errors of law or fact prejudicial to the plaintiff. It follows the order is

Petition dismissed.

All concurred.

Note on the Taxation of Utility Property

New Hampton illustrates some of the problems of determining the "fair market value" of property owned by a regulated public utility. Generally, regulatory agencies calculate the rate of return allowed on the utility's investment based on the property's depreciated original cost and not its current market value. In addition, regulators often require that property purchased from another utility be included in the purchasing utility's rate base at this depreciated original cost (or "net book value") even if the actual purchase price of the used property is higher. Because of this, utilities often take the position that the taxable value of their property should be limited to its net book value, for that would govern the amount of future income a prospective purchaser could expect to earn.

On the other hand, currently useful property that would be replaced if lost has a value to its owner based on that replacement value, adjusted for depreciation. A motorist damaging a utility pole can expect to receive a claim based on the cost of replacement, not on the pole's net book value.[4] The conflict between these two viewpoints arises in numerous property tax valuation cases.

In *Transcontinental Gas Pipe Line Corp. v. Bernards Township,* 111 N.J. 507, 545 A.2d 746 (1988), the New Jersey Supreme Court found that net book value (depreciated original cost), although used in the rate-setting process, was an inappropriate basis for property taxation. In response to evidence that most pipelines were sold at prices reflecting book value, the opinion stated:

[I]t does not appear that such transactions reflect all of the interests in the property of a regulated utility. Almost all such sales are from one natural gas pipeline company to another, and are subject to the approval of FERC [the

---

4. See, e.g., L. Simross, "An Unexpected Cost of Accidents," *Los Angeles Times,* August 9, 1989, Part 5, p. 1 ("[I]f you're the unlucky motorist who dings a hydrant, damages a power or telephone pole or wipes out a freeway guard rail, you've got a nasty surprise coming. You'll have to pay for the mess. And chances are it won't be cheap."). The article recounts the case of a driver billed $4,766.79 by Southern California Edison "'to repair and/or replace facilities damaged on March 3, 1989.' The wreck actually had damaged only one $13.17 part of the power pole's guy wires. But the utility claimed it required the labor of nine men to repair the total damages. Labor costs: $4,107.43."

Federal Energy Regulatory Commission], which prevents the new purchaser from including in the purchasing utility's rate base any value for the pipeline in excess of the purchased pipeline's book value. The reason for this is that the cost of an asset owned by a utility is eventually charged to the ratepayers as a cost through depreciation, and to allow a purchaser to increase its rate base to reflect the purchase price would force the ratepayers to pay twice for the same asset.* Due to the fact that FERC allows such property to be depreciated over a time period considerably shorter than its functional life, however, this totally depreciated property in fact has a significant value to the consumers that would not be reflected in the purchase price paid by an investor for the undepreciated assets of the utility. For these reasons, we find that taxpayers' evidence of comparable sales had no probative weight either as direct evidence of value or corroborative evidence of the validity of the results of other valuation methods.

*In cases where the acquired property will not be used to provide service to its original customers, however, no question of double payment is presented, and FERC will allow the full acquisition cost to be included in the rate base. See, for example, *Black Hills Power & Light Co.*, 40 F.P.C. 166 (1968); *Virginia Electric Power & Light Co.*, 38 F.P.C. 487, 488 (1967).

The opposing position is represented by cases such as *State ex rel. Wisconsin River Power Co. v. Board of Review*, 125 Wis.2d 94, 370 N.W.2d 580 (Wis.Ct.App. 1985), and *Boston Edison Co. v. Board of Assessors*, 393 Mass. 511, 471 N.E.2d 1312 (1984), which found as a factual matter that regulatory limitations on earnings set the market price for utility property. The Wisconsin court stated that it "recognizes that factors other than the return on investment allowed by law have affected the value of some properties, but requires a showing that those factors can reasonably be expected to affect the value of the property in question."

New York courts have dealt with this issue by finding utility property a "specialty," appropriately valued by the cost approach. In *Tenneco, Inc. v. Town of Cazenovia*, 104 A.D.2d 511, 479 N.Y.S.2d 587, 590 (1984), the court wrote:

That petitioner is a regulated utility does not alter this conclusion. Petitioner argues that since its income is based in part on the original cost of the pipeline less depreciation, the pipeline cannot have a fair market value derived by using a reproduction cost which is more than three times the original cost. Petitioner's income, while regulated, is not fixed; if for some reason, petitioner were required to replace the pipeline at today's costs, its rate base would increase and its rates would be allowed to increase to generate the necessary income to provide the approved rate of return. Thus, the value of the pipeline should not be limited by petitioner's current income.

The division among the courts on this issue reflects a basic disagreement as to the meaning of "fair market value" in these circumstances, requiring an interpretation of this term in light of the purposes of the taxing statute.

Questions

1. The *New Hampton* case addressed the distinction between value to the owner and resale value in finding "that the price an electric utility, including the plaintiff itself or a buyer in its position, would pay to an assumed third person may be considered." An individual's sentimental or eccentric attachment to a specific property is generally considered irrelevant to value for tax purposes. Is value to the owner a more legitimate consideration where, as here, the owner is a large commercial enterprise?

2. The *New Hampton* opinion noted that "in rate base disputes the interest of the utility is to show the value of its property at the maximum while that of the rate payers is to establish the lowest possible value. In tax cases the situation is exactly reversed." Should market value be defined in the same way for rate-setting and taxation purposes? On what basis can a court distinguish between two identical statutory references to "fair market value" in these different contexts? If a governmental unit took utility property in an exercise of its power of eminent domain, would the utility be satisfied with an award in the amount of depreciated original cost? Would a utility limit its insurance or tort claim to this amount if the property were damaged through accident or negligence? In the large eminent-domain case dealing with assembly of the site for Lincoln Center in New York City, the Appellate Division wrote:

> A certain degree of cynicism is no doubt warranted by the very general practice of landowners who have applied for writs [for property-tax reductions] of putting down estimates that vary widely from the claims that they make when the property is about to be condemned. As these figures cannot be reconciled, the conclusion is inescapable that one estimate or the other, and possibly both, bear little relation to the true opinion of the owner, and his statement that the estimate represents his opinion is false. But the constitution makes no provision for distinguishing the compensation to be given to an honest applicant and one who lets his desires outrun standards of common honesty. "Just" compensation does not mean compensation limited to the just.[5]

3. If a utility provides services to all business and residential customers in a given jurisdiction, and if the public regulatory commission allows the full amount of property taxes as a cost in setting the utility's rates, what is the net effect on the residents of any increase or decrease in the utility's property taxes?

---

5. *In re Lincoln Square Slum Clearance Project*, 15 A.D.2d 153, 222 N.Y.S.2d 786, 795 (1961), *aff'd*, 240 N.Y.S.2d 30, 12 N.Y.2d 1086, 190 N.E.2d 423 (1963), *aff'd*, 260 N.Y.S.2d 439, 16 N.Y.2d 497, 208 N.E.2d 172 (1965).

4. In *Transcontinental Gas Pipe Line Corp. v. Bernards Township*, 111 N.J. 507, 545 A.2d 746, 759 (1988), discussed above, the utility argued that assessment of its property on an amount higher than net book value would be discriminatory, because landlords subject to rent control were taxed only on the market value their property commanded in light of these income limitations. The court offered three responses. First, it distinguished the situations factually, because the amount of service the utility could offer was not limited, whereas rent control presupposes the availability of a finite number of apartments. Second, the court questioned whether utility regulation set an artificial limit on income, given testimony that the utility could not raise its rates without losing business. Finally, the court asserted that rent control affects assessments only in the adjustment of sales and income data derived from comparable but uncontrolled apartments, whereas this case involved no market or income data or comparisons to unregulated pipelines. Do you find these responses satisfactory? Can you suggest any other basis for distinguishing the two situations? What do you understand the court to have meant when it said of sales between power companies, "[I]t does not appear that such transactions reflect all of the interests in the property of a regulated utility"? Does this offer a parallel to the sale of a rent-controlled building?

Special-Purpose Property and the Cost Approach

MASHPEE WAMPANOAG INDIAN TRIBAL COUNCIL, INC. v. ASSESSORS OF MASHPEE
379 Mass. 420, 398 N.E.2d 724
Supreme Judicial Court of Massachusetts, 1980

WILKINS, Justice.

The Appellate Tax Board (board) determined that a parcel of land owned by the Mashpee Wampanoag Indian Tribal Council, Inc. (council), had no fair cash value because of restrictions contained in the deed by which the council acquired the parcel from the town of Mashpee. The assessors have appealed. We rule that the deed restrictions do not compel a determination as a matter of law that the parcel has no value. We reverse the board's decision and remand the proceedings for further consideration.

On May 28, 1975, pursuant to town meeting authorization and for a consideration of $500, the town conveyed the premises to the council, a Massachusetts charitable corporation, "for the use of the grantee as common land for tribal purposes." The grant further conditioned the use of the premises by the council to charitable purposes. The deed also provided that the conveyance "shall become void in the event said premises are subdivided, cease to be used by said grantee for said purposes, or in the event of the dissolution of the grantee." In the event of any one of these conditions occurring, "title shall thereupon revest in the grantor."

We reject the council's argument that, because it cannot effectively convey the premises to any other person or entity and can only use the premises for its purposes, the premises can have no assessed value. The issue here is not whether the parcel is exempt from taxation because the council is a charitable entity. The board did not reach that issue, which will be open for consideration in further proceedings before the board. The question is whether, as a matter of law, the land can have no "fair cash valuation" (General Laws, ch. 59, sec. 38) because of the deed restrictions.

Obviously, in light of the deed restrictions, the premises cannot be assessed by the consideration of fair cash value in terms of the highest price that a willing purchaser, not under peculiar compulsion, would pay to a willing seller who also is not under compulsion. However, the fact that land is not salable does not mean it must have no "fair cash value." *Beale v. Boston*, 166 Mass. 53, 55, 43 N.E. 1029 (1896).[1] In tax cases where there is no right, in the ordinary sense, to sell the assessed property, "the words 'fair cash value' must be given a somewhat more elastic significance" than normally attributed to them. *Massachusetts Gen. Hosp. v. Belmont*, 233 Mass. 190, 208, 124 N.E. 21, 27 (1919). If fair cash value cannot be ascertained by reference to sales of comparable property, it is proper to determine fair cash value from the intrinsic value of the property, including "any and all the uses to which the property is adapted in the hands of any owner." *Tremont & Suffolk Mills v. Lowell*, 163 Mass. 283, 285, 39 N.E. 1028, 1028– 1029 (1895). Of course, the existence of restrictions on the use of property may reduce its value below that which would be appropriate in the absence of such restrictions. *Lodge v. Swampscott*, 216 Mass. 260, 263, 103 N.E. 635 (1913) (deed restriction against building any structure on certain land reduces its fair cash value).

The board must consider the fair cash value of the land in light of the views expressed in this opinion. It may be that the council can prove that the land in fact has no value. It may be that, passing this issue, the council can establish that it is entitled to a charitable exemption. In any event, it does not follow, as a matter of law, that the deed restrictions render the land valueless.

The board's order determining that the council's parcel has no value is reversed, and the proceedings are remanded to the board.

So ordered.

PEOPLE EX REL. NEW YORK STOCK EXCHANGE BLDG. CO. V. CANTOR
221 A.D. 193, 223 N.Y.S. 64
New York Supreme Court, Appellate Division, 1927
aff'd mem., 248 N.Y. 533, 162 N.E. 514 (1928)

FINCH, J.

This appeal from an order in certiorari proceedings brings up for review a reduction in the real property assessment for the year 1921 from $9,800,000 to $8,900,000

---

1. The standard of "fair cash value" used in tax assessment cases is ordinarily the same as that used to fix damages for a taking by eminent domain. *Assessors of Quincy v. Boston Consol. Gas Co.*, 309 Mass. 60, 63, 34 N.E.2d 623 (1941). However, in some circumstances property might have a different value for tax purposes from that for eminent domain purposes. *See Massachusetts Gen. Hosp. v. Belmont*, 233 Mass. 190, 207, 124 N.E. 21 (1919).

(consisting of a reduction in the value of the land as unimproved from $7,750,000 to $6,850,000) upon lot 19, in section 1, block 23, borough of Manhattan, being the property known as the New York Stock Exchange. The relator appeals because the building was held to add any value at all to the land as unimproved, and because the assessment of the land as unimproved was not further reduced to $6,200,000.

The defendants, constituting the board of taxes and assessments of the city of New York, cross-appeal because of the reduction of the assessment, contending that the assessments of $7,750,000 as unimproved and $9,800,000 as improved should be confirmed. The facts necessary to show the reasons for the decision are briefly as follows:

The land affected is located on the southerly side of Wall Street, running from Broad Street to New Street, and contains 31,473 square feet. Upon the southerly portion of this land there was erected a building equal in height to eight stories and used exclusively by the New York Stock Exchange Association. This building was adapted to the needs of the said Association and its members. Upon the northerly portion of this land there was in process of erection an extension to said building, but no value therefor was properly included in the assessment, as the building was in course of construction. The assessment of the land and of the completed building upon the southerly portion thereof was tentatively fixed by the defendants for the year 1921 as follows: Unimproved, $7,750,000. Improved, $9,800,000. The valuation included for the building on the southerly portion of the land was thus fixed at $2,050,000.

Within the proper time the relator filed with the defendants a petition, duly verified by its president, wherein the relator objected to the valuation of both land and building, and stated that "the full and true value of said property for the year 1921 was $7,500,000, . . . and the amount for which it should have been assessed." The printed form of application required the relator to furnish the defendants with the costs of the improvements erected on the land, but the relator did not furnish such information as required. After a hearing, the assessment was confirmed, and the relator obtained a writ of certiorari to review the assessment.

The relator urges that the building does not enhance the value of the land, except "as a tear-down proposition, . . . and to that extent constitutes an incumbrance, which diminishes the value of the land to a greater extent than such value is increased by the construction cost of the building," because any purchaser of the property on the tax day, namely, October 1, 1920, would have been forced to tear down the building and erect one of a different character, since the building was only adapted to the one use, namely, that of the New York Stock Exchange. In support of its claim, the relator called three well-known real estate men as witnesses, two of whom testified that the land unimproved was of the value of $6,000,000, and the third that it was of the value of $6,144,199, and all three that the land with the improvements was worth no more. The defendants, on the other hand, also called three well-known experts, who testified that the value of the land unimproved was $8,360,000, $8,300,000, and $8,100,000, respectively.

The trial court found that the building was constructed between the years 1900 and 1903, and cost $3,250,000. There was evidence, which was not met, that on October 1, 1920, the fair and reasonable cost of reproduction of said building, exclusive of the portions demolished in the erection of the addition to said building, was $4,816,000. The defendants sought to introduce evidence of depreciation, so as to arrive at the value of the improvement by the method of showing cost, less depreciation; but this evidence was excluded, and an exception given to the defendants upon the objection of the relator.

We will first take up the value of the land as unimproved. The value as sworn to by the relator as the full and true value on the tax day, and as the value at which the premises should be assessed, was $7,500,000. As the relator contends that the improvements add nothing to the value of the land, the relator has thus in effect sworn to the value of the land unimproved as $7,500,000. The assessors have valued the land unimproved at $7,750,000. As the relator has thus sworn that the value of the land unimproved was $7,500,000, the learned Special Term was not justified in fixing the same at $6,850,000. Moreover, the experts for the defendants fixed the value of the land unimproved between $8,100,000 and $8,360,000. Preponderating evidence in the record sustains the valuation as fixed by the assessors. The learned trial court was in error, therefore, when it fixed the value of the land unimproved at less than the sum of $7,750,000.

Taking up now the question whether the improvements add anything to the value of the land, the Special Term has found that the improvements did add to the value of the land in the amount fixed by the assessors, namely, $2,050,000. The Special Term has also found that the building was an adequate improvement. There is no suggestion of inadequacy of the structure or mislocation. On the contrary, it is peculiarly adapted to the purposes of its use and in the best possible situation in the financial district. The relator contends that the building did not enhance the value of the land, because under section 889 of the Greater New York Charter (Laws 1901, c. 466, as amended by Laws 1911, c. 455), it was the duty of the defendants to assess this value year by year at its actual market value, no more and no less, and that, as this building can only be adequately used by the New York Stock Exchange and not by any one else, not even the other exchanges, therefore there is no actual market value, and hence the building adds nothing to the value of the land. A complete answer to this contention, however, is that section 6 of the Tax Law (as amended by Laws 1914, c. 277), provides: "All real and personal property subject to taxation shall be assessed at the full value thereof . . . ."

The relator makes no reference to this provision of the Tax Law, but relies solely on the language of section 889 of the Greater New York Charter, requiring deputy tax commissioners to assess all taxable property and to furnish to the board of taxes and assessments "the sum for which, in their judgment, each separately assessed parcel of real estate under ordinary circumstances would sell."

Under the principle which requires that statutes in pari materia must be read together, real property must be assessed at its full value, whether or not there is an ascertainable market value. As was said in *People ex rel. Waclark Realty Co. v. O'Donnel,* affirmed 130 App. Div. 880, 114 N. Y. S. 1142; affirmed 196 N. Y. 521, 89 N. E. 1110:

> The provisions of this section of the charter (section 889, providing for assessment at an amount for which real property under ordinary circumstances would sell) do not change the general tax law of the state that real property shall be assessed at its full value. I do not understand that, under the provisions of the charter, simply because the property cannot be sold under ordinary circumstances, it is therefore to escape taxation. See opinion of Mr. Justice Leventritt in *People ex rel. Consolidated Gas Co. v. Wells and Others,* 54 Misc. Rep. 322, 105 N. Y. S. 1006. It seems to me that, if the building is of such a character that it cannot be sold except under extraordinary circumstances, it is still the duty of the deputy tax commissioner in the first instance in ascertaining the value of the property, and of the commissioners of taxes in imposing the assessment, to determine its actual value from such material as the circumstances of the case afford. *People ex rel. Manhattan Railway Co. v. Barker,* 146 N. Y. 304, 312 [40 N. E. 996].

The same principles were likewise applied by the court in other cases, namely, *People ex rel. Union Club v. O'Donnel,* 126 App. Div. 916, 110 N. Y. S. 1141, where the cost was resorted to in order to fix the full value, it appearing that the Club building had a small commercial value, but nothing like its real value; also in *People ex rel. Delaware, L. & W. R. R. Co. v. Clapp*, 152 N. Y. 490, 46 N. E. 842, 39 L. R. A. 237, where the headnote says: "The rule to be ordinarily applied in assessing the value of the real estate of a railroad company for local taxation is the cost of replacing the portion of the road and appurtenances situated within the jurisdiction of the assessors, in the condition in which they are found by the assessors at the time of making the assessment."

In such a case the market value would be difficult, if not impossible, to find, and yet the property is not permitted for this reason to escape taxation. The same question has been met in the same way in other states. In *Massachusetts General Hospital v. Inhabitants of Belmont*, 233 Mass. 190, 124 N. E. 21, the taxing statute required assessments at "fair cash value." In such a case the court recognized that original cost, replacement cost, and production power were all legitimate elements to be considered.

All these cases follow the well-known fundamental principle that, where the detail of amount is to be ascertained, such as amount of damage or amount of value, the true amount in question and the method of its ascertainment is that which appears as possible and practicable under the circumstances of the case. If here we take the reproduction cost of the building on the tax day, namely, October 1, 1920, and allow for depreciation, we reach the result that the value of the building was at least the amount for which the tax commissioners have assessed the building, namely, $2,050,000.

Furthermore, only the total assessment of land and building can be reviewed. The learned Special Term therefore was in error in disregarding the evidence as to the total value of the land and improvements, and in directing a reduction of the assessment solely because the court was satisfied that the land unimproved was overvalued by the defendants in making the assessment. What the court should have found was that the total assessment was too great. Subdivision 3 of section 21 of the Tax Law (added by Laws 1914, c. 277, as amended by Laws 1916, c. 323), provides: "In all cities there shall be an additional column in the assessment roll before the column in which is set down the value of real property, and in such additional column there shall be set down the value of the land exclusive of the buildings thereon. The total assessment only can be reviewed."

Unless the total assessment is too large, the person assessed cannot be said to be aggrieved. Looked at, therefore, from the viewpoint of the total assessment, we find that the relator is in no sense aggrieved.

. . . .

The order appealed from should be reversed, with $10 costs and disbursements to the defendants, the writ of certiorari dismissed, and the assessment confirmed, with costs. Settle order on notice. All concur.

Notes on "Specialty" Valuation

1. The *Mashpee* and *New York Stock Exchange* cases illustrate the problem of finding the "fair market value" of unsalable property. What would be the "full value" of the Stock Exchange property if it were accepted that the building would be of no use to another purchaser and would simply reduce the market value of the bare land by the costs of demolition? The New York court considered this problem only a "detail of amount." If, however, two separate amounts could be computed in detail, (1) the high construction cost of the property and (2) its low current sale value, how should a

choice between them be made for purposes of tax assessment? Does a statute calling for assessment on "full value" resolve this question?

2. Recall in *New Hampton* that the court permitted the taxpayer itself to be considered a potential purchaser of the property in order to determine "market value." Could the same approach be taken in these cases? For example, a hypothetical purchaser might bid an amount just below construction cost for the stock exchange building, planning then to sell it back to the Stock Exchange itself. You can see that the term "market value" has no inherent meaning in such situations where no market exists but property has a significant value to its owner. Bonbright wrote:

> [T]he cases disclose two very different interpretations of the willing buyer–willing seller verbiage, although many of the reported opinions leave one in doubt as to which of the two is accepted by the judge who uses the phrase. The first interpretation is that the court is merely guarding the jury against the acceptance of "forced-sale" prices, and possibly also against the acceptance of "holdup" prices and "boom" prices. With these qualifications, however, the court is still seeking the price for which the present owner of the property could really sell it, rather than the price for which he would be able to sell it if he could find some buyer who does not exist in fact . . . .
>
> The second interpretation of "willing" buyer and seller goes much further, in that it *assumes* a market that does not really exist. It implies that property which is peculiarly adapted to the uses of its present owner, and which is therefore actually unsalable except perhaps at a very low figure, may nevertheless be deemed to have a high market value. In this case, one must assume the existence, contrary to the facts, of some person other than the present owner, for whose uses the property is adapted, and who is therefore willing to pay a correspondingly high price for it.
>
> When a court adopts this second version of the willing-buyer standard, it is resorting to a *tour de force* by which to bridge the gap between the realization value of a property and its value to the owner. In extreme cases, market value thus becomes a mere synonym for value to the owner. More frequently, however, the two ideas are confused rather than identified; for the courts still make a distinction without indicating its precise nature.[6]

Does Bonbright's logic suggest that the *New York Stock Exchange* result is incorrect, or does his logic simply imply that the result should not be considered a calculation of "market value"?

3. The New York Stock Exchange has architectural as well as tax significance. Designed by George Post and built in 1903, it combines a classical facade with an innovative all-glass curtain wall providing light for the trading floor. Although the Greek-temple appearance of a center of modern

---

6. J. Bonbright, *The Valuation of Property* (1937), vol. 1, p. 60.

commerce has been ridiculed as "stage set architecture,"[7] the Exchange itself takes the public aspect of this building most seriously. The American Institute of Architects (AIA) *Guide to New York City* reports, "The original mythological figures of the pediment became so deteriorated that their stone was replaced with sheet metal, secretively, so that the public would not know that any facet of the Stock Exchange was vulnerable."[8]

TUCKAHOE WOMAN'S CLUB v. CITY OF RICHMOND
199 Va. 734, 101 S.E.2d 571
Supreme Court of Appeals of Virginia, 1958

BUCHANAN, J., delivered the opinion of the court.

The City of Richmond assessed the appellant's real estate for 1955 at the sum of $105,000, being $5,000 for the land and $100,000 for the improvements. The appellant filed in the court below its application for a reduction of the assessment, alleging that the fair market value of the property was not more than $85,000 and asking for a refund of the tax paid by it in excess of the amount due on a proper assessment. The court heard evidence *ore tenus* and being of opinion that the assessment was not erroneous entered an order denying relief and dismissing the application. The issue on appeal is whether the assessment represents the fair market value of the property.

The lot, which is located at the corner of Dover Road and Avon Road in Windsor Farms, Richmond, was conveyed to the appellant, Tuckahoe Woman's Club, a nonstock corporation, in 1947, subject to a restrictive covenant which expires in 1977 under which the property can be used only as a woman's club. The clubhouse was built thereon in 1954 of brick with a slate roof and consisting in the main of a large auditorium with small balcony, stage, reception hall and small caterer's kitchen.

To establish the fair market value of the property the appellant offered the testimony of three experienced real estate men and the contractor who constructed the building. One was Frank W. Heindl, who had been appraising property for the last twenty years, including property in Windsor Farms, for the City of Richmond, Federal and State governments, banks, insurance companies and other corporations and individuals. He had inspected this property in 1955 for the purpose of determining its fair market value. He was then informed that the building cost $124,500 and the land $10,000. He testified that it was adapted primarily for its use as a club building, not easy to sell and in his judgment it would bring not more than $75,000 to $80,000 or $85,000 at a free sale. On cross-examination he said that if the City should want to acquire it by condemnation it should not pay more than $75,000 to $85,000 for it; that it was not worth more than that sum for any purpose.

George B. Snead, in the real estate business for twenty-seven years, was experienced in appraising and familiar with values in Windsor Farms. He inspected the property in 1955 for the purpose of arriving at its fair market value. He said that property built for

---

7.   P. Goldberger, *The City Observed: A Guide to the Architecture of Manhattan* (1979), p. 21.

8.   E. Willensky and N. White, eds., *AIA Guide to New York City*, 3d ed. (1988), p. 19.

a special use such as this when put on the market invariably had to be sold for less than reproduction cost or what it would appear to be worth, and if this property became for sale the owners would do well to get from $75,000 to $85,000 for it. On cross-examination he testified that if there were another club ready, able and willing to buy it for the same purpose, the appellant would be fortunate to get $75,000 to $85,000 for it, and if he were on a condemnation commission that would be his valuation of it.

J. Guthrie Smith, who had been a real estate broker in Richmond for thirty-six years, engaged in all phases of real estate business, was the president and sales manager of Windsor Farms, the appellant's grantor, from 1934 to 1954, and made the sale to the appellant. Testifying as to the value of this property for sale purposes, he said his experience in appraising had led him to believe there was no fair market value for clubs or lodges or churches or things of that nature; that they do not enjoy a market like other types of property, and when asked for the fair market value of them "you more or less pull it out of the air"; that his idea of a fair selling price for this property would be $75,000, based on his thirty-six years of experience in dealing with all types of real estate. "It is just one of those things that is a matter of judgment." On cross-examination he said he did not consider the value of the property to the Tuckahoe Woman's Club itself because use value was "another one of those things you pull out of the air." He illustrated that view by saying "A guy's false teeth might be worth a lot to him but they wouldn't mean anything to me."

J. Leonard Moore, the contractor on the building, said the cost of construction was in the neighborhood of $112,000. He was reasonably familiar, he said, with the fair market value of property in Richmond and had done some appraising but not on a paid basis. Based on his experience he did not think the building would possibly sell for more than $75,000.

The only witness for the City was J. Edward Routrey, its assessor of real estate who made this assessment. He had held that position since 1954 and had twelve years of experience in appraising property. He described the building and introduced photographs of it. He explained the basis of his assessment of $105,000, saying in substance that it would cost some $125,000 to reproduce the building plus the cost of the land, from which amount he made certain deductions because a building serving the same purpose and equally efficient would not cost more than $100,000. He said his purpose was to equalize the tax burden which he believed was the intent of the law in stating that property shall be assessed at its fair market value; that there are many properties for which there is no market value except to their owners; that the principle involved here assumes that the only market for the property is the present owner. "If these people abandoned it, our approach to the assessment would be entirely different. But so long as they use it we try to arrive at use to the present owners just like anything of a very special purpose nature." He said the property could never be rented for any purpose "and I cannot conceive of it ever being sold in our lifetime because there is no other club that would want it so our only guide which is acceptable is a depreciated reproduction cost. I have depreciated it as far as I can justify and that is the way we have arrived at $105,000.00. That is the way we have arrived at the valuation of all special purpose properties located in the city."

On cross-examination he was asked: "You say you base this appraisal on the depreciated reproduction cost?" He answered, "Right." He was asked whether he included any element of value to the present owner and he replied, "The value to the present owner is the only value I have to go by. It has no market value elsewhere that could be compared or justified."

Section 169 of our Virginia Constitution provides that "all assessments of real estate and tangible personal property shall be at their fair market value." In *Seaboard Air Line v. Chamblin,* 108 Va. 42, 60 S.E. 727, 729, this court adopted the definition given by *Lewis on Eminent Domain* (2d ed., p. 478) that the fair market value of property "is the price which it will bring when it is offered for sale by one who desires, but is not obliged, to sell it, and is bought by one who is under no necessity of having it." That definition has been repeated without change in many subsequent cases, a recent one being *Skyline Swannanoa v. Nelson County,* 186 Va. 878, 885, 44 S.E.2d 437, 441.

In estimating that value, as said in the first-named case, all the capabilities of the property and all the uses to which it may be applied or for which it is adapted, are to be considered, but it is not a question of the value of the property to the owner.

In *Lehigh Portland Cement Co. v. Commonwealth,* 146 Va. 146, 135 S.E. 669, it was said that in most cases an assessment based on the original value of the property less depreciation would afford an equitable basis of taxation, but would ignore the plain provisions of Section 169 of the Constitution that all assessments shall be at their fair market value, and whatever the rule may be in other jurisdictions the rule laid down in Section 169 is "the only legal rule provided by law for the assessment of real estate and tangible personal property situated in this Commonwealth." 146 Va. at 151, 135 S.E. at 670–671.

In that case the assessment was reduced on proof that lands in the district where the company's plants were located were uniformly assessed at only 50% of the actual value. The reduction was on the ground that Section 169 of the Constitution must be read in connection with Section 168, which requires that taxes be uniform on the same class of subjects within the territory of the taxing authority, and where it is impossible to secure both the standard of the true value and the uniformity and equality required by law, the latter requirement is to be preferred as the just and ultimate purpose of the law. That principle was reiterated in *Skyline Swannanoa v. Nelson County, supra,* 186 Va. at 881, 44 S.E.2d at 439. But that does not mean that property in any taxing jurisdiction may be assessed in excess of and without relation to its fair market value as required by the Constitution. It means only that a taxpayer whose property is assessed at its true market value has a right to have the assessment reduced to the percentage of that value at which others are taxed so as to meet the uniformity required by Section 168 of the Virginia Constitution as well as by the Equal Protection Clause of the Fourteenth Amendment.
. . . .

In the case at hand there is no real conflict in the evidence as to fair market value, which is the controlling standard for the assessment. The appellant's witnesses, qualified and experienced, placed the fair market value of appellant's property at $75,000 to $85,000. The city's assessor, and only witness, stated in a letter to plaintiff's counsel in October, 1955, that he agreed that if the property was then offered on the market it would not bring more than $75,000 to $85,000, but that he believed it had a value in use to the present owners somewhat in excess of $100,000, and he did not believe it would be fair to other property owners to assess it for any less. He stated on his cross-examination that if the owners desired to sell it he could not conceive of its bringing more than $85,000.

Section 58-1145 of the Code provides that on an application of this sort the burden of proof is on the taxpayer to show that the property in question is assessed at more than its fair market value or that the assessment is not uniform in its application. In *Washington County Nat. Bank v. Washington County, supra,* we said that courts are reluctant to override the judgments of assessors and that the judgment of the trial court is entitled to great weight, "but, with all of this in mind, in the final analysis we follow the evidence." 176 Va. at 222, 10 S.E.2d at 518..

In *City of Norfolk v. Snyder*, 161 Va. 288, 293, 170 S.E. 721, 723, we said that the conclusion of the assessor would not be disturbed "unless it appears that there has been a manifest error in the manner of making the estimate, or that evidence which should be controlling has been disregarded." Here the city assessor very frankly stated that his assessment of $105,000 was based on depreciated reproduction cost as representing the value of the property to the present owner, which he said was the only value he had to go by. That is not the basis for assessment fixed by the Constitution. Depreciated reproduction cost may be an element for consideration in ascertaining fair market value, but it cannot of itself be the standard for assessment. The assessor conceded that here it produced an amount in excess of what the property could be sold for. The value of the property to the owner is not the question and the answer to it does not supply the answer to the essential inquiry as to what is the fair market value.

For the reasons stated we hold that the 1955 assessment of the appellant's property was excessive and erroneous; that such assessment should have been in the sum of $85,000, and that the court below should have reduced the assessment to that amount and ordered a refund of any excess tax paid in consequence thereof. Code sec. 58-1148. The order appealed from is therefore reversed and the case is remanded for entry of an order granting that relief.

Reversed and remanded.

IN THE MATTER OF GREAT ATLANTIC & PACIFIC TEA COMPANY, INC. V. KIERNAN

42 N.Y.2d 236, 397 N.Y.S.2d 718, 366 N.E.2d 808
Court of Appeals of New York, 1977

GABRIELLI, Judge.

In this tax certiorari proceeding the issue presented for review is the proper method of valuation of appellant's property, one of the world's largest food processing plants. Respondent tax officials contend that the property is a specialty and thus the reproduction cost-less depreciation method should be utilized in establishing the value of the property for tax assessment purposes, while appellant maintains that the traditional market value approach will yield its true legal and full value.

The subject property is located in the Town of Horseheads, Chemung County, in that area of New York State known as the "Southern Tier." The structure was designed and constructed for appellant to accommodate its food processing, warehousing and shipping operations on a regional scale; and the plant, which has a floor area of 1,544,916 square feet, serves a large portion of the eastern United States. It contains 73 truck loading docks, several interior railroad sidings, laboratories, offices, cold storage and refrigeration facilities, in addition to other fixtures utilized in appellant's food processing enterprise. The building is divided into large open areas on the main floor while mezzanine walkways above the main floor provide employee access to working areas, and tunnels beneath it furnish utility services.

In 1973, respondents fixed the assessment of the property in the amount of $4,683,000 at an equalization rate of 21%, thus yielding a full value of $22,300,000. Appellant commenced this proceeding to declare the assessment void, or in the alternative to have it reduced to a proper level. At trial, real estate appraisers and experts produced by appellant, espousing the market value approach, testified that the value of the property was $13,900,000 while respondents' appraiser fixed the value at $19,200,000. In arriving at their valuation, appellant's appraisers relied upon sales of similar properties located in the eastern United States, which were some 500 to 1,000 miles distant from the subject property. The trial court, relying on the unchallenged testimony of the appellant's appraisers that the market for the subject property was regional in nature, found that there was an active market for the type of building here involved throughout the eastern United States. Significantly, the court also found that, while the subject property was built to serve the particular purposes of appellant's business, "the building is easily convertible to other industrial uses. It can readily be subdivided into smaller units, if desired. No heavy expenditure is called for to remove present fixtures or install others and the manner in which the building is constructed and laid out lends itself to simple alteration." Thus, the court, holding that the market value approach was proper in this case and that valuation of the subject property could be based upon sales of comparable properties beyond its immediate area, adopted the appellant's appraisers' value of $13,900,000.

Without disturbing the trial court's findings, the Appellate Division reversed and held that the property should be valued as a "specialty" because of the above-described features adapting it to appellant's use and, further, because no sales of similar property in the immediate locale could be found. The Appellate Division thus remitted the matter for a further hearing in which the value of the property was directed to be determined by the reproduction cost-less depreciation method of valuation. Following this hearing, the trial court fixed the value of the property, according to the method mandated by the Appellate Division, at $16,700,000. This latter determination, of course, is not subject to review on this appeal, as we are here concerned only with the original, nonfinal order of the Appellate Division from which this appeal is taken pursuant to CPLR 5601 (subd.[d]).

Section 306 of the Real Property Tax Law requires that all property be assessed at its full value and, generally, it is "market value" which provides the most reliable valuation for assessment purposes. However, where there is no reliable market data, other methods are available such as the capitalization of income method which is utilized in valuing rental property, or the reproduction cost-less depreciation method which is utilized when the subject property may properly be categorized as a "specialty" (see *People ex rel. New York Stock Exch. Bldg. Co. v. Cantor*, 221 App.Div. 193, 197, 223 N.Y.S. 64, 69, *aff'd*, 248 N.Y. 533, 162 N.E. 514). While various definitions have been advanced, a specialty may perhaps be best defined as a structure which is *uniquely* adapted to the business conducted upon it or use made of it and cannot be converted to other uses without the expenditure of substantial sums of money. Property has been categorized as a specialty where some intangible element such as the owner's prestige or good will inheres in its value (see, e.g., *G.R.F., Inc. v. Board of Assessors of County of Nassau*, 41 N.Y.2d 512, 513–514, 393 N.Y.S.2d 965, 967; *Matter of Seagram & Sons v. Tax Commission of City of New York*, 18 A.D.2d 109, 238 N.Y.S.2d 228, *aff'd*, 14 N.Y.2d 314, 318, 251 N.Y.S.2d 460, 462, 200 N.E.2d 447, 448).

On the other hand, property does not qualify as a specialty where it possesses certain features which, while rendering the property suitable to the owner's use, are not truly unique to his business but, in fact, make the property adaptable for general industrial use. Thus, if no great expense would be entailed in converting the property from the present owner's use to other business and industrial uses and if a market value may be ascertained, property should not be valued as a specialty merely because it contains such features as interior railroad sidings, truck loading docks or other amenities and fixtures which are not truly unique to the owner's business. Such "special features" do not, without more, require departure from the market value approach to valuation (cf. *G.R.F., Inc. v. Board of Assessors of County of Nassau*, 41 N.Y.2d p. 515, 393 N.Y.S.2d p. 968). In *McDonald v. State of New York*, 52 A.D.2d 721, 722, 381 N.Y.S.2d 929, 930, *aff'd*, 42 N.Y.2d 900, 397 N.Y.S.2d 990, 366 N.E.2d 1344 (1977), an animal hospital equipped with "kennels, dog runs, (and) an incinerator" was held not to be a specialty. Similarly, such "special features" as "dehumidifying equipment" and "recessed lighting" did not mandate valuation of property as a specialty in *Matter of City of New York (Lincoln Sq. Slum Clearance Project)*, 15 A.D.2d 153, 222 N.Y.S.2d 786. And, in a recently decided condemnation case, we rejected the owner's argument that, inter alia, interior truck loading docks and luxury office space qualified the property as a specialty (*Dormitory Auth. of State of N. Y. v. 59th St. & 10th Ave. Realty Corp.*, 51 A.D.2d 953, 381 N.Y.S.2d 500, *aff'd*, 41 N.Y.2d 1037, 396 N.Y.S.2d 179, 364 N.E.2d 843).

In the instant case, those facilities such as utility tunnels, employee walkways, truck loading docks, refrigeration facilities or the like do not render the subject property a specialty incapable of valuation according to the normal market value method. There was testimony by witnesses on both sides that these so-called "special features" would not interfere with the use of the property for other industrial purposes and, indeed, respondents concede that the property may be so used. Moreover, the features relied upon by the Appellate Division in categorizing the plant as a specialty could be utilized in a wide variety of industrial uses and, in fact, there was testimony that some of them, such as utility tunnels, employee walkways and temperature control systems, made the plant more flexible and adaptable. The property, therefore, was not so uniquely suited to appellant's business as not to be reasonably adaptable to other industrial uses; and this conclusion finds further support in the trial court's finding, not disturbed by the Appellate Division, that the property could be converted to general industrial use without a substantial expenditure of funds.

The Appellate Division reasoned that the reproduction cost-less depreciation method of valuation should be utilized since there were no reliable indicia of market value because of the lack of evidence of comparable sales in the immediate area. That court also rejected the trial court's reliance on appellant's out-of-State comparable sales . . . . Whether evidence should be received of comparable sales which are some distance away from the subject property depends, of course, on the nature and character of the property involved. It would not be proper, for example, to look beyond New York City in valuing an office building located therein because such a building would obviously have a local market. Here, however, there is no local market for appellant's facility but the record is clear, and the Trial Judge so found, that there was a broad regional market for this type of industrial plant. Under these circumstances, we think that it was not error to depart from the ordinary rule with respect to location of comparables and, thus, the trial court properly relied upon the out-of-state comparable sales utilized by appellant's appraiser in determining the value of the property by the market value approach. The ordinary or general rule should not blind us to the fact that the ultimate purpose of valuation, whether in eminent domain or tax certiorari proceedings, is to arrive at a fair and realistic value of the property involved. The reproduction cost method of valuation may result in serious overvaluation of the property due to rising construction costs and its failure to adequately account for factors such as functional obsolescence and physical deterioration (see *G.R.F., Inc. v. Board of Assessors of County of Nassau*, supra). Thus, reproduction cost should be utilized only in those limited instances in which no other method of valuation will yield a legally and economically realistic value for the property (see, generally, 1 Bonbright, *Valuation of Property*, pp. 175–176).* Here, because of the lack of any local market and the existence of a broad regional market for appellant's type of property, it is proper to depart from the ordinary rule relating to the proximity of comparables in order to arrive at a more realistic value than would be obtained by the reproduction cost method. To reject a sound and valid approach to valuation where the normally applicable rule has no relevance under the circumstances of a particular case, is to abandon the economic realism which should characterize valuation and embrace a rigid, dogmatic approach which will not yield fair and equitable results. As we recently stated in *G.R.F., Inc. v. Board of Assessors of County of Nassau, supra*, 41 N.Y.2d p. 515, 393 N.Y.S.2d p. 968, "[p]ragmatism . . . requires adjustment when the economic realities prevent placing . . . properties in neat logical valuation boxes" (citations omitted).

Finally, with respect to the Appellate Division's objection that no adjustments were made by the appraisers for differences in the localities in which the out-of-State comparable sales were located, it should be noted that there was testimony indicating that conditions such as business climate, labor, transportation and availability of public utilities were taken into account, and, in certain cases no adjustments were necessary. There was also testimony that if adjustments were made for differing conditions, the result would have been a reduction in value since conditions in the localities of the comparables were all more favorable than those in the Town of Horseheads, the location of the subject property.

Accordingly, the order appealed from should be reversed and the order of Supreme Court, Chemung County, entered July 3, 1974, reinstated, with costs.

BREITEL, C. J., and JASEN, JONES, WACHTLER, FUCHSBERG and COOKE, JJ., concur. Order reversed, with costs, etc.

Notes

1. The court states that the 1973 assessment of the property was "in the amount of $4,683,000 at an equalization rate of 21%, thus yielding a full value of $22,300,000." In other words, with assessments averaging 21% of full market value, the assessed value indicated that the assessors considered the full value of the plant to be $22.3 million. The conflict between such fractional assessments and §306 of the New York Real Property Tax Law, which required assessment at "full value," was the subject of *In re Hellerstein v. Assessor of Islip*, 37 N.Y.2d 1, 332 N.E.2d 279, 371 N.Y.S.2d 388 (1975), discussed later in this volume.

2. The footnote dealing with the use of the cost approach as an upper limit to value touches on a long-standing position of the New York courts.[9] In

---

*Of course, reproduction cost-less depreciation may always be introduced to establish the upper limit of value (see *G.R.F., Inc. v. Board of Assessors of County of Nassau, supra*, 41 N.Y.2d p. 514, 393 N.Y.S.2d p. 967; *People ex rel. Manhattan Sq. Beresford v. Sexton*, 284 N.Y. 145, 29 N.E.2d 654).

---

9. See W. Gifford, Jr., "Should Replacement Cost Impose a Ceiling on Real Property Tax Assessments?" *Journal of Taxation* 26 (1967):314.

People ex rel. Delaware, Lackawanna & Western R.R. Co. v. Clapp, 152 N.Y. 490, 46 N.E. 842 (1897), the Court of Appeals considered an attempt by local assessors to value seven miles of railroad track within their jurisdiction by reference to the earnings of the entire railroad system. The court held that reproduction cost less depreciation must serve as an upper bound to valuation:

> The cost of reproducing these seven miles of railroad seems to us to be the just and reasonable rule of valuation. There is no reason that we can perceive for assessing this property at a greater sum than the cost of replacement. It may not in every case be worth what it would cost to reproduce it. That would depend upon the income or earning capacity of the road after it is built. But this is the case of a paying railroad, and, when valued at what it would cost to procure the land, construct the roadbed, put down the ties and rails and erect the buildings and other structures, all new, it is difficult to see any ground for assessing it at a larger sum.

Note that (1) the court uses "reproduction" and "replacement" as synonyms in this case, and (2) the problem of valuing a small section of an integrated larger system has led many states to value railroad and other utility property on a statewide basis; that total is then apportioned among the localities where this property is located.

Note on the *Xerox* Case

The implications of the *A & P* case were investigated further in *Xerox Corporation v. Ross*, 71 A.D.2d 84, 421 N.Y.S.2d 475 (1979), *leave to appeal denied*, 49 N.Y.2d 702 (1980). Xerox attempted to use *A & P* to its advantage in order to avoid classification of a research, manufacturing, and warehousing complex as a "specialty."

The Xerox property resembled a small town, with 55 buildings on 1,032 acres of land, 72 acres of parking lots, 154 acres of landscaping, 68 acres of recreational facilities, and its own sidewalks, sewers, telephone lines, and utility distribution systems. The parties' disagreement as to valuation was of a similarly impressive scale. The complex was assessed for tax purposes at $129,195,200. Xerox's first valuation, based on the cost approach, was $92,749,820, but at trial it argued for a comparable-sales approach valuation of $40,000,000. It relied primarily on the same transactions that convinced the court in *A & P* that there existed a nationwide market for large, specialized structures of the type at issue there. In response, the town produced a cost-based appraisal valuing the property at $164,473,500.

The appellate division upheld the lower court's ruling that the sales which established a market for the A & P plant could not be used for the same purpose by Xerox:

The court was correct in holding that these sales, even as adjusted, were not comparable to the Xerox complex and were not reliable indicators of its value. The present case is sufficiently distinguishable from the A & P case in that, even though these sales were reliable comparables to the A & P plant, they are not comparable to the Xerox complex. First, the A & P plant and all of the sales are single buildings whereas the Xerox complex comprises 55 separate buildings. Second, the A & P plant, at 1,500,000 square feet, was only slightly larger than the largest of the sales which ranged from 400,000 to 1,200,000 square feet, while the Xerox complex, at 5,500,000 square feet, is several times the size of even the largest sale. Third, the Xerox complex acreage is many times larger than that of the A & P plant and the sales. Fourth, the A & P plant and all of the sales were manufacturing and warehousing facilities, while the Xerox complex comprises a variety of manufacturing, warehousing and laboratory buildings. Finally, the disparity between the $16,700,000 cost approach appraisal and the $13,900,000 market value approach appraisal of the A & P plant was not as severe as the disparity between the $40,000,000 market approach appraisal and Xerox's own $92,749,820 cost approach appraisal.

. . . .

Xerox's appraisal which proceeded upon this theory was unreliable for several reasons. First, its major comparable sales comprised only manufacturing and warehousing buildings. Second, instead of using comparables to arrive at values for different parts of the Xerox complex, then aggregating them to arrive at a value for the entire complex, the Xerox appraisal attempted to adjust each sale to the complex as a whole. In doing this, the appraisal decreased the value of the Xerox complex, through functional utility adjustments, for the complex's high percentage of laboratory and office space, notwithstanding that laboratory space is more expensive to construct than manufacturing and warehouse space.

Perhaps the most interesting aspect of the *A & P* and *Xerox* cases concerns the taxpayers' efforts to prove the existence of a "market." It might be expected that a property owner would seek instead to demonstrate the *lack* of any market for property being valued. Generally, the less active the market the lower the price, as fewer prospective purchasers bid against one another. Cases such as the *New York Stock Exchange* decision, however, show unwillingness to restrict the taxable value of costly and useful specialized property to the low price it might command if actually offered for sale. Substitution of a cost-based value, the "full value" cited in the *New York Stock Exchange* opinion, meant that in the absence of a market, property might be judged a "specialty" and assigned a cost-based value for tax purposes. This encourages owners to avoid the specialty designation by demonstrating that some market—even a distant one, as in *A & P*—exists for their property. In light of the amount of money at stake in these disputes, are cases such as *A & P* and *Xerox* sufficiently clear as to which buildings will be judged to be specialties and which will not?

"Prestige" Structures and the Cost Approach

FIRST FEDERAL SAVINGS & LOAN ASSOCIATION OF FLINT V. CITY OF FLINT
415 Mich. 702, 329 N.W.2d 755
Supreme Court of Michigan, 1982

PER CURIAM.

The City of Flint assessed improvements to property owned by First Federal Savings & Loan Association of Flint on the basis of historical cost. The Tax Tribunal and the Court of Appeals, 104 Mich.App. 609, 305 N.W.2d 553, approved the assessment, reasoning that the improvements had value to First Federal because they enhanced its image. Because the constitution and the General Property Tax Act require that property tax assessments be based on market value, not value to the owner, we reverse.

I

First Federal owns a building in downtown Flint that was constructed in 1926 and purchased by First Federal in 1966. First Federal occupies the first three floors of the building, and the remaining floors are closed.

After purchasing the building for $675,000, First Federal spent approximately $475,000 to renovate the building, adding the types of improvements suitable to a bank's image.

Because there have been no recent sales of comparable properties, the parties have used other methods to determine value. First Federal made its own appraisal of the property, computed from rents paid by other banks in Flint. Capitalizing those comparable rents, First Federal calculated the value of its property to be $447,000.

Flint's appraiser rejected the use of the income approach because the rents First Federal had used were either based on old leases or for less favorable locations. The city appraiser instead relied upon the cost approach. The cost of the building and its improvements, after depreciation, yielded a property value of $750,000.

A Tax Tribunal hearing officer upheld Flint's use of the cost approach, reasoning that the improvements had value to First Federal because they enhanced a financial institution's image of stability and success.[1] The Tax Tribunal adopted the decision of the hearing officer.

The Court of Appeals affirmed the judgment of the Tax Tribunal and held that the income approach was inappropriate because the property had a unique value to First Federal.

---

1. The hearing officer said:

The income approach does not provide for the inclusion of value which may be present in the form of enhancement of the purchaser's image. Petitioner is a financial institution whose success in business depends upon its image to a great degree. *If* its main office building has value in the form of enhancement of petitioner's image, there is no place in the income approach in which such value will be reflected.

It must be presumed that petitioner did not expend $1.15 million dollars in the acquisition and renovation of quarters which it occupies itself for the purpose of realizing rental profits. What petitioner sought (and what it got) was suitable premises for its banking operations. If petitioner is not realizing profits from the property, then there must be other value present in this property which accounts for such expenditure. That value is in the form of enhancement of petitioner's business. (Emphasis in original.)

II

The constitution requires that property tax assessments reflect "true cash value".[2] The General Property Tax Act defines that term to mean "the usual selling price" of the property.[3]

While actual and reproduction cost are some evidence of value, the constitutional and statutory standard is market-based.

The Tax Tribunal erred in adopting the hearing officer's reasoning that the value should include amounts expended for physical improvements that the hearing officer found were made to enhance the bank's "image" or "business," without regard to whether the expenditures added to the "cash" or "usual selling price" of the property. The law does not tax expenditures that merely enhance the image or business of the owner, only expenditures that add to the cash value or selling price of the property.

It can be anticipated that, if a bank puts fine hardwood and marble throughout a building, those expenditures may not enhance the selling price of the building in an amount equal to their cost. While the expenditures may add to the selling price of the building, they may not add dollar-for-dollar. A building is sometimes worth less the day after completion of construction than its cost of construction. Ordinarily overimprovements are built by government,[4] not by private entrepreneurs who, in theory at least, would not construct an improvement unless they thought it was worth at least what it cost to build.[5]

The Constitution and statute do not authorize a tax on the value of lumber or marble incorporated into a building, but on the market value of the completed structure and land.[6]

We do not hold that the income approach advocated by First Federal's appraiser should govern, nor do we fault the city's appraiser or the Tax Tribunal for *considering* historical

---

2. Const. 1963, art. 9, sec. 3.

3. M.C.L. sec. 211.27; M.S.A. sec. 7.27.

4. Governments, not infrequently for reasons of policy, build schools, hospitals, and indeed private housing in neighborhoods where private entrepreneurs will not build, which are worth less on the market than they cost to construct.

5. If the government were to sell an overimprovement to a private person, market price rather than the cost of construction would govern for ad valorem tax purposes. If the government subsidizes a private enterprise in constructing such structures, the market value rather than cost would govern.

This issue can also arise where a private landowner, for personal reasons or simple improvidence, overbuilds for the neighborhood. He constructs a house that costs $150,000 in a neighborhood where all the other houses are worth about $75,000. In the relevant market, the house costing $150,000 may be worth $125,000 or $100,000, but not $150,000. Because it is an overimprovement for the neighborhood, the house, although brand new, should be valued at the market value, not at what it cost.

Merely because the owner may have constructed an improvement that cost more than the improvement is worth on the market should not subject the owner to a higher ad valorem tax.

6. Even if the structure is not an overimprovement, expenditures on it do not necessarily enhance its value dollar-for-dollar. A greenhouse, a gazebo, a tennis court, or a hot tub, while of value to the owner, do not necessarily add dollar-for-dollar to the usual selling price.

cost. Rather, we reject the notion that it is proper to include, in determining value, expenditures made, as the Tax Tribunal found, to enhance plaintiff's image and business without regard to whether they add to the selling price of the building.

Absent more persuasive evidence, such as comparable sales, historical cost or reproduction cost can be considered in arriving at the usual selling price, but historical or reproduction cost that merely enhances image or business but not selling price is not subject to taxation.

We find an "error of law or the adoption of wrong principles" within the meaning of Const. 1963, art. 6, sec. 28, and reverse and remand to the Tax Tribunal for further proceedings.

FITZGERALD, C.J., and RILEY, LEVIN, KAVANAGH, WILLIAMS, COLEMAN and RYAN, JJ., concur.

IN RE JOSEPH E. SEAGRAM & SONS, INC. V. TAX COMMISSION

18 A.D.2d 109, 238 N.Y.S.2d 228
New York Supreme Court, Appellate Division, 1963
aff'd, 14 N.Y.2d 314, 251 N.Y.S.2d 460, 200 N.E.2d 447 (1964)

STEUER, Justice.

The appeal is from an order confirming the assessments for tax purposes for the tax years 1956–57 to 1961–62, inclusive, on the real estate located at 375 Park Avenue. At the outset it is well to bear in mind a fundamental distinction between a proceeding of this character and one to ascertain the value for the purposes of condemnation. In the latter proceeding the court is obligated to find the value of the property. In this proceeding the value need only be found if the petitioner shows that it is less than the value fixed by the appraisers.

Considering first the land values, these progress from $3,800,000 in the earliest year to $5,000,000 in the latest. The present owner acquired the greater part of the land in 1951 for $4,000,000. The balance, consisting of an adjacent plot on East 52nd Street, was acquired in 1955 for $900,000. It is not disputed that between the time of purchase and the years under review real estate values have been steadily rising. Under the circumstances, an attack on the assessments for the land could not succeed without a showing that the price paid was grossly excessive. The petitioner has sought to do this by two means: through the medium of comparative sales, and circumstances attending its own purchases of this land. As to the latter, it is not subject to dispute that petitioner is a large corporation with experienced executives and had occasion to supplement its own knowledge with capable real estate advice. It makes no claim that it was overreached by the sellers. What it does assert is that in 1950 its lease on the office space it occupied was about to expire and that necessity prevented it from making a bargain at realistic prices. The leisurely pace at which the acquisition proceeded was quite enough to allow Special Term to give little credence to this explanation. The testimony in regard to comparative sales was far from conclusive and, as against the sale of the property under review, carried practically no weight.

The building in question is an unusual one in its nature, though not unique. It has these distinctive features which are the hallmarks of its class: It is generally known by its name (having relationship to the owner) instead of a street address; it is constructed of unusual and striking materials; its architecture is noteworthy; and it is well set back from the streets on which it fronts, the space involved being employed in distinctive decorative effects. The net effect is that this building, and the limited number that resemble it, gives up a substantial fraction of the land that might be built upon, with a consequent diminution of the rentable space, and its construction involves a cost materially in excess of utilitarian standards.

These buildings serve their owners in a fourfold way: 1. They house their activities. 2. They provide income from the rental of the space not used by the owner. 3. They advertise the owner's business. 4. They contribute to the owner's prestige.[1]

Just how a building whose construction is designed to serve these particular purposes is to be appraised, presents certain difficulties. The enhancement of the owner's ego is not a factor that can have a market value. In this city at present buildings in this special category, though few, are not unique. The time may come when they are so numerous that they become subject to sale, rent and the other transactions of commerce, so that by trading a market price which reflects the extra-commercial aspect can be ascertained. Meanwhile in this proceeding it must first be determined whether a valuation based on the special character is necessary. It would not be necessary if the building, as a conventional office building, is of a value at least equal to the assessments.

The assessments for the last three years are the only ones in question. There is little material difference in the relevant figures, so a calculation for a single year will suffice to make the determination based on capitalization of net income. For the year ending July 31, 1960, the actual income was $3,005,510. This does not include any income for the space occupied by the owner. Petitioner's expert appraised this space as having a rental value of $927,850, giving a total income of $3,933,360. Petitioner further claims a vacancy allowance of 5%, which would not be unreasonable. The net estimated return would therefore be $3,735,692. Expenses would vary somewhat. Petitioner's average for the three years is $1,401,000. This includes an item of $288,000 in each year for tenant changes. The city has taken the position that this item is not allowable because the improvements are personalty and not a part of the realty, relying on *Matter of 666 Fifth Corporation v. Tax Commission*, 11 N.Y.2d 915, 228 N.Y.S.2d 670, 183 N.E.2d 76. We find the argument inappropriate. The figure represents a maintenance charge. Whether it has to do with realty or personalty is immaterial. We question the figure on a different ground. Petitioner, having the burden of proof, must justify its calculations. The record is not clear as to how the expert estimated this figure, nor what it includes. It may be gathered that the figure is the total expenditure on behalf of tenants amortized over a period of years—just what period is by no means certain. But the record does show that it includes expenditures of sums which might be considered so far beyond the range of ordinary tenant accommodation in a commercial venture as to be considered fantastic. Expenditures in excess of a million dollars went into the fitting of a restaurant. Some explanation would be required to show that these amounts were proper business charges and that there was a reasonable expectation that rents would be enhanced or made

---

1. In this connection they exemplify a well known economic theory (see T. Veblen, *The Theory of the Leisure Class*). Though the author did not foresee this particular manifestation of his "Doctrine of Conspicuous Waste," it comes well within the specifications he provides for its successful application: "In order to impress these transient observers . . . the signature of one's pecuniary strength should be written in characters which he who runs may read. It is evident, therefore, that the present trend of the development is in the direction of heightening the utility of conspicuous consumption as compared with leisure." Modern Library Edition, p. 87.

possible through them. In the absence of any attempt at justification, they must be rejected. This reduces the expenses to $1,113,000 annually, with a net income of $2,623,000 (figure rounded out). Using petitioner's capitalization figures for the land and the taxes thereon there is a residual income for the building of $2,186,000. Petitioner claims the proper capitalization rate is 8% (made up of 6% for income and 2% for depreciation) plus taxes. Aside from the claim, this rate is not supported, and the city offered no proof on the subject. These figures represent the conservative view of an investor's expectations and, while they might be subject to revision in the special circumstances here presented, the record is barren of any proof upon which any lesser rate might be adopted. Using these figures, the value of the building would be $17,802,000. While this exceeds the petitioner's estimate by almost $4,000,000, it is still $3,200,000 under the assessment, and only about half the actual cost of construction.

It would seem to follow beyond the hope of successful contradiction that the traditional method of ascertaining value by capitalization is not applicable in this situation. Nowhere in the record is it explained how just two years before the period under review an experienced owner employing a reliable contractor and having the services of outstanding architects put $36,000,000 into a structure that was only worth $17,800,000. Such a startling result requires more than speculation before it can be accepted as fact.

The conclusion, therefore, is that petitioner proceeded upon an untenable theory and failed to show error in the assessments which calls for affirmance of the confirmation by the referee. It would, however, be unfair to leave the impression that a building of this sort presents an insoluble problem and that the owner is never in a position to contest the assessment of the city's appraisers. Nor is it necessary to await the day when the number of buildings of this kind reaches a point where they can be determined to have a market or rental value in consonance with their special features. Naturally, determination will have to await a proper presentation of the issue, but it will not be idle to indicate the lines along which presentation might be made.

Two possible theories occur. The first, and perhaps more obvious, is that advanced by the city here, namely, replacement value—the reasonable cost of construction less depreciation. To date this method of appraisal has been limited to two situations, in both of which the logic of its use is impregnable. The first is where the building is unique and would, if destroyed, have to be replaced (*People ex rel. New York Stock Exchange Building Co. v. Cantor*, 221 App.Div. 193, 223 N.Y.S. 64, *aff'd* 248 N.Y. 533, 162 N.E. 514). The second situation is where the owner claims it as the highest value which can be put on the building (*Matter of 860 Fifth Ave. Corp. v. Tax Comm'n*, 8 N.Y.2d 29, 200 N.Y.S.2d 817, 167 N.E.2d 455). Neither of these categories embraces the issue here. But an approach to that method of valuation may be found through them. Buildings that are unique through their design for a special purpose which not only serves that purpose but renders them unsuitable for any other use are unsalable if the owner is the only one engaged in that enterprise or the number of persons is so few that the practical effect is the same. Likewise, the owner cannot replace the building by purchase. Consequently its value to him is the cost of replacement. Buildings so specialized as to have a restricted use, that is, a use by a limited number of people, are appraised similarly where there is an absence of proof of what such buildings sell or rent for (*Matter of City of N.Y. [Kramer Realty]*, 16 A.D.2d 148, 226 N.Y.S.2d 288). While here the special features do not restrict the use, they do affect the value and the absence of proof of that effect could well lead to a valuation on replacement value as a last resort.

Another approach would be through the rental value of the space occupied by the owner. We have seen that the peculiar feature of this building and the few that resemble it is the identification in the public mind of the magnificent structure, and the consequent effect it has on the aesthetic improvement of the neighborhood, with the owner. The public does not know or care about the actual ownership of the fee. The same effect could be produced if the building were identified in the public mind by the name of a tenant. In calculating the income of the building the additional increment that a tenant who could afford and would be willing to pay for such a privilege should be included. This increment could be added to the estimated rental of the owner-occupied space. Having determined this figure, capitalization of the result should produce a scientific appraisal.

The order should be affirmed, with costs.

Order, entered on May 8, 1962, unanimously affirmed with $20 costs and disbursements to the respondent.

All concur in result and concur in opinion by STEUER, J., with respect to land value assessments and the treatment of tenant-changes.

VALENTE and EAGER, JJ., concur in concurring opinion by BREITEL, J. P.

BREITEL, Justice Presiding (concurring).

I concur in affirmance of the order. I also agree with the views expressed by Mr. Justice STEUER concerning the land value assessment and the so-called tenant-changes. It is with respect to the building value assessment that I find it necessary to express my own views.

Taxpayer has argued cogently that the value of the building should be determined in the usual way by capitalization of the net income, using 6% as the rate of capitalization and 2% as the rate of depreciation. The 6% rate of income capitalization, the only rate proven in the case, is a modest, presumptively proper, return in the absence of any proof that financial and real estate market conditions justify a lower rate. A commercial building is an investment that is being amortized and it is unlikely that a prudent investor would regard anything more than 50 years as a conservative basis on which to gamble physical depreciation, technological obsolescence, area deterioration, or other physical devaluation (Am. Inst. of Real Est. App., *The Appraisal of Real Estate* [3rd ed.], ch. 14, esp. at pp. 204–205; 1 Bonbright, *Valuation of Property*, ch. X). Hence, the 2% rate, in the absence of proof to the contrary, would seem reasonable. Because of the leverage in rates of capitalization and amortization one must be especially cautious before adjusting them, and, in no event, should it be done without objective basis in the record.

The recent cost of construction of this building stands out, however, as a seeming contradiction of the result derived by capitalization of net income. It is because of this that the City has attempted to resolve the problem by the concept of a limited specialty— and to base value on replacement cost less depreciation. At this point it is not necessary to reach that hurdle. It has been held with respect to new buildings that the cost of construction is a highly significant indicator of value.

. . . .

Given a profit-minded owner with available experience and resources, and a competent builder, the cost of construction is likely to represent the value of the newly-finished product. Consequently, in the absence of credible qualifying explanation, for a new building the cost of construction is, *prima facie*, the true value. Indeed, because it would escape this fact, the taxpayer is in the anomalous position of urging that vast corporate funds were used to construct a building of much less value. This, if so, is never satisfactorily explained and does not do much credit to the sagacity of the corporate managers.

The maximum assessment for the building for the years in question was $21 million. The building, according to the City's examination of the taxpayer's books, cost $36 million to complete. Even if one were to eliminate the cost of all tenant improvements at taxpayer's figure of $9.5 million, contrary to what has already been concluded with respect to tenant-changes, there would be a residue of $26.5 million. Taxpayer's expert, without knowledge of the actual costs, gave $19 million as the reproduction cost of the building before depreciation, excluding all tenant installations. Adding only a part of the cost of the tenant installations it would match the assessment; adding all the tenant installations the cost would exceed the building assessment generously. Interestingly enough, the taxpayer's expert, despite his lower cost figure, had only praise for the competence of the architect, engineers, and builders of this building. Consequently, in the absence of any satisfactory explanation to show excessive costs, the construction cost establishes value, *prima facie*—a value substantially in excess of the building assessment.

But the discrepancy here between capitalized rental income and cost of construction merits further analysis. The capitalized rental income as computed by taxpayer, using 6% as the rate of capitalization and 2% as the rate of depreciation, but including as an amortized expense the rejected tenant-changes, is $14.5 million. Excluding adjustments for tenant-changes the result would be $17 million—$4 million short of the building assessment, and up to $19 million short of the construction cost. Given a new building, prudently constructed for commercial purposes, the answer must be that the rental value assigned to the owner-tenant is too low, and, perhaps too, that the building as a whole bearing the name of its owner includes a real property value not reflected in commercial rental income. Of course, this would mean that, to begin with, the owner did not build for commercial rental-income purposes alone, and, as a consequence, capitalization of such income without adjustments produces a false result. Of course, the formula for capitalization of commercial rental income is relevant when commercial property is held only for such income, or when its market value is determinable solely by its potential for such income. This is merely a corollary of the principle that income capitalization is valid only for property held for or measurable only by its income. In short, when dealing with commercial property one must not confuse investment for commercial rental income with investment for some other form of rental value unrelated to the receipt of commercial rental income.

It is self-evident that an owner who builds, as did this taxpayer, a prestige (monumental) building for itself, requires the leasing to other commercial tenants simply as an important way of bearing the heavy costs involved. The prestige building has a rental value not based alone on commercially rented space, but on the building's value in promoting the economic interests of an owner. Thus, such an owner is not wasting assets. Rather, it is investing in a real estate project that will contribute to the production of income in its principal enterprise. Since this practice is becoming a common feature of urban areas, such investment has ceased to be idiosyncratic and is undoubtedly translatable into market value terms. Typically, such value would be related to owner-occupancy of principal or prestige offices with choice space, the continued power to control its choice of space, and most often, identification by name of the building with that of the owner.[1]

---

1. Where, as sometimes happens, a major tenant's name is borne by the building, presumably, the rental paid reflects the name-bearing value. Or, in another situation,

On this view the rental value assigned to the taxpayer's space is understated, if there is merely charged to that space the prorated value assigned to other tenants. And, undoubtedly too, there is value to be assigned to the building as a whole, independent of commercial rental income, since the building, qua building, is also held for business purposes, unrelated to the receipt of commercial rental income.

At this time, it is not necessary to work out the values last discussed, so long as, the building being new, the cost of construction, otherwise unexplained, suffices to justify the building assessment. With the passage of time both the taxpayer and the City will have, with respect to future assessments, the burden of providing proof and testimony bearing on such values. If there is sufficient evidence of market values, that may do. If not, reproduction cost less appropriate adjustments may have to be utilized to find the value of so much of the property as definably is not held for commercial rental income purposes—perhaps with the present ratio between adjusted original cost and capitalized commercial rental income as a starting point. In this connection it would be likely, although not necessarily so, that the prestige or monumental value of the building would depreciate economically at a much greater rate than the value attributed to the rental income potential.

It is unlikely, however, that a formulation based upon the physical ratio of owner-occupied space to commercially rented space would be valid. The reason is simply that an owner's quantitative need for space may be wholly unrelated to the economic value to it of the building as a whole, either as a prestige monument or as the seat of power to control the choice and use of space.

Worth discarding, although urged, is the argument that because a building does not occupy all of the assembled land, there is an inadequate improvement. This does not follow. The improvement is inadequate to the land only if that is not a sound economic way to construct a building. Indeed, a discernible trend in modern prestige building, for at least a quarter of a century, may make construction to the building line an inadequate improvement—economically. Exclusively utilitarian construction may produce more "rentable" space, but not more valuable space.

VALENTE and EAGER, JJ., concur.

In re Joseph E. Seagram & Sons, Inc. v. Tax Commission
14 N.Y.2d 314, 200 N.E.2d 447, 251 N.Y.S.2d 460
Court of Appeals of New York, 1964

DESMOND, Chief Judge.

In this proceeding to review tax assessments the contest is as to the values ($20,500,000 in two of the years, $21,000,000 in the third year) assigned by the Tax Commission to the building which was completed just before the first of these tax years at a cost of $36,000,000. Summarized, the position of appellant is that capitalization of rental income, including estimated rent for the offices occupied by appellant itself, would not justify a building value of more than about $17,000,000.

---

it may be that the tenant's name is used to enhance the prestige of the building; but in that case the rental income of the other tenants will reflect that value. The permutations are many, and whether the increased value attaches to the real estate or to business good-will may well, in some cases, present problems difficult of solution.

Unlike many of the real property tax proceeding orders reviewed in this court, this order comes to us from an Appellate Division affirmance of Special Term so that questions of fact and of weight of evidence are not before us. We cannot reverse or modify in such a situation unless the record is without any substantial evidence to support the conclusion below or there has been error of law in the use of an erroneous theory of valuation, or otherwise. We find no such errors here.

Although we do not concur in everything said in the two Appellate Division opinions, we agree that for an office building like this, well suited to its site, the actual building construction cost of $36,000,000 is some evidence of value, at least as to the tax years soon after construction. Petitioner urges, however, that for a building built to rent and rentable, capitalization of net income is the only basis for valuation and that the building assessment here can be justified only by assigning an inflated value to the office space occupied by petitioner itself. This, says petitioner, really means that petitioner, having for its own reasons constructed an unusually costly and beautiful building, is being taxed ostensibly for building value but really for the prestige and advertising value accruing to petitioner because the "Seagram Building" has become world-renowned for its striking and imposing beauty. We do not agree with this interpretation of the opinions and order of the Appellate Division.

Usually, the assumed rent for the space occupied by a building owner would for purposes of capitalization of net rent income be computed at about the same rate as the rents actually paid by other tenants. But there can be many reasons why, as both of the Appellate Division opinions state, "the building as a whole bearing the name of its owner includes a real property value not reflected in commercial rental income" since "the owner did not build for commercial rental-income purposes alone, and, as a consequence, capitalization of such income without adjustments produces a false result" and, therefore, "one must not confuse investment for commercial rental income with investment for some other form of rental value unrelated to the receipt of commercial rental income." In other words, the hypothetical rental for owner-occupied space need not be fixed at the same rate as paid by tenants. This does not mean that advertising or prestige or publicity value is erroneously taxed as realty value. It certainly does not mean that a corporate sponsor of esthetics is being penalized for contributing to the metropolis a monumental and magnificent structure.

The order should be affirmed with costs.

BURKE, Judge (dissenting).

We do not suggest that cost of construction is not relevant, that it may not be taken into consideration as bearing on value. That it may be so considered is an old rule recognized in many cases . . . .

We do criticize as erroneous in law the holding of the Appellate Division—and also the holding of this court insofar as it refuses to meet the issue—that cost of construction is prima facie evidence of value in the case of "a newly-erected structure built especially for prestige and advertising value as well as for the headquarters use of its owner." (*Matter of Pepsi-Cola Co. v. Tax Comm. of City of New York*, 19 A.D.2d 56, 59, 240 N.Y.S.2d 770, 774–775.)

While the well-settled rule is that capitalized net income is the best measure of the value of commercial rental property,* it has now been decided that this measure must be

---

*The city offered no testimony as to economic value, i.e., capitalization of net income.

displaced as "false" where the building is of such renown that the court feels that its owner must benefit economically thereby, over and above the rental commanded by the building. In such a case, it is said, the rental value of the space occupied by the owner-tenant, Seagram, must be valued not in proportion to the value of space occupied by the other tenants but at some higher value that reflects the business advantage accruing to one whose name is associated with such an outstanding and well-known building. Since the petitioner failed to so value its space it is held to have failed to carry the burden of showing excessive assessment.

. . . .

The narrow and highly technical character of the rule applied by the Appellate Division may be highlighted by comparison with *Matter of Pepsi-Cola Co. v. Tax Comm. of City of New York*, 19 A.D.2d 56, 240 N.Y.S.2d 770, *supra*, decided by the same court three months after the instant case. There, the court was confronted with a brand new structure quite similar in novelty to the Seagram Building in that it "is unusually distinctive and individualistic in appearance, (and) is set back approximately 14 feet on Park Avenue and 34 feet on 59th Street to provide on said sides a promenade and plaza ornamented with plants and shrubbery." Yet the court held that it is not "in the same category as the Seagram Building, that is, a newly-erected structure built especially for prestige and advertising value as well as for the headquarters use of its owner." Since both are new, held for business rental, and used as headquarters for the owner, the only difference is the presumed benefit accruing to the Seagram Company from having its name associated with an architecturally superior and well-known building.

"Value" under section 306 of the Real Property Tax Law, Consol. Laws, c. 50-a, is market value given willing sellers and buyers. In our view, this approach to value necessarily excludes any element that is unique to the present owner of a building. Any increment in Seagram's outside business enterprises deriving from public appreciation of the Seagram Building will not pass to a buyer of the building in a sale. Such an element would disappear if the building were sold to another investor, engaged in another business or in no business at all, other than real estate investment. The good will follows Seagram and cannot be regarded as real property value inherent in the building itself.

Of course, the prestige of the Seagram Building undoubtedly enhances the value of the building in any hands. This is undoubtedly real estate value—value which is transferable in a sale, and for which a buyer will pay. Such value also affects the rental commanded by the building. But, if tenants are willing to pay more for space in the Seagram Building than for similar space elsewhere, that is fully reflected in the capitalization of earnings. In turn, it would seem to follow that such capitalization adequately comprehends any increase in value that the building would bring in a sale—without resorting to concepts foreign to real estate value.

By the consideration of a so-called value element without regard to its place in light of the ultimate statutory norm of market value, and thereby displacing income capitalization as an acceptable measure of value and giving undue prima facie effect to cost, the Appellate Division has committed legal error for which the order appealed from should be reversed and the case remitted for reconsideration without regard to any supposed theory that the building is a specially built structure representing more of a real estate investment in its owner-occupant's business than a commercial office building.

DYE, FULD and BERGAN, JJ., concur with DESMOND, C. J.

BURKE, J., dissents in a separate opinion in which VAN VOORHIS and SCILEPPI, JJ., concur.

Order affirmed.

Notes on the *Seagram* Case

The Seagram Building has been described as "one of New York's, and the country's, great works of modern architecture . . . [designed] by Mies van der Rohe and Philip Johnson, as handsomely proportioned and serene a tower as the twentieth century has conceived."[10]

> Rarely has a building been designed with such painstaking care all the way through. No doorknob, lavatory or tap, no sign, mail chute was left to accident . . . . Works of art were bought or specially commissioned for the Seagram Company's own floors . . . . Seagram was an expensive building, possibly the most expensive skyscraper per square foot, ever built up to that time. Yet it seemed to repay much of its cost in terms of good public relations and other intangibles, and the paved plaza in front of the building gave it such nobility and "prestige" that numerous banks offered large sums to the Seagram Company for the right to build branch offices on the plaza . . . .[11]

This happy combination of profitability and excellence in design extended to the Four Seasons restaurant as well. Recall that the appellate division questioned the business justification for the amount spent there:

> Expenditures in excess of a million dollars went into the fitting of a restaurant. Some explanation would be required to show that these amounts were proper business charges and that there was a reasonable expectation that rents would be enhanced or made possible through them.

Time has diminished both the seeming extravagance of this sum and any suspicion that it was not justified by business considerations. In 1988, the *Wall Street Journal* reported that the restaurant, anxious to avoid any changes in decor that might startle its wealthy clientele, spent a half million dollars on "new table lamps, china, salt and pepper bowls, new upholstery, and many little things specifically meant to be nearly imperceptible."

> According to a *Wall Street Journal* survey last year, it is the favorite restaurant *anywhere* of chief executives of big corporations . . . .
>
> The Four Seasons, designed three decades ago at a cost of $4.5 million by the eminent architect Philip Johnson, is considered by some to be a paragon of modern architecture.
>
> It isn't surprising that this busy restaurant makes money, even though it is located at street level in the Seagram Building, in a decidedly high-rent neighborhood. The owners won't say what their lease costs them. But their revenue has risen to about $14 million a year from $2 million 15 years ago . . . .[12]

---

10. P. Goldberger, "Three Ways to Get a Sense of Extraordinary New York," *New York Times*, August 8, 1980, p. C9.

11. P. Blake, *Mies van der Rohe, Architecture and Structure* (1960), pp. 108–10.

12. R. Ricklefs, "The Four Seasons Needed Sprucing up, But Change Is Risky," *Wall Street Journal*, November 16, 1988, p. 1.

A 1980 restaurant review described the restaurant's setting:

For sheer physical grandeur the restaurant may be unmatched by any in the world. The scale throughout is formidable, with ceilings set at stratospheric levels above tracts of space that, in prohibitively pricey premises, have been disposed and appointed with an alarming disregard for bottom-line realities. The approach to the dining room, for example, in itself entails a tour of more real estate than most whole restaurants occupy . . . . Horticultural displays, made up of mature trees and, when appropriate, extensive flower beds, are alternated seasonally at staggering expense, as are menus, table appointments, and staff uniforms. Matched-grain panels of fine, superbly burnished wood soar to improbable heights while equally lofty windows combine with a ceaseless ripple of chain-brass to bathe the space with softly filtered light by day and veil it from the outside world by night. Museum-caliber contemporary art punctuates the outsized planes of Philip Johnson's architecture, dispelling what otherwise might be the discomfiting impression that one mistakenly has wandered into the nave of Laon Cathedral.[13]

The plaza in front of the Seagram building, although presented in the property tax litigation as an uneconomic use of expensive Park Avenue space, was a similarly successful urban design innovation. Acclaim for this amenity encouraged revision of the New York City Zoning Resolution to permit more intensive development of sites where a plaza or arcade was incorporated into the building plan. Unfortunately, many of these open spaces proved to be of little benefit to the public.

Some are not built to specifications or are unusable or unwelcoming, some are frequented by drug dealers or vandals, and some are closed off by their owners or are in out-of-the-way locations. Meanwhile, the owners continue to enjoy the use of the extra floor space.[14]

The proliferation of badly designed or poorly maintained plazas, accompanied by higher buildings and a consequent loss of sunlight at the street level, led to harsh criticism and subsequent revision of this "incentive zoning" measure.[15]

---

13. J. Jacobs, "Spécialités de la Maison: New York," *Gourmet*, July, 1980, p. 8.

14. D. Dunlap, "Policies Reworked as Open Spaces Go Unused," *New York Times*, August 8, 1988, page B1.

15. The Seagram plaza and its relationship to New York City zoning incentives are examined in detail in William H. Whyte's two books, *The Social Life of Small Urban Spaces* (1980) and *City: Rediscovering the Center* (1988)—particularly Chapter 16, "The Rise and Fall of Incentive Zoning." Whyte discusses a study by Jerold S. Kayden, *Incentive Zoning in New York City: A Cost-Benefit Analysis* (1978), in which Kayden calculated that between 1961 and 1973 New York City developers realized an additional $48 of floor space for each dollar spent on plazas constructed to qualify for this incentive program.

The Seagram Building was sold in 1980 to the Teachers Insurance & Annuity Association of America (TIAA) for $86,460,000. The new owners successfully petitioned the New York City Landmarks Preservation Commission to designate the building itself a landmark, but brought suit against the city when the restaurant interior was given landmark status as well. The restaurant owners, with a lease term scheduled to expire in 1999, sought landmark designation, which TIAA charged "will have the practical effect of forcing TIAA to continue to operate the space as a restaurant."[16] Again, the most efficient use of this space was at issue, for TIAA argued that preservation of the interior was in effect preservation of a use, restricting future changes in the function of the restaurant space. The appellate division affirmed the validity of the landmark designation, stating, "The fact that occupancy other than that of a restaurant might not constitute optimum commercial utilization of the space does not require the conclusion that the designation is in effect a preservation of prior use." *Teachers Insurance and Annuity Association of America v. City of New York*, 185 A.D.2d 207, 586 N.Y.S.2d 262 (1992), *appeal dismissed,* 81 N.Y.2d 759, 610 N.E.2d 391, 594 N.Y.S.2d 718 (1992).

Critical reaction to the *Seagram* decision was voiced in law reviews.[17] *New York Times* editorial writers let their displeasure with the decision be known as well: "When it serves society badly, there is something wrong with the law. A clear illustration is in the New York State Court of Appeals decision upholding a lower court judgment that Joseph E. Seagram & Sons is to be penalized in the form of higher taxes for building an extravagantly handsome structure that has become one of the city's chief ornaments. For New York this decision is a catastrophe."[18]

Notes and Questions

1. What does the success of the Seagram Building indicate about the financial benefit of a prestigious address? The appellate division opinion suggested, "The public does not know or care about the actual ownership of the fee. The same effect could be produced if the building were identified in the public mind by the name of a tenant." After 1981 the Seagram Company was a tenant in this building. Would association with the building name affect the amount it would be willing to pay to rent space there? Would tenants other than the Seagram Company pay the same premium to rent that space? What benefit from association with the Seagram name could be offered to future purchasers?

---

16. D. Dunlap, "Building Owner Fights Landmark at 4 Seasons," *New York Times,* February 4, 1990, p. 39.

17. J. Murphy and E. Rook, "State and Local Taxation," *Syracuse Law Review* 15(1964):223, 225; and note, *Fordham Law Review* 33(1964):121.

18. *New York Times,* June 13, 1974, p. 22.

2. Similarly, what does the success of the Seagram Building indicate with regard to the assessment at issue in the *First Federal Savings & Loan* case? Does it increase your skepticism toward the bank's claims that expenditures "to enhance image and business" do not increase the value of the building itself, or do you find the cases distinguishable? Should the *Seagram* approach be limited to buildings of outstanding architectural merit? Consider in this regard Judge Burke's comment concerning the *Pepsi-Cola* decision. The Pepsi-Cola headquarters, like the Seagram Building, was architecturally distinguished, associated with its owner's name, and located on a Park Avenue plaza, yet the appellate division simply concluded that it was not "in the same category" for property tax purposes. The Pepsi-Cola headquarters, at 500 Park Avenue, was designed by the firm of Skidmore, Owings and Merrill. Paul Goldberger, architecture critic for the *New York Times*, described it as "an elegant box of glass and aluminum floating on piers . . . . Like the Seagram Building it is a jewel of metal and glass that works best when it can be played off against older masonry buildings."[19] In fact, the Pepsi-Cola Building was later sold to Olivetti and renamed the Olivetti Building.

3. Larger economic developments also affect the financial situation of "prestige" buildings of this type. In 1990 the *Wall Street Journal* reported:

> They are the structures that ego built, and they've helped shape the skyline of America. Corporate chieftains have built skyscrapers with studied indifference to the bottom line. Cost was secondary to image—personal and corporate.
>
> But something's happened.
>
> . . . .
>
> Today, few showy headquarters buildings are in the pipeline. Many of the biggest companies, the kind that built the biggest buildings, are in trouble. So are banks, which built some of the fanciest buildings in many cities. Even companies that have money aren't likely to show off in the sullen 1990s by strutting an edifice complex.
>
> "In the 1990s, corporations don't want to be opulent in any way or frivolous with shareholders' money," says Clive Chajet, chairman of the corporate image consulting firm Lippincott & Marguiles. "Opulence and glitz are not the corporate values of the 1990s."[20]

How might developments of this sort affect the valuation of such buildings for tax purposes? What specific evidence should taxpayers and assessors examine in order to establish these effects?

---

19. P. Goldberger, *The City Observed: A Guide to the Architecture of Manhattan* (1979), p. 154.

20. N. Barsky, "What Will Become of Skylines without Edifice Complexes?" *Wall Street Journal*, February 20, 1990, p. A1.

4. Consider again the relationship of the "specialty" category to the concept of functional obsolescence as a means of reconciling the sale value of a unique building and its cost less physical depreciation. For example, a theater built for live performances, complete with stage, dressing rooms, and storage space, might be later used only to show motion pictures. Should its valuation include an allowance for functional obsolescence? Can you distinguish the rationale for a reduced assessment here from that in *Seagram*? See *B. F. Keith Columbus Co. v. Board of Revision*, 148 Ohio St. 253, 35 Ohio Ops. 244, 74 N.E.2d 359 (1947). If a town once supported two theaters of identical design and now only one continues to offer live performances, the second being used for movies, should they be assigned different values for property tax purposes? Will destruction of the first building cause the second to be valued as a "specialty," with a consequent increase in its assessment? Should the owner of the operating theater purchase the second at a low price, and argue that this sets the "market value" for both buildings? What if movies turn out to be more profitable than live shows? The *B. F. Keith* case is discussed in "Functional Obsolescence as a Factor in Valuation," *University of Cincinnati Law Review* 17(1947):165, 172.

5. What is the difference between a claim of "obsolescence" in the case of a building not used for its intended purpose, such as the theater in the previous example, and a structure such as the Seagram Building or the New York Stock Exchange? How does the Seagram Building differ from the Stock Exchange in terms of marketability? Should any of these differences affect "fair market value" for tax purposes?

Valuation Disputes and Specialty Property: The General Motors-North Tarrytown Experience

The difficulty of valuing industrial plants gives rise to many tax disputes, and when large amounts are at issue these disputes can take on political importance. Some of these complexities were illustrated by a decade of public attention to the property taxes on a General Motors (GM) automotive assembly plant in North Tarrytown, New York. GM initiated litigation challenging these taxes in the fall of 1982, claiming an overvaluation of more than $30 million. The negotiations that followed eventually produced a complex arrangement under which GM made reduced payments in lieu of taxes in exchange for continuing operations at that site.[21]

---

21. Otherwise unannotated factual data in the following section are based on research and interviews undertaken in 1986 for the Lincoln Institute of Land Policy by Ken Zimmerman.

The GM assembly plant occupied ninety-seven acres of land along the Hudson River and had been critical to the local economy since it began producing Stanley Steamers a century ago. GM was the county's largest employer, with two shifts totalling 5,000 employees and a payroll of over $124 million. A negotiated settlement in 1979 had already reduced the plant's valuation by 25 percent to $70 million. The new litigation followed GM plans to reduce production in response to decreased demand and a GM study ranking the Tarrytown facility among the least efficient of all its plants. Contributing factors included high prevailing wage rates, electricity costs more than double the national average, a lack of land for expansion, and, in particular, the highest property taxes of any GM plant. The plant management shared these results with local officials as they announced the layoff of the entire second shift.

Local managers sought both a reduction in current tax payments and a ceiling on assessments for future improvements, such as paint shop renovations to meet Clean Air Act standards. The managers felt that investment in a new paint shop was critical to the plant's future. They also knew that Ford Motor Company had recently received a $32.5 million tax refund on its Dearborn, Michigan, plant.

GM paid taxes to four local jurisdictions: the incorporated village of North Tarrytown, the town of Mt. Pleasant, the Union Free School District, and Westchester County. Property taxes supplied more than half these units' revenue, and GM was the largest single Tarrytown taxpayer. The region had recently lost a major portion of its tax base when the Rockefeller family estate, encompassing 40 percent of the total village area, was converted to a tax-exempt state reservation. The village had failed in its efforts to obtain compensating state payments in lieu of taxes on the reservation. Even if an increase in the tax rate on other property were politically feasible, village taxes were limited by the state constitution to 2 percent of the assessment roll.

Mt. Pleasant levied taxes for itself, the school district and the county. The village assessed property independently and levied its own taxes. These jurisdictions varied in their dependence on GM. The North Tarrytown plant provided $1.5 million of the $3.0 million raised by the village in property taxes for its overall $4.2 million budget. GM contributed $2.5 million of the school district's $12 million in property taxes. The town and county, however, received only minimal revenue from the plant.

State and local authorities had to weigh the loss of tax revenue against the danger of plant closure. They did not know how large a reduction in taxes would be necessary to keep the plant operating. Nor were state and local interests identical. Local governments were primarily concerned with revenue loss; state officials, with the regional business climate.

GM attorney Fred Martin stated that the actual market value of the plant was not an issue because "GM demanded that the maximum effective value of the plant be $40 million." Local officials never argued that GM was mistaken in its $30–40 million estimate; instead, their position was based on their need for revenue. State officials, although convinced that the plant was overvalued, concentrated on keeping it in North Tarrytown rather than on determining its fair market value.

Ironically, GM's position was strengthened by a 1980 New York State Board of Equalization and Assessment study valuing the plant at $37 million, with a 50 percent allowance for functional and economic obsolescence. The village itself had concluded that residential property occupying a comparable area paid only $30,000 in property taxes annually.

Had the case gone to court, GM attorney Fred Martin planned a two-part claim patterned on the *Xerox* case. He would first have taken the position that the plant was not specialty property and that market data could be used to show its overassessment. Following *A & P*, he would use detailed descriptions of the buildings, grounds, and equipment to show that the plant could be converted to other uses. In the alternative, he would argue that even if the plant were a specialty, its assessment should be reduced to reflect functional obsolescence. Martin felt the depressed value of industrial plants in the area would provide strong grounds for the first approach, and Tarrytown's labor, transportation, and utility costs would assist in the second. The Tarrytown plant was over seventy years old and had been renovated only infrequently. The difficulty of measuring functional obsolescence left all parties uncertain whether GM could justify the 50 percent allowance necessary to reduce its assessment to $37 million. However, the amount of revenue at stake encouraged local officials to negotiate. If successful, GM would have been entitled to refunds compounded at 9 percent interest, totalling $4.5 million for the village and $7.2 million for the school district.

GM invited local officials, including union representatives and village, town, and county politicians, to a discussion of the plant's future. GM then presented a "laundry list" of incentives needed to keep the plant competitive, including tax reductions, rail clearance improvements, investment tax credits, job training funds, exemption from state sales taxes, and access to less expensive power from the FitzPatrick nuclear plant on Lake Ontario. The state responded by convening an intergovernmental task force including the village mayor, the town supervisor, county officials, and representatives of state agencies. The state commerce department drafted a package of incentives that included investment tax credits, sales tax exemptions, rail clearances, highway improvements, subsidized power, and job training funds. However, this initial proposal of May 1984 did not address the property tax issue.

The school district attempted to participate in the negotiations but failed. The town represented the school district in most tax disputes, but the amount of revenue at stake here led the district to seek a more active role. Unlike most districts in affluent Westchester County, the Union Free School District incurred high costs relative to its property tax base and had a large number of non–English-speaking students. Its costs for remedial and special education were among the highest in the country, and it had suffered an annual loss of $225,000 when the earlier GM refund claims were settled without its participation in 1979. The district enlisted the aid of the state teachers' union, undertook a public relations campaign, and even threatened to file for bankruptcy. However, state and local officials resisted this pressure, and the task force never included a school representative.

After studying the state's initial proposal, GM headquarters in Detroit responded that it could make no commitment to the plant without resolution of the assessment dispute. The state then set out to convince the local governments to accept a tax reduction rather than risk a much greater loss through an unsuccessful court battle. In the following months, state officials employed a combination of threats and promises to persuade the local governments to accept a compromise. To their earlier concerns for promoting business location in New York was added the pressure of a closely contested gubernatorial campaign. Yet state officials were also anxious to avoid setting any precedent of compensation for local property tax reductions.

At a meeting with representatives of local governments, state officials proposed saving the plant $1 million in taxes by reducing its valuation while increasing residential and commercial assessment ratios. Although local officials responded favorably, GM did not. Fred Martin said that Detroit management assumed the package would improve as a court date neared. "We needed to show that we were aggressively pressing our legal options to communicate the seriousness of the problem." The corporation was also concerned that the offer did not bar future assessment increases. GM rejected the proposal.

The village and town presented a more generous package to GM in February, offering to reduce the plant's annual tax to $3.5 million, with further reductions to reflect changes in the state equalization rate. Pending claims would be settled for $2.1 million—roughly half the maximum amount GM stood to win if its petition were completely successful. A series of meetings in April resulted in a deadlock. The parties remained $30 million apart in their estimate of value.

After the April meetings, town supervisor Mike Rovello became convinced that the issue "could be resolved only outside the arena" of conventional tax settlements. He proposed that the plant be purchased by the state Industrial Development Authority (IDA) and leased back to GM. IDA real estate is exempt from local property taxes. IDA purchases of construction materials are also exempt from New York sales tax, a benefit worth over $1 million to GM. In addition, tax-exempt financing would be available for the pollution abatement equipment in the paint shop. The state would provide 10,000 kilowatts of electric power from the FitzPatrick plant, saving GM approximately $1 million on its annual $15 million electric utility charges. The federal government also agreed to designate the plant a "foreign trade subzone," saving $1.7 million annually on duties on imported goods.[22]

In return, Rovello proposed that GM make two sets of payments: lease payments sufficient to satisfy the annual amount due on the bonds that would finance IDA's purchase of the plant, and payments in lieu of property taxes to the local jurisdictions. Rovello did not inform the village and school district of these negotiations, in order to avoid public debate until "GM acceptance was imminent." Instead, he met privately with the county executive, state officials, and GM representatives.

Subsequent negotiations set GM's payments in lieu of taxes at $3.5 million annually for ten years, slightly higher than Detroit's demand, but less than the local governments had anticipated (see table 2).

Table 2
Terms of the Settlement Compared with Taxes

	Existing 1985 taxes	New York State proposal	Final payment in lieu of taxes
Town	$ 43,099	$ 0	$ 43,099
County	1,049,851	764,991	278,860
Village	1,550,500	250,000	1,300,550
Schools	2,859,563	1,000,000	1,859,563
Total	$5,497,013	$2,014,991	$3,482,022

GM representatives approved this settlement because it offered predictable taxes for ten years without GM relinquishing the right to petition for a refund. Moreover, despite the nominal form of a sale-leaseback, the company retained sufficient control over the plant to satisfy its commitments to lenders and shareholders.

In November 1986 GM announced that it would shut eleven plants employing 29,000 workers. Tarrytown was to remain open, and was awarded the job of assembling the GM minivan. In return, the state agreed to raise

---

22. J. Feron, "G.M. to Produce New Mini-Vans in Upstate Plant," *New York Times*, February 4, 1987, p. B2.

twenty-three bridges over railroad tracks and enlarge seven railroad tunnels serving the plant, at a cost of $22 million.[23] The minivan had originally been planned for a GM plant in Framingham, Massachusetts; in November 1987 GM announced the closing of that plant, putting 3,700 employees there out of work.[24]

The Tarrytown school district faced the greatest difficulty in adjusting to the terms of the GM settlement. The school superintendent said, "If we had said 'no' to the settlement and chose to go to court instead, we would have had the Governor and everybody else saying that we weren't being a good community member."[25] A member of a Tarrytown residents' association, Save Our Schools, wrote in 1990:

> Here in the Tarrytowns, we've learned that Japanese corporations, and not American ones, make the best neighbors.
>
> In 1978 the General Motors plant in North Tarrytown began a series of attempts to lower its taxes by lowering its assessed value. By 1983 it claimed to have overpaid local taxes by almost $7 million, an amount that neither the town nor the school district could possibly repay. Encouraged by Gov. Mario Cuomo, the local taxing authority was forced in 1985 to accept an agreement in which GM was no longer assessed for any taxes. Instead it only had to make small "payments in lieu of taxes" for a 10-year period.
>
> . . . .
>
> Hitachi America Limited, a subsidiary of Hitachi Limited in Tokyo, has been based in Tarrytown for six years. It has never filed a tax certiorari case.[26]

News reports stated:

> Big tax cuts won by General Motors here and by two companies in neighboring Tarrytown are forcing residents to decide whether to make painful cuts in their

---

23. "Raising the bridges about two feet and enlarging the tunnels will give triple-stacked carriers access to the Albany area, beyond which the minivans can be distributed by rail throughout the United States. The plant now distributes all its vehicles—the midsized Buick Century and Pontiac 6000 models—by truck, which is more costly." J. Feron, "G.M. to Produce New Mini-Vans in Upstate Plant," *New York Times*, February 4, 1987, p. B2.

24. M. Kranish and B. Mohl, "GM to Close Framingham Plant Nov. 30," *Boston Globe*, November 5, 1987, p. 1.

25. L. Foderaro, "Corporate Tax Cuts Burden School System," *New York Times*, March 8, 1990, p. B1.

26. C. Rubenstein, "The Deadbeat of America," *New York Times*, March 17, 1990, p. 27. In response, the GM plant manager asserted that the agreement was "hailed by all parties involved as a positive solution," and pointed to the company's waiver of $10 million in refunds, and its donations of vehicles and components worth $300,000 to local educational institutions in 1989. A. M. Beirne, Letter, *New York Times*, April 7, 1990, p. 24.

joint school system, the Union Free School District of the Tarrytowns, or shoulder a sharp tax increase.[27]

The other two companies, Technicon Instruments and Consolidated Edison, won their victories through court decisions and court-approved settlements of tax litigation. A spokesman for the New York State Division of Equalization and Assessment presented the view that had guided the state's handling of the GM negotiations:

> Large companies had for a long time adopted a good-neighbor policy in which they looked the other way, knowing full well they were being overassessed. Somewhere along the way the competition became so great that the bottom line is now more important than community spirit.[28]

After voters twice rejected proposed school budgets for Tarrytown in 1990, the schools opened with only a 1 percent budget increase. As a result, "dozens of teachers, secretaries and administrators were laid off, and there is no money for new school supplies, library books, routine repairs or for extracurricular activities, from the yearbook to the debate team."[29]

1991 reports found morale at the Tarrytown plant good:

> The plant is the only one assembling the Chevrolet Lumina APV, the Pontiac Trans Sport and the Oldsmobile Silhouette—sleek, futuristic-looking minivans designed mainly for families that used to rely on station wagons. The plant's singular status has provided it considerable protection, auto industry analysts said. For the plant to be shut permanently, G.M. would have to pull out of the mini-van market altogether or retool a different plant, neither of which is likely, they said.[30]

Described as "struggling but hopeful," plant workers "found comfort in the fact that the North Tarrytown plant is the only plant producing the General Motors line of minivans."[31] Although GM fell short of its commitment to maintain Tarrytown jobs, New York State authorities ruled this to be due to extenuating circumstances and continued to provide low-cost power allocations.[32]

---

27. L. Foderaro, "Corporate Tax Cuts Burden School System," *New York Times*, March 8, 1990, page B1.

28. *Ibid.*

29. L. Foderaro, "Tarrytown Making Do in Schools," *New York Times*, September 6, 1990, p. B1.

30. A. Hearth, "A Bad Year, But the G.M. Plant in North Tarrytown Hangs on," *New York Times*, September 1, 1991, §12WC (Westchester Weekly), p. 1.

31. A. Hearth, "G.M. Plant Is Struggling but Hopeful," *New York Times*, March 10, 1991, §12WC (Westchester Weekly), p. 1.

32. PR Newswire, July 30, 1991, "Power Supplies Cut to Two Companies by New York Power Authority."

Nonetheless, in February 1992 GM announced that the Tarrytown plant would close permanently in 1995.[33] Ironically, disappointing sales of the minivan were blamed for this result. "Viewed in hindsight, the General Motors Corporation's assembly plant in North Tarrytown, N.Y., was probably doomed the moment the company decided in 1987 to manufacture its plastic-bodied minivans there."[34]

This news caused reconsideration of the tax agreement by some commentators:

> The stunning decision by the General Motors Corporation to close its 91-year-old assembly plant here, coming after 15 years of huge subsidies aimed at keeping big business in the region, has provoked bitter criticism of the taxpayer support of corporation and which, if any, industries should qualify.
>
> GM announced February 24 that it would shutter the North Tarrytown plant in 1995, eliminating 3,400 jobs in a region where manufacturing, once dominant, has been in harrowing decline.
>
> . . . .
>
> Many experts say GM's decision primarily reflected its shrinking share of the global automobile market and the high costs of doing business in a region where even generous public incentives cannot give manufacturers a competitive edge.
>
> "The question may be, 'Why are we trying to retain these dying industries?'" said Vincent Tese, president of New York State's Urban Development Corporation and Gov. Mario M. Cuomo's chief economic adviser, in an interview last week.[35]

One year later, in February 1993, a Michigan judge enjoined GM's planned closing of its Willow Run plant in Ypsilanti Township, reasoning that tax benefits the company had received left it responsible to keep the plant in operation.[36] Although the decision did not hold the agreement between the township and the corporation to constitute a contract, it found "promissory estoppel" sufficient to enjoin any transfer of production from Willow Run to another facility. Judge Donald Shelton of the Washtenaw County Circuit Court wrote:

---

33. P. Ingrassia and J. White, "GM Posts Record '91 Loss of $4.45 Billion and Identifies a Dozen Plants for Closing," *Wall Street Journal,* February 25, 1992, p. A3.

34. D. Levin, "Vehicle's Design Doomed Van Plant," *New York Times,* February 26, 1992, p. C1.

35. T. Lueck, "Business Incentives: A High-Priced Letdown," *New York Times,* March 8, 1991, p. 16.

36. Lawyers for the township argued that the company had received more than $1.3 billion in tax abatements from the township and the county since 1975. W. Brown, "Judge Rules GM Can't Close Michigan Plant," *Washington Post,* February 10, 1993, p. C1.

The rigid and technical rules of conventional contract law are designed to provide the framework for a Court to adjudicate the rights of parties in a contractual dispute. As with other generalized principles, these rigid rules sometimes fail us in our attempt to wring justice from a specific dispute between people whose expectations of each other are not fulfilled. Fortunately, our common law has evolved concepts of equity which are designed to allow a Court the flexibility, which is the true hallmark of fairness, to do justice in such situations.

. . . .

The plaintiffs in this case contend that, regardless of whether the statute and application form [for tax abatements] created a contract by their own terms, General Motors, by its statements and conduct in connection with those and other applications, represented that it would provide continuous employment at the Willow Run plant if the government continued to provide tax abatement subsidies.

The issue, in promissory estoppel terms, is whether those representations indeed constitute a promise and whether it is the type of promise that should be enforced by this Court to prevent an injustice.

. . . .

There would be a gross inequity and patent unfairness if General Motors, having lulled the people of the Ypsilanti area into giving up millions of tax dollars which they so desperately need to education their children and provide basic governmental services, is allowed to simply decide that it will desert 4,500 workers and their families because it thinks it can make these same cars a little cheaper somewhere else. Perhaps another judge in another court would not feel moved by that injustice and would labor to find a legal rationalization to allow such conduct. But in this Court it is my responsibility to make that decision. My conscience will not allow this injustice to happen.[37]

GM immediately appealed this ruling. The company also denied that tax benefits to its North Tarrytown plant restricted its ability to move from that jurisdiction. "In response to the threat of a state lawsuit, a GM spokeswoman, Margaret G. Holmes, said GM felt it would win such a suit because, in return for abatements, it had promised to stay in Tarrytown only until 1995."[38] The injunction was lifted by the Michigan Court of Appeals on August 3, 1993, and an appeal was denied by the Michigan Supreme Court one month later.[39]

---

37. *Township of Ypsilanti v. General Motors Corp.*, Michigan Circuit Court No. 92-43075-CK (February 9, 1993), reprinted in full in *State Tax Notes*, March 3, 1993, 93 STN 41-11, Doc. 93-50425.

38. J. Berger, "Incentive Plan Seeks to Save G.M. Plant," *New York Times*, February 24, 1993, p. B1.

39. *Township of Ypsilanti v. General Motors Corp.*, 201 Mich. App. 128, 506 N.W.2d 556 (1993), *leave to appeal denied*, 443 Mich. 879, 509 N.W.2d 152 (1993).

Questions

1. How did the assessment dispute fit within the intermingled political, social, economic, and legal aspects of these negotiations? Does this study imply that industrial valuation disputes are too complex to be handled as property tax matters? Are they too political to be addressed by the courts?

2. When, if ever, should a taxpayer be able to set the level of its future assessments without regard to changes in market value? Would GM have been able to achieve this through litigation alone, however successful? What other items on its "laundry list" could it have obtained through its legal action?

3. What guidance do *A & P* and *Xerox* provide to parties contemplating a challenge to the assessment of "specialty" structures? What guidelines could a court provide that would assist in these disputes?

4. Would anything in this narrative indicate to you that at the time of the disputed assessments New York law called for taxation of all property at a uniform percentage of full market value? Would anything indicate that the tax was based on market value at all?

5. The importance of the property to local governments is based on its status as an independent revenue source. What diminished that independence in this case? Was this diminution appropriate, given that most residents of North Tarrytown and the neighboring villages were not GM employees? Had the plant shut down, which social and economic costs would have been borne by the taxing jurisdictions, and which by the state?

6. Is any purpose served by having two overlapping tax districts, such as North Tarrytown and Mt. Pleasant, simultaneously attempting independent appraisals of the same complex industrial property?

7. Would the state equalization rate in itself reveal anything about the value of the GM plant? The company argued that a declining equalization rate for the town indicated that its property suffered an increase in its effective valuation. Is this necessarily so? What additional information would be required to determine whether this was so?

6 SPECIAL PROBLEMS IN THE INCOME APPROACH

Introduction

Property purchased for its income-producing potential, such as commercial office buildings, will command a price based in large part on the buyer's estimate of future rent levels. This is why the New York court stated in *People ex rel. Parklin Operating Corp. v. Miller*, 287 N.Y. 126, 129–130, 38 N.E.2d 465 (1941):

> Evidence of income derived, or which can be derived from real property may at times constitute more persuasive evidence of the price at which the income-producing property can be sold in ordinary circumstances than evidence of actual sales of more or less similar property under more or less similar conditions, for we know that in ordinary circumstances investors will pay for income-producing property a price measured in large part by the amount and certainty of the income which can be obtained from such property.

Even where the income capitalization approach is agreed to be appropriate, it can present complex computational challenges. The income to be capitalized for purposes of real property taxation should be the return on real property itself, excluding the amount attributable to business enterprise value or managerial effort. The investment return to be capitalized must be net of fixed costs, operating expenses, and vacancy allowances. Small differences in the choice of a capitalization rate can have a large effect on the ultimate value figure.[1]

The most important legal issues concerning the income method deal with problems in defining the relevant property income. These problems reflect uncertainties in the legal definition of the property to be taxed. The first set of cases in this chapter considers the valuation of property subject to a long-term lease calling for rents that have fallen below full current market levels. This situation does not present a court with a computational challenge, but with a legal one: a choice between a definition of taxable property that is limited to the landlord's interest, and thus undeniably affected by the unfavorable lease, or a definition that encompasses both the landlord's interest and the tenant's interest. A new owner who purchased both of these interests together would hold the property free of any lease, and therefore free of the reduction in value caused by the unfavorable rental terms.

---

1. On the technical aspects of income analysis and capitalization, see International Association of Assessing Officers, *Property Appraisal and Assessment Administration* (1990), Chapters 11 and 12.

Many other problems concerning the valuation of property subject to divided legal interests follow the basic pattern of the long-term lease cases. The second section of this chapter considers disputes in which owners suffered restrictions on their potential income from taxable property as a result of voluntary agreements conveying part of their interest in the property to other parties. The *Twin Lakes* case is a dramatic example of the problematic results of a simple, straightforward, and perhaps simplistic, approach to this issue. In the later *Sahalee* case, the same court met a similar situation with a long and complex opinion that provided ample opportunity for the facts and circumstances of the case to prevent consideration of the theoretical issue dealt with so succinctly in *Twin Lakes*.

The final section of this chapter considers a special variation on the long-term lease problem: the assessment of government-subsidized housing subject to restrictions on the income that can be charged to low-income tenants. On the one hand, this can be seen as a more sympathetic case for a reduction in valuation, as the income restrictions are the result of government action and not a private agreement. At the same time, it is a less compelling case in that the investors responsible for the tax voluntarily agreed to below-market rent levels in exchange for generous income tax advantages.

Although these cases explore only a small portion of the legal issues concerning the income approach to valuation, they illustrate the problems in the definition of taxable property raised by this method.

Valuation of Property Subject to a Long-Term Lease

The first set of cases in this chapter deals with property subject to a long-term lease unfavorable to the landlord. If the "property" subject to tax is deemed to encompass both the landlord's and tenant's interests, the amount by which the landlord's interest is reduced is equal to the amount by which the tenant's interest is enhanced: the present value of the difference between fair market rent (sometimes called "economic" rent[2]) and the rent required by the lease (sometimes called "contract" rent) over the remaining term of the rental agreement.   The computational question therefore depends on a prior determination of the composition of the "property" to be taxed. If it includes only the landlord's interest, the fair market value is affected by the long-term lease, although there may be a question of whether the lease was an arm's-length agreement. If the property to be valued includes both the tenant's and landlord's interests, its fair market value is not affected by the lease.

---

2.   This nomenclature is common in valuation decisions but causes some confusion because it is unrelated to "economic rent" as that term is used in economic literature. For example, *The MIT Dictionary of Modern Economics* (D. Pearce, ed., 4th ed. [1992]) defines "economic rent" as "A payment to a factor in excess of what is necessary to keep it to its present employment."

IN THE MATTER OF MERRICK HOLDING CORP. V. BOARD OF ASSESSORS
45 N.Y.2d 538, 382 N.E.2d 1341, 410 N.Y.S.2d 565
Court of Appeals of New York, 1978

FUCHSBERG, Judge.

Merrick Holding Corp., the owner of land improved by a 29-store shopping center complex in Nassau County, brought this consolidated certiorari proceeding to review the amount at which the property was assessed for the 1968–1975 tax years. The valuation had been arrived at by the income capitalization method. However, instead of accepting actual rental income as a basis for its computations, the county's board of assessors first increased it by amounts, termed "leasehold bonuses," which reflected the difference between the rentals payable to Merrick under long-term leases with three major tenants and the appreciably higher market rental value of the leased spaces. The dispute between the parties focused on the validity of these add-ons.

Special Term, though decreeing some reductions on the basis of other issues not here relevant, upheld the application of the leasehold bonuses and entered judgment accordingly. But the Appellate Division, pointing out that the county's appraiser had conceded that the three leases "were 'not necessarily improvident when they were made'" and taking the view that, without proof of improvidence, it was "improper to apply the leasehold bonus principle to a selected portion of leases in a shopping center in the absence of (undefined) special circumstances," reversed on the law and remanded for a new determination. On remand, Special Term then granted the taxpayer's motion for summary judgment, eliminated the add-ons and entered a new judgment reducing the assessment correspondingly. On the county's appeal to us, we now conclude that the order of the Appellate Division should, in turn, be reversed and the matter remitted for review of the facts. Our reasons follow.

The command of section 306 of the Real Property Tax Law that all property be assessed at full value does not pronounce an inelastic approach to valuation. Nor does the legislative directive specify a particular method for establishing value. And courts, being under no compunction to do so, have not confined assessors to any one course. To ensure that the existence of varied and multifaceted patterns of land use and ownership does not frustrate the design that each contribute equitably to the public fisc, courts have upheld any fair and nondiscriminatory method that appears most likely to achieve that end.

Thus, though commonly the most accurate standard is provided by the sales prices of comparable properties located within the same or similar competitive area in which a parcel being assessed is located, in the absence of sufficiently reliable market data, alternative methods, such as income capitalization or, where necessary, reproduction cost, may be employed. Not surprisingly, as to income producing property, income capitalization has been the preferred mode.

Consequently, the board's employment of income capitalization rather than cost or market in the present case was not exceptional (see, generally, Graham, "Market Valuation of a Regional Shopping Center," 32 Appraisal J. 589). But the appropriateness of this method does not take away from the reality that its application, calling as it does for the exercise of judgment by the appraiser, furnishes, at best, no more than an estimate of the present worth of the benefits to be reaped from the property at issue (1 Bonbright, *Valuation of Property*, p. 218). The goal at all times remains full value. To that end, assessors may devise reasonable methods that assure that the income they accept as the basis for capitalization is as close a reflection of true value as possible.

Our recent holding in *G.R.F., Inc. v. Board of Assessors of County of Nassau*, 41 N.Y.2d 512,.393 N.Y.S.2d 965, 362 N.E.2d 597, reflects this flexible approach to problems of valuation. Having found that the circumstances warranted no hard and fast choice between a strict income capitalization approach and one based on cost of reproduction, we there emphasized that "[p]ragmatism . . . requires adjustment when the economic realities prevent placing the properties in neat logical valuation boxes" (*G.R.F., Inc. v. Board of Assessors of County of Nassau*, 41 N.Y.2d 512, 515, 393 N.Y.S.2d 965, 968, 362 N.E.2d 597, 599, *supra*).

In short, categorization must yield to more exact means of arriving at value. Since other factors may tend to qualify the reliability of actual income as a sole measure of value, the per se rule articulated by the Appellate Division, which would interdict them, must be rejected. For, though realized income will often turn out to be the surest indicator of full value, when fair market rents exceed rental income the latter may, in whole or in part, be made to defer to more precise means of fixing a base on which to compute capitalization (see *Encyclopedia of Real Estate Appraising* [Friedman ed., 1968], pp. 40–41; 1 Bonbright, *Valuation of Property*, p. 229; see Babcock, *The Valuation of Real Estate*, pp. 384–385).

So, if examination discloses that rent has been arbitrarily set without regard to the market rental value whether through self-dealing, as, for example, where a landlord and tenant are business affiliates or property is owner-occupied (*Woolworth Co. v. Commission of Taxation*, 26 A.D.2d 759, 272 N.Y.S.2d 257), or, certainly, where there is any indication of collusion, the rent arrangement will be of little, if any guidance to sound appraisal.

On the other hand, in arriving at their valuations, assessors may always consider below market rents that result from arm's length bargaining carried out in good faith. Courts recognize, however, that reliance on contract rents, particularly those involving property subject to below market long-term leases, may yield distorted valuations and that an assessor, therefore, may apply compensatory measures calculated to adjust such income figures to a point at which they become reliable indicators of full value. It was permissible, therefore, for the board of assessors here to try to accomplish that by tempering its use of rental income with leasehold bonuses in amounts representing the differential between the actual rent and the market rent for each of the three stores in question.

In doing so, the board fulfilled its obligation to assess Merrick's shopping center at full value undiminished by the leases by which the property was burdened. Put another way, all the interests in the property save those assessed separately, such as easements, were to be treated conceptually, for real estate tax purposes, as a single "bundle of rights" (*Encyclopedia of Real Estate Appraising* [Friedman ed., 1968], p. 133). Presumably, to the extent that any of the center's leases called for below market rents, that fact would be reflected in a lower value of the landlord's interest and a correspondingly higher value of the tenants' interests (1 Bonbright, *Valuation of Property*, pp. 495–497). The leasehold bonuses added by the county were designed to take into account the value deriving from the tenants' interests—a component of full value that it found did not emerge from actual income figures supplied by the landlord. The utilization of a single assessment encompassing both interests, with the tax payable entirely by the landlord, is consonant with this underlying unitary concept of value.

The net result is that a landlord, despite low income occasioned by below market leases, nevertheless remains obligated to pay taxes on the market value of the property taken as a whole. At first blush, this may appear to penalize the unsuccessful entrepreneur for a lack of business acumen. But it must always be remembered that an underlying aim of valuation is to assure that, in providing for public needs, the share reasonably to be borne by a particular property owner is based on an equitable proportioning of the fair value of his property vis-à-vis the fair value of all other taxable properties in the same tax jurisdiction. Otherwise, the landlord who fails to realize the fair potential of his property would, in effect, shift part of his tax burden to the shoulders of his fellow taxpayers.

We recognize that when it developed its shopping area in 1952 and 1953, Merrick may have been required to grant bargain leases to induce nationally known tenants to locate in its center in the expectation that higher rents could be exacted from smaller stores eager to profit from the greater number of patrons the "flagship" stores would draw (see *G.R.F., Inc. v. Board of Assessors of County of Nassau, supra*). Each of the three key tenants— Food Fair, F. W. Woolworth and National Shoes—is a retail chain organization commanding ready recognition from members of the consuming public. Their leases (and that of one other tenant), in the aggregate, embrace fully 45% of the desirable street level shopping center store area. Besides providing for low rents, the leases negotiated between the three tenants and Merrick lacked escalation clauses affording meaningful protection to the landlord against tax increases or other contingencies. It is not surprising then that the proof showed that during the tax periods in question each of these tenants were paying, for other comparable space in the same county a prevailing price nearly twice as much.

The fact remains that the advantageous leases were yielded to the three tenants with the landlord's eyes open and no doubt directed towards its own short or long-range profit. The county was not a party to these plans; nor was it, or is it, a coentrepreneur who was required to share in Merrick's good or bad fortune. Clearly, the county tax authorities need not depend for valuation purposes on the uncertain results of managerial banes or boons.

For all these reasons it cannot be said that the board's use of leasehold bonuses was inappropriate. Of course, in arriving at the value of the entire property, if Merrick's leases with its lesser tenants were at above market rents these should be offset against the below market rentals received from the three flagship tenants. In that connection, in remitting for review of the facts we note that, though the record contains proof that the rentals paid by Merrick's numerous lesser tenants were not below market, there is no finding as to whether these exceed market and, if so, the extent to which such excess counterbalanced the below market stream of income that flowed from the three major leases to which the bonuses were applied.

Accordingly, the judgment appealed from and the order brought up for review should be reversed and the matter remitted to the Appellate Division for further proceedings as provided by CPLR 5613.

JASEN, GABRIELLI, JONES, WACHTLER and COOKE, JJ., concur with FUCHSBERG, J.

BREITEL, C. J., concurs in result and so much of the opinion as states the rule that the county is entitled to assess the full value of the property regardless of whether the property is burdened by disadvantageous leases.

Judgment appealed from and order of the Appellate Division brought up for review reversed, with costs, and the matter remitted to the Appellate Division, Second Department, for further proceedings in accordance with the opinion herein.

DARCEL, INC. v. CITY OF MANITOWOC BOARD OF REVIEW
137 Wis.2d 623, 405 N.W.2d 344
Supreme Court of Wisconsin, 1987

STEINMETZ, Justice.

This is a review of a decision of the court of appeals affirming the order of the trial court. The question before the court is whether the City of Manitowoc Board of Appeals (the board) erred by affirming a property tax assessment based on "market" rental income when there was a recent arms-length sale of the property from which to determine fair market value. We conclude that an arms-length sale price is the best indicator to determine fair market value for property tax purposes and an approach that considers factors extrinsic to the arms-length sale is not statutorily correct and therefore in error as a matter of law.

All the stock of Darcel, Inc. was sold on August 10, 1983, for $4,100,000. The only asset of Darcel, Inc. was the Mid-Cities Mall. On January 1, 1984, the city of Manitowoc assessed the fair market value of the mall at $5,231,000 for the 1984 tax year. This assessment was based in part on what the assessor determined to be the fair market value of the store rental property. According to the city assessor, the market value was much greater than contract value of many of the leases because certain leases were long-term leases entered into in 1968 at the fair market value at that time.

Darcel, Inc. (the new owners) filed a written objection to the assessment pursuant to sec. 70.47(7), Stats., following which the Board of Review convened, took evidence, and sustained the assessor's estimates by a vote of four to three. Darcel then petitioned the Manitowoc county circuit court for a writ of certiorari. The writ was granted by the Honorable Fred H. Hazelwood, who remanded the case to the board for further consideration. Judge Hazelwood held that the board ignored the competent evidence of an arms-length sale, and the board's conclusion was not supported by any evidence in the record.

The board appealed the trial court's decision to the court of appeals which affirmed the trial court. The court of appeals, after determining that the board would be in error as a matter of law if it considered extrinsic factors in the presence of an arms-length sale, determined that the sale of the Mid-Cities Mall was indeed an arms-length transaction. *Darcel,* 128 Wis.2d at 214, 381 N.W.2d 575. The board petitioned for review of that decision to this court.

. . . .

The board argues that, because the long-term leases on this property were several dollars per square foot below the "going rate" for mall rental space in similar malls, the recent sale price was not the "full value which could *ordinarily* be obtained therefor at private sale."[2] (Emphasis added.) The board contends that, although the buyer

_____

2. Section 70.32(1), Stats., states: "*Real estate, how valued.* (1) Real property shall be valued by the assessor in the manner specified in the Wisconsin property assessment manual provided under s. 73.03(2a) from actual view or from the best information that the assessor can practicably obtain, at the full value which could ordinarily be obtained therefor at private sale. In determining the value the assessor shall consider, as to each piece, its advantage or disadvantage of location, quality of soil, quantity of standing timber, water privileges, mines, minerals, quarries, or other valuable deposits known to be available therein, and their value; but the fact that the extent and value of minerals

purchased all the rights the seller possessed to sell in an arms-length transaction, the leaseholder owned valuable rights that were not included in the sale price. Some long-term leases were generating only $1.09 per square foot rent while other space inside the mall and in other malls generated between $6 to $10 per square foot. Indeed, one long-term tenant renting space for $1.09 per square foot was subletting the space for $5.75 a square foot. Thus, the presence of the long-term leases artificially lowered the sale price to less than "full value." The board asserts the only way the assessor could determine "full value" was to use the income approach and use a fair market rent to determine property value.[3] While the board admits that the sales transaction was arms-length, it insists that not all of the "bundle of rights" that make up the property were transferred to the new owners because some of the value of the rights was retained by the long-term tenants. However, these were rights of the tenants, not the seller-owner.

The mall owners argue that they did buy all the "bundle of rights" that comprised the property. They purchased the land the buildings stood on, the physical plant, the right to the rental income through the leases, and the reversions when the leases expired. Since the mall owners had to bear the burden of honoring the leases that did not generate market rent, they must have purchased all the contractual rights accompanying such a lease.

It is immaterial that the lease was a detriment to the property; it was transferred to the new mall owners, and its value was reflected in the sales price of the property. Thus, the sale was an arms-length transaction and clearly the best evidence of the "full value" of the property.

Fair market value or full value of property is consistently defined as: "[T]he amount it will sell for upon arms-length negotiation in the open market, between an owner willing but not obliged to sell, and a buyer willing but not obliged to buy." *State ex rel. Mitchell Aero*, 74 Wis.2d at 277, 246 N.W.2d 521.

The Property Assessment Manual for Wisconsin Assessors, Vol. I, page 7-3 (Revised 12/82) states the conditions necessary for a sale to be considered a "market value" transaction:

"1. It must have been exposed to the open market for a period of time typical of the turnover time for the type of property involved.

"2. It presumes that both buyer and seller are knowledgeable about the real estate market.

"3. It presumes buyer and seller are knowledgeable about the uses, present and potential, of the property.

"4. It requires a willing buyer and a willing seller, with neither party compelled to act.

---

or other valuable deposits in any parcel of land are unascertained shall not preclude the assessor from affixing to such parcel the value which could ordinarily be obtained therefor at private sale . . . ."

3. The Property Assessment Manual for Wisconsin Assessors, Vol. I, at 7–19, 19–20 (Revised 12/82) describes the income approach to valuation as: "The income approach is the conversion of anticipated future benefits (income) into an estimate of the present worth of a property. This process is called capitalization. When there is no sale of the subject and no comparable sales are available the income approach can be used along with other information to make an assessment."

"5. Payment for the property is in cash, or typical of normal financing and payment arrangements prevalent in the market for the type of property involved."

Although the board contested the satisfaction of these conditions in the lower courts, it concedes here that the sale of the Mid-Cities Mall was an arms-length transaction, at least as to the rights sold in that transaction. This court has previously held that it is error for an assessor to use other means to assess the value of property in the presence of an arms-length sale. *State ex rel. Geipel v. Milwaukee*, 68 Wis.2d 726, 737, 229 N.W.2d 585 (1975). However, this assessor did have a duty to determine if the sale was at arms-length and properly investigated further. While his investigation uncovered some "red flags" that could have indicated an other-than-arms-length sale, these "red flags" were later explained to the satisfaction of the circuit court, and did not appear to be the basis of the board's findings.[4]

The mere claim of an arms-length sale should not foreclose the assessor from further investigation to determine the nature of the sale. Only through investigation and comparison can an assessor determine if the sale is truly at arms-length. From the record it appears that the Manitowoc city assessor entered his comparative study of shopping malls with just such an investigation in mind. However, such an investigation should only be given credence if it produces the "best information" possible, and better information than a facially arms-length sale. Because of the nature of shopping malls and like property that are unique in nature, a sale that meets the arms-length qualifications stated previously will represent the full value of the property. Any comparative information about other shopping malls would be, at best, speculative, and at worst, totally subjective.[6] Information that would suggest that the mall was not being used to the highest and best use speculates about the ability of the owners to rent the property. While this may not be true of all property with leases, the sale price should be conclusive of market price unless there is evidence that the leases themselves were not entered into at arms-length and in good faith. Sale-leaseback situations, for instance, may be undertaken with terms to avoid property tax and might not be entered at arms-length.

Since the board initially asserts that not all the property rights were transferred, it is necessary to determine what those property rights were before the sale. First, the prior owner had fee simple of all the actual real estate, including the mall area and parking areas. It is clear that the areas in fee simple were purchased in an arms-length sale.

---

4. At the board and at the lower court, the assessor challenged the arms-length character of the sale by citing numerous outstanding bills the prior owner had, that the prior owner was being pursued by creditors for these bills, and that the property was soon to be subject to foreclosure. The circuit court found that since the five factors stated in the Assessor's Manual were met, any suspicion of an other-than-arms-length sale was overcome.

6. Prior to 1980, the Mid-Cities Mall's assessed value was $2,895,600. On January 1, 1980, as part of a reassessment of the whole city, the mall was reassessed by an outside assessment contractor at $5,231,900. The 1980 assessment was not challenged by the prior owners of the mall and remained the same until the 1984 assessment. The city assessor's actual comparative results were higher than this figure by nearly $500,000; he reduced them as "close enough" to the prior assessed value.

These facts suggest that the city assessor was not making a totally independent valuation of the property but striving to support someone else's prior high assessment.

Second, the prior owner had leased certain areas of the property. By doing so, the right of occupation of the leasehold was contracted away for a right to a certain amount of rent. In addition, the prior owner retained the reversion of the leasehold estate. It is clear that the new owner received: 1) the same right to collect rent that the prior owner had retained as a result of entering the lease agreements, and 2) the reversion of the leasehold estate. This, too, was part of an arms-length transaction.

Third, all other encumbrances (such as easements) that might have been present on the property were transferred. These are not at issue in the present action.

From this analysis, it is clear that all of the "bundle of rights" that made up the property were transferred in this sale. The new owners received exactly those rights possessed by the former owners.

The board's complaint, however, is that the prior owners did not own the "full value" of the tenant's leasehold. By operation of the rental marketplace, like the marketplace for real estate itself, the value of the tenant's leasehold has increased independent of the contract itself. This increased value is evidenced by the difference between the rent specified by the long-term lease and "market" rental. Since the prior owners never "owned" this increased value, the prior owners could not transfer this value to the new owners, even though all the rights that made up the property were transferred. Although the rights themselves were transferred, some of the value of the rights were not transferred. Therefore, the argument is the price paid by the new owners to the prior owners did not reflect the true value of all the rights in the property.

The city assessor based his conclusion that not all the rights were being sold or that not all the value was being conveyed on his survey of eleven shopping malls over the state of Wisconsin and their sales prices in recent years. From this, the assessor derived a weighted average rental value per square foot. This, he concluded, was the "market price" of mall rental space that could be applied to the Mid-Cities Mall.

We find this analysis not acceptable. The assessor's "value" theory is entirely dependent on what comparable market rates are for rent. However, what the parties contracted for was a leasehold, not just a month-to-month tenancy, but a long-term lease with terms and conditions that made it unique when compared to other kinds of leases. When an assessor judges the value of real estate without a recent sale, he often looks at "comparable sales"—"properties that are similar to the subject property in age, condition, use, type of construction, location, number of stories, and physical features. The more similar the sold property is to the subject, the more valid is the sale price as an indicator of the value of the subject property."

When an assessor is assessing the value of leaseholds, he is not justified in simply comparing the "bottom line," that is, what is the rent charged on the leases. If the assessor wishes to establish comparable leaseholds, he must examine other elements about the lease: the location of the rental property within a mall, whether the lease was for an "anchor" store or for a smaller store within the mall, the type and age of the mall that the leasehold is in, relative vacancies in the malls, and the length and terms of the lease that created the leasehold. If the assessor finds that the rental rate per square foot is not substantially lower than other leases that were contracted in the same historical period, his inquiry is at an end. If the lease price per square foot is historically justified, the sale price of the real estate is the best information about full value of the property for tax purposes.

However, there is no evidence whatsoever that the long-term leases in the Mid-Cities Mall were not entered into at arms-length or were below market value for long-term leases of that type. The city attorney, appearing for the board, admitted at oral argument that there was no evidence that the long-term leases were not entered into at arms-length or were below market value at the time of their inception. The leases in the Mid-Cities Mall that are allegedly below market leases were entered into in 1968 for a period of fifteen years with options. If the leases were entered into at arms-length when drafted, sale of the leases represented the full value of the leasehold. Since both the full value of the leasehold interests and the prior owner's interests were sold to the new owners of the Mid-Cities Mall, all the interests in the property were transferred. The price for these interests was the price paid at the arms-length sale, $4,100,000. That price represents the best information about the full market value of the property because it is the full market value of the property.[9]

If an encumbrance on the subject land would equally subject all potential buyers to the same decreased use or rent of the property, and the encumbrance was entered into at arms-length for a fair market price at the time it was entered, it should be considered to lower the full market price of the property. This means that any current market value of the encumbrance should not be allowed to distinguish an otherwise arms-length sale of the property itself, and the presence of such an encumbrance should be considered when assessing the full market value of the encumbered land.

We are not convinced by the precedent that the board cites from other jurisdictions that this approach is incorrect.[10] In most of the cases cited, the courts did not have the advantage of considering an otherwise arms-length sale when considering the assessment. In these cases, the taxpayer, by introducing evidence of lower-than-market rents, attempted to distinguish the estimate of true market value, based on market rents rather than contract rents. In other words, the taxpayer attempted to supplant one estimate

---

9. The new owners willingly admit an additional $30,000 of improvements to the property since the date of the sale and do not contest inclusion of the new improvements in the eventual assessment. Improvements that have taken place after the recent arms-length sale of the property would have to be assessed and the value of those improvements added to the arms-length sale price.

10. *Caldwell v. Department of Revenue,* 122 Ariz. 519, 596 P.2d 45 (1979); *Clayton v. County of Los Angeles,* 26 Cal.App. 390, 102 Cal.Rptr. 687 (1972); *Martin v. Liberty County Bd. of Tax Assessors,* 152 Ga.App. 340, 262 S.E.2d 609 (1979); *Springfield Marine Bank v. Property Tax Appeal Bd.,* 44 Ill.2d 428, 256 N.E.2d 334 (1970); *Oberstein v. Adair County Bd. of Review,* 318 N.W.2d 817 (Ia. App. 1982); *Donovan v. City of Haverhill,* 247 Mass. 69, 141 N.E. 564 (1923); *Crossroads Center, Inc. v. Commission of Taxation,* 286 Minn. 440, 176 N.W.2d 530 (1970); *Demoulas v. Town of Salem,* 116 N.H. 775, 367 A.2d 588 (1976); *Parkview Village Association v. Collingswood,* 62 N.J. 21, 297 A.2d 842 (1972); *People ex rel. Gale v. Tax Commission,* 17 A.D.2d 225, 233 N.Y.S.2d 501 (1962); *In Re Property of Pine Raleigh Corp.,* 258 N.C. 398, 128 S.E.2d 855 (1963); *Wynwood Apartments v. Board of Review of Cuyahoga County,* 59 Ohio St.2d 34, 391 N.E.2d 346 (1979); *Swan Lake Moulding Company v. Department of Revenue,* 257 Or. 622, 480 P.2d 713 (1971); *Kargman v. Jacobs,* 113 R.I. 696, 325 A.2d 543 (1974); *Yadco, Inc. v. Yankton County,* 89 S.D. 651, 237 N.W.2d 665 (1975); *Rowland v. City of Tyler,* 5 S.W.2d 756 (Tex. Com. App. 1928); *Board of Supervisors of Fairfax County v. Nassif,* 223 Va. 400, 290 S.E.2d 822 (1982).

We note that *C.A.F. Inv. Co. v. Tp. of Saginaw,* 410 Mich. 428, 302 N.W.2d 164 (1981), supports the use of actual rental income and rejects any reference to potential income when estimating the fair market value of the property. The Michigan court concluded that such a rule was valid even in the absence of a recent arms-length sale of the property.

with another estimate. In the current case, the assessor attempted to supplant the actual arms-length sale price with an estimate based on non-comparable property. While the principles involved may be the same, the injustice of taxing the current market value of the leasehold is most clearly demonstrated when a sale has occurred.

In two cases cited a recent sale had occurred. In *Pepsi-Cola Bottling Co. v. Bd. of Assessors*, 397 Mass. 447, 491 N.E.2d 1071 (1986), Pepsi had built the original building in 1957 and sold it under a "lease-back" arrangement. Under the terms of this leaseback, Pepsi was to pay the "owner" of the property $1.44 per square foot during the duration of the long-term lease period, but Pepsi retained the option to renew the lease at $0.63 per square foot. Additionally, Pepsi was to pay all property taxes and assessments, all fire and liability insurance premiums, all utility charges, ordinary and structural repairs and maintenance. Pepsi leased and occupied the entire property and improvements.

The regular term of the lease expired in December, 1982, and Pepsi exercised its option and began paying $0.63 per square foot rent. In February, 1983, the property was sold in an otherwise arms-length transaction for $310,000. The assessment board found comparable properties under lease for $2.80 to $3 and applied the $2.80 rate to the Pepsi property.

While the *Pepsi* court approved using market rates because the tenant's rights were not "valued" in the sale, the *Pepsi* sale can be distinguished from the sale of the Mid-Cities Mall and the leases therein. In *Pepsi*, whether the original lease was at arms-length is questionable because of the sale-leaseback agreement. Clearly, even if the market rate of leases were $1.44 per square foot, no reasonable arms-length lease agreement would provide for an additional cut in rent after more than two decades. In addition, since Pepsi was responsible for the property taxes instead of the owner, it was in Pepsi's best interest to drive the value of the property as low as possible. Moreover, Pepsi as lessee had so many of the duties of an owner it was almost indistinguishable from an owner. Under the terms of the lease, the only thing the eventual owner could do was collect rent and take the eventual reversion.

The leases in Mid-Cities Mall, however, are conceded by the board to be arms-length leases of a small portion of the mall undertaken with terms, conditions, and rents similar to leases in many other malls at the time they were signed.

In the second case, *People v. Tax Commission of City of New York*, 17 A.D.2d 225, 233 N.Y.S.2d 501 (1962), the New York court simply made a policy choice. The lease was entered into during the depression for twenty-one years with a renewal for an additional twenty-one years at the same rate. The property was sold, while still under the lease, for $225,000 in 1954. The taxing authority fixed the value at $365,000. The court recognized that:

> "Of course, an outstanding bona fide lease and the rental income established thereby are matters to be considered in determining 'the full value' of the whole property, land and improvements. Value arrived at by capitalization of the fair rental value is, in ordinary cases, the surest guide to a sound appraisal. In that connection, the actual rent realized is significant as an important factor in determining what the fair rental value is. But when there is evidence that factors such as long-term leases made under distress or boom conditions affect the actual rent, the weight to be given to the actual rent must be discounted accordingly."
> *Id.* at 230, 233 N.Y.S.2d at 507. (Citations omitted.)

Fluctuating economic conditions are too uncertain and varying in time to determine if a lease was made in a "boom" or "bust" era or to form a basis for passing judgment on the business decisions of persons who are not available to defend those decisions. The value in the presence of long-term leaseholders may be difficult to set since they serve as magnet stores for all other stores in the mall. Also, such long-term leaseholders may give stability to a mall which may or may not be financially attractive depending on continually changing economic circumstances. When agreed to, the square footage charges may very well have been economically attractive for the mall owner and tenant. As one of the board members commented, there was a good possibility that if the original builders of the Mid-Cities Mall had not entered the long-term leases under the terms they did, the mall itself might never have begun construction or started as a business entity. Then the city never would have had the mall within its tax base. Should the board or this court be allowed to declare the terms of that lease a "bad business decision" simply because overall inflation caused rents to rise in a fashion no one could predict? We reject the invitation of the New York court to require businesspersons to be equipped with precognition; we refuse to second guess their business judgments, as long as such judgments were entered into at arms-length.

The Wisconsin Constitution requires in Article VIII, sec. 1: "The rule of taxation shall be uniform . . . ." If the city taxes property on the basis of the income the assessor theorizes the property might produce rather than the actual rent the property does produce, the principle of uniform taxation would be violated. Other landowners would be taxed on the basis of what their property will sell for, but the landowner with long-term leases will be taxed on what the assessor believes the land might produce, not what the land will sell for in an arms-length transaction.

We do not hold that actual rents will always control an estimate of property value; however, we hold that actual rents of arms-length leases must be considered as a factor in determining market value. Primarily we hold that a recent arms-length sale of the property is the "best information" to arrive at the full tax assessment value of that property, and capitalization of so-called "market" rent is not the best evidence of value in the presence of such a sale. As the board did not consider the "best information" in arriving at its valuation of the Mid-Cities Mall, we affirm the decision of the court of appeals.

The decision of the court of appeals is affirmed.

BABLITCH, Justice (dissenting).

Seventeen states that have considered the issue presented here, see Majority Opinion p. 349 n. 10, including California, New York, Minnesota and Illinois, disagree with the conclusion reached by the majority of this court. Each of those courts support the proposition that fair market rents rather than contract rents are to be used in determining fair market value of income producing properties for tax assessment purposes. The majority cites only one other state which agrees with its conclusion. My research reveals no other. The overwhelming authority disagrees with the majority for good reason.

If the long term leases on this property provided for fair market rents, the property is undisputably worth $5.2 million. However, the leases provided woefully inadequate rents, and therefore the selling price was $1.1 million less than the full value. Because the majority concludes that the full value of the property for purposes of taxation is $4.1 million, $1.1 million worth of otherwise taxable property is removed from the property tax rolls. The property taxes that would have been paid on that additional $1.1 million must now be borne by all other property taxpayers in the City of Manitowoc. The majority says the law compels this result. I think not.

The majority opinion is in error in three respects: 1) it is contrary to the requirement of sec. 70.32(1), Stats., that value be determined at the full value which could ordinarily be obtained at private sale; 2) it is contrary to the requirement of the Wisconsin Property Assessment Manual for Wisconsin Assessors which provides that assessors are to value all rights in the real estate regardless of whether the property owner possesses the entire bundle of rights; and 3) it is contrary to the objective of uniformity and consistency in taxation. Accordingly, I dissent.

I will address each of these errors in turn.

I.

Section 70.32(1), Stats., provides in part that real property must be assessed "at the full value which could *ordinarily* be obtained therefor at private sale." (Emphasis added.) Thus, the law recognizes that there are circumstances in which an arms length selling price will not control the determination of full value. Such is the case here. This was far from an "ordinary" sale. Long-term leases provided for rents that were substantially lower than fair market rents. Stores at a comparable competing shopping center across the street were paying rents ranging from $7.50 to $10.00 per square foot. By contrast, the two largest tenants in this property were only paying $1.09 per square foot under leases negotiated in 1968, and which would not terminate until approximately the year 2000. The majority's conclusion necessarily implies that this price was the full value which could "ordinarily" be obtained. Rather than being "ordinary," I assume that this set of circumstances in which contract rents are substantially lower than fair market rents is extraordinary. The "ordinary" sale price would ordinarily reflect that contract rents are substantially equivalent to fair market rents. Because these contract rents are so substantially different from fair market rents, the selling price here is not that which could "ordinarily" be obtained. Thus, we must look further to determine the fair market value. The answer lies in sec. 70.32(1) and the Wisconsin Property Assessment Manual for Wisconsin Assessors.

II.

Section 70.32(1), Stats., provides that property shall be assessed "in the manner specified in the Wisconsin property assessment manual . . . ." The Wisconsin Property Assessment Manual for Wisconsin Assessors (the Manual) is prepared by the Wisconsin Department of Revenue. It provides that "even though a property owner may not possess the entire bundle of rights, the value that is being sought is market value . . . includes all rights and privileges." Wisconsin Assessment Manual for Wisconsin Assessors, 7-2, Dec. 1985. Here, Darcel could not purchase all rights. Darcel was obligated to honor the long-term leases. The lessees, despite the sale, maintained their rights to lease the stores at contract rents that were substantially lower than fair market rents. The value of those rights was presumably $1.1 million, the difference between the value of the property if leased at fair market rent ($5.2 million) and the actual sale price ($4.1 million).

The statute directs that property be assessed according to the Manual. The Manual requires that assessment include the full value of all the rights (referred to as "the bundle of rights") including leasehold interests. The majority, by finding that the full value was the selling price of $4.1 million fails to take into account in any respect the value of the leasehold interest. The $1.1 million dollars worth of property is therefore off the tax rolls. This is not only contrary to Wisconsin law, it is contrary to the conclusion of 17 other states that have decided this issue.

Therefore, I conclude that the statutes as well as the Manual support the finding of the Manitowoc Board of Review that the full value of this property for tax assessment purposes is $5.2 million. This conclusion is further supported by a longstanding principle: the principle of uniformity and consistency in taxation.

III.

The Wisconsin Constitution, article VIII, sec. 1, provides that "[t]he rule of taxation shall be uniform . . . ." This principle has been part of the Wisconsin Constitution since 1848. Section 73.03, Stats., directs the Wisconsin Department of Revenue to provide "more nearly uniform and more consistent assessments of property at the local level."

The Georgia court of appeals succinctly and correctly addressed this concern:

"If tax assessments on the same property were to fluctuate according to the varying terms of a lease, the computation of ad valorem taxes on the basis of such assessments would result in a tax penalty for one who, through business acumen or fortuity, succeeds in leasing his property for an amount in excess of its 'fair market value' and a tax windfall to one who, through bad business judgment, leases far below his property's 'fair market value.' Such a method of evaluation would hardly produce assessments which were 'fairly and justly equalized' as between taxpayers." *Martin v. Liberty Cty. Bd. of Tax Assessors*, 152 Ga.App. 340, 262 S.E.2d 609, 612 (1979).[1]

The error of the majority is readily seen by a hypothetical posed in appellant's brief:

"Assume the following facts: There are two 20 year old shopping centers across the street from each other. They are identical with respect to area, location and all other characteristics, except that one shopping center is encumbered by leases which do not have the flexibility to generate market rents. The leases at this shopping center produce an annual net operating income of $400,000.00. The leases for the other shopping center produce market rents generating an annual net operating income of $600,000.00. Each of the shopping centers is sold on the same date at an arm's length sale price equal to ten times annual net operating income. That is, one shopping center is sold for $4,000,000.00; the other shopping center is sold for $6,000,000.00.

As the Appellant understands the rationale of the court of appeals, the assessment on one shopping center should be $4,000,000.00 while the assessment on the other shopping center is $6,000,000.00. This would be so even though the physical characteristics of the two shopping centers are identical. The Appellant submits that to limit the assessment on the shopping center encumbered by the bad leases to $4,000,000.00 would violate the uniformity requirements of the Wisconsin constitution and the Wisconsin Statutes." Appellant-petitioner's supreme court brief, pp. 22–23 (June 3, 1986).

I agree.

In conclusion, I would hold that Darcel must pay property taxes based on a value that reflects fair market rents rather than woefully inadequate contract rents, i.e., the assessed value of $5.2 million established by the City of Manitowoc Board of Review.

---

1. If these long-term leases provided for substantially higher contract rents than fair market rents, I doubt whether Darcel, Inc. would argue that contract rents should control its assessment.

Would this result lead to an unfair burden on Darcel or others similarly situated? Hardly. The negotiated selling price in a free market will reflect the property taxes that new owners will have to pay notwithstanding unrealized rents from financially inadequate long-term leases. Presumably the selling price to Darcel reflected just that.

Would this result lead to an unfair burden on the seller? Burden? . . . yes. Unfair? . . . no. The lower selling price results because of the seller's own misjudgments in negotiating the leases.

Unfortunately, the majority places the burden of the costs of those past misjudgments squarely where it should not rest: on the City of Manitowoc property taxpayers.

Accordingly, I dissent.

I am authorized to state that Chief Justice NATHAN S. HEFFERNAN joins in this dissent.

VALENCIA CENTER, INC. V. BYSTROM
543 So.2d 214
Supreme Court of Florida, 1989

SHAW, Justice.

We have on appeal *Valencia Center, Inc. v. Bystrom*, 526 So.2d 707 (Fla. 3d DCA 1988), in which the district court found section 193.023(6), Florida Statutes (1987), unconstitutional. We have jurisdiction. Art. V, §3(b)(1), Fla. Const. We affirm.

This case presents two issues: whether section 193.023(6) is constitutional, and whether the property appraiser arrived at a proper assessment for shopping center property for the years 1981, 1982, 1984, and 1985. We hold that the statute is unconstitutional and that the property appraiser correctly arrived at a proper assessment.

Valencia Center owns real property developed for use as a shopping center. Current zoning allows office buildings up to thirteen stories high and neighboring properties have been developed for such use. Valencia attempted to develop the property at issue for thirteen-story use but was precluded from doing so by a judicial determination that a pre-1965 lease to Publix Supermarkets, which is highly favorable to Publix, restricts development. Active market demand indicates the property's highest and best use is for thirteen-story buildings, and throughout the tax years in question, the appraiser has based his assessment of the property's value on recent sales of comparable properties zoned for thirteen-story use. Were the assessment to be based on the property's current use as a shopping center and the income from the lease to Publix, the assessment undoubtedly would be reduced. This dispute has been ongoing and, during its course, the 1986 legislature enacted section 193.023(6), which provides:

> (6) In making his assessment of improved property which is subject to a lease entered into prior to 1965 in an arm's length, legally binding transaction, not designed to avoid ad valorem taxation, and which has been determined by the courts of this state to restrict the use of the property, the property appraiser shall assess the property on the basis of the highest and best use permitted by the lease and not on the basis of a use not permitted by the lease or of income which could be derived from a use not permitted by the lease. This subsection shall apply to all assessments which are the subject of pending litigation.

Our decision on the constitutionality of this statute is controlled by *Interlachen Lake Estates, Inc. v. Snyder*, 304 So.2d 433 (Fla. 1974). There, we determined that the legislature cannot establish different classes of property for tax purposes other than those enumerated in article VII, section 4 of the Florida Constitution, which provides:

Section 4. Taxation; assessments. —By general law regulations shall be prescribed which shall secure a just valuation of all property for ad valorem taxation, provided:

(a) Agricultural land or land used exclusively for non-commercial recreational purposes may be classified by general law and assessed solely on the basis of character or use.

(b) Pursuant to general law tangible personal property held for sale as stock in trade and livestock may be valued for taxation at a specified percentage of its value, may be classified for tax purposes, or may be exempted from taxation.

The statute in issue in *Interlachen* provided a favored taxing standard for unsold lots in platted subdivisions. Section 193.023(6) in the instant case creates a similar favored classification for property that is subject to a pre-1965 lease. This is an "unreasonable and arbitrary" classification. *Interlachen*, 304 So.2d at 435. Section 193.023(6), therefore, is unconstitutional.

While the legislature cannot arbitrarily classify property for favored tax treatment, it can establish the just valuation criteria that are to be applied to all property. *Id.* at 434. To accomplish this, the legislature has enacted section 193.011, which provides:

193.011 Factors to consider in deriving just valuations. —In arriving at just valuation as required under sec. 4, Art. VII of the State Constitution, the property appraiser shall take into consideration the following factors:

(1) The present cash value of the property, which is the amount a willing purchaser would pay a willing seller, exclusive of reasonable fees and costs of purchase, in cash or the immediate equivalent thereof in a transaction at arm's length;

(2) The highest and best use to which the property can be expected to be put in the immediate future and the present use of the property, taking into consideration any applicable local or state land use regulation and considering any moratorium imposed by executive order, law, ordinance, regulation, resolution, · or proclamation adopted by any governmental body or agency or the Governor when the moratorium prohibits or restricts the development or improvement of property as otherwise authorized by applicable law;

(3) The location of said property;

(4) The quantity or size of said property;

(5) The cost of said property and the present replacement value of any improvements thereon;

(6) The condition of said property;

(7) The income from said property; and

(8) The net proceeds of the sale of the property . . . .

—193.011, Fla.Stat. (1987).

This Court has found that the just valuation at which property must be assessed under the constitution and section 193.011 is synonymous with fair market value, i.e., the amount a purchaser, willing but not obliged to buy, would pay a seller who is willing but not obliged to sell. In arriving at fair market value, the assessor must consider, but not necessarily use, each of the factors set out in section 193.011. The particular method of valuation, and the weight to be given each factor, is left to the discretion of the assessor, and his determination will not be disturbed on review as long as each factor has been lawfully considered and the assessed value is within the range of reasonable appraisals.

In challenging the assessment, Valencia argues that the property's potential use for thirteen-story buildings should not be considered in valuation because it does not represent the present or immediate future use of the property under section 193.011(2). This Court has addressed this particular issue long ago in *City of Tampa v. Colgan*, 121 Fla. 218, 230, 163 So. 577, 582 (1935), in which we ruled: "Prospective value alone cannot be made the substantive basis of an assessment, but can be considered to the extent that it enters into, or is reflected in, present value."

In arriving at fair market value, a willing buyer most certainly would consider that Valencia's property is zoned for thirteen-story buildings. The appraiser properly considered this potential future use.

As to whether the assessment should be decreased because of the below-market lease to Publix, this issue too has already been addressed by this Court. In *Department of Revenue v. Morganwoods Greentree, Inc.*, 341 So.2d 756, 758 (Fla.1977), we stated:

> We reaffirm the general rule that in the levy of property tax the assessed value of the land must represent all the interests in the land. This means that despite the mortgage, lease, or sublease of the property, the landowner will still be taxed as though he possessed the property in fee simple. The general property tax ignores fragmenting of ownership and seeks payment from only one "owner."

(Citations omitted.) Here, the overall interest consists of two parts: the interest remaining in the hands of the owner-lessor, Valencia, and the interest held by the lessee, Publix. The amount a willing buyer would pay for the "fee simple" equals the value of both the lessor's and lessee's interests. The owner in this case, Valencia, has simply transferred a large part of the property's value to the lessee. Failing to consider the transferred interest would result in an assessment below fair market value.

We affirm the district court decision.

It is so ordered.

EHRLICH, C.J., and BARKETT and GRIMES, JJ., concur.

McDONALD, J., dissents with an opinion, in which OVERTON and KOGAN, JJ., concur.

McDONALD, Justice, dissenting.

I dissent. The just valuation clause of the Constitution was not meant to be infused by the courts with a particular appraisal methodology which ignores other reasonable appraisal factors. Section 193.023(6), Florida Statutes (1987), is a constitutionally drawn tax statute that is reasonably related to just property valuation, as urged by amicus in this cause. I believe that this statute simply confines the property appraiser's measurement of highest and best use of property encumbered by a long-term lease to the highest use allowed by the lease. In many ways, section 193.023(6) is simply a refinement of factor two listed in section 193.011, which requires lease-encumbered property to be valued in a manner consistent with the traditional income capitalization method for appraising property. The legislature can prescribe such a framework.

. . . .

OVERTON and KOGAN, JJ., concur.

Notes and Questions

1. Is the difference in result between the Wisconsin and New York cases explained by any evident difference in the applicable statutes in those states?

2. Does the *Darcel* opinion adequately rebut the New York court's position that the taxing jurisdiction is not a co-entrepreneur sharing in the business owner's success or failure? How should the assessment be affected by the fact that the unfavorable leases may have made construction of the mall, and therefore its inclusion in the city tax base, possible?

3. What is the property that is being assessed in these cases? Does the fact that the new owner obtained all the rights held by the prior owner establish that a sale conveyed "all the 'bundle of rights' that made up the property"?

4. If the approach of *Darcel* were to be adopted, should the tenant be taxed on the property right that it holds? How would the market value of this right be calculated? If the tenant were not taxed, would the owner of identical property leased at full market rents be in a position to argue that the requirement of uniformity in taxation had been violated by this disparity?

5. How should the assessment of property subject to a long-term lease at *above*-market rents proceed in New York? In Wisconsin?

6. In *C.A.F. Investment Co. v. Township of Saginaw*, 410 Mich. 428, 302 N.W.2d 164 (1981), the Michigan Supreme Court took a position similar to that later adopted by the Wisconsin court in *Darcel*. One justice wrote,

> Adding an enhanced value of the lessee's interest to the lessor's interest where the property is bound to a long-term lease and taxing them together is as unjustified as the Internal Revenue Service saying to a taxpayer that he was imprudent to buy long-term Treasury bonds a number of years ago at 5% when he could now buy 90-day Treasury bills at 15% and that his income from those bonds, for tax purposes, will be deemed to be 15%.[3]

How would you respond?

7. How, if at all, should a finding that a long-term lease was not "improvident when made" influence the outcome of a case of this type?

8. The dissenting opinion in *Darcel* refers to *Martin v. Liberty Cty. Bd. of Tax Assessors*, 152 Ga.App. 340, 262 S.E.2d 609 (1979). In that case, following reasoning similar to that in *Merrick*, the court ruled that valuation of the taxpayer's property could not be reduced by reason of an unfavorable thirty-five-year lease.

---

3. 302 N.W.2d at 175 (concurring opinion).

Appellant's argument that consideration should be given to the existence of the lease and its adverse effect on the "fair market value" of the property would focus on what *his* remainder interest in the property would bring at a cash sale. Assuming, however, that the lease results in a decreased value of appellant's interest in the property, there would be a proportional increase in the "fair market value" of the leasehold. The "fair market value" of the estates merge to establish the "fair market value" of the fee.[4]

One of the most intriguing aspects of that case concerned the rent schedule, under which the owner "elected to receive cash payments totalling $216,540 during the first four years of the term and an annual rent in the amount of $2.75 per acre thereafter." *Ibid.* at 610. If the owner chose to receive the entire present value of the rent due under a long-term lease at the outset of its term, would there be a basis for valuing the property at the nominal value a prospective purchaser would offer for it? How should an assessor in Wisconsin treat such property in order to be consistent with *Darcel*?

Valuation of Property Subject to Other Legal Restrictions

The long-term lease cases pose a question as to whether the "property" to be taxed consists of the landlord's interest alone, or the landlord's and tenant's interests together. This problem of identifying the legal interests that compose the property subject to tax arises in many other contexts as well. An income-based valuation for tax purposes requires a decision, even if implicit, on this point whenever legal restrictions limit the return realized by property owners.

TWIN LAKES GOLF AND COUNTRY CLUB V. KING COUNTY
87 Wash.2d 1, 548 P.2d 538
Supreme Court of Washington, 1976

FINLEY, Associate Justice.

This is an appeal from a decision of the King County Superior Court declaring that the plaintiff-respondent's golf course has no taxable "fair market value" and that certain real property taxes assessed against the golf course and collected under protest by the county must be refunded to the taxpayer.

The dispositive issue is whether the golf course has a "fair market value" for tax assessment purposes. The property is encumbered with both zoning and conveyancing restrictions regarding use and nonalienation of the realty, and has a history of operating at a substantial, apparently unavoidable, financial loss every year.

------

4. 262 S.E.2d at 611.

On January 1, 1972, the King County Assessor made an assessment regarding the 18-hole golf course owned by Twin Lakes Golf and Country Club for the 1973 tax year. He determined that the golf course had a value of $660,600. The King County Treasurer levied taxes on the golf course in the sum of $16,387.10. The Country Club paid the taxes under protest pursuant to RCW 84.68.020, then unsuccessfully appealed the assessment first to the King County Board of Equalization and then to the State Board of Tax Appeals.

The golf course was constructed and essentially has been operated as an integral part of the Twin Lakes Development, a residential community located in the Federal Way area in South King County. The development is composed of 5 subdivisions which contain 1,006 single-family residential lots, 289 of which are adjacent to the golf course. The realty, i.e., the golf course, subject to the assessment involves no buildings or structures. It includes an irrigation system but otherwise consists solely of fairways, greens, and sand traps and is surrounded by homes in the development.

Four of the subdivisions, together with the golf course, were developed and constructed as a planned unit development (PUD) pursuant to the King County zoning code. To obtain PUD zoning, the developer was required to set aside and reserve certain lands for "common open space" as required by the King County zoning code.[1] The King County Council approved the developer's request and zoned four of the subdivisions, including the golf course, as a PUD. The ordinances adopted by the county required the developer to construct a golf course on the realty and to reserve it for common open space and golf course use for the benefit of the lot owners in the development.

The developer, prior to conveying the lots, filed with the King County Auditor a declaration of covenants, conditions and restrictions which provided that each lot owner would have the right to use and enjoy the golf course. The covenants provided that the restrictions were to run with and bind the land for a period of 20 years and automatically were renewed for 10-year periods unless 75 percent of the lot owners terminated the covenants. The deeds given by the developer to lot purchasers referred to the covenants and with each deed purchasers of a lot acquired the right to become a member of the golf club and to use the golf course. The deeds also referenced certain plat maps. The plat maps were recorded by the developer for all five subdivisions and indicated that the property would remain "open space" land free of buildings and other structures.

The Twin Lakes Golf and Country Club was incorporated in 1966 and since then consistently has incurred losses from the operation of the clubhouse, the golf course, and other club facilities. Primarily as a result of the club's lack of income and because of a lack of data on comparable sales of golf courses, the assessor computed and determined the value of the realty by the cost approach, i.e., cost of reproduction, appraisal method. This method is used by the assessor in valuing all other golf courses in King County, Washington. In computing the value of the golf course, the assessor made no reduction in valuation relative to the restrictions upon the use of the realty created by PUD zoning or the protective covenants or by the recorded plat maps. In the assessor's opinion, these restrictions did not affect the value of the realty.

The trial court found and concluded: (1) These restrictions encumbered the property and made the realty a servient estate for the benefit and use of all lots in the development and substantially and adversely affected the value of the golf course. (2) The Country Club cannot alter the present recreational use of the open space. (3) The club consistently has incurred losses from the operation of the golf course, ranging from $22,331 to

---

1. King County Code, ch. 21.56.

$44,734 per year. (4) The use of the property as a golf course has been unprofitable and will continue to produce losses. Finally, the trial court concluded that, as of January 1, 1972, the golf course had no "fair market value" for purposes of the assessment of county real-estate taxes.

RCW 84.40.030 establishes the standard of valuation. It provides, in part: "All property shall be valued at . . . its true and fair value in money and assessed on the same basis unless specifically provided otherwise by law."

The words "true and fair value in money" have consistently been interpreted by our courts to mean "fair market value." *Bitney v. Morgan*, 84 Wash.2d 9, 14, 523 P.2d 929 (1974). "Market value means the amount of money which a purchaser willing, but not obliged, to buy would pay an owner willing, but not obligated, to sell, taking into consideration all uses to which the property is adapted and might in reason be applied." *Mason County Overtaxed, Inc. v. Mason County*, 62 Wash.2d 677, 683—84, 384 P.2d 352, 356 (1963). The market value of realty is to be measured by considering benefits to be garnered from the use of the property and the burdens placed upon it. Burdens are restrictions which may arise from zoning ordinances or other legal limitations on the use of land. See *Pier 67, Inc. v. King County*, 78 Wash.2d 48, 57, 469 P.2d 902 (1970).

In *Tualatin Dev. Co. v. Department of Revenue*, 256 Or. 323, 473 P.2d 660 (1970), the court concluded that a golf course in a planned adult residential community had no market value for tax purposes. The court reached this result because the use of the land as a golf course had been unprofitable and would continue to be so, zoning restrictions required the property to be maintained as open space, and lots were advertised and sold with reference to the inclusion of the golf course in the development plan. Although King County argues otherwise, we find no significant distinction between the instant case and *Tualatin*. When the use of land is so restricted that its ownership is of no benefit or value; the assessment for tax purposes should be nothing. *Tualatin Dev. Co. v. Department of Revenue*, supra at 329, 473 P.2d 660. See *Supervisor of Assessments v. Bay Ridge Properties, Inc.*, 270 Md. 216, 310 A.2d 773 (1973); *Crane-Berkley Corp. v. Lavis*, 238 App.Div. 124, 263 N.Y.S. 556 (1933).

An assessment may be set aside if the assessor, by failing to take into account the restrictions on the use of the property and its lack of past and potential profitability, so grossly overvalues the property as to result potentially in a constructive fraud upon its owner. See *Boise Cascade Corp. v. Pierce County*, 84 Wash.2d 667, 672, 529 P.2d 9 (1974); *Pier 67, Inc. v. King County*, supra, 78 Wash.2d at 58, 469 P.2d 902.

We are persuaded that the trial court properly concluded (1) that the golf course had no fair market value as of January 1, 1972, and (2) that the taxes in question should be refunded.

The judgment of the trial court should be affirmed. It is so ordered.

STAFFORD, C.J., and ROSELLINI, HUNTER, HAMILTON, WRIGHT, UTTER, BRACHTENBACH and HOROWITZ, JJ., concur.

SAHALEE COUNTRY CLUB, INC. V. STATE BOARD OF TAX APPEALS
108 Wash. 2d 26; 735 P.2d 1320
Supreme Court of Washington, 1987

En Banc. Durham, J. Pearson, C.J., Utter, Dolliver, Dore, Andersen, Callow, and Goodloe, JJ., and Hamilton, J. Pro Tem., concur. Brachtenbach, J., did not participate in the disposition of this case.

DURHAM, J. The Sahalee Country Club has appealed from a decision by the Board of Tax Appeals (Board) valuing its golf course at $3.1 million for tax purposes. The valuation of golf courses and similar open spaces has apparently been the source of some controversy in this state's tax tribunals since our opinion in *Twin Lakes Golf & Country Club v. King Cty.*, 87 Wash.2d 1, 548 P.2d 538 (1976). Today we reemphasize that the critical element of *Twin Lakes* is the subject property's market value. Any other factor is relevant only to the extent that it can be shown to affect market value. Because the Sahalee golf course was shown to have a fair market value of $3.1 million, we affirm the Board's decision.

The Sahalee golf course is owned by Sahalee Country Club, Inc., a nonprofit private corporation with 500 shareholding members. The club itself consists of a golf course, clubhouse, parking lots and other improvements. It occupies approximately 212 acres on a plateau east of Lake Sammamish. The course consists of 27 holes and is of championship quality. In fact, Golf Digest each year recognizes Sahalee as one of the best 100 courses in the country.

In this case, taxation of the course requires an understanding of the course's relationship to its surroundings. The golf course is an integral part of a residential community consisting of approximately 500 single family homes and condominiums. The community almost completely surrounds the course. The lots were sold with the promise that the golf course would remain in perpetual existence. Other than that promise, however, the lot owners have no control over the management of the club's property. Lot owners do not acquire any ownership of the course merely by owning a lot. Lot owners are treated no differently than the general public if they apply for membership in the club. There are no recorded restrictions on alienation of the club nor any restrictive covenants as to use of the course. Sale of the club would require no consent from surrounding lot owners. Lot owners cannot use the course for any purpose without joining the club.

The club's property is zoned for single family residential use, which includes use as a golf course. Although zoning regulations would allow converting the club's property to a residential subdivision, practical restrictions (such as the configuration of the course and the limited access) limit the property to use as a golf course.

The King County Assessor appraised the club's fair market value at approximately $3.3 million for assessment years 1982 and 1983. Sahalee disagreed with this appraisal because it believed that its property value should be zero under principles outlined in *Twin Lakes*. In *Twin Lakes*, this court held that the Twin Lakes Country Club had zero value because legal restrictions in favor of neighboring landowners limited the property's use to that of a golf course, which use resulted unavoidably in financial loss. The King County Board of Equalization agreed with Sahalee's argument and valued its property at zero. The assessor appealed this decision to the Board of Tax Appeals. After hearing 2 weeks of testimony, the Board of Tax Appeals overturned the Board of Equalization's zero valuation and placed a $3.1 million value on the club's property. Sahalee sought judicial review in Thurston County Superior Court.[1] The case was then certified for direct review to the Court of Appeals and again certified from the Court of Appeals to this court.

---

1. The assessor has also cross-petitioned for correction of two of the Board's factual assertions. We agree with the assessor's position. The Board's opinion refers to the course being "landlocked" by the residential community, although the record reveals that in two places the course abuts a county road. The Board also found that the course

Sahalee has presented an array of objections to the Board's valuation of its golf course. Some of these objections concern details of the Board's calculations, which if meritorious would require some adjustments in the Board's $3.1 million. These objections will be treated later in the opinion. Two of Sahalee's arguments, however, strike at the very heart of the Board's decision, seeking not an adjustment in the Board's valuation, but a decision that the golf course has no market value at all. Both of these arguments are based on *Twin Lakes*, to which we now turn.

INTERPRETATION OF TWIN LAKES

The starting point for real property valuation is RCW 84.40.030, which provides that all real property "shall be valued at one hundred percent of its true and fair value in money and assessed on the same basis unless specifically provided otherwise by law." *Twin Lakes* explained this language as follows:

> The words "true and fair value in money" have consistently been interpreted by our courts to mean "fair market value." *Bitney v. Morgan*, 84 Wn.2d 9, 14, 523 P.2d 929 (1974). "Market value means the amount of money which a purchaser willing, but not obliged, to buy would pay an owner willing, but not obligated, to sell, taking into consideration all uses to which the property is adapted and might in reason be applied." *Mason County Overtaxed, Inc. v. Mason County*, 62 Wn.2d 677, 683-84, 384 P.2d 352 (1963). The market value of reality [*sic*] is to be measured by considering benefits to be garnered from the use of the property and the burdens placed upon it. Burdens are restrictions which may arise from zoning ordinances or other legal limitations on the use of land. See *Pier 67, Inc. v. King County*, 78 Wn.2d 48, 57, 469 P.2d 902 (1970).

Twin Lakes, at 4.

In *Twin Lakes*, we applied these general market value principles to the peculiar facts of that case. The Twin Lakes golf course was built as an integral part of a housing community. Covenants restricted the use of the golf course for the benefit of the lot owners in the development. Specifically, the property was restricted to use as a golf course and was additionally restricted as to its alienation. The golf course had consistently been operated at a financial loss and would continue to do so in the future. *Twin Lakes*, at 2-4. This court applied the familiar principle that real property's market value "is to be measured by considering benefits to be garnered from the use of the property and the burdens placed upon it." *Twin Lakes*, at 4. This court finally concluded that the Twin Lakes Golf Course had a zero market value because the use of the property was so restricted that its ownership was of no benefit or value. *Twin Lakes*, at 5.

Twin Lakes, therefore, clearly states that the bottom line is market value. Therefore, to obtain a zero valuation, a taxpayer must show more than restrictions on the use of its property and a history of unprofitability; the taxpayer must also show that these factors deprive the property of all market value.

---

is not owned "to any large extent" by the surrounding lot owners as part of their lot ownership. This statement wrongly implies that ownership of a lot automatically includes some ownership of the golf course. The record shows that lot ownership by itself does not include any golf course ownership. In all other respects, we affirm the Board's factual findings.

Sahalee argues that it should have a zero market value because the facts of its case are comparable to those in *Twin Lakes*. Sahalee points out that in each case, the use of a private golfing club was restricted in favor of neighboring residential lots, and in each case, the club was operated at a financial loss. The Twin Lakes Club was valued at zero, and Sahalee seeks the same. This argument has some initial intuitive appeal because a property should be valued at zero when its use is restricted to an operation that loses money. Sahalee's argument, however, has two flaws. As an initial matter, the record shows that Sahalee is not the financial problem it claims to be, but rather has an annual net operating income of over $100,000.[2] More importantly, however, Sahalee has ignored the key consideration here, i.e., market value. The record clearly shows that Sahalee has market value despite the restrictions and the questionable profit history. First, similarly restricted golf courses around the western United States had significant market values. Second, a "sophisticated lender" took the property as security for a $925,000 loan in 1969. Third, expert testimony established that investors would be interested in the property if it were listed for sale. Those investors would be able to change the operation of the course into a money-making venture, partially through expanding the number of its members. Given this market value evidence, the zero valuation of *Twin Lakes* certainly cannot apply to Sahalee.

Sahalee's second argument is that *Twin Lakes* is based on the theories of "shifting value" and "double taxation." Sahalee argues that its golf course increased the property values of neighboring residential lots by a total of $13 million, an amount far in excess of the cost of building the golf course. Sahalee contends that $13 million in value had shifted from the course to the residential lots, which would leave the golf course without value. Sahalee argues that taxing the golf course as well as taxing the residences for the additional $13 million would amount to double taxation. Under this argument, Sahalee focuses on the dollar amount of the benefit that accrues to the neighboring lot owners, not the dollar amount of the burden that this relationship places on the golf course.

This argument, however, misinterprets *Twin Lakes*. *Twin Lakes* did not mention the concepts of "shifting value" or "double taxation" in its analysis.[3] Rather, this court's analysis focused on the extent to which the golf course retained any market value, not on the extent to which neighboring properties were increased in value. While we agree that value sometimes is transferred from burdened to benefited properties, there is no

---

2. The parties disagree as to Sahalee's profit history because they are each measuring it differently. The assessor argues that Sahalee had an annual net operating income of between $140,000 and $230,000, after excluding depreciation and interest from expenses. The assessor's expert testified that this is the figure which is used by appraisers in determining value through income capitalization. Sahalee counters by arguing that the club's average annual net income was $23,000, which was more than offset by the $800,000 in deferred maintenance obligations which have accumulated in the last 10 years. Sahalee, however, has not presented any evidence to show the appropriateness of calculating income in this manner. We, therefore, find the assessor's evidence to be more credible.

3. Although *Twin Lakes* did not mention these concepts, Sahalee argues that they form the basis for that decision. In support of this argument, Sahalee points out that the briefs in *Twin Lakes* discussed these concepts, and that our opinion relied on a case that discussed shifting value. See *Crane-Berkley Corp. v. Lavis*, 238 A.D. 124, 127, 263 N.Y.S. 556 (1933). Neither of these arguments is sufficient for us to imply into *Twin Lakes* concepts which were not necessary to its analysis.

necessary dollar-for-dollar correlation between the decrease in value of the burdened property and the increase in value of the benefited property. See *Borough of Englewood Cliffs v. Estate of Allison*, 69 N.J. Super. 514, 529, 174 A.2d 631 (1961); *Alvin v. Johnson*, 241 Minn. 257, 263, 63 N.W.2d 22 (1954). As Professor Bonbright pointed out:

> One should note that there is no necessary equivalence between the damage a landowner suffers by being subjected to an easement and the benefit other land obtains from that easement. An easement of passage over *A*'s forest land to the road may greatly enhance the value of *B*'s hotel property without correspondingly depreciating *A*'s land; while on the other hand an easement of light over *C*'s lot may merely make *D*'s backyard slightly pleasanter while preventing *C* from building an apartment house.

1 J. Bonbright, *Valuation of Property* 497 (1937).

Although some older cases held that the increased value of benefited property was relevant in valuing the burdened property,[4] modern cases, such as *Twin Lakes*, have not used this analysis. These cases have expressly rejected such a theory. See *Beaver Lake Ass'n v. County Bd. of Equalization*, 210 Neb. 247, 257, 313 N.W.2d 673 (1981); *Lake Cy. Bd. of Review v. Property Tax Appeal Bd.*, 91 Ill. App. 3d 117, 122, Ill. Dec. 451, 414 N.E.2d 173 (1980).

We join in rejecting this theory. It erroneously focuses on the market value of neighboring properties rather than on the market value of the subject property. Once again, we must reiterate that the *Twin Lakes* focus is on the subject property's market value, not on other considerations. Other considerations, such as restrictions on property use, unprofitability, and neighboring property values, are relevant only insofar as they affect the subject property's market value. Given the independent evidence in the record establishing that Sahalee had some market value, the Board correctly rejected Sahalee's arguments for zero valuation.

Having determined that the Sahalee golf course had some market value, the Board next had to calculate the amount of that value, taking into account the appropriate benefits and burdens. In order to better explain the Board's decision, we will first outline some general principles of property valuation.

GENERAL METHODS OF PROPERTY VALUATION

Real property is to be valued according to its "highest and best use," which is the most profitable, likely use to which a property can be put. WAC 458-12-330. In estimating the highest and best use, an assessor may consider the property's particular adaptation to a particular use. WAC 458-12-330; *Samish Gun Club v. Skagit Cty.*, 118 Wash. 578, 579-80, 204 P. 181 (1922).

Fair market value is determined by one or more of three general methods: market data, cost, and income capitalization. RCW 84.40.030(1), (2). The market data approach involves appraising property by analyzing sale prices of similar property. American Institute of Real Estate Appraisers, *Golf Courses: A Guide to Analysis and Valuation* 103 (1980) (AIREA). Of the three methods, the market data approach is the most reliable, as long as adequate data is available. B. Boyce & W. Kinnard, Jr., *Appraising Real Property* 199 (1984).

---

4. See *People ex rel. Poor v. Wells*, 139 A.D. 83, 87, 124 N.Y.S. 36, *aff'd*, 200 N.Y. 518, 93 N.E. 1129 (1910), and to a far lesser extent, *Crane-Berkley Corp. v. Lavis*, 238 A.D. 124, 127, 263 N.Y.S. 556 (1933) (mentioning a shift in value).

The second method, cost, can also take the form of cost less depreciation or reconstruction cost less depreciation. RCW 84.40.030(2). This approach estimates what it would cost a typically informed purchaser to produce a replica of the property in its present condition. B. Boyce & W. Kinnard, Jr., at 269. The cost approach usually involves adding an estimate of the depreciated reproduction cost of the property's improvements and buildings to an estimated value of the land if vacant. AIREA, at 104.

Finally, fair market value can be estimated through capitalization of income. Under this method, value is assumed to be approximately equal to the present value of the future benefits of property ownership. AIREA, at 106. Application of the appropriate annual rate of capitalization to the forecast of annual net income generates an estimate of that present value. B. Boyce & W. Kinnard, Jr., at 230.

The final step in the appraisal process is the reconciliation of the values determined through the different methods outlined above. Usually, more than one method is employed, even if only as a check on accuracy. These methods usually produce a range of estimates. The appraiser calculates a final value estimate by placing greatest emphasis on the value generated by the method deemed to be most reliable. AIREA, at 107-08.

THE BOARD'S VALUATION OF SAHALEE

The Board relied primarily on the assessor's cost analysis in valuing Sahalee's property, which was conducted as follows. The assessor first valued the site as if it had no improvements. This was done by looking at comparable bare land sales in the area. The assessor determined that the most comparable land sales, those with limitations on intensive developments, ranged in price from $6,500 to $7,500 per acre. Consequently, Sahalee's land was valued at $7,500. The assessor then valued the golf course improvements (e.g., fairways, greens, traps, etc.) by determining replacement cost estimates and subtracting all depreciation amounts. The assessor arrived at a value for the improvements of $56,000 per hole. The combined value of land and course improvements was $75,000 per hole. By adding together the values for the land, the course improvements, and the buildings,[5] the assessor arrived at a total value of $3.1 million. The Board accepted this figure with only minor changes.[6]

The assessor also used the market data approach in valuing Sahalee. This approach estimates property value by using the sales prices from sales of comparable properties. RCW 84.40.030(1). Comparable properties were determined to be those which were restricted, either legally or practically, to use as a golf course. Sales of such courses occur rarely; hence, the assessor had to look to sales occurring around the western United States. The most comparable sales ranged in adjusted sales prices from roughly $70,000 to $140,000 per hole. Accordingly, the valuation of Sahalee at $75,000 per hole for land and improvements fits in at the lower end of this range. The Board used the market data approach only as a way of confirming the value determined under the cost approach.

The Board considered, but then rejected, the income capitalization method because capitalization of the meager income generated by golf courses usually does not accurately estimate their market value.

---

5. The valuation of the buildings is not in dispute here. The parties agree on that aspect of the club's valuation.

6. The assessor sought a value of $3,172,500, while the Board concluded that the value was $3,131,900.

SAHALEE'S OBJECTIONS TO ITS VALUATION

Sahalee maintains that the Board's valuation does not give sufficient consideration to the burdens imposed on the golf course. Sahalee's property was restricted in two ways to use as a golf course. First, the conditional use permit states that the land will be used as a golf course in perpetuity. Second, practical considerations such as the peculiar layout of its property and limited access also rendered unlikely other uses, such as residential development. However, the Board took this factor into consideration when it valued the golf course. Sahalee's bare land value was valued per acre at $7,500, rather than the $15,000 to $30,000 range which property capable of residential development was valued at. The lower figure reflects Sahalee's special limitation.

Sahalee argues that the income capitalization method should have been used. However, there are many reasons why this argument is unpersuasive. First, the income capitalization method is inappropriate when, as here, the subject property is not designed as a profit-making venture. See *Boise Cascade Corp. v. Pierce Cy.*, 84 Wash.2d 667, 677-78, 529 P.2d 9 (1974); B. Boyce & W. Kinnard, Jr., at 436; *Encyclopedia of Real Estate Appraising* 614 (1959); AIREA, at 102, 107. Sahalee is a nonprofit corporation. Second, the cost approach is often the best one for estimating the value of special-purpose properties (those constructed to fit the peculiar needs of a particular occupant). B. Boyce & W. Kinnard, Jr., at 253. Country clubs are considered to be special-purpose properties. AIREA, at 28. Third, the cost approach is particularly applicable where the property is being used at its highest and best use, as it was in the instant case. Finally, the Board generally uses the cost method to value golf courses, so its use in the present case is not arbitrary.

Furthermore, the assessor "should be afforded considerable discretion" in her choice of the proper valuation method(s). *Folsom v. County of Spokane*, 106 Wash.2d 760, 769, 725 P.2d 987 (1986); *Chief Seattle Properties, Inc. v. Kitsap Cy.*, 86 Wash.2d 7, 25, 541 P.2d 699 (1975); *King Cy. v. Department of Rev.*, 32 Wash. App. 617, 621, 649 P.2d 126 (1982). Given the superiority of the cost approach in the present case, the Board's use of it in valuing Sahalee's property certainly was not an abuse of discretion.

Sahalee also objects to the use of data from sales of golf courses throughout the western United States (specifically Arizona, California, Oregon and Washington) under the market data approach. Remember that the market data method involves examination of sales of similar properties. Sahalee argues that only similar properties in the immediate area should have been considered, and further, that sales of courses in "sun-belt" states are not relevant because those courses earn money all year. The Board concluded, however, that there is a nationwide market for golf course investments. Substantial evidence supports this conclusion, primarily the testimony of one expert as to large investment companies interested in golf courses throughout the western states. Furthermore, similar properties from outside the immediate geographical area can be used as a comparison if the number of similar sales in the immediate area is inadequate for analysis. WAC 458-12-301(1). The other properties need not be identical, but any differences should be taken into account, as they were in Sahalee's case. The sales figures of year-round courses in the sun-belt states were adjusted for a number of factors, including climatic and geographical differences, before they were used as a guide for Sahalee's valuation. Differences in the comparability of one property to another goes to the weight, not the admissibility, of the sales data. *Chase v. Tacoma*, 23 Wash. App. 12, 17, 594 P.2d 942 (1979). The admission of comparable sales is within the trial court's discretion. *State v. Hobart*, 5 Wash. App. 469, 474, 487 P.2d 635 (1971). The use of out-of-state data did not represent an abuse of discretion.

Sahalee also objects to the properties used for comparison purposes under the cost approach. As discussed earlier, one step in the cost approach involves valuing the land as if it had no improvements. Sahalee argues that the properties used for comparison purposes in estimating the bare land's value were dissimilar. The Board, however, found them to be similar, and gave corresponding weight to those values depending on the relative degrees of similarity. Sahalee did not submit any data of its own with which to contravene the assessor's evidence. Substantial evidence, therefore, supports the assessor's valuation of Sahalee's bare land at $7,500. Furthermore, as shown above, the Board had discretion in admitting the comparable sales data, and that discretion was not abused.

Finally, Sahalee also argues that the evidence of one of the assessor's experts was flawed because he incorrectly assumed that the property had alternative uses, including residential subdivision. However, the expert's assumption, if error, is harmless because he found the property's highest and best use to be that of a golf course. Property is to be valued according to its highest and best use. WAC 458-12-330. Therefore, the expert's assumption about alternative uses could not have affected his ultimate appraisal value.

The Board's decision is affirmed.

Notes and Questions

1. The taxing jurisdiction presented a detailed analysis of the country club's finances in *Sahalee*. In *Twin Lakes*, by contrast, the court faced a far more abstract legal valuation question. To what extent is the difference between their outcomes attributable to this distinction? For example, the court was considerably more skeptical of the golf course's money-losing situation in the later case. In *Lomas Santa Fe, Inc. v. Comm'r*, 74 T.C. 662 (1980), *aff'd*, 693 F.2d 71 (9th Cir. 1982), *cert. denied*, 460 U.S. 1083 (1983), which dealt with federal income taxation, a real estate developer seeking to depreciate his retained interest in a subdivision golf course explained that there was a legitimate business reason for this arrangement. He explained that if he relinquished control over the golf course, it would not be operated "in the style required for promotion of a luxury residential community," and so could not serve as a "marketing tool and sales vehicle in the offer of residential properties." 74 T.C. at 665, 671. Once all subdivision units had been sold, he planned to dispose of his interest in the golf course. Is it possible that if members of the homeowners' association in *Twin Lakes* had been willing to assess themselves higher dues, the annual deficit could have been eliminated? How would you investigate this possibility? How, if at all, should it influence the property tax assessment?[5]

---

5. For background on the use of golf courses as marketing tools for residential developments, see R. Hylton, "Can Builders Rely on a Fairway View to Sell Homes?" *New York Times*, March 24, 1991, Sec. 3, p. 10.

2. The dramatic finding of zero value in *Twin Lakes* led to many similar cases, particularly in Washington State. Carol Logan, in *Slash Property Taxes*, explained the *Twin Lakes* ruling:

> Nine state Supreme Court justices threw open the door in 1976. Unanimously upholding the Twin Lakes Golf and Country Club, they handed down a landmark decision. The high court thundered that the King County Assessor's $660,000 valuation was wrong. Greens have zero value. Refund those taxes and cease sending bills, the tribunal ordered . . . . PUDs have blossomed in King County, and elsewhere, suggesting that more common areas could gain zero value, if criteria are satisfied.

> Indeed, others jumped on the Twin Lakes bandwagon. Holly Hills Association, for one, gained zero value, forever ending its $184,000 greenspace valuation in 1979. The state board also granted zero value to Innis Arden Club Inc. greenspace in 1978. That meant farewell forever to $354,000 per year. They will pay no taxes on $33.5 million for the first 100 years.

> "One who focuses narrowly can reach a conclusion of tax avoidance," Twin Lakes' lawyer John Piper said. "But we proved that the whole PUD brought in more taxes than it would have if each home had taken a little more open space: Value migrated to the home. When their value goes up, taxes go up."[6]

The cover of *Slash Property Taxes* contains both a picture of a homeowner attacking a monster with a club and an endorsement from the International Association of Assessing Officers: "We like the author's positive attitude."

3. Does a zero-value assessment differ qualitatively from a nominal assessment? In a case factually similar to *Twin Lakes* the New Jersey Tax Court criticized the taxpayer for requesting a zero-value assessment in "the absence of proof that the plaintiff has been deprived of *all* beneficial interest in the subject property." *Tower West Apartment Ass'n, Inc. v. Town of West New York*, 2 N.J. Tax 565 (1981), *aff'd*, 5 N.J. Tax 478 (App. Div. 1982). The 1961 *Allison* case cited in *Sahalee* (*Borough of Englewood Cliffs v. Estate of Allison*, 69 N.J. Super. 514, 529, 174 A.2d 631 [1961]) valued land available to the public as a park at 10 percent of its unencumbered value. This calculation was criticized by the Oregon Supreme Court even as it approved the general approach of reducing assessment to reflect such encumbrances. "Assigning a money value to such a speculative possibility [i.e., sale of land in its encumbered state] seems to us unnecessary; the figure could only be arrived at arbitrarily." *Tualatin Dev. Co. v. Dep't of*

---

6. C. Logan, *Slash Property Taxes: Born Free—Taxed to Death* (1986), Chapter 3, pp. 23–24.

Revenue, 256 Or. 323, 332, 473 P.2d 660 (1970). *Tualatin* then assigned a zero value to a golf course, a result cited as precedent in *Twin Lakes.* But New Jersey courts have been reluctant to adopt the zero-value conclusion, as cases dealing with property contaminated by hazardous waste demonstrate. In a dispute dealing with the value of a beach within a residential subdivision, a witness testified that it

> has no value . . . . But I must say that it does, it has to have some value . . . . I don't think it could be sold. Well, it probably could be sold in the market, but it certainly couldn't be sold for very much money, because there are too many strings attached to the property . . . . I would say it has zero value. But I am trying to be practical about this thing. It must have some value for taxation purposes.[7]

Must it?

4. The legal issues in the valuation of property encumbered for the benefit of another taxable parcel are more convoluted than those encountered in the context of a long-term lease. A taxing jurisdiction may take the position that the division of interests between landlord and tenant do not affect the valuation of the entire property for tax purposes. Refusal to value restricted property at its diminished sale price can be inconsistent, however, with valuation of the benefited parcel (such as the residential lots in *Twin Lakes*) at its enhanced sale price. At the same time, as the quotation from Bonbright in *Sahalee* demonstrates, a legal restriction does not "transfer" some quantity of value from one parcel to another. The development of Washington case law from *Twin Lakes* to *Sahalee* is in some respects a reflection of the difficulty of these issues, as the court moved from a definitive position on this theoretical issue to a far more ambiguous stance, relying on the specific facts of the particular dispute before it. For examples of other approaches to this problem, see *Recreation Centers of Sun City, Inc. v. Maricopa County,* 162 Ariz. 281, 782 P.2d 1174 (1989); *Lake County Board of Review v. Property Tax Appeal Board,* 91 Ill.App.3d 117, 46 Ill.Dec. 451, 414 N.E.2d 173 (1980); *Locke Lake Colony Ass'n, Inc. v. Town of Barnstead,* 126 N.H. 136, 489 A.2d 120 (1985); and *Beckett Ridge Ass'n No. 1 v. Butler County Board of Revision,* 1 Ohio St. 3d 40, 437 N.E.2d 601 (1982).

5. What effect, if any, should a taxpayer's successful effort to obtain a zero-value assessment have in the calculation of an award in eminent domain in the event of a later taking of the same property?

---

7. *In re Appeal of Neptune Township,* 86 N.J. Super. 492, 496, 207 A.2d 330 (1965).

IN THE MATTER OF TRINITY PLACE COMPANY V. FINANCE ADMINISTRATOR
38 N.Y.2d 144, 341 N.E.2d 536, 379 N.Y.S.2d 16
Court of Appeals of New York, 1975

FUCHSBERG, Judge.

The question before us is whether the City of New York may reflect in its tax assessments the benefits it has afforded to a private owner under zoning resolutions which provide for incentive zoning developments, where the owner has dedicated part of its land to the public under these resolutions in return for substantial advantages which the dedication directly confers on its remaining land.

Appellant leases two city blocks in downtown Manhattan, on which it constructed, in 1970, a large office building and an open plaza. The original owner of the land, United States Steel Corporation, had planned to construct two office buildings, one on each block, but was forced to consider other alternatives when some of the tenants on the southern block refused to move. Its solution, arrived at with the aid of special city zoning provisions, was to build only one office building, located on the northern block, but a building with as large a floor area as would ordinarily be permitted on both lots together, and to dedicate at least 50% Of the land area, including the entire southern block as well as the remaining portion of the northern block, as an open plaza for use by the public.

City zoning ordinances permit such a compromise. (Zoning Resolution, sec. 74—74.) Under these provisions, the two-block parcel is treated as a single, unitary "zoning development." The plaza is exacted as the price for the permit to build a much larger structure than is otherwise allowed on the remaining land. (Sec. 74—742.)

The appellant nevertheless challenged its tax assessment for the years 1970—1974 on the grounds that the plaza portion of the land is now, for all intents and purposes, valueless and should be so assessed. That portion was taxed on an assessed valuation of $6,500,000 during the years in question. The land under the northern block was, during those years, assessed at $13,700,000. These figures represent the same assessment values which obtained before the rezoning permitted the combined building and plaza arrangement; they have not been altered to reflect the complementary use of the two blocks.

The special referee, noting that, under the agreement with the city, the plaza area may not be utilized for any other purpose without the city's permission, held that the land was indeed valueless and burdened with an easement which rendered it totally unmarketable. The referee then applied hornbook law to the effect that land which is unmarketable may not be taxed as though it were salable, and reduced its assessed value for the four years in question, from $6,500,000 to $150,000, citing *People ex rel. Poor v. Wells* (139 App.Div. 83, 124 N.Y.S. 36, *aff'd* 200 N.Y. 518, 93 N.E. 1129); *People ex rel. Topping v. Purdy* (143 App.Div. 389, 128 N.Y.S. 569, *aff'd* 202 N.Y. 550, 95 N.E. 1137); and *People ex rel. Gale v. Tax Comm'n of City of N.Y.* (17 A.D.2d 225, 233 N.Y.S.2d 501).

The Appellate Division reversed, two Justices dissenting. The majority found that the provision that no change in use be made with respect to the plaza area without city permission was not such a restriction as might make the land totally unmarketable and noting, properly, the extent to which the zoning law treats the parcel as a single unit. (46 A.D.2d 373, 362 N.Y.S.2d 475.) The dissenters agreed with the special referee.

We affirm the order of the Appellate Division. In enumerating the factors which are relevant here, we find the following ones significant.

First, the city resolution under which the "zoning development" is created not only states in terms that it applies to parcels composed of two or more separate city blocks (sec. 74–741, subd. [a]) but also notes that the resulting development is not expected to correspond to the definition of a "lot" as shown on the tax maps of the city. (sec. 12–10.) In so doing, it acknowledges that there may be potential conflicts and, as we read it, resolves these in favor of recognition of the unitary nature of the zoning development it creates.

Second, the tax assessments on these two blocks have not changed since the zoning regulation was applied. The two blocks are assessed now at the same rates which applied in 1969; thus there has been no compensating increase in the rates applied to the northern block to allow for the oversized building. Instead, the city continues to treat the two parcels as though each were capable of supporting the ordinary-sized office building. In our view, this is an entirely permissible method of treating, for tax purposes, the quid pro quo entered into between United States Steel and the city, since the floor area added to the northern portion, over and above what would ordinarily be allowed, is precisely the floor area originally determined for the plaza block.

Third, the two separate blocks were originally purchased by a U.S. Steel Corporation nominee, were then sold to U.S. Steel as a single parcel and were subsequently resold by it to the present owner. The resale price for the assembled package, after rezoning, exceeded by a very considerable margin the sum of the original acquisition prices for the two blocks separately, further indicating that the southern or plaza block is, under the zoning arrangement, anything but worthless. Moreover, appellant's rental agreement reflects the same pro rata recognition of the value of the southern block. (See *Matter of Seagram & Sons, Inc. v. Tax Comm. & City of N.Y.*, 18 A.D.2d 109, 238 N.Y.S.2d 228, *affd.* 14 N.Y.2d 314, 251 N.Y.S.2d 460, 200 N.E.2d 447.)

Fourth, we are not called upon here to determine how the southern block should be assessed if it were held by a separate owner. It is not so held now. The case law cited by the referee below to support the proposition that, where an owner cannot market land encumbered with easements creating a park, he may not be taxed as though it were marketable, dealt exclusively with situations in which the owners of the park land were distinct from the owners of the land benefited by the easements. There was, in those cases, no equitable or legal reason why such an owner, whose land has not assumed the burdens as compensating benefit for other advantages, should pay taxes, for he owns nothing of value. Here, however, the land is all held by one owner, who benefits from its larger building while it yields the use of the plaza land. Such an owner may not ignore the real and continuing interrelationship between the block that carries the building and the one that locates it on an open plaza. Just as the application to have the two parcels declared one zoning unit was made in order to meet the owner's needs, so also may it, and any subsequent owners, be held accountable for the results of that decision. It may not now disavow the deal for tax purposes.[2]

Finally, the fact that the plaza land may not be used for other purposes without city permission is not determinative of its value. It is true that this restriction constitutes a very real limitation on the separate marketability of the plaza land, but, as we have already pointed out, the owner has recouped this loss on the northern block. In addition, we note that such a provision for future use with city permission is not a mere detail. If, in the future, when the office building on the northern block has outlived its usefulness,

---

2. These conclusions also suffice to dispose of appellant's contention that the tax assessment on the northern block is not before the court procedurally and cannot therefore be utilized to off-set the disputed assessment of the southern block.

a different arrangement on the two-block parcel is desired, it is more than likely that the city will stand ready to renegotiate the use of the entire parcel, just as it has made an effort to accommodate the owner in this instance. What has been zoned can be rezoned. The presence in the agreement with the city of the provision permitting a change at a later date is thus an important one, since it reflects the negotiated, mutually accommodating nature of the agreement under which the disputed plaza exists.

The negotiated nature of the agreement cannot be overemphasized. The city resolutions under which this arrangement is made possible are an example of what various commentators have denominated "incentive" zoning or "bonus" zoning. While the techniques embodied in such incentive zoning programs are not without their problems, as is to be expected when new ways are developed to meet new conditions, they provide a valuable and flexible tool whereby cities may obtain amenities which they may not otherwise demand of private owners and, at the same time, owners may obtain highly desirable economic advantages. Given the difficulties in land use control and regulation which presently plague our older cities, we should be very careful not to nullify the usefulness of incentive zoning by undercutting the city's half of the bargain in the manner urged upon us here by appellant.

For all these reasons, we affirm the order of the Appellate Division reinstating appellant's tax assessments.

BREITEL, C.J., and JASEN, GABRIELLI, JONES, WACHTLER and COOKE, JJ., concur.

Order affirmed, with costs.

Notes and Questions

1. Does restriction of one parcel in order to permit more intense development of another parcel present a "transfer of value" of the same type as was at issue in *Twin Lakes*?

2. What weight should be given to "the negotiated nature of the agreement" in such a case, if the agreement did not deal with property taxation?

3. In reinstating the earlier assessment that did not take into account the development restriction, was the New York court following the path of the *Hackensack* case, where a thirty-year-old cost figure was reinstated as the basis for taxation? If the court had required a market-value assessment of the restricted parcel, could the city have responded by raising the assessment of the parcel on which the building was located?

Valuation of Subsidized Housing

REBELWOOD, LTD. V. HINDS COUNTY
544 So.2d 1356
Supreme Court of Mississippi, 1989

Before ROY NOBLE LEE, C.J., and ROBERTSON and ANDERSON, JJ.
ROBERTSON, Justice, for the Court:

I.

This is a dispute over the assessed value placed upon a federally subsidized low-income housing complex. Our question is whether the public assessor, when making such an assessment for purposes of ad valorem taxation, may consider enhancements to value flowing from benefits enjoyed by the property in the form of various federal subsidies. Because our law mandates that property be valued and assessed according to its true value, we answer in the affirmative.

II

A.

This appeal concerns protests filed by Rebelwood, Ltd., a Mississippi limited partnership (hereinafter "Taxpayer"). Taxpayer's managing general partner is Das A. Borden and Company, an Alabama corporation. Taxpayer is the owner of a 161-unit, multi-family complex of apartments known as Rebelwood and located in Jackson. Taxpayer makes complaint against the City of Jackson and Hinds County, Mississippi, regarding the true value and assessed value assigned Taxpayer's property for two consecutive years: 1984 and 1985. Rebelwood is Class II real property[1] which by law is assessed at fifteen percent of true value. Miss. Const. Art. 4, sec. 112 (1890, as amended); Miss.Code Ann. 27-35-4(2) (Supp.1988). Both the County and the City have for those years assigned Rebelwood a true value of $4,044,950 and an assessed value of $606,740. The two protests were consolidated for trial in the Circuit Court of Hinds County.[2]

The bottom line is taxes. If, as the public assessors maintain, the value of federal benefits enjoyed by Rebelwood are included in the estimate of Rebelwood's true value, Taxpayer for 1984 owes taxes as follows:

City of Jackson	—	$45,202
Hinds County	—	$15,248

If, as Taxpayer maintains, Rebelwood is assessed as a free market apartment complex and the federal subsidy program ignored, Taxpayer's 1984 tax bills are

City of Jackson	—	$30,371
Hinds County	—	$10,245

The record does not reflect the 1985 tax differentials, although we assume they are similarly proportioned.

B.

Rebelwood was completed in 1981. As a result of federal participation under the National Housing Act, 12 U.S.C. sec. 1715*l*(d)(4), Taxpayer was able to finance the cost of construction at a 7.5% mortgage rate. In addition to this mortgage subsidy, Taxpayer operates Rebelwood under a housing assistance program authorized by Section 8 of the Housing Act of 1937. 42 U.S.C. sec. 1437f. This program is managed by the U.S.

---

1. Class II includes all real property other than single-family, owner-occupied, residential property and public utility property owned or used by public service corporations. Miss. Const. Art. 4, sec. 112 (1890, as amended).

2. Hinds County took the lead in resisting Taxpayer's appeal before the Circuit Court and before this Court. By agreed orders entered by the Circuit Court on July 7, 1986,

Department of Housing and Urban Development (HUD) and provides housing for elderly and low-income people.

The federal assistance program begins when a private developer files an application with HUD in which the developer forecasts the replacement costs of the building, proposed "contract rent," and projected expenses necessary for operation and maintenance. "Contract rent" is defined under HUD regulations as the total amount of rent specified in the developer's contract with HUD and is comprised of (a) the actual rent paid by the tenant and (b) the housing assistance subsidy paid by the government. 24 C.F.R. sec. 880.201 (1988). The amount of the contract rent varies depending on the cost of construction, projected operation expenses, and mortgage expenses. 24 C.F.R. sec. 880.308(a)(8) (1988). The contract rent may exceed what HUD has determined to be the neighborhood's "fair market rent" by as much as twenty percent. 24 C.F.R. sec. 880.203 and sec. 880.204(b)(1)(ii)(B) (1988).

The tenants who occupy such subsidized housing pay as rent a percentage of their income, not to exceed thirty percent. 24 C.F.R. sec. 813.107 (1988). The difference between the rent actually paid by the tenant and the "contract rent" as contained in the developer's application is subsidized by the federal government. In most instances, the contract rent exceeds rents paid by similarly situated tenants in the vicinity of the development. One motivation for investing in apartments participating in this subsidized housing program is the rather favorable tax treatment generated by the depreciation schedules permitted under federal tax law.

These benefits are of considerable value. In exchange therefor, owners and developers must build the units to HUD specifications and accept tenants based upon HUD guidelines. In addition, the developer's revenues are limited by various HUD regulations. 24 C.F.R. sec. 880.205 (1988).

Testimony regarding the operation of Rebelwood showed an annual gross income of approximately $670,000. Of this figure, $110,000 represented rents actually paid by the tenants while $560,000 was received in the form of a federal rental subsidy. As with most subsidized housing, Rebelwood is an attractive place to live for those with marginal incomes and has a waiting list for prospective tenants. The average occupancy rate for Rebelwood is 98%. As such, the operating statement for 1983 may be considered representative of the income-generating capacity for Rebelwood for the life of the federally-subsidized mortgage—40 years. Since the subsidy benefits conferred by the participation in the federal program are transferable, any future purchasers of the Rebelwood complex would also acquire them.

C.

At trial, appraisers for each party studied Rebelwood under the three statutorily-authorized approaches to value: the cost approach, the income capitalization approach and the market data or comparative sales approach. Miss.Code Ann. sec. 27-35-50(2) (Supp.1988). These approaches do not, considered singly, establish value. Each rather is one approach to value, with the appraiser's estimate of value being, in the end, an opinion which is the product of a reconciliation of the indications yielded by the three approaches. That opinion is and must be of the value of the property, not its owners or management, for it is the property that is being valued, assessed and taxed.

We will consider separately each approach to value and the evidence adduced at trial.

---

the true value of Rebelwood finally established in this litigation will be accepted by Taxpayer and the City of Jackson as true value for city ad valorem tax purposes for the years 1984 and 1985.

Cost Approach

The cost approach[5] is a method by which the value of the property is derived by estimating the replacement cost of the improvements and deducting from that figure the estimated physical depreciation and any form of obsolescence, if appropriate. This figure is then added to the market value of the land to yield an overall valuation of the realty.

Taxpayer's appraisers suggest that the cost approach indicates a value of the Rebelwood complex at $2,042,000. Hinds County's appraisers offered an opinion that the cost approach indicates a value of $4,044,900.

The disparity between these two figures can be attributed primarily to the inclusion by Taxpayer's appraisers of some $1,535,000 in "functional economic obsolescence." The appraisers reasoned that, because Rebelwood was built pursuant to HUD specifications, including various non-competitive floor plans (e.g., five-bedroom apartments), and the amenities provided are minimal (e.g., no air-conditioning), the complex would not be an attractive investment if placed on the open market.

The appraisers for the County testified that functional depreciation has no application to the use to which the property was put for the tax years in question, 1984 and 1985, a use, we might add, which will presumably continue for the next 35 years. Further, as one of the County's appraisers testified: "This property was operating at better than 95% occupancy—97% occupancy—and there was no way to measure functional or economic depreciation when you have that situation." The thrust of the testimony of the County's appraisers was that the functional obsolescence of the complex was hypothetical (at best) because Rebelwood exists as a subsidized housing complex, not as one operating in a free market environment.

Market Data or Comparative Sales Approach

Market data or comparative sales approach[6] is, as its alternative names imply, an approach to value in which the value estimate is predicated upon prices actually paid in open market transactions for various properties similar to the one at issue in the appraisal.

---

5. The cost approach involves a determination of the "current" cost of reproducing property less loss in value from deterioration and functional and economic obsolescence—accrual depreciation. There are five basic steps involved in this approach:
  1. The estimate of the *land value* as if vacant
  2. The estimate of the current *cost of reproducing or replacing* the existing improvements
  3. The estimate of accrued depreciation from all causes
  4. Deduction of accrued depreciation estimate to arrive at indicated value of improvements
  5. The addition of the land value to the indicated value of the improvements to develop indicated property value.

[American Institute of Real Estate Appraisers,] *The Appraisal of Real Estate,* at 71, 345-404 [9th ed. 1987]; [International Association of Assessing Officers], *Property Assessment Valuation,* at 131-83 [1977]. *See also* W. Kinnard, *Income Property Valuation]* at 347-77 [1971]; R. Suter, *The Appraisal of Farm Real Estate* 329-50 (1974).

6. The market data approach involves an analysis of actual arm's length sales of property similar to the subject property. An application of this approach involves five basic steps:
  1. [Seek] out similar properties for which pertinent sales, listings, offerings, and/or rental data are available.

The price paid for a similar apartment complex would then be evaluated with reference to the yearly gross income that such a property could expect to earn. The multiplier resulting from such an evaluation is used to account for variations existing between the properties recently sold regarding size (number of units), age and location.

The appraiser for Hinds County analyzed the recent sales of similar subsidized housing, compared them against their respective gross incomes and arrived at a multiplier in the range of 5.5 to 7.0. The appraiser chose to employ a multiplier in the lower end of this range—6.0. The gross income, as reflected in the operating statement for Rebelwood, was then multiplied by 6.0 and yielded a value indication of $4,039,998.

Taxpayer's appraisers also employed the market data approach, but began their analysis with a somewhat different assumption. The comparative sales analyzed by Taxpayer's appraisers included no subsidized housing. The appraisers also disregarded the rental subsidy income received by Rebelwood as well as the cash-flow advantages of Rebelwood's 7½% mortgage. The rationale behind this exclusion was explained by Taxpayer's appraiser:

> The sale of a HUD . . . for a practical matter, if any had sold they would have almost surely sold with the low interest rate mortgage going, with all the subsidies going and the real estate. Now if I were appraising a HUD for sale of all three together, yes, but I'm not. I'm appraising it for the real estate only. Had I had a sale of a HUD property, I can think of no practical ways to separate the three items so that I could back it into the real estate only. And since I am appraising for real estate only, I found sales that were of real estate only, not sales that included things other than the real estate. And that's why I didn't use any HUD sales.

By using the recent sales of non-subsidized housing as a comparison and by excluding the advantages the complex possessed by virtue of its rent and mortgage subsidies, Taxpayer's appraisers testified that the market data approach suggests a value of $1,892,000.

Income Capitalization Approach

In the income capitalization approach[7] the anticipated net income which the property is expected to generate over its usable life is capitalized and processed to indicate the capital investment which produces the net income. In this approach, more than either

---

2. [Ascertain] the nature of the conditions of sale, including the price, terms, motivating forces, and its bona fide nature.

3. [Analyze] each of the comparable properties' important attributes with the corresponding ones of the property being appraised, under the general divisions of time, location and other characteristics, including physical and economic.

4. [Consider] the dissimilarities in the characteristics disclosed in Step 3, in terms of their probable effect on the sale price.

5. [Formulate] in the light of the comparisons thus made, an opinion of the relative value of the subject property as a whole, or, where appropriate, by applicable units, compared with each of the similar properties.

The Appraisal of Real Estate, supra, at 70–71, 311–42; Property Assessment Valuation, supra, at 105–30; W. Kinnard, supra, at 329–43; R. Suter, supra, at 293–326.

7. The income or earnings approach determines value by reference to the property's income-producing capacity under *typical* management. See *Crocker v. Mississippi State*

of the others, it is important to keep well in mind that it is the property that is being valued and assessed and not management.

The Hinds County appraisers offered their opinion that the income approach indicates a value for Rebelwood at $3,978,780. The starting point for these appraisers was that the estimated net income as deduced from Rebelwood's operating statement for 1982—$437,665—was a representative figure and this amount of income would continue in the future.

Taxpayer's appraisers began their income analysis with the assumption that Rebelwood was not a subsidized complex, eschewing the income figures from the operating statement in favor of a hypothetical income which Rebelwood could be expected to earn on the open market. In addition, Taxpayer's appraisers hypothesized that the vacancy rate would be greater—in the neighborhood of 5%. One appraiser explained the rationale for this adjustment:

> Right now it's very simple to keep it fully rented because the tenants are not paying their own rent. They are offered virtually free rent. It's very easy under those conditions to find people who want to move into these apartments. They keep a waiting list, a serious waiting list of people who are ready to move in just like that . . . . Now in the free world, when somebody moves out, what you've got to do is run ads in the paper, get people in, show it to them, persuade them to part with $280 a month to live there, and you run into a much higher vacancy that way than you do under one where somebody else is paying the man's rent.

Using this postulated gross income figure, Taxpayer's appraisers found that the income capitalization approach indicates a value of $1,860,000.

D.

After a two-day trial where the parties' experts offered widely conflicting evidence regarding the value of the property, the jury returned a finding that the "true value" of the property was $3,180,000. The Circuit Court on October 7, 1986, entered judgment in accordance with the verdict.

Highway Commission, 534 So.2d 549, 553 (Miss.1988); *Georgia Pacific Corp. v. Armstrong,* 451 So.2d 201, 207 (Miss.1984). In a commercial rental context, the four steps basically followed are:

1. Obtain the rent schedules and the percentage of occupancy for the subject property and for comparable properties for the current year and for several past years. This information provides gross rental data and the trend in rentals and occupancy. This data is then compared and adjusted to an effective estimate of gross income which the subject property may reasonably be expected to produce.
2. Obtain expense data, such as taxes, insurance and operating costs being paid by the subject property and by comparable properties. The trend in these expenses is also significant.
3. Estimate the remaining economic life of the building to establish the probable duration of its income, or, alternately, estimate the suitable period of ownership before resale.
4. Select the appropriate capitalization method and the applicable technique and appropriate rate for processing the net income. *The Appraisal of Real Estate, supra,* at 71–72, 407–558; *Property Assessment Valuation, supra,* at 203–75; W. Kinnard, *supra,* at 383–436; R. Suter, *supra* at 293–326.

Taxpayer now appeals to this Court and files nine assignments of error. In its brief, Taxpayer treats these assignments as directed to two essential issues:

(1) The Circuit Court erred in instructing the jury to consider the value of any federal subsidy received by the taxpayer in determining a "true value" for the housing complex.

(2) A valuation which considers the amount of federal subsidy received by the taxpayer violates the Uniformity and Equalization in Value Clause of the Mississippi Constitution and the Equal Protection Clause of the Fourteenth Amendment to the United States Constitution.

Hinds County has cross-appealed, claiming that the determination of value rendered by the jury was not based upon any competent evidence in the record. We affirm on direct appeal and reverse and render on Hinds County's cross-appeal.

III.

Inclusion or exclusion of the value of federal subsidies, inuring to the Taxpayer as owner of Rebelwood, dictates vastly disparate estimates as to Rebelwood's "true value." Consideration of these subsidies in the assessment of value is the *sine qua non* of the appeal.

Our point of beginning is the recognition that value in today's setting is a function of positive, and not natural law. See *General Motors Corp. v. State Tax Commission*, 510 So.2d 498, 500 (Miss. 1987); *Mississippi State Tax Commission v. Dyer Investment Co., Inc.*, 507 So.2d 1287, 1290 (Miss. 1987). Natural or economic indicia of value are of consequence only insofar as they have been recognized in our positive law. Happily, we find much in our law that is consonant with sound economic and appraisal theory.

Our state's law on the point finds its source in Miss. Const. Art. 4, sec. 112 (1890, as amended) which provides, *inter alia*, that property of the sort before us today "shall be . . . [assessed] according to current use, regardless of location." The constitutional mandate has been implemented in Miss. Code Ann. sec. 27-35-50 (Supp. 1988), which twice reiterates the current use concept.[8] Rebelwood in 1984 and 1985 was used as a federally subsidized low-income housing project.

Of greater importance is a second provision found in the legislative directive, as reflected in the above-mentioned statute. Our public assessors are directed to consider

---

8.   In relevant part, Miss.Code Ann. sec. 27-35-50 (Supp.1988) reads:

(1) True value shall mean and include, but shall not be limited to, market value, cash value, actual cash value, proper value and value for the purposes of appraisal for ad valorem taxation.

(2) With respect to each and every parcel of property subject to assessment, the tax assessor shall, in ascertaining true value, consider whenever possible the income capitalization approach to value, the cost approach to value, and the market data approach to value, as such approaches are determined by the State Tax Commission . . . . The choice of the particular valuation approach or approaches to be used should be made by the assessor upon a consideration of the category or nature of the property, the approaches to value for which the highest quality data is available and, the *current use* of the property.

(3) Except as otherwise provided in subsection (4) of this section, in determining the true value of land and improvements thereon, factors to be taken into consideration are the proximity to navigation, to a highway, to a railroad, to a city, town, village, or road, *and any other circumstances that tend to affect its value,* and not what it might bring at a forced sale, but what the owner would be willing to accept and would expect to receive for it if he were disposed to sell it to another able and willing to buy.

(4) In arriving at the true value of all Class I and Class II property and improvements, the appraisal shall be made according to *current use,* regardless of location.

. . . .

certain specific factors affecting value of subject property and are then told to consider "any other circumstances that tend to affect its value." Federal subsidies received by Taxpayer on account of Rebelwood—both those designated for rental payments as well as those for debt retirement—qualify as "any other circumstances that tend to affect" the value of this property. This language codified the view accepted by this Court in *McCardle's Estate v. City of Jackson*, 215 Miss. 571, 579, 61 So.2d 400, 402 (1952), where the Court announced that "[a]ll of the facts as to the condition of the property, its surroundings, its improvements, and capabilities may be considered." 215 Miss. at 579, 61 So.2d at 402.

This case concerns the assignment of value for specific years: 1984 and 1985. One relevance of the "use" inquiry is to determine the assessment ratio for each year and to fix our focus upon the actual and not the hypothetical. All single-family, owner-occupied, residential real property, labeled Class I property, must be assessed at ten percent (10%) of true value. Miss. Const. Art. 4, sec. 112 (1890, as amended); Miss. Code Ann. sec. 27-35-4(1) (Supp. 1988). Class II includes all other real property, except that owned by public utilities. State law provides that Class II real property shall be assessed at fifteen percent (15%) of true value. Miss. Const. Art. 4, sec. 112 (1890, as amended); Miss. Code Ann. sec. 27-35-4(2) (Supp. 1988). Rebelwood is Class II real property.

Beyond this, the function of the current use requirement is quite limited. It makes clear that the concept of highest and best use, familiar in such contexts as eminent domain and fair market appraisals of value generally, has no place in this state's ad valorem taxation system.[9] The most familiar illustration is farm land lying in the immediate path of growth of a municipality. The highest and best and most valuable use of such land will often be development of a residential subdivision. Our law allows the owner to continue to farm the land, if he wishes, and tells him the land will be taxed as farmland so long as he continues to use it as such, even though as farmland it has a lower true value than it would be assigned if it were treated as residential property. By the same token, if, hypothetically, the area surrounding Rebelwood were used for high rise commercial office buildings—so that Rebelwood's fair market value were greatly increased over its value as an apartment complex—our law would mandate that it continue to be assessed as an apartment complex—until such time as Taxpayer saw fit to convert it to the higher use by demolition and new construction or by sale.

Seen in this light, the sound and fury over Rebelwood's current use label is seen signifying nothing. It matters not whether we employ as a use label "open market apartment complex," "federally subsidized low income housing," "multi-family dwellings" or whatever. The battle is over value. Our question is whether the federal benefits enjoyed by Rebelwood affect its value—to Taxpayer or in the open market. Because those benefits make ownership of the property by Taxpayer more desirable than without,

---

In determining the true value based upon current use, no consideration shall be taken of the prospective value such property might have if it were put to some other possible use. [Emphasis added]

Rebelwood is Class II real property. Miss. Const. Art. 4, sec. 112 (1890, as amended); Miss. Code Ann. sec. 27-35-4(2) (Supp.1988).

9. For a brief summary of use value as compared with fair market value, see *The Appraisal of Real Estate, supra*, at 16-21; and Robertson, *Problems of Valuation and Equalization in Mississippi's Ad Valorem Tax System*, 48 Miss.L.J. 201, 217 (1977); *see generally* Posner, *Economic Analysis of Law* 459 (3d ed.1986).

they must sensibly be considered in assessing value in use. And because those benefits may be transferred to purchasers, the same obtains for Rebelwood's value in exchange. The point is made clear by thought of the factors affecting value.

> Value is extrinsic to the commodity, good or service to which it is ascribed; it is created in the minds of individuals who constitute a market. The relationships that create value are complex, and values change with changes in the factors that are most influential. Typically, four interdependent economic factors create value: *utility*, scarcity, desire, and *effective purchasing power*. All four factors must be present for a property to have value.[10]

Rebelwood's utility to Taxpayer in the years in question was greatly enhanced by the package of federal benefits Taxpayer enjoyed. In this sense, Rebelwood's value was enhanced.

Effective purchasing power is equally important. This factor affecting value refers to

> *the ability of an individual or group to participate in a market—that is, to acquire goods and services with cash or its equivalent.* A valid estimate of the value of a property includes an accurate judgment of the market's ability to pay for the property.[11]

Our law's insistence that property be valued according to current use does not change this. Think of the value of a residence if there were no financing available, public or private. What an individual could sell his or her house for would be drastically reduced. The willing buyer/willing seller test of value necessarily incorporates the idea that willingness is a function of effective purchasing power, i.e., it is idle to suggest that I am willing to pay $100,000 for your house if I have no way of obtaining access to more than $10,000 with which to pay you. The experience of the past century surely makes clear that changes in the availability of financing radically affects the values of properties.

In the context of a federally subsidized low income housing project, these considerations also obtain. No one would build a Rebelwood if it were not for the federal benefits and subsidies. The availability of the federal programs makes it economically feasible and desirable to engage in such an enterprise. Indeed, that is precisely the reason the Congress authorized such a program, to provide incentives to people to invest in low income housing projects and thus increase the availability of such housing. But if you take away the federal programs, Rebelwood goes broke tomorrow. Its value is far less without the federal programs. And, if in future tax years the federal programs be stripped away, Rebelwood's assessment will be reduced as its value is reduced.

Still, Taxpayer advances the argument that this state should frame its public policy so as to encourage federally subsidized low-income housing investment and that taxation of these benefits received in the form of subsidies would somehow discourage this sort of investment. Of course, Congress has already provided quite adequate incentives to such housing. The point is seen ephemeral, as the federal regulations controlling the owners' return on investment take into account local property tax increases.[12]

---

10. *The Appraisal of Real Estate, supra,* at 22. [Emphasis supplied].

11. *The Appraisal of Real Estate, supra,* at 23. [Emphasis in original].

12. The applicable HUD regulation reads:
(a) *Automatic annual adjustment of contract rents.* Upon request from the owner to the contract administrator, contract rents will be adjusted on the anniversary date of the contract . . . .

We have canvassed the reported decisions in other states and find that the majority by far subscribe generally to the view we accept. See, e.g., *Executive Square, Ltd. v. Board of Tax Review*, 11 Conn.App. 566, 528 A.2d 409, 413 (1987); *In re Johnstown Assoc.*, 494 Pa. 433, 431 A.2d 932 (1981); *Kankakee County Board of Review v. Property Tax Appeal Board*, 163 Ill.App. 3d 811, 114 Ill. Dec. 851, 855, 516 N.E.2d 1006, 1010 (1987); *Steele v. Town of Allenstown*, 124 N.H. 487, 471 A.2d 1179, 1182 (1984); *Antisdale v. City of Galesburg*, 420 Mich. 265, 362 N.W.2d 632, 639 (1985). Only Ohio appears to take the view urged by Rebelwood. See *Canton Towers v. Board of Revision of Stark County*, 3 Ohio St.3d 4, 444 N.E.2d 1027 (1983); *Alliance Towers v. Stark County Board of Revision*, 37 Ohio St.3d 16, 523 N.E.2d 826, 832—33 (1988). We have reviewed the Ohio decisions and find them unpersuasive.

We hold that the value of any federal subsidy or benefits enjoyed by Taxpayer by reason of its ownership of Rebelwood must be considered in establishing true value for each year in which such subsidy or benefits are in fact enjoyed. The assignment of error is denied.

IV.

We turn now to Taxpayer's charge of discrimination: that incorporation into Rebelwood's true value of the value of federal subsidies offends Taxpayer's rights under the amended Uniformity and Equality Clause of this state's constitution. See Miss. Const. Art. 4, sec. 112 (Supp.1984). Also implicated is the Equal Protection Clause of the federal constitution.

The goal of these constitutional mandates is a fair and equitable distribution of the tax burden. Our history tells of two ways that goal may be thwarted. First, we have seen widely varying assessment ratios—the ratio of assessed value to true value—though the properties may have been of like kind, quality and value. This form of discrimination has been largely eradicated, although to an extent legalized, by the 1986 amendments to Section 112 of the Mississippi Constitution. No charge is made here of that form of assessment discrimination. Rebelwood, like all other Class II property, is assessed at fifteen percent of true value.

The second form of assessment discrimination has been at once more subtle and blatant—and more difficult to detect and correct. We refer to discrimination in the assignment of true value—before the assessment ratio is ever applied. Where properties, superficially similar but in fact having widely varying true values, are assigned the same true value, this form of discrimination occurs. A familiar example is the assessment of all cultivatable agricultural acreage at the same dollars per acre value. Conversely, such discrimination occurs when properties of like kind, quality and value are assigned widely varying true values.

Taxpayer charges this latter form of discrimination. To support its argument, Taxpayer posits the following illustration:

> Two properties (property A and property B) sat side by side. Both properties were multi-family complexes. Both properties were in virtually the same location . . . . The only difference between property A and property B was the fact that

---

(b) *Special additional adjustments.* For all projects, special additional adjustments will be granted, to the extent determined necessary by HUD, to reflect increases in the actual and necessary expenses of owning and maintaining the assisted units *which have resulted from substantial general increases in real property taxes, assessments,* utility rates, and utilities not covered by regulated rates, and which are not adequately compensated for by annual adjustments under paragraph (a) of this section.

24 C.F.R. sec. 880.609 (1988) (emphasis added).

property A was a conventional, non-subsidized housing project constructed by means of conventional market financing and operating without housing assistance payments from the federal government. Property B, on the other hand, was developed with below-market financing under HUD's sec. 221(d)(4) [12 U.S.C. sec. 1715] program and received housing assistance payments under HUD's Section 8 program . . . .

Under the scenario described above, Mr. Barnes [the County's appraiser] testified that his office would tax property A at a lower assessed value than property B. This tax inequality would exist despite the fact that the properties were identical in every respect except for the existence of government subsidies.

Section 112 of the Mississippi Constitution requires uniformity and equality in taxation. This requirement is satisfied when, in establishing true value, the public assessor considers all factors affecting the value of the property, and employs the same assessment ratio. The federal subsidies enjoyed by Rebelwood affect its value to Taxpayer, and because transferrable, to a prospective purchaser as well. Absent a showing that other federally subsidized housing projects are treated differently, or that, in the case of free market apartment complexes, the Hinds County assessor does not consider all factors affecting value, Section 112 affords Taxpayer no right to relief. See *Lavecchia v. Vicksburg*, 197 Miss. 860, 20 So.2d 831 (1945), holding that the assessed valuation of a taxpayer's property be equal and uniform with that of other *like* property in the city. See also *Peterson v. Sandoz*, 451 So.2d 216, 219 (Miss.1984):

[T]axes should be uniformly and equally collected from a class of *similarly situated taxpayers* if it is to provide those within the class to equal and constitutional treatment under the law. [Emphasis added]

The Supreme Court of the United States has for at least seventy years enforced in this context rights secured by the Equal Protection Clause. A taxpayer is entitled to relief if he proves that his property has been assigned an assessed value substantially higher than similar properties. This Court as well has recognized historically the function of the Equal Protection Clause in assessment equalization jurisprudence. But where, as here, Taxpayer's property has been valued and assessed according to the value the same as other like properties, the Equal Protection Clause affords no relief.

Taxpayer relies on *Stuart v. Board of Supervisors*, 195 Miss. 1, 11 So.2d 212 (1943), as standing for the proposition that the County's standard for determining functional and economic depreciation discriminates against subsidized housing and, therefore, the County's appraisal of Rebelwood violates Section 112 and the Equal Protection Clause. In actuality, *Stuart* supports Hinds County's argument. Section 112 requires, as *Stuart* states, that no parcel of real property shall be assessed at more than actual value. As demonstrated, Rebelwood's actual value is the value that it has on the open market, the value that a willing buyer and willing seller would put on the property, assuming its current use as subsidized housing. If no actual functional obsolescence exists, Section 112 does not require that deductions be allowed. The result desired by Taxpayer, that Rebelwood be treated differently from other commercial housing and its income ignored in place of a fictional income, would itself be violative of Section 112's requirement of uniformity, and, as well, of the Equal Protection Clause.

As with Taxpayer's first assignment, there are no Mississippi cases directly on point. Indeed, we find but one case where the owner of a federally subsidized complex challenged the assessment based upon a constitutionally-mandated equalization scheme.

In *In re Johnstown Assoc.*, 494 Pa. 433, 431 A.2d 932 (1981), the Supreme Court of Pennsylvania responded to this argument as follows:

> The Pennsylvania Constitution, art. VIII, sec. 1, states that "all taxes shall be uniform on the same class of subjects . . ." Indeed, this Court has held that the constitutional requirement of uniformity is satisfied so long as the taxing authority assesses all property at the same percentage of its actual value; by maintaining such a uniform ratio, each property will be held accountable for its pro rata share of the burden of local government . . . . *The uniformity standard is not violated by allowing variations, between buildings, with respect to ratios of taxes to income.*

In re Johnstown Assoc., 431 A.2d at 934 (emphasis added).

As in Pennsylvania, property valuation in this state may consider the gross income generated by the property as an indicator of value. *McArdle's Estate v. City of Jackson*, 215 Miss. 571, 579, 61 So.2d 400, 402 (1952). It is not, therefore, a constitutional violation to value differently otherwise identical properties if the disparate values result from disparate revenue-generating capabilities. The constitutional issue raised in Taxpayer's appeal is without merit.

V.

Hinds County presents a cross-appeal. The County argues that the Circuit Court erred when it refused to hold, as a matter of law, that for the years in question, the true value of Rebelwood Complex was $4,044,950. Procedurally, Hinds County argues that the Circuit Court erred when it refused to direct a verdict in the County's favor on the issue of value, and, thereafter, when it refused to correct this error via post-trial motion for judgment notwithstanding the verdict.

Hinds County bases this claim on its view that Taxpayer's valuation witnesses ignored the legal mandate that all factors affecting value be considered. More fully, Hinds County's point is that, without contradiction, the federal subsidy and benefits enjoyed by Rebelwood have a substantial value and that Taxpayer's "experts admit that they made no attempt to appraise the property according to current use, choosing instead to create a hypothetical situation and appraise Rebelwood as if it were a free-market type apartment complex."

Put otherwise, Hinds County's point is that there is no credible evidence in the record from which the jury may have concluded that the true value of Rebelwood was $3,180,000. Either the legal definition of true value required inclusion of the value of federal subsidy and benefits, in which event true value would be the County's figure of approximately $4,000,000, or any such subsidy and benefits were properly excludable and Rebelwood would be treated as "a free-market type apartment complex," in which event true value of Rebelwood would necessarily be Taxpayer's figure of slightly less than $2,000,000. Our review of the record convinces us that there truly is no middle ground and that everything turns on the correct interpretation of the definition of true value found in Section 27-35-50. We have considered and resolved the point in Part III above.

Because we are concerned with an attack on a jury verdict, our scope of review is as limited as it is familiar. We have recently reiterated that scope of review in *Guerdon Industries, Inc. v. Gentry*, 531 So.2d 1202 (Miss. 1988) as follows:

> . . . [W]hen a trial court, or the Supreme Court . . . [on appeal], considers such a motion [for directed verdict or judgment notwithstanding the verdict] it must do so "in the light most favorable to the party opposed to the motion." The non-

movant must also be given the benefit of all favorable inferences that may reasonably be drawn from the evidence. If the facts and inferences so considered point so overwhelming in favor of the defendant [movant] that reasonable men and women could not have arrived at a verdict for the plaintiff [non-movant], granting the motion is required. The burden upon the movant in such cases is great, for if there is "substantial" evidence opposed to the motion, which would allow reasonable and fair-minded men and women to reach differing conclusions, the motion must be denied.

531 So.2d at 1205; *Stubblefield v. Jesco, Inc.,* 464 So.2d 47, 54 (Miss. 1984); *Paymaster Oil Mill Co. v. Mitchell,* 319 So.2d 652, 657 (Miss. 1975). This rule is necessary so that Taxpayer's right to trial by jury be respected the same as in any other civil case. *City of Jackson v. Locklar,* 431 So.2d 475, 478 (Miss. 1983). This view obtains in property tax appeals heard *de novo* in the circuit court the same as in any other civil case tried before a jury. *Board of Supervisors of Jackson County v. Standard Oil Company,* 353 So.2d 1137, 1138 (Miss. 1977); see also *Calhoun County Board of Supervisors v. Grenada Bank,* 543 So.2d 138, 140 (Miss. 1988) (petition for rehearing pending).

In the ordinary case where each litigant presents an all or nothing point of view and where the jury returns a verdict "somewhere in between," we will be slow to intervene. Where, for example, in an automobile collision case a plaintiff contends that the defendant was the sole party at fault and where the defendant in return argues that the accident was entirely caused by the plaintiff's negligence, often the evidence will quite comfortably permit a conclusion that each party was partially to blame. Here, however, we perceive no basis for a compromise. Everything turns on the definition of true value. As explained above, we resolve that issue in favor of Hinds County and hold on this record, as a matter of law, that the value of any federal subsidy or benefits enjoyed by Taxpayer by reason of its ownership of Rebelwood must be included in establishing its true value for each year in which such subsidy or benefits are in fact enjoyed. This being the case, there is no way on this record that our hypothetical, rational juror who gave all good fidelity to the rule of law could have reached any conclusion other than that the true value of the property for the years in question was approximately $4,000,000.

In settling upon the precise true value to be assigned this property for 1984 and 1985, we must give close attention to the lowest figure, i.e., the true value estimate most favorable to Taxpayer, that the jury could rationally have returned. Hinds County appears to argue that its assessment of $4,000,000 is entitled to a presumption of correctness and, because Taxpayer's appraisers ignored current use, the original assessment should stand. However viable such a presumption may be at earlier stages of the process, it evaporates in light of the extensive proof offered by both sides before the Circuit Court and its jury.

We reiterate that the values suggested by an appraiser following one of the approaches to value is not in and of itself an appraisal. A professionally and legally acceptable assessment of value is an opinion which is the product of a reconciliation of—and not an averaging of—the values indicated by each of the three approaches to value. Rare is the day when a competent appraisal may be based on a single approach. We consider in this light the indications of value as found by those appraisals which correctly assigned current use. These are:

Cost Approach	$4,044,900
Market Data Approach	$4,039,998
Income Capitalization Approach	$3,978,780

Having well in mind our limited scope of review and that we must give Taxpayer every benefit of the doubt where the evidence is disputed—so long as we apply the correct legal standard regarding current use, we hold that no hypothetical, rational juror could have concluded on this record that for the years 1984 and 1985 Rebelwood had a true value of less than $3,978,780. Emphasis upon the income capitalization approach to value is particularly appropriate here in that the primary reason why Taxpayer holds such property is for the production of income. Moreover, the quality of data available makes credible the income capitalization approach to value.

By reason of the foregoing, we regard Hinds County's cross-appeal as well taken. We vacate the judgment of the Circuit Court insofar as it adjudges the true value of the Rebelwood Complex and we now hold as a matter of law that for the years 1984 and 1985 the true value of Rebelwood was $3,978,780.

One feature of the property assessment valuation process should ease Taxpayer's pain a bit. The assessment of value is not permanent. We are today concerned only with the true value of Rebelwood for the years 1984 and 1985, years in which no one disputes that the complex was used as a federally subsidized low income housing complex and enjoyed valuable federal benefits. If for any reason in the future the federal government pulls the rug out from under Rebelwood, that no doubt would affect its value. Because Taxpayer, like any other property owner, is entitled to have its property valued and assessed each year, any such change will surely be reflected in the succeeding year's valuations and assessments. If we should reach a point in time in the future when Rebelwood's functional obsolescence really does affect true value, the law no doubt would afford Taxpayer the right to a substantially reduced assessed value. So long, however, as Rebelwood enjoys the benefits of the federal subsidies and a 98 percent occupancy rate, however, Taxpayer's approach to value will remain quite hypothetical at best, and when we consider that federal regulations allow Taxpayer adjusted benefits for Rebelwood to reflect changing property tax obligations, Taxpayer's argument before this Court appears a bit disingenuous.

AFFIRMED ON DIRECT APPEAL; REVERSED AND RENDERED ON CROSS-APPEAL.

ROY NOBLE LEE, C.J., HAWKINS, P.J., and ANDERSON, J., concur.

DAN M. LEE, P.J., concurs to Parts I, II, III and IV and dissents to Part V.

PITTMAN, J., HAWKINS, P.J., and SULLIVAN, J., specially concur by separate written opinion.

BLASS and PRATHER, JJ., not participating.

PITTMAN, Justice, specially concurring:

The majority opinion rightfully would include a rental income as part of the total assessment. Though our inclusion of federal subsidies as a part of property valuation for tax purposes breaks new ground in the area of taxation, the rental income inclusion is not inconsistent with prior methods of assessment or holdings of this Court. *McArdle's Estate v. City of Jackson*, 215 Miss. 571, 579, 61 So.2d 400, 402 (1952).

However, the tenor of the majority opinion would include all federal subsidies for tax valuation and from its dicta could have each tax assessor looking at mortgage interest rates to tax the more favorable mortgages by inclusion in tax valuation and looking behind various and changing farm subsidies to include them specifically in tax valuation. The federal subsidies for Rebelwood are easily isolated and are included and taxed. Not so for many other federally sponsored subsidies; therefore, this opinion should be limited to income or rental value only and not so sweeping as to include interest subsidies or possibly farm subsidies or other creative financing programs sponsored by the federal government. The majority opinion reaches the right result, but this is new ground and could produce new types of taxation. *Tradewinds East Associates v. Hampton Charter Township*, 159 Mich.App. 77, 406 N.W.2d 845 (1987).

HAWKINS, P.J., and SULLIVAN, J., join this opinion.

<hr/>

KANKAKEE COUNTY BOARD OF REVIEW v. PROPERTY TAX APPEAL BOARD
131 Ill.2d 1, 544 N.E.2d 447, 136 Ill.Dec. 76
Illinois Supreme Court, 1989

<hr/>

Justice WARD delivered the opinion of the court:

This appeal arises from an administrative review proceeding. Riverwoods Associates (Riverwoods) filed a complaint with the Kankakee County Board of Review (Review Board) alleging that the assessor of Kankakee County had overassessed its property in 1984. The Review Board determined that the property had a fair market value of $7,904,735 and under section 20 of the Revenue Act of 1939 (Ill.Rev.Stat. 1983, ch. 120, par. 501) should be assessed at one-third of that value, or $2,632,722. The Review Board refused to reduce the assessment, and Riverwoods appealed to the Illinois Property Tax Appeal Board (PTAB). The PTAB conducted a hearing pursuant to its statutory authority (Ill.Rev.Stat. 1987, ch. 120, par. 592.3) and reduced the valuation of the property from $7,904,735 to $2,325,000, finding that the rent subsidy Riverwoods received pursuant to a contract with the Illinois Housing Development Authority should not be considered in determining the value of the property for tax purposes. The PTAB accordingly reduced the tax assessment on the property from $2,632,722 to $775,388. The Review Board filed a petition in the circuit court of Kankakee County for administrative review of the PTAB's decision (Ill.Rev.Stat.1987, ch. 110, par. 3—104) and the circuit court affirmed the PTAB's decision. The Review Board appealed and the appellate court reversed, holding that the PTAB erred as a matter of law in adopting a valuation approach which ignored the subsidy Riverwoods received from the Illinois Housing Development Authority. (163 Ill.App.3d 811, 114 Ill.Dec. 851, 516 N.E.2d 1006.) We granted the PTAB's petition for leave to appeal in No. 66396 and Riverwoods' petition for leave to appeal in No. 66397. 107 Ill.2d R. 315(a).

Riverwoods Apartments is a 125-unit building located in the city of Kankakee. The building is rented exclusively to elderly residents, whose rent is subsidized under an agreement with the Illinois Housing Development Authority. The terms of the subsidy agreement are not part of the record. The property owner, Riverwoods Associates, appeared before the Kankakee County Board of Review (the Review Board) complaining that the assessor had improperly assessed the value of the property and requesting a tax reduction. The Review Board denied its complaint and Riverwoods appealed to the PTAB.

At an administrative hearing held before the PTAB, both Riverwoods and the Review Board introduced written appraisals of the fair market value of Riverwoods' property. Riverwoods also presented the testimony of its appraiser. Both appraisals applied the three methods of valuation in calculating the fair market value of the property: the market data approach, the reproduction cost approach and the capitalization of net income approach.

At issue here is the proper method for calculating the fair market value of property under the capitalization of net income method of valuation. Under this approach, the fair cash value of property is determined by applying a capitalization rate to the property's estimated net annual income. There is no dispute concerning the proper capitalization rate. Rather, we are asked to determine whether the rent subsidy which Riverwoods receives under its contract with the government should be considered in estimating the net annual income of the apartment building.

Nicholas Muros, who prepared the appraisal submitted by Riverwoods at the hearing before the PTAB, testified that he did not take the government subsidy into account in estimating the net annual income of the apartment building for purposes of the income approach. He explained that, in 1984, Riverwoods received an average monthly rent of $123 per apartment directly from tenants. In addition, Riverwoods received a substantial rental subsidy pursuant to a Federal subsidy agreement. Although the subsidy agreement is not part of the record, the trial court's memorandum states that the subsidy provides approximately 80% of Riverwoods' income. Muros stated that he did not consider the rent subsidy as part of the rental income on the property, because he viewed the subsidy as income earned from the government contract, rather than income earned by the property itself. Instead, he surveyed the average rent paid for comparable non-subsidized apartment units in the Kankakee area, and arrived at a gross potential rent figure of $300 to $350 per apartment, or a gross income of $457,800. He then adjusted this figure for vacancy losses and expenses, and arrived at a "net income" of $274,500. He then capitalized this figure at a rate of 11.8%, and arrived at a value of $2,326,271, which he rounded down to $2,325,000. As stated, Muros' report also developed estimates of value under the market data approach ($2,300,000) and under the reproduction cost approach ($2,325,000). He concluded, however, that the income approach produced the most accurate method of valuation. His final opinion that Riverwoods' property had a fair market value of $2,325,000 coincides with his estimate of value under the income approach.

Walter Stoutamoyer prepared the appraisal which the Review Board submitted to the PTAB. Although Stoutamoyer did not appear before the PTAB to explain his data or methodology, his appraisal indicates that he did consider the subsidy in estimating the net annual income of Riverwoods' property for purposes of the income approach. Accordingly, he determined that the property had a much higher fair market value of $5,900,000 under the net income approach. In applying the income approach, however, Stoutamoyer did not use the rent Riverwoods received from tenants plus the government subsidy as the gross income figure. Instead, he considered the rents paid at comparable properties in the Kankakee and Central Illinois areas. Although his appraisal does not state whether or not these comparable properties were subsidized, Riverwoods' attorney conceded that the properties Stoutamoyer considered were subsidized housing projects. Stoutamoyer estimated that Riverwoods received an average potential rent of $520 per month per apartment, and a potential gross annual income of $781,800. He then adjusted this figure for vacancy losses and expenses and arrived at a net income figure of $620,219. He then capitalized this figure at a rate of 10.5% and arrived at a value of $5,906,848, which he rounded down to $5,900,000. Although Stoutamoyer's appraisal considered the income approach, his value estimate was based almost exclusively upon the reproduction cost approach, under which the depreciated cost of the improvements to the land is added to the value of the land itself. His conclusion that Riverwoods' property had a fair market value of $6,665,875 coincided with his estimate of value under the reproduction cost approach. Stoutamoyer's appraisal also determined that Riverwoods' property had a value of $5,504,000 under the market data approach, although he disregarded this estimate of value as unreliable under the circumstances.

The PTAB adopted the appraisal that Muros prepared for Riverwoods and found the fair market value of the subject property was $2,325,000. The PTAB rejected Stoutamoyer's appraisal, stating that it relied too heavily upon the reproduction cost approach, which is not favored under decisions in our State in situations where the income and market approaches to determining value may be applied. The PTAB then concluded that Muros' use of market rent, rather than actual or contract rent, in calculating the fair market value of Riverwoods' property was consistent with the principles set forth in *Springfield Marine Bank v. Property Tax Appeal Board*, (1970), 44 Ill.2d 428, 256 N.E.2d 334. The PTAB interpreted *Springfield Marine* as holding that property subject to an encumbrance which distorts the property's rental income above or below market value must be valuated as unencumbered. The PTAB therefore relied upon the appraisal introduced by Riverwoods as the best estimate of value and determined that the property had a fair market value of $2,325,000.

The trial court upheld the PTAB's decision. The Review Board argued that the PTAB erred when it relied upon an appraisal which did not consider the rent subsidy Riverwoods received from the government. The court stated, however, that the Review Board had failed to subpoena the subsidy contract or present any evidence before the PTAB regarding the terms of the agreement. The court found that it was virtually impossible for the PTAB to appraise the effect of the subsidy contract in the absence of any evidence as to its terms. The court also stated that the principles set out in *Springfield Marine* should be applied in cases such as this, where the encumbrance at issue increased, rather than decreased, the value of the property. The court thus concluded that Riverwoods' property should be valued apart from the subsidy agreement. The court finally concluded that the PTAB was justified in refusing to follow Stoutamoyer's appraisal in view of its undue emphasis on reproduction cost and that the PTAB's decision therefore was not against the manifest weight of the evidence.

The appellate court reversed. (163 Ill.App.3d 811, 114 Ill.Dec. 851, 516 N.E.2d 1006.) Although it did uphold the PTAB's adoption of the income approach as the most reliable method for determining fair market value in this case, the court reversed on the legal issue of what factors should be considered when determining the fair market value of property under the income approach. Specifically, the court held that three types of rent should be considered in determining the fair market value of property under the income approach: "economic rent," that is, rent which the property would probably command in the open market; "restricted rent," rent actually paid by the tenants; and "contract rent," that is, the actual rent that property owners receive from tenants plus the rent subsidy they receive from the government. The court determined that all three types of rental income are entitled to consideration under the income approach, although no one amount may be controlling. The court observed that "economic," or market, rent is determined by analyzing the property at issue with reference to "comparable" properties. Because the record did not clearly show that the properties Muros considered were "comparable" to Riverwoods' property, or whether the economic rent of Riverwoods' property truly reflected its income-earning capacity, the court found no sound basis for the PTAB's adoption of Muros' appraisal. The court also concluded that the subsidy should be considered in determining the fair market value of Riverwoods' property because it would be considered by a willing and able buyer and seller, and because ignoring the subsidy would amount to a judicially mandated tax subsidy by the local government beyond that established by legislative policy. The court concluded that the

PTAB erred as a matter of law in accepting a valuation approach, which the appellate court found "totally disregarded the subsidy aspects of the Riverwoods Apartments." 163 Ill.App.3d at 818—19, 114 Ill.Dec. 851, 516 N.E.2d 1006.

The Revenue Act states that real property shall be valued at one-third of its "fair cash value." (Ill.Rev.Stat. 1987, ch. 120, par. 501.) This court defined "fair cash value" as the price the property "'would bring at a voluntary sale where the owner is ready, willing and able to sell but not compelled to do so, and the buyer is ready, willing and able to buy but not forced so to do . . . .'" (Springfield Marine, 44 Ill.2d at 430, 256 N.E.2d 334, quoting People ex rel. McGaughey v. Wilson (1937), 367 Ill. 494, 496, 12 N.E.2d 5.) Although both parties agree that the income approach to valuation is a reliable indicator of the property's fair market value, they disagree regarding the proper method of calculating the gross income of subsidized property for purposes of this approach.

The Review Board argues that "contract rent," or the actual rent that Riverwoods receives from tenants plus the rent subsidy it receives from the government, should be used in calculating Riverwoods' gross annual income under the income approach. Riverwoods and the PTAB, on the other hand, argue that the "market rent," or that rent which the property would probably command on the open market as indicated by current rents being paid for comparable space, should be used in calculating Riverwoods' gross annual income under the income approach. Riverwoods argues that the PTAB's use of market rent, rather than contract rent, in calculating the fair market value of the subject property was consistent with the principles set forth in this court's opinion in Springfield Marine Bank v. Property Tax Appeal Board (1970), 44 Ill.2d 428, 256 N.E.2d 334.

In Springfield Marine, the taxpayer's predecessor in title subjected the property to long-term leases which had approximately 10 years to run at the time of the court's decision. The value of the property had appreciated significantly after the leases were executed, so that the rent designated in the leases was substantially below that which could be obtained in the open market at the time the property was assessed. (44 Ill.2d at 429, 256 N.E.2d 334.) The taxpayer contended that its property tax assessment was too high because it failed to reflect the unfavorable leases which diminished the property's rental income. The PTAB refused to reduce the assessed valuation of the parcels. The trial court, however, concluded that the PTAB's decision was contrary to the manifest weight of the evidence and reduced the assessed valuation of the property to reflect the disadvantageous leases. On direct review, this court reversed, stating:

> It is clearly the value of the 'tract or lot of real property' which is assessed, rather than the value of the interest presently held by the owner. In determining the value of the property, rental income may of course be a relevant factor. However, it cannot be the controlling factor, particularly where it is admittedly misleading as to the fair cash value of the property involved. (44 Ill.2d at 430-31, 256 N.E.2d 334.)

The court acknowledged that many factors may prevent a property owner from realizing an income return from property which accurately reflects its true earning capacity, but concluded that "it is the capacity for earning income, rather than the income actually derived, which reflects 'fair cash value' for taxation purposes." (44 Ill.2d at 431, 256 N.E.2d 334.) The court accordingly reinstated the assessment approved by the PTAB and reversed the trial court's conclusion that the assessment was contrary to the manifest weight of the evidence.

Relying upon *Springfield Marine*, Riverwoods and the PTAB argue that "contract rent," or that rent that Riverwoods receives from tenants and pursuant to its contract with the government, must be disregarded in this case because it does not reflect the rent which the property would command in the open market. They argue that, instead, the income that property would generate in the open market absent the benefits or burdens of any of the current owner's contractual obligations should be considered in determining the fair cash value of property. They acknowledge the distinction between the unfavorable leases at issue in *Springfield Marine* and the favorable subsidy contract here. They argue, however, that the principles of *Springfield Marine* should apply with equal force to contracts which artificially inflate rents above, rather than below, market value. To hold otherwise, they argue, would penalize the competent and the diligent and reward the incompetent.

The Review Board responds that the principles set forth in *Springfield Marine* do not apply in this case, because the subsidy at issue is not an "encumbrance" but rather is rent which substantially benefits Riverwoods and so must be considered in the same manner that rent collected from tenants is considered in the income approach. It argues that Riverwoods' actual income must be considered because it reflects the property's income-earning capacity in the marketplace of subsidized housing. The Board argues that the subsidy reflects an agreement between Riverwoods and the government as to what this type of subsidized housing is worth in the open market.

Amicus curiae, the Lake County Board of Review, likewise argues that income-earning capacity of subsidized housing projects and the income which the owners of such housing actually derive are identical because the government controls the income earned by controlling the amount of rent that can be charged and the amount of the subsidy. Amicus argues that market-derived rent does not accurately reflect subsidized property's earning capacity, because such property is planned, built and operated outside the traditional marketplace. Amicus argues that a number of decisions from other jurisdictions hold that subsidy income must be considered in valuation. *Executive Square Limited Partnership v. Board of Tax Review* (1987), 11 Conn.App. 566, 528 A.2d 409; *Steele v. Town of Allenstown* (1984), 124 N.H. 487, 471 A.2d 1179.

Before we consider the merits of the parties' arguments, we must determine the appropriate standard of review. The PTAB is required by statute to conduct hearings and decide each case before it based upon equity and the weight of the evidence presented. (Ill. Rev. Stat. 1987, ch. 120, par. 592.4.) Its decisions are then subject to review under the provisions of the Administrative Review Law (Ill. Rev. Stat. 1987, ch. 110, par. 3—101 et seq.). The Act limits the scope of judicial review by providing that "[t]he findings and conclusions of the administrative agency on questions of fact shall be held to be prima facie true and correct." (Ill. Rev. Stat. 1987, ch. 110, par. 3—110.) Thus, the usual standard for judicial review of an administrative decision is whether it is contrary to the manifest weight of the evidence, and a court will not intervene in a case where there is simply a difference of opinion as to the actual value of property. The Review Board contends, and the appellate court held, however, that this case involves an improper method of valuation rather than simply a difference of opinion as to the market value of Riverwoods' property. The Review Board argues that the PTAB erred in concluding that, under *Springfield Marine Bank v. Property Tax Appeal Board* (1970), 44 Ill.2d 428, 256 N.E.2d 334, the value of Riverwoods' property had to be determined without considering the subsidy income Riverwoods receives pursuant to its contract with the government. Accordingly, we must determine whether the PTAB erred as a matter of law when it determined that the subsidy income Riverwoods receives pursuant to its contract with the government may not be considered when determining the fair market value of Riverwoods' property for taxation purposes.

Riverwoods and the PTAB concede that the contract rent Riverwoods receives under the government subsidy contract is a relevant factor to "consider" in determining the fair cash value of property for tax purposes. They argue, however, that actual rent or contract rent must be disregarded where it does not accurately reflect rents obtainable in the open market for comparable property. They cite decisions from other jurisdictions which support the conclusion reached in *Springfield Marine* as authority for this argument. Riverwoods and the PTAB interpret *Springfield Marine* as holding that contract rent is irrelevant in determining the fair cash value of property where contract rent is not reflective of rents obtainable on the open market. Although we agree that the principles set out in *Springfield Marine* are relevant in this case, we disagree with the manner in which the PTAB applied those principles to the facts here.

Springfield Marine does not stand for the proposition that contract rent is irrelevant where it is different from market rent. Rather, that case simply held that, when property is subject to an unfavorable lease, the contract rent or actual rental income must be disregarded in determining the property's fair market value when the actual rental income does not reflect the property's capacity for earning income. Thus, under *Springfield Marine*, a property's income-earning capacity is the most significant element in arriving at "fair cash value." (*Springfield Marine*, 44 Ill.2d at 431, 256 N.E.2d 334.) When actual rental income does not reflect the income-earning capacity of property, it may be disregarded, and the taxing authority may look to rents obtainable for comparable property in the open market. Where actual income truly reflects the income-earning capacity of the property, however, it may not be ignored simply because it does not coincide with rents obtainable on the open market.

As stated, the standard for determining the fair market value of property is the price at which ready, willing and able buyers and sellers would agree. (*Springfield Marine*, 44 Ill.2d at 431, 256 N.E.2d 334.) In this case, the rent subsidy that Riverwoods receives pursuant to its contract with the government enhances the property's income-earning capacity. A willing buyer would most certainly consider the guaranteed income rate set by the Federal government when determining the fair cash value of the property. To ignore actual income would be to ignore the effect of the subsidy on a prospective investor's judgment regarding the fair market value of the property. Because the rent subsidy Riverwoods receives pursuant to its contract with the government affects the earning capacity, and thus the fair cash value, of Riverwoods' property, we conclude that the PTAB erred as a matter of law in accepting a valuation that relied only on the rent the property would command in the open market of unsubsidized housing. A government subsidy contract that enhances the income-earning capacity of a particular piece of property must be considered in assessing the fair cash value of that property for taxation purposes.

We do not mean to suggest that the tax assessor, in applying the income approach to valuation, is limited to and must accept the actual rental figure under the government subsidy contract as the sole measure of projected income. In most cases, such an approach would lead to a distorted measure of fair cash value. Factors such as the transferability of the subsidy contract, the remaining term of the contract and restrictions on the amount of return on capital investment would certainly affect the value of the property. A valuation approach which considers the subsidy income, but does not consider the negative aspects of a subsidy agreement upon the earning capacity of subsidized property, would be inappropriate. The taxing authority must weigh both the positive and the negative aspects of the subsidy agreement and adjust the actual income figure to accurately reflect the true earning capacity of the property in question. As stated, "it is the capacity for earning income, rather than the income actually derived, which reflects 'fair cash value' for taxation purposes." *Springfield Marine*, 44 Ill.2d at 431, 256 N.E.2d 334.

In this regard, we note that the appraisal that the Review Board submitted to the PTAB did not use Riverwoods' actual income or the contract rent it receives under the subsidy agreement ($736 per month per apartment) in calculating the gross annual income of Riverwoods' property under the income approach. Rather, the appraisal compared Riverwoods' property to similar subsidized housing and calculated that the property had a potential gross income of only $520 a month per apartment, approximately $200 less than the rent Riverwoods actually receives pursuant to its contract with the government. The Review Board now claims, however, that Riverwoods' contract rent or actual income is equivalent to the property's income-earning capacity. There is no evidence in the record to support this contention. The evidence suggests only that the government subsidy enhances the income-earning capacity of Riverwoods' property, and should be considered in determining the fair cash value of Riverwoods' property. Accordingly, we do not hold that Riverwoods' actual income coincides with the property's income-earning capacity. We simply hold that the PTAB erred as a matter of law when it failed to consider the effect of the subsidy agreement on the income-earning capacity and thus the fair market value of Riverwoods' property. On remand, the PTAB must consider the effect which the subsidy agreement has upon the earning capacity of Riverwoods' property.

Riverwoods and the PTAB argue that the rental income that Riverwoods receives under the subsidy agreement should not be considered in valuating the property, because it is earned by virtue of Riverwoods' personal contract with the government, rather than by the property itself. They argue that any projected income figure which considers the rent subsidy values Riverwoods' interest in the property, rather than the earning capacity of the property. This court has held, however, that the fair cash value of property should be determined according to the use for which the property is designed and which produces its maximum income. In *State v. Illinois Central R.R. Co.* (1861), 27 Ill. 64, 67-68, this court stated:

> Where property has a known and determinate value . . . , there can be no difficulty [in fixing valuation]. But there are many kinds of property, as to which the assessor has no such satisfactory guide. Such is peculiarly the case with railroad property, and other similar property, constructed not only for the profit of the owners, but for the accommodation of the public, under the sanction and by the exercise of the sovereign power of the State. *In such cases, the inquiry should be, what is the property worth to be used for the purposes for which it is constructed,* and not for any other purpose to which it might be applied or converted, or for which it might be used. In such cases, if the property is devoted to the use for which it was designed, and is in a condition to produce its maximum income, one very important element for ascertaining its present value is discovered, and that is its net profits. (Emphasis added.)

In this case, the evidence shows that Riverwoods' property was designed for use as subsidized housing. The appraisers for both parties agreed that the best and highest use of the property is its current use as subsidized housing. Although the subsidy agreement is not part of the record on this appeal, there is no evidence to suggest that a prospective purchaser could not also use the property as subsidized housing if it was sold on the open market today. Riverwoods' appraiser testified at the hearing before the PTAB that government subsidy contracts such as that at issue here are generally transferable to prospective purchasers with the consent of the government. Because the evidence suggests that the property is available to others for use as subsidized housing, and that the subsidy agreement affects the property's income-earning capacity, we conclude that the subsidy agreement must be considered when calculating the fair market value of Riverwoods' property.

Riverwoods and the PTAB urge this court to ignore the government subsidy, and to instead consider the rental income that the property would command in the open market of unsubsidized housing. Rents established in the market of unsubsidized housing, however, do not accurately reflect the earning capacity of subsidized housing, because subsidized housing is conceived, constructed and operated outside the forces of the traditional marketplace. Both parties agree that the market rents in the area would not have justified building the project and that the project would not have been feasible without the government subsidies. The subsidy enhances the earning capacity of government subsidized housing above market levels to provide owners with an incentive to build low-income housing. Thus, the subsidy cannot be ignored in determining the earning capacity, and thus the fair cash value, of subsidized housing.

Several other jurisdictions have likewise concluded that rental subsidies must be considered in calculating the fair cash value of government subsidized housing. See *Executive Square Limited Partnership v. Board of Tax Review* (1987), 11 Conn.App. 566, 528 A.2d 409; *Steele v. Town of Allenstown* (1984), 124 N.H. 487, 471 A.2d 1179. But see *Canton Towers, Ltd. v. Board of Revision* (1983), 3 Ohio St.3d 4, 444 N.E.2d 1027 (where the Ohio Supreme Court held that rents obtainable for comparable unsubsidized housing in the open market, rather than actual rental income, were properly used to calculate the gross annual income of subsidized housing under the income approach to valuation).

Riverwoods and the PTAB next contend that a valuation approach which considers the effect of a government subsidy agreement upon the fair market value of subsidized housing would violate the constitutional guarantee of uniformity of taxation set forth in article IX, section 4, of the Illinois Constitution of 1970 (Ill. Const. 1970, art. IX, sec. 4). They argue that it violates the principle of uniformity to consider the actual rental income when valuating Riverwoods' property and subsidized housing in general, while valuating all other property according to rents charged for comparable property in the open market. Article IX, section 4(a), of the Constitution of 1970 provides: "Except as otherwise provided in this Section, taxes upon real property shall be levied uniformly by valuation ascertained as the General Assembly shall provide by law."

The principle of uniformity of taxation requires equality in the burden of taxation. This court has held that an equal tax burden cannot exist without uniformity in both the basis of assessment and in the rate of taxation. The uniformity requirement prohibits taxing officials from valuating one kind of property within a taxing district at a certain proportion of its true value while valuating the same kind of property in the same district at a substantially lesser or greater proportion of its true value.

We reject Riverwoods' claim that consideration of the subsidy agreement in assessing the fair market value of subsidized housing violates the rule of uniformity. The principle of uniformity of taxation requires that similar properties within the same district be assessed on a similar basis. The cornerstone of uniform assessment is the fair cash value of the property in question. As stated, a property's income-earning capacity is an important factor in determining its fair cash value. Thus, uniformity is achieved only when all property with the same income-earning capacity and fair cash value is assessed at a consistent level. In most instances, the income-earning capacity and fair cash value of unsubsidized property may be accurately determined with reference to rents charged for comparable property in the open market. Market rents, however, do not necessarily reflect the income-earning capacity of subsidized property. The subsidy agreement must be considered to determine the true income-earning capacity, and thus the true value, of subsidized property. Riverwoods did not present any evidence to show that consideration of the subsidy agreement will cause its property to be assessed at anything other than one-third of its fair cash value. Failure to consider the subsidy agreement would permit subsidized property to be taxed at less than its fair cash value, in violation of the principle of uniformity.

Riverwoods also argues that the Review Board violated the rule of uniformity because it overassessed its property in relation to other comparable subsidized properties. As support of this argument, Riverwoods claims that the Review Board valued its property at $63,812 per unit, whereas two other subsidized apartment complexes in the Kankakee area were valued at $14,108 and $21,230 per unit respectively. The taxpayer who objects to an assessment on the basis of lack of uniformity bears the burden of proving the disparity of assessment valuations by clear and convincing evidence. Riverwoods failed to sustain their burden of proof in this case. There is no evidence in the record to suggest that the two subsidized projects are comparable to Riverwoods' property. Nor is there evidence showing that Riverwoods will be required to bear a disproportionately greater tax burden than owners of other comparable subsidized properties if the subsidy agreement is considered in calculating the fair market value of their property. Riverwoods cannot establish a lack of uniformity in taxation or a violation of constitutional rights by simply asserting that the Review Board determined that their property had a greater actual value than other subsidized properties.

Riverwoods finally argues that consideration of the subsidy revenue when determining the value of Riverwoods' property for property tax purposes will result in double taxation in violation of article IX, section 4, of the Illinois Constitution (Ill. Const. 1970, art. IX, sec. 4). Riverwoods asserts that the subsidy revenue is taxed as income and therefore should not be subject to an additional ad valorem property tax. It adds that a government rent subsidy is an intangible asset which cannot properly be subject to taxation as real property. This court has held that double taxation means "'taxing twice, for the same purpose, in the same year, some of the property in the territory in which the tax is laid, without taxing all of it a second time.'" (*People ex rel. Hanrahan v. Caliendo* (1971), 50 Ill.2d 72, 83—84, 277 N.E.2d 319, quoting *People ex rel. Toman v. Advance Heating Co.* (1941), 376 Ill. 158, 163, 33 N.E.2d 206.) The subsidy income at issue in this case is not real property, nor is it taxed as such. Rather, the subsidy revenue, like the rent paid by tenants, is simply used to determine the fair market value of Riverwoods' property under the income approach to valuation. The fact that Riverwoods pays income tax upon the subsidy revenue does not prohibit the taxing authority from considering that revenue when calculating the fair market value of Riverwoods' property for taxation purposes. Because the subsidy is not taxed as both income and as real property, we reject Riverwoods' double taxation claim.

We hold that the PTAB erred as a matter of law in failing to consider the effect of the subsidy agreement upon the income-earning capacity, and thus the fair market value, of Riverwoods' property for taxation purposes. Accordingly, we affirm the judgment of the appellate court.

Nos. 66396 & 66397—Appellate court affirmed.

CALVO, J., took no part in the consideration or decision of this case. Ill., 1989.

Notes and Questions

1. Consider the income limitations on federally subsidized housing as a form of rent restriction similar to a long-term lease. Should a court's position on the long-term lease question control the valuation of subsidized housing in that state? What should be the effect of finding that (1) investment in the housing project was not "improvident," (2) investors were aware of the income limitations at the time the development was planned, (3) some portion (or all) of property taxes may be passed on to tenants in the form of higher rents? See *Community Development Co. of Gardner v. Board of Assessors*, 377 Mass. 351, 385 N.E.2d 1376 (1979); *Kargman v. Jacobs*, 113 R.I. 696, 325 A.2d 543 (1974); *Kargman v. Jacobs*, 122 R.I. 720, 411 A.2d 1326 (1980).

2. How should a state's position on (1) the valuation of property subject to a long-term lease and (2) the valuation of rent-restricted subsidized housing affect the valuation of property subject to local rent control ordinances?

3. How should a state's position on the valuation of public utility property subject to rate limitations affect the valuation of subsidized housing? See *Royal Gardens Co. v. City of Concord*, 114 N.H. 668, 328 A.2d 123 (1974), in which a majority of the court held that it could not "distinguish for valuation purposes a state and federally regulated utility from a federally regulated housing project which limits the income to be received by the owner."

4. The late Professor Stanley Surrey, who served for eight years as Assistant Secretary of the Treasury for tax policy, testified in 1973 against the practice of offering tax incentives to private developers as a means of constructing low-income housing.

> There is something terribly amiss when to provide low-income housing for the shelter of the poor, we at the same time shelter tax millionaires . . . . If it is low-income rental housing we are considering, we must ask if we would pay out funds to well-off professional people or executives so that they will turn over some of the dollars to the developers as their compensation but will keep enough to provide a 15–20 percent rate of return on the after-tax profits . . . .[8]

These tax incentives have remained in force in part because they are supported even by housing advocates who acknowledge the logic of Professor Surrey's position. One such proponent was unusually candid as to the reasons for this support:

---

8. Committee on Ways and Means, Panel Discussion on Tax Reform, 93d Cong., 1st Sess. (February 5, 1973), pp. 71, 100–101.

Usually, one of the strengths of direct subsidies over tax incentives is their high degree of visibility and political accountability. In the present political climate, which is witnessing increasing demands for lower taxes and less government spending, visibility and political accountability must be counted as liabilities. The present Administration would be committing political suicide to propose new and costly housing programs. Because tax incentives are subject to less government scrutiny than direct government subsidies, Congress apparently has taken the less politically risky route to provide government assistance. While tax incentives are not the most equitable, effective or efficient method of providing an adequate supply of low-income housing, at present, they are the only method."[9]

The recurrence of the same themes in this debate through decades of tax legislation is only dramatized by the fact that the author meant by the "the present administration" the Carter presidency.[10]

---

9.   D. Stevenson, "Tax Reform and Real Estate Tax Shelters: Consequences for Low-Income Housing," *University of Cincinnati Law Review* 48 (1979):99.

10. With regard to property tax incentives for low-income housing, see M. Durchslag, "Property Tax Abatement for Low-Income Housing: An Idea Whose Time May Never Arrive," *Harvard Journal on Legislation* 30 (1993):367, a reevaluation after thirty years of the positions taken in N. Alpert, "Property Tax Abatement: An Incentive for Low Income Housing," *Harvard Journal on Legislation* 11 (1973):1.

7 LEGAL CHALLENGES TO PROPERTY TAX SYSTEMS

Introduction

Although this book deals primarily with legal issues concerning the valuation of property for tax purposes, entire systems of property taxation are themselves equally the subject of legal challenge. This chapter introduces cases dealing with three such types of disputes: federal constitutional challenges to assessments based on acquisition price, rather than current market value, state constitutional challenges to fractional valuation schemes, and state constitutional challenges to the use of the property tax as a major source of funding for local public schools.

Federal Constitutional Challenges to Acquisition-Value Taxation

California instituted a type of acquisition-value property tax through passage of "Proposition 13" in 1978. This measure basically froze property tax values at their 1975–76 levels, with reassessment only upon a later change in ownership.[1] Interim inflation adjustments were limited to 2 percent annually. Ironically, much of the political impetus for this measure stemmed from the extremely efficient nature of California's tax administration, which was able to estimate changes in market values more accurately than in any other state. As a result, homeowners saw the rapid value increases of the 1970s reflected almost immediately in their tax bills.

> In the sixteen years before 1978, assessed values in California tripled, tax rates increased by 51 percent, and property taxes themselves more than quadrupled .... In 1977 the price of homes in many parts of California ran wild. Increases of 25 to 50 percent in one year were not uncommon. By mid-1978 the average price of a home in Southern California was nearly double the national average. Homeowners found their assessed values escalating without any corresponding reduction in rates. Some were literally being put out of their homes by the tax assessments.[2]

The existence of a large state surplus available to cushion the loss of local revenue contributed to popular support for Proposition 13.

---

1. Special provisions, some adopted through later referendum measures, deal with reduction in base year value, and with the definition of "change in ownership" or "new construction" in cases of inheritance, divorce, reconstruction after a natural disaster, and many additional circumstances. See generally Ehrman and Flavin, *Taxing California Property* (1979 and 1988).

2. K. Ehrman and S. Flavin, *Taxing California Property*, 2d ed. (1979), §2.1.

Soon after its enactment, Proposition 13 was challenged in state court on an array of state and federal constitutional grounds. In this case, *Amador Valley Joint Union High School District v. State Board of Equalization*,[3] six judges of the California Supreme Court found no constitutional impediment to an acquisition-value tax base:

> Not only does an acquisition value system enable each property owner to estimate with some assurance his future tax liability, but also the system may operate on a fairer basis than a current value approach. For example, a taxpayer who acquired his property for $40,000 in 1975 henceforth will be assessed and taxed on the basis of that cost (assuming it represented the then fair market value). This result is fair and equitable in that his future taxes may be said reasonably to reflect the price he was originally willing and able to pay for his property, rather than an inflated value fixed, after acquisition, in part on the basis of sales to third parties over which sales he can exercise no control. On the other hand, a person who paid $80,000 for similar property in 1977 is henceforth assessed and taxed at a higher level which reflects, again, the price he was willing and able to pay for that property. Seen in this light, and contrary to petitioners' assumption, section 2 [defining taxable value under Proposition 13] does not unduly discriminate against persons who acquired their property after 1975, for those persons are assessed and taxed in precisely the same manner as those who purchased in 1975 namely, on an acquisition value basis predicated on the owner's free and voluntary acts of purchase. This is an arguably reasonable basis for assessment.[4]

The recently appointed Chief Justice, Rose Bird, dissented in finding the acquisition-value basis a violation of equal protection. The unpopularity of this position was dramatized when she later lost her position on the California Supreme Court by failing to obtain the voter approval required in that state.[5]

Through legislation and subsequent constitutional amendments the reach of Proposition 13 has been extended significantly. For example, a 1980 amendment excluded reconstruction of property after a disaster loss from the category of "new construction," and also permitted reductions in valuation to reflect "damage, destruction or other factors causing a decline in value." Interspousal transfers and the purchase of stock in a corporation holding title to real estate have similarly been excluded from the definition of a "change in ownership." Many additional exclusions prevent various types of transfers or

---

3.　22 Cal. 3d 208, 149 Cal. Rptr. 239, 583 P.2d 1281 (1978).

4.　Ibid.

5.　The major political issue in Chief Justice Bird's defeat was her consistent refusal to uphold any death penalty convictions during her tenure on the court. Her removal in 1986 came by a 2-to-1 margin. See H. Scheiber, "Innovation, Resistance, and Change: A History of Judicial Reform and the California Courts, 1960–1990," *Southern California Law Review* 66(1993):2049.

construction from increasing the taxable value of real property. In November 1986, voters approved a constitutional amendment providing that the purchase and transfer between parents and children of the principal residence and the first $1 million of other property do not constitute a "purchase" or "change in ownership" for property tax purposes.[6]

No appeal of the *Amador Valley* case was sought to the United States Supreme Court. More than a decade later, however, new interest in this issue was raised by the Court's decision in *Allegheny Pittsburgh Coal Co. v. Webster County*,[7] which found an equal protection violation in the more common situation in which a de facto acquisition-value system arises from an assessor's failure to update property valuations in the absence of a sale. In that case, Chief Justice Rehnquist wrote:

> The Webster County tax assessor valued petitioners' real property on the basis of its recent purchase price, but made only minor modifications in the assessments of land which had not been recently sold. This practice resulted in gross disparities in the assessed value of generally comparable property, and we hold that it denied the petitioners the equal protection of the laws guaranteed to them by the Fourteenth Amendment.
>
> . . . .
>
> This approach systematically produced dramatic differences in valuation between petitioners' recently transferred property and otherwise comparable surrounding land. For the years 1976 through 1982, Allegheny was assessed and taxed at approximately 35 times the rate applied to owners of comparable properties. After purchasing that land, Kentucky Energy was assessed and taxed at approximately 33 times the rate of similar parcels. From 1981 through 1985, the County assessed and taxed the Shamrock-Oneida property at roughly 8 to 20 times that of comparable neighboring coal tracts. These disparities existed notwithstanding the adjustments made to the assessments of land not recently conveyed. In the case of the property held by Allegheny and Kentucky Energy, the County's adjustment policy would have required more than 500 years to equalize the assessments.
>
> . . . .
>
> The County argues that its assessment scheme is rationally related to its purpose of assessing properties at true current value: when available, it makes use of exceedingly accurate information about the market value of a property—the price at which it was recently purchased. As that data grows stale, it periodically adjusts the assessment based on some perception of the general change in area property values. We do not intend to cast doubt upon the theoretical basis of such a scheme. That two methods are used to assess property in the same class is, without more, of no constitutional moment. The Equal Protection Clause "applies only to taxation which in fact bears unequally on persons or property

6. See generally K. Ehrman and S. Flavin, *Taxing California Property* (3d ed. 1988), chap. 2.

7. 488 U.S. 336 (1989).

of the same class." *Charleston Fed. Savings & Loan Assn. v. Alderson*, 324 U.S. 182, 190, 65 S.Ct. 624, 629, 89 L.Ed. 857 (1945).

. . . .

But the present case is not an example of transitional delay in adjustment of assessed value resulting in inequalities in assessments of comparable property. Petitioners' property has been assessed at roughly 8 to 35 times more than comparable neighboring property, and these discrepancies have continued for more than 10 years with little change. The County's adjustments to the assessments of property not recently sold are too small to seasonably dissipate the remaining disparity between these assessments and the assessments based on a recent purchase price.

. . . .

A taxpayer in this situation may not be remitted by the State to the remedy of seeking to have the assessments of the undervalued property raised. "The [Equal Protection Clause] is not satisfied if a State does not itself remove the discrimination, but imposes on him against whom the discrimination has been directed the burden of seeking an upward revision of the taxes of other members of the class." [citations] The judgment of the Supreme Court of Appeals of West Virginia is accordingly reversed, and the case remanded for further proceedings not inconsistent with this opinion.

The *Allegheny Pittsburgh* case is discussed by W. Cohen[8] and J. Vitha.[9] Perhaps the most provocative response came from Professor Glennon,[10] who argued that "*Allegheny's* analytic tests epitomize judicial interventionism in the service of conservative political ends," harkening back to the Supreme Court's position a century ago as "a handmaiden to railroads and large corporations."

In 1990 the Supreme Court agreed to hear a case in which Macy's department store argued that the higher California property taxes borne by new property owners under Proposition 13 violated both the equal protection clause and the commerce clause, by impeding the free movement of business across state lines.[11] In another example of the extraordinary popularity of Proposition 13, the Macy company withdrew the case after antitax protesters in California threatened to boycott the store if it pursued this appeal.[12]

8. W. Cohen, "State Law in Equality Clothing: A Comment on *Allegheny Pittsburgh Coal Company v. County Commission.*" *University of California Law Review* 38 (1990):87.

9. J. Vitha, "Comment: *Allegheny Pittsburgh Coal Co. v. County Commission of Webster County, West Virginia:* The Supreme Court Gives 'Welcome Stranger' Tax Assessments a Cold Reception," *Brooklyn Law Review* 56(1991):1383.

10. R. Glennon, "Taxation and Equal Protection," *George Washington Law Review* 58 (1990):261.

11. *R.H. Macy & Co., Inc. v. Contra Costa County*, 226 Cal. App. 3d 352, 276 Cal. Rptr. 530 (1990), *cert. dismissed*, 11 S.Ct. 2923 (1991).

12. "The store said it dropped the case after it realized many California homeowners

An individual homeowner, Stephanie Nordlinger, did bring a similar challenge to Proposition 13 on equal protection grounds. Because she brought this case as an individual homeowner, however, and not in connection with a commercial undertaking, her case did not present the commerce clause issues raised by the Macy challenge.

In *Nordlinger v. Hahn*,[13] Justice Blackmun wrote[14]:

In 1978, California voters staged what has been described as a property tax revolt[1] by approving a statewide ballot initiative known as Proposition 13. The adoption of Proposition 13 served to amend the California Constitution to impose strict limits on the rate at which real property is taxed and on the rate at which real property assessments are increased from year to year. In this litigation, we consider a challenge under the Equal Protection Clause of the Fourteenth Amendment to the manner in which real property now is assessed under the California Constitution.

I

A

Proposition 13 followed many years of rapidly rising real property taxes in California. From fiscal years 1967–1968 to 1971–1972, revenues from these taxes increased on an average of 11.5 per cent per year. In response, the California Legislature enacted several property tax relief measures, including a cap on tax rates in 1972. The boom in the State's real estate market persevered, however, and the median price of an existing home doubled from $31,530 in 1973 to $62,430 in 1977. As a result, tax levies continued to rise because of sharply increasing assessment values. Some homeowners saw their tax bills double or triple during this period, well outpacing any growth in their income and ability to pay.

By 1978, property tax relief had emerged as a major political issue in California. In only one month's time, tax relief advocates collected over 1.2 million signatures to qualify Proposition 13 for the June 1978 ballot. On election day, Proposition 13 received a favorable vote of 64.8 percent and carried 55 of the State's 58 counties. California thus had a novel constitutional amendment that led to a property tax cut of approximately $7 billion in the first year. A California

---

would be hurt if the Supreme Court voided Proposition 13 entirely. Observers, however, say the store was driven-off by a torrent of angry letters and cut-up charge cards from customers who like Proposition 13....[W]hatever Macy's would have earned by winning the case, $1 or $2 million, they would have lost a billion dollars in the state." R. Freilich, L. Vaskov, and F. Ernst, "1991-1992 Supreme Court Review: The Court's New Path— The Middle Ground," *The Urban Lawyer* 24(1992):669, 737–38 [footnotes omitted].

13. 112 S.Ct. 23326, 120 L.Ed.2d 1 (1992).

14. References to the pages numbers in briefs, appendices, and oral argument transcripts have been omitted from these excerpts.

1. See *N.Y. Times*, June 8, 1978, p. 23, col. 1; *Washington Post*, June 11, 1978, p. H1.

homeowner with a $50,000 home enjoyed an immediate reduction of about $750 per year in property taxes.

As enacted by Proposition 13, Article XIIIA of the California Constitution caps real property taxes at 1% of a property's "full cash value." Sec. 1(a). "Full cash value" is defined as the assessed valuation as of the 1975—1976 tax year or, "thereafter, the appraised value of real property when purchased, newly constructed, or a change in ownership has occurred after the 1975 assessment." Sec. 2(a). The assessment "may reflect from year to year the inflationary rate not to exceed 2 per cent for any given year." Sec. 2(b).

Article XIIIA also contains several exemptions from this reassessment provision. One exemption authorizes the legislature to allow homeowners over the age of 55 who sell their principal residences to carry their previous base-year assessments with them to replacement residences of equal or lesser value. Sec. 2(a). A second exemption applies to transfers of a principal residence (and up to $1 million of other real property) between parents and children. Sec. 2(h).

In short, Article XIIIA combines a 1% ceiling on the property tax rate with a 2% cap on annual increases in assessed valuations. The assessment limitation, however, is subject to the exception that new construction or a change of ownership triggers a reassessment up to current appraised value. Thus, the assessment provisions of Article XIIIA essentially embody an "acquisition value" system of taxation rather than the more commonplace "current value" taxation. Real property is assessed at values related to the value of the property at the time it is acquired by the taxpayer rather than to the value it has in the current real estate market.

Over time, this acquisition-value system has created dramatic disparities in the taxes paid by persons owning similar pieces of property. Property values in California have inflated far in excess of the allowed 2% cap on increases in assessments for property that is not newly constructed or that has not changed hands. As a result, longer-term property owners pay lower property taxes reflecting historic property values, while newer owners pay higher property taxes reflecting more recent values. For that reason, Proposition 13 has been labeled by some as a "welcome stranger" system—the newcomer to an established community is "welcome" in anticipation that he will contribute a larger percentage of support for local government than his settled neighbor who owns a comparable home. Indeed, in dollar terms, the differences in tax burdens are staggering. By 1989, the 44% of California home owners who have owned their homes since enactment of Proposition 13 in 1978 shouldered only 25% of the more than $4 billion in residential property taxes paid by homeowners statewide. If property values continue to rise more than the annual 2% inflationary cap, this disparity will continue to grow.

B

According to her amended complaint, petitioner Stephanie Nordlinger in November 1988 purchased a house in the Baldwin Hills neighborhood of Los Angeles County for $170,000. The prior owners bought the home just two years before for $121,500. Before her purchase, petitioner had lived in a rented apartment in Los Angeles and had not owned any real property in California.

In early 1989, petitioner received a notice from the Los Angeles County Tax Assessor, who is a respondent here, informing her that her home had been reassessed upward to $170,100 on account of its change in ownership. She learned that the reassessment resulted in a property tax increase of $453.60, up 36% to $1,701, for the 1988-1989 fiscal year.

Petitioner later discovered she was paying about five times more in taxes than some of her neighbors who owned comparable homes since 1975 within the same residential development. For example, one block away, a house of identical size on a lot slightly larger than petitioner's was subject to a general tax levy of only $358.20 (based on an assessed valuation of $35,820, which reflected the home's value in 1975 plus the up-to-2% per year inflation factor).[2] According to petitioner, her total property taxes over the first 10 years in her home will approach $19,000, while any neighbor who bought a comparable home in 1975 stands to pay just $4,100. The general tax levied against her modest home is only a few dollars short of that paid by a pre-1976 owner of a $2.1 million Malibu beachfront home.

. . . .

II

The Equal Protection Clause of the Fourteenth Amendment, sec. 1, commands that no State shall "deny to any person within its jurisdiction the equal protection of the laws." Of course, most laws differentiate in some fashion between classes of persons. The Equal Protection Clause does not forbid classifications. It simply keeps governmental decisionmakers from treating differently persons who are in all relevant respects alike.

. . . .

At the outset, petitioner suggests that her challenge to Article XIIIA qualifies for heightened scrutiny because it infringes upon the constitutional right to travel. In particular, petitioner alleges that the exemptions to reassessment for transfers by owners over 55 and for transfers between parents and children run afoul of the right to travel, because they classify directly on the basis of California residency. But the complaint does not allege that petitioner herself has been impeded from traveling or from settling in California because, as has been noted, prior to purchasing her home, petitioner lived in an apartment in Los Angeles . . . . Petitioner has not identified any obstacle preventing others who wish to travel or settle in California from asserting claims on their own behalf, nor has she shown any special relationship with those whose rights she seeks to assert, such that we might overlook this prudential limitation. Accordingly, petitioner may not assert the constitutional right to travel as a basis for heightened review.

---

2. Petitioner proffered to the trial court additional evidence suggesting that the disparities in residential tax burdens were greater in other Los Angeles County neighborhoods. For example, a small 2-bedroom house in Santa Monica that was previously assessed at $27,000 and that was sold for $465,000 in 1989 would be subject to a tax levy of $4,650, a bill 17 times more than the $270 paid the year before by the previous owner. Petitioner also proffered evidence suggesting that similar disparities obtained with respect to apartment buildings and commercial and industrial income-producing properties.

B

The appropriate standard of review is whether the difference in treatment between newer and older owners rationally furthers a legitimate state interest. . . .

As between newer and older owners, Article XIIIA does not discriminate with respect to either the tax rate or the annual rate of adjustment in assessments. Newer and older owners alike benefit in both the short and long run from the protections of a 1% tax rate ceiling and no more than a 2% increase in assessment value per year. New owners and old owners are treated differently with respect to one factor only—the basis on which their property is initially assessed. Petitioner's true complaint is that the State has denied her—a new owner—the benefit of the same assessment value that her neighbors—older owners—enjoy.

We have no difficulty in ascertaining at least two rational or reasonable considerations of difference or policy that justify denying petitioner the benefits of her neighbors' lower assessments. First, the State has a legitimate interest in local neighborhood preservation, continuity, and stability. The State therefore legitimately can decide to structure its tax system to discourage rapid turnover in ownership of homes and businesses, for example, in order to inhibit displacement of lower income families by the forces of gentrification or of established, "mom-and-pop" businesses by newer chain operations. By permitting older owners to pay progressively less in taxes than new owners of comparable property, the Article XIIIA assessment scheme rationally furthers this interest.

Second, the State legitimately can conclude that a new owner at the time of acquiring his property does not have the same reliance interest warranting protection against higher taxes as does an existing owner. The State may deny a new owner at the point of purchase the right to "lock in" to the same assessed value as is enjoyed by an existing owner of comparable property, because an existing owner rationally may be thought to have vested expectations in his property or home that are more deserving of protection than the anticipatory expectations of a new owner at the point of purchase. A new owner has full information about the scope of future tax liability before acquiring the property, and if he thinks the future tax burden is too demanding, he can decide not to complete the purchase at all. By contrast, the existing owner, already saddled with his purchase, does not have the option of deciding not to buy his home if taxes become prohibitively high. To meet his tax obligations, he might be forced to sell his home or to divert his income away from the purchase of food, clothing, and other necessities. In short, the State may decide that it is worse to have owned and lost, than never to have owned at all.

. . . .

Petitioner argues that Article XIIIA cannot be distinguished from the tax assessment practice found to violate the Equal Protection Clause in *Allegheny Pittsburgh*. Like Article XIIIA, the practice at issue in *Allegheny Pittsburgh* resulted in dramatic disparities in taxation of properties of comparable value. But an obvious and critical factual difference between this case and *Allegheny Pittsburgh* is the absence of any indication in *Allegheny Pittsburgh* that the policies underlying an acquisition-value taxation scheme could conceivably have been the purpose for the Webster County tax assessor's unequal assessment scheme. In the first place, Webster County argued that "its assessment scheme is rationally related to its purpose of assessing properties at true current value" (emphasis added). Id., at 488 U.S., at 343. Moreover, the West Virginia "Constitution and laws provide that all property of the kind held by petitioners shall be taxed at a rate uniform throughout the State according to its estimated market value," and the Court found "no suggestion" that "the State may have adopted a different system in practice from that specified by statute." Id., at 345.

To be sure, the Equal Protection Clause does not demand for purposes of rational-basis review that a legislature or governing decisionmaker actually articulate at any time the purpose or rationale supporting its classification. Nevertheless, this Court's review does require that a purpose may conceivably or "may reasonably have been the purpose and policy" of the relevant governmental decisionmaker. *Allegheny Pittsburgh* was the rare case where the facts precluded any plausible inference that the reason for the unequal assessment practice was to achieve the benefits of an acquisition-value tax scheme. By contrast, Article XIIIA was enacted precisely to achieve the benefits of an acquisition-value system. *Allegheny Pittsburgh* is not controlling here.[8]

Finally, petitioner contends that the unfairness of Article XIIIA is made worse by its exemptions from reassessment for two special classes of new owners: persons aged 55 and older who exchange principal residences, and children who acquire property from their parents. This Court previously has declined to hold that narrow exemptions from a general scheme of taxation necessarily render the overall scheme invidiously discriminatory. For purposes of rational-basis review, the "latitude of discretion is notably wide in . . . the granting of partial or total exemptions upon grounds of policy."

The two exemptions at issue here rationally further legitimate purposes. The people of California reasonably could have concluded that older persons in general should not be discouraged from moving to a residence more suitable to their changing family size or income. Similarly, the people of California reasonably could have concluded that the interests of family and neighborhood continuity and stability are furthered by and warrant an exemption for transfers between parents and children. Petitioner has not demonstrated that no rational bases lie for either of these exemptions.

Petitioner and amici argue with some appeal that Article XIIIA frustrates the "American dream" of home ownership for many younger and poorer California families. They argue that Article XIIIA places start-up businesses that depend on ownership of property at a severe disadvantage in competing with established businesses. They argue that Article XIIIA dampens demand for and construction of new housing and buildings. And they argue that Article XIIIA constricts local tax revenues at the expense of public education and vital services.

---

8. In finding *Allegheny Pittsburgh* distinguishable, we do not suggest that the protections of the Equal Protection Clause are any less when the classification is drawn by legislative mandate, as in this case, than by administrative action as in *Allegheny Pittsburgh.* Nor do we suggest that the Equal Protection Clause constrains administrators, as in *Allegheny Pittsburgh,* from violating state law requiring uniformity of taxation of property.

Time and again, however, this Court has made clear in the rational-basis context that the "Constitution presumes that, absent some reason to infer antipathy, even improvident decisions will eventually be rectified by the democratic process and that judicial intervention is generally unwarranted no matter how unwisely we may think a political branch has acted." Certainly, California's grand experiment appears to vest benefits in a broad, powerful, and entrenched segment of society, and, as the Court of Appeal surmised, ordinary democratic processes may be unlikely to prompt its reconsideration or repeal. Yet many wise and well-intentioned laws suffer from the same malady. Article XIIIA is not palpably arbitrary, and we must decline petitioner's request to upset the will of the people of California.

The judgment of the Court of Appeal is affirmed.

This effort to distinguish the constitutionality of California's legislatively mandated acquisition-value tax base from that of West Virginia's administratively imposed acquisition-value tax base drew sharp criticism from Justice Thomas, who concurred in the judgment but who found *Allegheny Pittsburgh* constitutionally equivalent. He wrote:

Allegheny Pittsburgh . . . does not prevent the State of California from classifying properties on the basis of their value at acquisition, so long as the classification is supported by a rational basis. I agree with the Court that it is, both for the reasons given by this Court and for the reasons given by the Supreme Court of California in *Amador Valley Joint Union High School District v. State Board of Equalization*, 22 Cal. 3d 208, 583 P. 2d 1281 (1978). But the classification employed by the Webster County assessor, indistinguishable from California's, was rational for all those reasons as well . . . .

. . . .

Even if the assessor did violate West Virginia law (and that she did is open to question), she would not have violated the Equal Protection Clause. A violation of state law does not by itself constitute a violation of the Federal Constitution. We made that clear in *Snowden v. Hughes*, 321 U.S. 1 (1944), for instance, where a candidate for state office complained that members of the local canvassing board had refused to certify his name as a nominee to the Secretary of State, thus violating an Illinois statute. Because the plaintiff had not alleged, say, that the defendants had meant to discriminate against him on racial grounds, but merely that they had failed to comply with a statute, we rejected the argument that the defendants had thereby violated the Equal Protection Clause.

"Not every denial of a right conferred by state law involves a denial of the equal protection of the laws, even though the denial of the right to one person may operate to confer it on another . . . . Where the official action purports to be in conformity to the statutory classification, an erroneous or mistaken performance of the statutory duty, although a violation of the statute, is not without more a denial of the equal protection of the laws." *Id.*, at 8. See also *Nashville, C. & St. L. R. Co. v. Browning*, 310 U.S. 362 (1940).

. . . .

After today, however, a plaintiff might be able [to] invoke federal jurisdiction to have state actors obey state law, for a claim that the state actor has violated state law appears to have become a claim that he has violated the Constitution . . . .

I understand that the Court prefers to distinguish *Allegheny Pittsburgh*, but in doing so, I think, the Court has left our equal protection jurisprudence in disarray. The analysis appropriate to this case is straightforward. Unless a classification involves suspect classes or fundamental rights, judicial scrutiny under the Equal Protection Clause demands only a conceivable rational basis for the challenged state distinction . . . . Proposition 13, I believe, satisfies this standard—but so, for the same reasons, did the scheme employed in Webster County.

Justice Stevens, in turn, dissented with a biting opinion that characterized Proposition 13 as a windfall to those who invested in California real estate in the 1970s, whom Justice Stevens termed "the Squires."

. . . .

As a direct result of this windfall for the Squires, later purchasers must pay far more than their fair share of property taxes.

The specific disparity that prompted petitioner to challenge the constitutionality of Proposition 13 is the fact that her annual property tax bill is almost 5 times as large as that of her neighbors who own comparable homes: While her neighbors' 1989 taxes averaged less than $400, petitioner was taxed $1,700. This disparity is not unusual under Proposition 13. Indeed, some homeowners pay 17 times as much in taxes as their neighbors with comparable property. For vacant land, the disparities may be as great as 500 to 1. Moreover, as Proposition 13 controls the taxation of commercial property as well as residential property, the regime greatly favors the commercial enterprises of the Squires, placing new businesses at a substantial disadvantage.

As a result of Proposition 13, the Squires, who own 44% of the owner-occupied residences, paid only 25% of the total taxes collected from homeowners in 1989. Report of Senate Commission on Property Tax Equity and Revenue to the California State Senate 33 (1991) (Commission Report). These disparities are aggravated by section 2 of Proposition 13, which exempts from reappraisal a property owner's home and up to $1 million of other real property when that property is transferred to a child of the owner. This exemption can be invoked repeatedly and indefinitely, allowing the Proposition 13 windfall to be passed from generation to generation. As the California Senate Commission on Property Tax Equity and Revenue observed, "The inequity is clear. One young family buys a new home and is assessed at full market value. Another young family inherits its home, but pays taxes based on their parents' date of acquisition even though both homes are of identical value. Not only does this constitutional provision offend a policy of equal tax treatment for taxpayers in similar situations, it appears to favor the housing needs of children with homeowner-parents over children with non-homeowner-parents. With the repeal of the state's gift and inheritance tax in 1982, the rationale for this exemption is negligible." Commission Report, at 9-10. The Commission was too generous.

To my mind, the rationale for such disparity is not merely "negligible," it is nonexistent. Such a law establishes a privilege of a medieval character: Two families with equal needs and equal resources are treated differently solely because of their different heritage.

In my opinion, such disparate treatment of similarly situated taxpayers is arbitrary and unreasonable. Although the Court today recognizes these gross inequities, its analysis of the justification for those inequities consists largely of a restatement of the benefits that accrue to long-time property owners. That a law benefits those it benefits cannot be an adequate justification for severe inequalities such as those created by Proposition 13.

Like Justice Thomas, Justice Stevens found Proposition 13 constitutionally equivalent to the acquisition-value system overturned in *Allegheny Pittsburgh*. Where Justice Thomas would allow both systems to stand, Justice Stevens would invalidate both. He wrote, "If anything, the inequality created by Proposition 13 is constitutionally more problematic because it is the product of a state-wide policy rather than the result of an individual assessor's maladministration."

. . . .

In my opinion, Proposition 13 sweeps too broadly and operates too indiscriminately to "rationally further" the State's interest in neighborhood preservation. No doubt there are some early purchasers living on fixed or limited incomes who could not afford to pay higher taxes and still maintain their homes. California has enacted special legislation to respond to their plight. Those concerns cannot provide an adequate justification for Proposition 13. A state-wide, across-the-board tax windfall for all property owners and their descendants is no more a "rational" means for protecting this small subgroup than a blanket tax exemption for all taxpayers named Smith would be a rational means to protect a particular taxpayer named Smith who demonstrated difficulty paying her tax bill.

Notes and Questions

1. Proposition 13 was a political response to increasing property taxes, the housing inflation of the 1970s, a large state government surplus in California, and an efficient tax administration that kept pace with rising market values. Prices for single-family homes in the San Francisco area rose 18 percent annually between 1973 and 1978. In the same period Southern California experienced even more rapid increases, about 30 percent annually between 1973 and 1978.[15] The incendiary effect of the state surplus was such that twelve years later it was cited against former California Governor Jerry Brown in his campaign for president, as Propo-

---

15. D. Sears and J. Citrin, *Tax Revolt: Something for Nothing in California* (1985), p. 22.

sition 13 critics harbored "the deep-seated suspicion that the deconstructionist movement it spawned could have been avoided had Brown found a way to return a whopping $7.3 billion budget surplus to school districts and local governments."[16] The efficiency "problem" is in some respects the most complex. Note that the 1975 *Hellerstein* case, reprinted below, cited California as a state requiring full-value assessment, a system introduced in 1966 after a series of scandals involving agreements between assessors and business taxpayers. Some commentators concluded after passage of Proposition 13 that the former system of "extralegal" assessments was a preferable alternative.

> The origin of California's recent dilemma was its rigid, highly reformed property-tax system. The performance of this system in the 1970s reemphasized what every working politician should know: In government one should not rely too heavily on rules to replace political discretion. Had California's assessors retained some of their pre-1965 authority to set assessments, they could have mediated at least some of the housing inflation. Homeowners would have been less battered. Local governments would have retained most of their powers.[17]

Do you share this admiration (or at least acceptance) of a system in which assessors have authority to set assessment levels? As an alternative, could California tax rates have been lowered to keep collections constant or rising slowly while the state experienced rapid increases in property values?

2. On the relationship of the *Nordlinger* and *Allegheny* cases, see S. Mandarino.[18]

3. In 1980 Massachusetts voters approved a property-tax limitation measure, termed "Proposition 2-1/2," that limited tax rates and total tax collections, but not assessed values. This was upheld by the Massachusetts Supreme Judicial Court against constitutional challenge in *Massachusetts Teachers Association v. Secretary of the Commonwealth.*[19] As a result of these two tax limitation measures, average property tax rates fell dramatically in both states. California, however, rejected current market value as a tax base, but Massachusetts assessments became far more accurate than they had been in the past (see table 1).

---

16. M. Ingrassia, "Jerry Brown, Man of Many Riddles," *Newsday*, March 29, 1992, p. 18.

17. F. Levy, "On Understanding Proposition 13," *The Public Interest*, Summer 1979, p. 66.

18. S. Mandarino, "Note, *Nordlinger* to *Allegheny*: 'This Town Ain't Big Enough for Both of Us,'" *Wisconsin Law Review* 1993 (1993):1195.

19. 384 Mass. 209, 424 N.E.2d 469 (1981).

Table 1
Average Effective Property Tax Rates—
Single-Family Homes with FHA-Insured Mortgages

	1971	1987
California	2.48%	1.05%
Massachusetts	2.43%	0.84%

4. In *Township of West Milford v. Van Decker*, 120 N.J. 354, 576 A.2d 881 (1990), the New Jersey Supreme Court cited *Allegheny* in holding that "spot assessment," or the practice of "increasing the assessed value only of homes purchased . . . and leaving the value of other homes undisturbed" was a violation of both the federal and state constitutions. Similarly, in *Krugman v. Board of Assessors*, 141 A.D.2d 175, 183-184, 533 N.Y.S. 2d 495 (1988), more than a decade after *Hellerstein*, the New York appellate division held that "the respondents', practice of selective reassessment of only those properties in the village which were sold during the prior year contravenes statutory and constitutional mandates . . . . The respondents' disparate treatment of new property owners on the one hand and long-term property owners on the other has the effect of permitting property owners who have been longstanding recipients of public amenities to bear the least amount of their cost."

State Constitutional Challenges to Fractional Valuation Systems

HELLERSTEIN V. ASSESSOR OF ISLIP
37 N.Y.2d 1, 332 N.E.2d 279, 371 N.Y.S.2d 388
New York Court of Appeals, 1975

WACHTLER, Judge.

Petitioner, an owner of real property located on Fire Island, claims that the entire assessment roll for the Town of Islip is void. The argument has been raised in a proceeding instituted pursuant to article 7 of the Real Property Tax Law, Consol. Laws, ch. 50a, which permits court review of an assessment upon a complaint of illegality, overvaluation or inequality (see Real Property Tax Law sec. 706). There is no claim of overvaluation or unequal treatment in the assessment of petitioner's property. She argues only that the assessments are illegal because they were not made in accordance with section 306 of the Real Property Tax Law which states: "All real property in each assessing unit shall be assessed at the full value thereof." This, we have held, means market value, unless that cannot be established "and then other tests of full value must be used." (*People ex rel. Parklin Operating Corp. v. Miller*, 287 N.Y. 126, 129, 38 N.E.2d

465, 466.) Here it is conceded that all assessments throughout the township are based on a *percentage* of market value.

The Supreme Court, Suffolk County, in an opinion, dismissed the petition. The Appellate Division, Second Department, affirmed, without opinion . . . .

Section 306 of the Real Property Tax Law has an ancient lineage. In 1788 the New York Legislature directed "the assessors of each respective city, town and place in every county of this State (to) make out a true and exact list of the names of all the freeholders and inhabitants and opposite the name of every such person shall set down the real value of all his or her whole estate real and personal as near as they can discover the same." (See L.1788, ch. 65, March 7, 1788.) . . . . Although the statute is one of the oldest in the State there does not appear to be any extant legislative history indicating what the full value requirement was intended to accomplish. And despite the fact that the custom of fractional assessments appears to be at least as old as the statute (see Kilmer, "Legal Requirements for Equality in Tax Assessments," 25 Albany L.Rev. 203, 210), it has prompted very little litigation. In several of the older cases the problem can be seen lurking in the background; but it is only during the last 10 years that we find the practice being directly challenged in the courts.

. . . .

One of the most peculiar aspects of the township's case is the narrowness of their defense of the practice of fractional assessments. They are satisfied to rest on the theory "thus it has been, thus it always must be," without making any effort to explain how the custom began, whether it serves any useful purpose, and what would happen if the assessors complied, or were made to comply, with the strict letter of the law. Our own cases do not discuss these points; but they have been extensively reviewed and debated by scholarly commentators and by the courts in other jurisdictions.

The vast majority of States require assessors, either by statute or constitutional prescription, to assess at full value, true value, market value or some equivalent standard. (See Note, 68 Yale L.J. 335—387). Two States have expressly provided by statute that this requires assessment at 100% of value (see 13 Ariz.Rev.Stat.Ann., sec. 42—227; California Revenue & Taxation Code, secs. 401, 408). Several States have specifically authorized fractional assessments, and this seems to be the modern trend. In 1917 there were four States in this latter category; by 1958 there were eight; and, as of 1962 15 States had enacted legislation providing for fractional assessments, either at a fixed percentage or according to local option.

Where full value is required, the standard has been almost universally disregarded. A 1957 study by the United States Census Bureau placed the average assessment ratio in the country at 30% of actual value (see Bird, *The General Property Tax: Findings of the 1957 Census of Governments* 40).

No one seems to know exactly how the practice of fractional assessment began. In an early case the Supreme Court suggested that: "If we look for the reason for this common consent to substitute a custom for the positive rule of the statute, it will probably be found in the difficulty of subjecting personal property, and especially invested capital, to the inspection of the assessor and the grasp of the collector. The effort of the landowner, whose property lies open to view, which can be subjected to the lien of a tax not to be escaped by removal, or hiding, to produce something like actual equality of burden by an underevaluation of his land, has led to this result" (*Cummings v. National Bank*, 101 U.S. 153, 163, 25 L.Ed. 903).

This may well explain the origin of the rule, but it does not account for its remarkable powers of endurance, especially in a State like New York, which has removed personal property from the tax rolls (Real Property Tax Law, sec. 300). Its survival depends on other factors none of which are particularly commendable.

Bonbright, in his treatise, lists (p. 498):

> "several reasons for the persistence of partial valuation. Gullible taxpayers associate a larger valuation with a larger tax, or at any rate are less contentious about a relatively excessive assessment if it does not exceed their estimate of true value. The ability to maintain a stable rate and to increase revenue by tampering with the tax base—a change which calls for less publicity and less opposition— is naturally desired by the party in power. Occasionally, partial valuation is intended as a substitute for a varied system of rates; i.e., different forms of property, while nominally taxed at the same rate, are in fact taxed at differing rates by being assessed at different proportions of full values. Undervaluation of realty is sometimes justified as compensating for the elusiveness of personalty; but even if the latter is assessed fully when caught, experience has shown that the net result is to furnish an additional incentive for evasion.

> "Another inducement to undervaluation has been that, since the state relies on the property tax for part of its revenue, the county assessors seek to lighten their constituents' burden at the expense of the rest of the state by assessing the local property at a lower percentage than is applied elsewhere. This process has often resulted in a competition between counties as to which could most nearly approach the limit of nominal valuation. With the increasing trend in some states toward reserving the property tax for the support of the local communities, and in other states toward the creation of state boards of equalization, the enthusiasm for percentage valuation has been dampened."

Most of these considerations have probably served to perpetuate the custom in New York; but there may be other factors at work.

This State, of course, does not depend on real property taxes as a source of State revenue. However the State does supply financial aid to communities based primarily on assessed valuation (State Finance Law, sec. 54, subd. 1, par. c; sec. 54, subd. 2, pars. a, c, Consol.Laws, ch. 56) and this undoubtedly furnishes "another inducement to undervaluation." The activities of the State Equalization Board are meant to correct this problem but as one commentator observes "possibly local tax officials believe that there is no harm in trying" (Johnson, "Fractional Ratios and Their Effect on Achievement of Uniform Assessment," *The Property Tax: Problems and Potentials*, Tax Institute of America, p. 210).

Since the State Constitution provides that "[a]ssessments shall in no case exceed full value" (N.Y. State Const., art. XVI, sec. 2) assessing at a percentage of value discourages claims of unconstitutional overvaluation. Then the taxpayer is left with the far more difficult task of proving comparative inequality.

Obviously these reasons are all good reasons for abolishing the custom. As Bonbright observes (pp. 497–498): "Theoretically the taxpayer's pocket is not in the least affected by uniform undervaluation or overvaluation. Systematic undervaluation diminishes the tax base and the tax rate must therefore rise in order to supply the required government revenue . . . . The objections to the practice of undervaluation are patent. In the first place, except where sanctioned by statute, it involves a generally known and sanctioned disregard by officials of the law requiring them to assess property at its full and fair value. The other great vice is that the percentage of undervaluation is rarely a matter of common knowledge, so that it is extremely difficult to ascertain whether there is uniformity in the proportion or whether, through incompetence, favoritism, or corruption of the assessors, some portions of the taxpaying body are bearing the others' burdens, as between either individuals or local groups."

In recent years the high courts in several States, noting the mounting criticism, have held that full value means what it says and that the practice of fractional assessments is illegal (see, e.g., *Switz v. Township of Middletown*, 23 N.Y. 580, 130 A.2d 15; *Ingraham v. Town & City of Bristol*, 144 Conn. 374, 132 A.2d 563; *Russman v. Luckett*, 391 S.W.2d 694 (Ky.); *Bettigole v. Assessors of Springfield*, 343 Mass. 223, 178 N.E.2d 10; *Walter v. Schuler*, 176 So.2d 81 (Fla.); *Southern Ry. Co. v. Clement*, 57 Tenn.App. 54, 415 S.W.2d 146).

In sum, for nearly 200 years our statutes have required assessments to be made at full value and for nearly 200 years assessments have been made on a percentage basis throughout the State. The practice has time on its side and nothing else. It has been tolerated by the Legislature, criticized by the commentators and found by our own court to involve a flagrant violation of the statute. Nevertheless the practice has become so widespread and been so consistently followed that it has acquired an aura of assumed legality. The assessors in Islip inherited the custom and it is conceded that they have continued it. Throughout the years taxes have been levied and paid, or upon default, tax liens have arisen, followed by foreclosure and ultimate transfer of title, all on reliance on the apparent legality of fractional assessments. Now we have before us a petition directly challenging the practice and seeking an order "declar[ing] the entire assessment roll of the Town of Islip for the year 1968-1969 as illegal, null and void." In the alternative the petitioner requests that we direct the township to "make future assessments of all property on the assessment rolls of said town at the full value."

The petitioner recognizes that if we invalidate the assessment roll this could bring "fiscal chaos to the Town of Islip." If the petitioner had sought mandamus this alone would be sufficient to deny relief, for we have long held that the courts should not act "so as to cause disorder and confusion in public affairs, even though there may be a strict legal right" (*Matter of Andresen v. Rice*, 277 N.Y. 271, 282, 14 N.E.2d 65, 70). We have not previously considered whether the same principle should apply to a claim of illegality brought pursuant to section 706 of the Real Property Tax Law. However since the nature of the relief and the public impact are identical, we believe it is incumbent on the courts, where their discretion is involved, to exercise the same degree of restraint whenever a settled assessment roll or property rights based thereon are challenged for illegality. And this should be true whether the proceeding be labeled mandamus or otherwise. It follows from this that we will not, in this action, on the equity side, disturb the settled assessment rolls. The taxes levied and paid, the tax liens, matured or pending, and completed transfers of foreclosed properties made in reliance on the assessment rolls are matters not now before the court and on which therefore it should not pass. We assume however that should these questions arise, the courts will exercise the sound discretion with which they are vested. To this extent we agree with the courts below that the petitioner was not entitled to have the past assessment rolls declared a nullity.

This does not mean however that we must indorse the practice or withhold relief insofar as future assessments are concerned. Future compliance with the full value requirement will undoubtedly cause some disruption of existing procedures, but time should cure the problem. The difficulty of transition is sufficient reason to defer relief, but not to deny it. The petitioner thus is entitled to an order directing the township to make future assessments at full value as required by section 306 of the Real Property Tax Law. The order however should not go into effect immediately. To make this transition, the township should be allowed a reasonable time, but not later than December 31, 1976. In the interim assessments may be made in accordance with the existing practice and any tax levies, liens, foreclosures or transfers based on such assessments shall not be subject to challenge for failing to comply with section 306 of the Real Property Tax Law.

Accordingly, the order of the Appellate Division should be modified to the extent of directing that, within a reasonable time, but in no event later than December 31, 1976, the respondent shall assess the real property within the township at full value.

JONES, Judge (dissenting).

I think the order of the Appellate Division should be affirmed.

While the long-standing practice of fractional assessments for real property taxation cannot be said to violate the constitutional mandate that "[a]ssessments shall in no case exceed full value" (N.Y. Const. art. XVI, sec. 2), there can be no blinking the fact that fractional assessment cannot be squared with the literal command of section 306 of the Real Property Tax Law—"All real property in each assessing unit shall be assessed at the full value thereof."

Were we now called on to interpret such a provision in a recently adopted statute or to pass on the propriety of an emerging practice of fractional valuation under an older enactment, we would be confronted with an entirely different question. Neither is the case now before us, however.

As is stated in the majority opinion, the literally explicit provision of section 306 which it is now sought for the first time in our court to enforce has an ancient lineage. As the majority also recognizes, however, paralleling the long history of statutory address to "full value" has been the equally venerable practice of fractional assessment. With but a few desultory exceptions, the custom of fractional assessment has been followed without challenge until recently. It appears that over the years a collector was held liable for taking property under a certificate based on a fractional assessment only in a single reported instance (*Van Rensselaer v. Witbeck*, 7 N.Y. 517). In *People ex rel. Board of Supervisors v. Fowler*, 55 N.Y. 252 the supervisors of Westchester County sought unsuccessfully to compel full value assessment by requiring the assessors to file a proper certificate of assessment. The court, taking note of uncontroverted proof that it had been the custom at least for several years not to assess at full value but rather to assess at about one third or in some cases at one fourth of full value, refused to require the assessors precisely to track the statutory language. "Courts do not sit to compel man to take false oaths, and whatever duty the assessors may have omitted, they owe no duty to the public to commit crime, and no public exigency can require it of them." (55 N.Y. at p. 254.) While the *Fowler* court commented critically on the discrepancy between statutory language and practice, as did the Appellate Division, Third Department, in the later case of *People ex rel. Congress Hall v. Ouderkirk*, 120 App.Div. 650, 105 N.Y.S. 134. ("But it is a custom not only wholly repugnant to the plain mandates of the statute, but also radically at war with the official oaths of the assessors, and also with their oaths to the assessment rolls" (p. 655, 105 N.Y.S. p. 138)) no judicial mandate was sought or granted to enforce strict conformity with the statutory language.

. . . . Although it may be accurate to say that our court has never squarely confronted the issue and held the practice of fractional assessment valid, more significant in my view, although obviously not conclusive, is the conspicuous fact that notwithstanding the ingenuity and dogged determination of taxpayers, sometimes on the flimsiest of arguments, to resist taxation thought to be illegal, the present is the first case in nearly 200 years in which our State's highest court has been invited to confront the issue head-on and to overturn fractional assessments.

From a different point of view we note that notwithstanding what we must assume has been the awareness of fractional assessment practice on the part of individual legislators (on few issues are voter pleas more continuous or persistent than those in search of tax relief) no legislation has been adopted over the years to require abandonment of the uniform, State-wide practice. As we said recently in *Engle v. Talarico* (33 N.Y.2d 237, 242, 351 N.Y.S.2d 677, 680, 306 N.E.2d 796, 799): "Where the practical construction of a statute is well known, the Legislature is charged with knowledge and its failure to interfere indicates acquiescence (RKO-Keith-Orpheum Theaters v. City of New York, 308 N.Y. 493, 127 N.E.2d 284)."

Not only has there been a failure on the part of the Legislature to interfere with fractional assessments; legislation has been enacted which was clearly predicated on the practice of fractional assessments. New York State began establishing equalization rates in 1859. From then until 1912 State equalization rates, set only for whole counties, were used to equalize assessed valuations of the various counties in order to apportion State property taxes among the counties during the period when the State was levying direct taxes on property. In 1912 the State began to establish equalization rates for individual cities, towns and villages. In 1958, in the same chapter in which it enacted present section 306 of the Real Property Tax Law, the Legislature also adopted article 12 of the Real Property Tax Law which provides for the establishment of State equalization rates. The critical significance of this continuing pattern of legislative activity, of course, is that it was all premised on the assumption that there was an existing practice of fractional assessments and the implicit expectation that the practice would continue. Had the Legislature intended to insist on State-wide full value assessment there would, of course, have been no occasion of equalization machinery or procedures.

It must be evident that the local boards of assessors, the agencies of government charged with responsibility for implementation of the statutory scheme for assessment of real property, construe the statutory provisions to authorize fractional assessments. In other contexts we have repeatedly held that if not irrational or unreasonable the construction given a statute by the agency charged with responsibility for its administration should be upheld (*Matter of Howard v. Wyman*, 28 N.Y.2d 434, 438, 322 N.Y.S.2d 683, 686, 271 N.E.2d 528, 530, and its progeny).

Today's decision of the majority will affect many more persons than the first instance taxpayers. The enthusiasm of purchasers at tax sales for nonpayment of taxes based on fractional assessments will be chilled. At a moment of the greatest strain on the public fisc in many years, I suggest that so to hinder the collection of taxes could be nothing short of disastrous. Less significantly, title examiners with the conspicuous distaste for bold adventure which has always characterized their activities can be expected to be hesitant to certify tax titles based on fractional assessments in the past after we have declared that such practice violates the statute. Additionally, I can visualize the filing of literally hundreds of protective claims.

I cannot believe there will not be other practical ramifications among many taxpayers and others, none of whom will be legally bound by the waiting period imposed on Pauline Hellerstein.

Nor, on the other hand, do I foresee any effective countermove to today's decision available to the Legislature. Even if a bill were passed tomorrow expressly authorizing fractional assessments, I know of no authority by which such an enactment could be given retroactive effect to disturb or modify property rights otherwise vested and fixed.

In short I see no way open to the court, as it would be to the Legislature were the court not to speak, to make a practically effective prospective-only determination with respect to the validity of fractional assessment practice. In my view for our court to attempt to do so will be to invite utter confusion, immediately, among taxpayers, assessors, tax collectors, purchasers of tax titles, title examiners, and others.

In these circumstances and in the light of the history of both enactment and failure to enact on the part of our State Legislature, of the construction uniformly placed on the statutory assessment procedures by those charged with direct responsibility thereunder, and of what I can only characterize as the general acceptance by taxpayers and municipal authorities alike of fractional assessments, I conclude that it ill becomes the judiciary, in what I conceive to be an exaggerated emphasis on the literal but long-ignored terminology of the statute, to overturn a practice of such venerable and broadly accepted status. No one questions that the Legislature could explicitly authorize and present practice; there would be no constitutional impediment. I agree that it would be desirable from various points of view were the Legislature unmistakably to express its views with reference to fractional assessment. I see no sufficient reason, however, to invalidate present practice for the purpose of forcing the issue, opening as it inevitably will a veritable Pandora's box of both foreseeable and unforeseeable complications. Attractive and persuasive as are some of the arguments in support of the principle of full value assessment (more appropriately, however, to be addressed to the Legislature), it must be conceded as a practical matter that the implementation of such a system could be achieved only by the expenditure of very large sums of money to defray the expense of what would have to be nearly State-wide reassessment procedures. On the one hand I see no warrant for the judicial imposition of such costs in the historical circumstances of this case. On the other, I see no justification or useful purpose to be served in forcing the Legislature to go through the ceremony of formally expressing what I can only believe is at least its tacit approval of present fractional assessment procedures.

I would, therefore, affirm the order of the Appellate Division. I am obliged additionally to observe that not only do I seriously question the wisdom of giving prospective-only effect to judicial determinations as does the majority in this case, more importantly I know of no sufficient legal authority for such a procedural disposition.

JASEN, FUCHSBERG and COOKE, JJ., concur with WACHTLER, J.

JONES, J., dissents and votes to affirm in a separate opinion in which BREITEL, C.J., and GABRIELLI, J., concur.

Order modified, without costs, in accordance with the opinion herein and, as so modified, affirmed.

Notes on the New York Response to *Hellerstein*

Consider the practical difficulties facing a taxpayer who attempts to persuade a court that his property is assessed at less than the constitutional or statutory full-value standard, but at a higher ratio to full value than that which prevails through the jurisdiction generally. In the past, taxing authorities have sometimes had no statistical data on the assessment ratio for their districts. See *In re Kents*, 34 N.J. 21, 166 A.2d 763 (1961). The expense of proving the assessment ratio through independent appraisals of selected parcels (as contemplated by section 720(3) of the New York Real Property Tax Law, reprinted in the materials above) was demonstrated in *860 Executive Towers, Inc. v. Board of Assessors*, 53 A.D.2d 463, 385 N.Y.S.2d 604 (1976), *aff'd mem. sub nom. Pierre Pellaton Apts., Inc. v. Board of Assessors*, 43 N.Y.2d 769, 401 N.Y.S.2d 1013, 372 N.E.2d 801 (1977). Having prevailed on the merits, the taxpayers there sought to recover their costs, and introduced evidence that their fifty-day trial required over two thousand hours of attorneys' time. Fees for appraisers and statisticians alone exceeded $281,000. The taxpayers requested a total reimbursement of $484,000 for their costs in proving the assessment ratio, and were awarded $435,000.

After the *Hellerstein* decision, the New York legislature took steps to limit taxpayer use of the state equalization ratio as a means of proving relative overassessment. Legislation permitting use of the state ratio only to show assessment rates for property of the same class as that under review was held unconstitutional in *Slewett & Farber v. Board of Assessors*, 97 Misc.2d 637, 412 N.Y.S.2d 292 (1978). The legislature then eliminated use of the state ratio in such proceedings altogether, except for cases involving the assessment of residential units housing three or fewer families. The preamble to this legislation declared, "[T]he equalization rate . . . was never intended to determine property values for taxing purposes, but was intended only to be used in connection with equalizing state aid and to compute constitutional tax and debt limits. Therefore, the use of such equalization rate for the purpose of quantifying the ratio of assessment to market value within a taxing district produces spurious and counter-productive results." The preamble justified the exception for small residential units as "an effort to provide a remedy which would enable the individual residential owner-petitioner to assemble and present in a summary and inexpensive manner evidence of inequality of assessment . . . ." *Slewett & Farber v. Board of Assessors*, 80 A.D.2d 186, 438 N.Y.S.2d 544 (1981), *modified,* 54 N.Y.2d 547, 430 N.E.2d 1294, 446 N.Y.S.2d 241 (1982), found it unconstitutional to permit residential taxpayers to use "spurious and counter-productive" evidence denied other owners. Legislation enacted in 1981 permitted all taxpayers to use the state equalization rate except in disputes involving property located in assessing units with a population of one million or more. Only New York City and Nassau County meet this description. The provision was upheld against an equal-protection challenge in *Colt Industries, Inc. v. Finance Administrator*, 54 N.Y.2d 533, 446 N.Y.S.2d 237, 430 N.E.2d 1290 (1982), *appeal dismissed,* 459 U.S. 983 (1982).

From 1978 to 1981 the New York legislature's response to *Hellerstein* was limited to a series of moratoriums on its reassessment order and temporary restrictions on the right of commercial and industrial property owners in New York City to protest their assessments—restrictions encouraged by the city's estimate that its potential refund liability might exceed $1 billion in the absence of such measures. In October 1981 the legislature addressed the assessment problem in a complex enactment designed primarily to prevent any large-scale shift of the property tax burden from businesses to homeowners. This measure established two different assessment systems, one for New

York City and Nassau County, and another for the rest of the state. New York City and Nassau County were divided into four assessment classes: residences housing up to three families, apartment buildings, utilities, and all other property, primarily industrial and office buildings, with each class responsible for the same proportion of total property tax revenue as it contributed in 1981. This proportion could be adjusted for future increases in property value, but not to remedy past underassessments. Increases in homeowners' assessments were limited to 6 percent annually, and 20 percent over the next five years. The other New York State jurisdictions were given permission to continue their past assessment practices, with the option of adopting a modified version of the New York City system.

Governor Carey vetoed this legislation. He stated in his veto message that "enactment of this bill would perpetuate rather than eliminate the inequities which have existed for too long a period in our real-property tax system. It would undermine—if not reverse—those advances toward a fair and equitable real-property tax system which have been made in various parts of the state in recent years. The approximately 600 towns and cities which are improving the quality of assessment administration through revaluation would be subject to pressures to reverse their direction and revert to prior practices." The legislature, anxious to resolve the uncertainty caused by *Hellerstein* in a manner acceptable to the state's homeowners, overrode the governor's veto, and the measure became law in early December.

The threat of an end to the relative underassessment of much residential property stimulated intense lobbying by New York homeowners' groups opposed to the *Hellerstein* decision. Consider the following excerpt from a letter to the *New York Times* from the cochairman of the "New York Suburban Coalition Against Reassessment." What would your response be to these concerns? How effectively do you think the New York legislation addressed them?

> At first sight, full value would seem to be the easiest and most equitable way to achieve [a uniform and equitable assessment system], but in practice it has proved to be a disaster. . . . [W]here commercial property owners had been traditionally assessed at higher percentages than residential property owners, the equalization resulted in unfair shifts of the tax burden onto homeowners. These are some of the inequities in full value.

> Homeowner groups began to ask the legislators, Why should a homeowner be forced to pay the same taxes as a business that passes that tax along in the goods and services that it sells? Who decides full value? The local assessor? A computer? And how often must a locality undergo a costly reassessment? Every year? The cost to taxpayers for this system would have been astronomical![20]

---

20. J. Asselta, Letter: "How to Protect the Homeowner," *New York Times,* December 2, 1981.

Nearly a decade later, a report by State Comptroller Edward Regan pointed to "a distressing lack of uniformity within every property class and within almost every neighborhood in the city . . . the less valuable the property, the more it is taxed in relation to its market value." Owners of houses worth less than $100,000 were found to pay an effective tax rate almost twice that of owners of houses worth more than $200,000. The *New York Times* reported:

> City and state officials blame history and politics for the inequities. As the value of houses rose over many decades, the city seldom revised its assessments. As a result, the tax on more expensive houses was based on a lower and lower percentage of their actual worth.
>
> In response to a court decision that would have forced the city to raise taxes on underassessed properties, the Legislature decided to protect homeowners. It approved a bill in 1981 that prohibits the city from raising assessments on one-, two-, and three-family houses more than 6 percent a year and more than 20 percent over five years.
>
> City officials now say that the law, which the Koch administration supported, severely limited them in doing what was needed to correct inequities: raising assessments on houses that grew rapidly in value in the unprecedented real-estate surge of the 80's.
>
> . . . .
>
> Finance Commissioner Carol O'Cleireacain said she was determined to address what she called "the blatant inequalities in the property tax. She promised to overhaul the system, but she did not say how.
>
> A wholesale revision of the property tax would need the approval of the City Council and the Legislature. But the Dinkins administration is not likely to find much support in either chamber. Both have repeatedly acted in the last 10 years to retain the status quo, in part because the beneficiaries of the system—many of whom would face steep increases if it were made more equitable—are determined to preserve it, and they constitute a large vocal voting bloc.
>
> . . . .
>
> Edward L. Sadowsky, former chairman of the Council's Finance Committee and the head of the city's Tax Study Commission, said political realities had made the property tax difficult to change.
>
> "My house is exhibit 1," said Mr. Sadowsky, who lives in Beechhurst, Queens. It has gone up eight-fold in value since I bought it in 1969, while the taxes on the house have maybe gone up 20 or 25 percent. It's a great deal."

The report concluded that the same political factors that blocked implementation of the *Hellerstein* decision were likely to perpetuate these inequalities in New York City assessments:

> The consensus among outside experts is that the city should move to full-market assessments. Buffalo and Rochester have done so, and Syracuse is shifting to it. But it seems unlikely that New York will follow soon.

. . . .

In a sense, the current system seems almost calculated to perpetuate itself. Its beneficiaries would pay more if the system were made more equitable, and so they fight to retain it. Victims often do not even know they are overtaxed. When they receive a notice of an assessment increase, they see that their home is assessed at a fraction of what it is worth and may think they are getting a break, unaware that others are assessed at far lower rates.

. . . .

"It's pure politics, in terms of who votes in this city, and one-, two-, and three-family homeowners vote," said Steven Spinola, president of the Real Estate Board of New York.[21]

A comprehensive contemporaneous study of the *Hellerstein* decision is contained in a three-part series of articles by Beebe and Sinnott,[22] which also reviews cases on fractional assessment and classification from other jurisdictions.

Notes and Questions

1. The *Hellerstein* case differs in form from the "welcome stranger" cases in that, as the New York court noted, the taxpayer brought "no claim of overvaluation or unequal treatment in the assessment of petitioner's property." However, as the opinion makes clear, fractional assessment is objectionable because it gives rise to overvaluation and unequal treatment. If all assessments were at the same fraction of full market value it would not distort any taxpayer's actual liability. This theoretical (and unrealistic) possibility lay behind New York's long acceptance of fractional valuation. For this reason, *Hellerstein* is often discussed as a rejection of "welcome stranger" assessment, as in a 1976 *Syracuse Law Review* article.[23]

2. Unlike similar cases overturning fractional assessment systems in other states, *Hellerstein* dealt with a legislative, not constitutional, requirement of full-value assessment. Why do you think the New York legislature did not simply overrule that decision by statute in the following session?

3. How would the practical and political effects of the *Hellerstein* case have differed if that court had continued the prior interpretation of "full value" as a "uniform percentage of full value"?

---

21. A. Finder and R. Levine, "When Wealthy Pay Less Tax Than the Other Homeowners," *New York Times*, May 29, 1990, p. A1.

22. Robert L. Beebe and Richard J. Sinnott, "In the Wake of *Hellerstein*: Whither New York?" *Albany Law Review* 43(1979):203, 411, 777.

23. "Comment, *Hellerstein v. Assessor of the Town of Islip*: A Response to Inequities in Real Property Assessments in New York," *Syracuse Law Review* 27(1976):1045, 1061.

4. Was the *Hellerstein* court correct when it wrote that the system of fractional assessment had "time on its side and nothing else"? Was the dissent correct in terming legislative ratification of fractional assessment an empty "ceremony"?

Legal Challenges to Financing Education through the Property Tax

Use of the property tax to fund local school systems has been challenged as a violation of state constitutions in a large number of cases in recent years, after *San Antonio Independent School District v. Rodriguez,*[24] found no federal equal protection violation in such a system. The *McDuffy* opinion that follows lists a number of such cases; since it was issued in mid-1993, additional challenges have been brought in Ohio and New Hampshire, and Michigan has adopted a legislative measure ending property tax funding of local education. A property tax limit adopted by Oregon voters in 1990 requires that state general funds replace all property tax losses for local education districts. In New York, a state where a constitutional attack on school financing was not successful, a special commission appointed by the governor to study the state's educational system recommended in 1993 that property tax revenues from nonresidential property be redistributed on a per-pupil basis among all school districts in the same county.

The following case provides a recent example of such litigation. Other examples can be found in its footnote 91 (the number of this footnote indicates how short an excerpt this is of the original opinion). Many articles on school finance litigation contain similar lists of state cases; a very inclusive compilation can be found in an article by T. Reynolds.[25]

McDUFFY V. SECRETARY OF THE EXECUTIVE OFFICE OF EDUCATION
415 Mass. 545; 615 N.E.2d 516
Supreme Judicial Court of Massachusetts, 1993

LIACOS, C.J. The Constitution of this Commonwealth, adopted by the people, provides:

> "Wisdom and knowledge, as well as virtue, diffused generally among the body of the people, being necessary for the preservation of their rights and liberties; and as these depend on spreading the opportunities and advantages of education in the various parts of the country, and among the different orders of the people, it shall be the duty of legislatures and magistrates, in all future periods of this

---

24. 411 U.S. 1 (1973).

25. T. Reynolds, " Note, Education Finance Reform Litigation and Separation of Powers: Kentucky Makes Its Contribution," *Kentucky Law Journal* 80 (1992):309, 310 n. 2.

Commonwealth, to cherish the interests of literature and the sciences, and all seminaries of them; especially the university at Cambridge, public schools and grammar schools in the towns; to encourage private societies and public institutions, rewards and immunities, for the promotion of agriculture, arts, sciences, commerce, trades, manufacturers, and a natural history of this country; to countenance and inculcate the principles of humanity and general benevolence, public and private charity, industry and frugality, honesty and punctuality in their dealings; sincerity, good humour, and all social affections, and generous sentiments among the people."

Part II, c. 5, sec. 2, of the Massachusetts Constitution.

In this case, sixteen students of the Commonwealth's public schools in sixteen different towns and cities of the Commonwealth sued the Board of Education, the Commissioner of Education, the Secretary of the Executive Office of Education, and the Treasurer and Receiver General, seeking a declaration of rights under G. L. [Massachusetts General Laws] c. 231A (1990 ed.) that the Commonwealth has failed to fulfil its duty to provide them an education as mandated by the Constitution. The plaintiffs claim that the State's school-financing system effectively denies them the opportunity to receive an adequate education in the public schools in their communities. This denial of the opportunity for an adequate education, the plaintiffs claim, violates both Part II, c. 5, sec. 2, and arts. 1 and 10 of the Declaration of Rights of the Massachusetts Constitution.

. . . .

We conclude that a duty exists. Second, we shall attempt to describe the nature of that duty and where it lies. Third, we shall consider whether on this record such a duty is shown to be violated. We take this approach because we are confident that the executive and legislative branches of government will respond appropriately to meet their constitutional responsibilities.[8]

The stipulated record contains 546 stipulations and six volumes of documentary material. The plaintiffs claim that this record supports their factual assertions, and that these facts, taken together, are sufficient to prove their legal claim that the school-financing scheme in Massachusetts violates Part II, c. 5, sec. 2, and arts. 1 and 10. The defendant education officials dispute both contentions: They deny that the stipulated record supports the plaintiffs' factual claims, and they argue that, even if it did, these facts would be insufficient to prove the plaintiffs' legal claims. The defendants also dispute the existence of the plaintiffs' legal claims under the Massachusetts Constitution. We outline briefly the plaintiffs' claims.

---

8. We note that both parties engage in a clash of views that focuses on whether the constitutional language requires an "adequate" education, whether the State provides an education which is "adequate," and if not, who is to blame. We decline to enter into this aspect of the debate . . . . The word "adequate" does not appear in the constitutional language and the struggle of the parties reveals, with good faith on all sides, necessary biases as to meaning. Thus, we strive to ascertain, as we should, the intention of the drafters of the constitutional language and to provide a frame of reference for the implementation of that intent in a modern society. Last, who is to "blame" between local governments or the Commonwealth appears to us to be totally irrelevant to the difficult questions put before us. We use the word "adequate" only to state the parties' arguments.

1. The plaintiffs' factual claims. The plaintiffs' key factual assertions concern: (1) the inadequacy of the education offered at the public schools they attend; (2) the insufficiency of funds for their schools; and (3) the State's school-funding system.

a. Adequacy. The plaintiffs assert that the educational opportunities offered to them in the towns and cities in which they live and attend public school are "inadequate." They assert further that "the education provided to the Plaintiffs is inadequate by any reasonable standard of adequacy." To support this inadequacy claim, the plaintiffs cite reports and affidavits of education professionals on the question of adequacy, and, in addition, using stipulations of record, they describe conditions in the plaintiffs' schools, and then compare them with conditions in three "comparison" communities (Brookline, Concord, and Wellesley). Among the reports which the plaintiffs cite to support their claim of inadequacy is a 1991 report of the Board of Education (one of the defendants). This report states that "schools in the Commonwealth of Massachusetts are in a state of emergency due to grossly inadequate financial support," and that the education offered in the public schools in some cities and towns of the Commonwealth is not "adequate" or "acceptable."

. . . .

b. Funding levels. The plaintiffs claim that the financial resources of the public schools in their towns and cities are substantially less than the financial resources of public schools in other towns and cities of the Commonwealth. They also claim that financial resources of the schools in their communities are so low as to render their schools unable to provide students "with the opportunity to receive an adequate education."

c. The school financing system. The plaintiffs claim that the school funding system— "a conglomeration of statutes, occasional emergency legislation, local appropriations, and ad hoc practices not codified by statute" fails to ensure that the schools in the plaintiffs' towns and cities have sufficient funds to provide an adequate education. The financing "system," the plaintiffs claim, is responsible both for the wide disparity in funding among the schools in different communities of the Commonwealth, and for the insufficiency of school funds in the towns and cities in which they live and attend school.

According to the plaintiffs, there are several, interrelated problems with the school funding system: First, under the existing "system," the principal source of funds for public schools is local funds, primarily the local real property tax, which is assessed, collected, and used locally. Towns and cities with low real estate valuations, such as those in which the plaintiffs live and attend school, are severely limited in their ability to raise local funds. Second, there is no State statute or regulation requiring towns and cities to contribute any particular amount, percentage of local funds, or any local funds to the support of schools in their communities. Third, although the Commonwealth provides various forms of "State aid" annually to towns and cities under General Laws, chapters 70 and 70A, to supplement funds raised locally, the amounts granted are insufficient to compensate for deficiencies in local funds. Fourth, State aid is unpredictable every year and, in some years, is not granted by the State until after the school year has begun. Fifth, State aid for schools is undifferentiated from State aid for other municipal purposes, and there is no requirement that towns and cities actually use State aid for schools to support schools and not for other municipal purposes.

2. The plaintiffs' legal claims. On the basis of these factual assertions, the plaintiffs claim that the Commonwealth, through its school-financing system, has effectively denied the plaintiffs the opportunity to receive an adequate education. The Commonwealth's failure to provide them with an adequate education, they claim, violates the duty imposed on the Commonwealth by Part II, c. 5, sec. 2, of the Massachusetts Constitution, which provides, inter alia, that "it shall be the duty of

legislatures and magistrates, in all future periods of this Commonwealth, to cherish . . . the public schools and grammar schools in the towns." The plaintiffs also claim that the failure to provide them with an adequate' education violates the equal protection guarantees of arts. 1 and 10.

The plaintiffs seek identical relief under both of their constitutional claims: a declaratory judgment that "the Commonwealth has an obligation to provide each public school child with the opportunity to receive an adequate education," and that "the Commonwealth has violated the Massachusetts Constitution by failing to fulfill its obligations to the Plaintiff school children."

. . . .

We note that the plaintiffs do not seek a judgment that the Commonwealth has an obligation to equalize educational spending across all towns and cities, or that the Commonwealth has an obligation to provide equal educational opportunities to all its students. Instead, they seek a declaratory judgment that these constitutional provisions require the State to provide every young person in the Commonwealth with an "adequate" education. The plaintiffs argue that Part II, c. 5, sec. 2, and arts. 1 and 10, each require "equal access to an adequate education, not absolute equality."

We turn now to an examination of Part II, c. 5, sec. 2, of the Massachusetts Constitution to determine whether, as the plaintiffs claim, its provisions impose on the State an enforceable obligation to provide to each young person in the Commonwealth the opportunity for an education.

. . . .

In determining the meaning of a constitutional provision, we look to the language and structure of the provision, so that it is "construed so as to accomplish a reasonable result and to achieve its dominating purpose." *Lincoln v. Secretary of the Commonwealth,* 326 Mass. 313, 317, 93 N.E.2d 744 (1950) . . . . Moreover, the Constitution "is to be interpreted in the light of the conditions under which it and its several parts were framed, the ends which it was designed to accomplish, the benefits which it was expected to confer, and the evils which it was hoped to remedy." . . . [T]he Constitution "is a statement of general principles and not a specification of details . . . . It is to be interpreted as the Constitution of a State and not as a statute or an ordinary piece of legislation. Its words must be given a construction adapted to carry into effect its purpose." *Cohen v. Attorney Gen.,* 357 Mass. 564, 571, 259 N.E.2d 539 (1970), quoting *Tax Comm'r v. Putnam,* 227 Mass. 522, 523-524 (1917).

B.

Part II, c. 5, sec. 2, of the Massachusetts Constitution was adopted as part of the Constitution of the Commonwealth in 1780 . . . . The plaintiffs argue that "the duty of legislatures and magistrates, in all future periods of this Commonwealth, to cherish . . . public schools and grammar schools in the towns" includes the duty to provide an adequate education to the young people of the State, and that this duty is "an enforceable obligation" of the Commonwealth. The defendant education officials argue that the language of the entire section is "aspirational" and a "noble expression of the high esteem in which the framers held education," but that it is not "mandatory."

We begin with the language and structure of the provision . . . . The two statements at the beginning of Part II, c. 5, sec. 2, state plainly the premises on which the duty is established: First, the protection of rights and liberties requires the diffusion of wisdom, knowledge, and virtue throughout the people. Second, the means of diffusing these qualities and attributes among the people is to spread the opportunities and advantages of education throughout the Commonwealth. . . .The duty established is, inter alia, placed on the "legislatures and magistrates, in all future periods of this Commonwealth." The common meaning of "duty" in 1780, according to a dictionary of the English language published that year, was "that to which a man is by any natural or legal obligation bound." T. Sheridan, *A General Dictionary of the English Language* 1780 (Scolar Press 1967) . . . . Hence, the "duty . . . to cherish the interests of literature and the sciences, and all seminaries of them; especially . . . public schools and grammar schools in the towns" is an obligation to support or nurture these interests and institutions. The breadth of the meaning of these terms ("duty . . . to cherish"), together with the articulated ends for which this duty to cherish is established, strongly support the plaintiffs' argument that the "duty . . . to cherish . . . the public schools" encompasses the duty to provide an education to the people of the Commonwealth. Part II, c. 5, sec. 2, states plainly that the duty to "cherish"—support—public schools arises out of the need to educate the people of the Commonwealth; it is reasonable therefore to understand the duty to "cherish" public schools as a duty to ensure that the public schools achieve their object and educate the people.

. . . .

Several features of Part II, c. 5, sec. 2, strongly suggest that the duty to cherish schools is mandatory. First, "duty," according to common usage in the late Eighteenth Century, meant, as indicated above, "obligation." Second, the language of Pt. II, c. 5, sec. 2, contains in essence a double injunction: It not only sets forth the "duty"; it also, by the use of the term "shall," mandates the duty: "it shall be the duty of legislatures and magistrates" (emphasis supplied). Third, the duty is enjoined "for all future periods of this Commonwealth." This unusual temporal reference underscores the continuing nature of the obligation and militates against a reading of "duty" as merely advisory. Fourth, the Constitution does not use the term "duty" lightly. None of the powers and responsibilities of the three branches of government is described or prescribed in the Constitution as a "duty."

. . . .

We have reviewed at great length the history of public education in Massachusetts so that we might glean an understanding of the meaning of c. 5, sec. 2. In doing so, we have considered the history of the colony, the province, the condition and concepts relating to education underlying the drafting of the Constitution of the Commonwealth and, in particular, c. 5, sec. 2. We have examined the intention of the framers, the language and the structure of the Constitution, the ratification process by the towns and also the words, acts, and deeds of contemporaries of that time, and, especially the views, addresses, and statutes of early Governors (magistrates) and the Legislatures. In this light, we have considered the proper meaning of the words "duty" and "cherish" found in c. 5, sec. 2. What emerges from this review is that the words are not merely aspirational or hortatory, but obligatory. What emerges also is that the Commonwealth has a duty to provide an education for all its children, rich and poor, in every city and town of the Commonwealth at the public school level, and that this duty is designed not only to serve the interests of the children, but, more fundamentally, to prepare them to participate as free citizens of a free State to meet the needs and interests of a republican government, namely the Commonwealth of Massachusetts.

This duty lies squarely on the executive (magistrates) and legislative (Legislatures) branches of this Commonwealth. That local control and fiscal support has been placed in greater or lesser measure through our history on local governments does not dilute the validity of this conclusion. While it is clearly within the power of the Commonwealth to delegate some of the implementation of the duty to local governments, such power does not include a right to abdicate the obligation imposed on magistrates and Legislatures placed on them by the Constitution.

We now turn to the remaining questions before us. In so doing, we consider briefly the statutory structures pertaining to the administration of the public schools and to the funding schemes presently utilized. Ultimately, we must decide two additional fundamental questions. First, what does the constitutional mandate entail? Second, on this record is that mandate being violated?

We shall then conclude by a brief discussion of what remedies may be appropriate for this court to require.

. . . .

The defendants argue before us that, if one looks to the administrative and financing schemes now in effect, that one must conclude, even if a constitutional duty is found, that the defendants are meeting their constitutional mandate. We disagree. The essential facts are not in dispute and we are entitled to draw our own proper inferences from them. We need not conclude that equal expenditure per pupil is mandated or required, although it is clear that financial disparities exist in regard to education in the various communities. It is also clear, however, that fiscal support, or the lack of it, has a significant impact on the quality of education each child may receive. Additionally, the record shows clearly that, while the present statutory and financial schemes purport to provide equal educational opportunity in the public schools for every child, rich or poor, the reality is that children in the less affluent communities (or in the less affluent parts of them) are not receiving their constitutional entitlement of education as intended and mandated by the framers of the Constitution.

For this conclusion, we need look no further than the parties' stipulations and the record appendix to conclude that the Commonwealth has failed to meet its constitutional obligation. In these documents, which include extensive stipulations, reports, and affidavits of education professionals (some of them defendants or former defendants in this case), we find statement after statement recounting the Commonwealth's failure to educate the children in the plaintiffs' schools and those they typify. The Commonwealth has not directed us to, nor have we discovered, any statements in the record tending to show otherwise. We briefly review the relevant portions of the record.

In their 1991 Report of the Committee on Distressed School Systems and School Reform, the defendant members of the board speak of a "state of emergency due to grossly inadequate financial support," and admit that "certain classrooms simply warehouse children at this time, with no effective education being provided." Arguably, this admission, by itself, suffices to establish the constitutional violations, but there is more. Harold Raynolds, Jr., the former Commissioner of Education (and a former defendant) has stated that "in many of the communities in Massachusetts, particularly less affluent communities such as the ones in which the plaintiffs attend school, Massachusetts is failing—and failing more than ever before—to achieve [the] goal [of providing every child with an opportunity for success in learning]." Peter Finn, the Executive Director of the Massachusetts Association of School Superintendents, affirms that "it is also clear that the education now offered in many of the poor communities, including the communities in which the plaintiffs attend school, is inadequate."

The parties have stipulated to the opinions of the superintendents of four of the plaintiffs' districts, which describe in some detail the Commonwealth's failure to educate the children in those districts. The parties have stipulated that the conditions in these schools are "typical" of the schools in the other twelve communities in which plaintiffs attend school. The superintendent in Brockton is of the opinion that "the Brockton Public Schools are unable to provide the programs, services and personnel that are necessary to meet the needs of its students"; that "Brockton is not adequately teaching its students to read"; that "shortcomings in the history and social studies programs in the Brockton public schools. . . have severely undercut the system's capacity to educate its students to understand the society in which they live and to help students become enlightened participants in the democratic process as they become adults."

The superintendent of the Leicester public schools states that "the Leicester public school system does not provide an adequate education to its students"; that class sizes in the third, fourth, and fifth grades in Leicester are "too large to provide the amount of individual attention and instruction needed by elementary students"; that guidance services in the schools "are inadequate and seriously jeopardize the future of [Leicester's] students"; that administrative support and management are "inadequate"; and that "most of the Leicester schools are in a terrible condition and that the high school is an extremely unsafe building."

The superintendent of the Lowell public schools states that class sizes in Lowell are "too large for teachers to be effective with elementary level students"; that the "low level of guidance offered in the Lowell public schools is inadequate to meet the needs of even an average suburban system, let alone the extreme needs of a system such as Lowell, with its unusually diverse population and large percentage of at-risk students."

Lastly, the parties stipulated that the superintendent of the Winchendon public schools is of the opinion that Winchendon "tends to end up with inexperienced and poor quality teachers"; that "there are not enough offerings for advanced students"; that "the science facilities are also poor, the textbooks are outdated and the middle school labs antiquated" and that "Winchendon is unable to provide an adequate science education for today's world to its students."

The parties have stipulated that students in the plaintiffs' districts are offered "significantly fewer educational opportunities and lower educational quality than" students in the schools in the "comparison" districts of Brookline, Concord, and Wellesley. The stipulations outline specific deficiencies in the plaintiffs' schools, such as: large classes; reductions in staff, inadequate teaching of basic subjects including reading, writing, science, social studies, mathematics, computers, and other areas; neglected libraries; inability to attract and retain high quality teachers; lack of teacher training; lack of curriculum development; lack of predictable funding; administrative reductions; and inadequate guidance counseling.

In contrast, the comparison districts are able to offer "significantly greater educational opportunities," including: multi-faceted reading programs; extensive writing programs and resources; thorough computer instruction; active curriculum development and review ensuring comprehensive and up-to-date curriculum; extensive teacher training and development; comprehensive student services; and a wide variety of courses in visual and performing arts. In short, the record indicates that these districts are able to educate their children.

It is clear that c. 5, sec. 2, obligates the Commonwealth to educate all its children. The bleak portrait of the plaintiffs' schools and those they typify, painted in large part by the defendants' own statements and about which no lack of consensus has been shown, leads us to conclude that the Commonwealth has failed to fulfil its obligation.[91]

---

91. Our conclusion that the Commonwealth is in violation of its constitutional duty to educate our children is not the first decision of its kind. The highest courts of some of our sister States have declared their educational systems to violate the education clauses, the equal protection provisions, or both clauses, of their Constitutions: *Dupree v. Alma*

The crux of the Commonwealth's duty lies in its obligation to educate all of its children. As has been done by the courts of some of our sister States, we shall articulate broad guidelines and assume that the Commonwealth will fulfil its duty to remedy the constitutional violations that we have identified. The guidelines set forth by the Supreme Court of Kentucky fairly reflect our view of the matter and are consistent with the judicial pronouncements found in other decisions. An educated child must possess "at least the seven following capabilities: (i) sufficient oral and written communication skills to enable students to function in a complex and rapidly changing civilization; (ii) sufficient knowledge of economic, social, and political systems to enable students to make informed choices; (iii) sufficient understanding of governmental processes to enable the student to understand the issues that affect his or her community, state, and nation; (iv) sufficient self-knowledge and knowledge of his or her mental and physical wellness; (v) sufficient grounding in the arts to enable each student to appreciate his or her cultural and historical heritage; (vi) sufficient training or preparation for advanced training in either academic or vocational fields so as to enable each child to choose and pursue life work intelligently; and (vii) sufficient level of academic or vocational skills to enable public school students to compete favorably with their counterparts in surrounding states, in academics or in the job market." *Rose v. Council for Better Educ., Inc.*, 790 S.W.2d 186, 212 (Ky. 1989).[92]

Sch. Dist. No. 30 of Crawford County, 279 Ark. 340 (1983); *Serrano v. Priest*, 18 Cal. 3d 728, 135 Cal. Rptr. 345, 557 P.2d 929 (1976), *cert. denied*, 432 U.S. 907 (1977); *Horton v. Meskill*, 172 Conn. 615, 376 A.2d 359 (1977); *Rose v. Council for Better Educ., Inc.*, 790 S.W.2d 186 (Ky. 1989); *Helena Elementary Sch. Dist. v. State*, 236 Mont. 44, 769 P.2d 684 (1989); *Abbott v. Burke*, 119 N.J. 287, 575 A.2d 359 (1990); *Robinson v. Cahill*, 62 N.J. 473, 303 A.2d 273 (1973); *Edgewood Indep. Sch. Dist. v. Kirby*, 777 S.W.2d 391 (Tex. 1989); *Seattle Sch. Dist. No. 1. v. State*, 90 Wash. 2d 476 (1978); *Washakie County Sch. Dist. v. Herschler*, 606 P.2d 310 (Wyo.), *cert. denied sub nom. Hot Springs County Sch. Dist. No. 1 v. Washakie County Sch. Dist. No. 1*, 449 U.S. 824, 66 L. Ed. 2d 28, 101 S. Ct. 86 (1980). While we do not undertake a comprehensive review of these cases, we note that several decisions relied on constitutional language and history less explicit than ours. See, e.g., *Robinson*, supra; *Rose*, supra.

For decisions of State Supreme Courts that have upheld their educational systems against constitutional challenges, see, e.g., *Shofstall v. Hollins*, 110 Ariz. 88, 515 P.2d 590 (1973); *Knowles v. State Bd. of Educ.*, 219 Kan. 271 (1976); *Hornbeck v. Somerset County Bd. of Educ.*, 295 Md. 597, 458 A.2d 758 (1983); *Milliken v. Green*, 390 Mich. 389, 212 N.W.2d 711 (1973); *Board of Educ., Levittown Union Free Sch. Dist. v. Nyquist*, 57 N.Y.2d 27 (1982), *appeal dismissed*, 459 U.S. 1138, 1139 (1983); *Board of Educ. of the City Sch. Dist. of Cincinnati v. Walter*, 58 Ohio St. 2d 368 (1979); *Danson v. Casey*, 484 Pa. 415, 399 A.2d 360 (1979); *Kukor v. Grover*, 148 Wis. 2d 469, 436 N.W.2d 568 (1989).

92. The precise nature of the remedy prescribed by the courts of our sister States that have declared their educational systems unconstitutional varied with the facts presented and the relevant constitutional provisions. Ultimately, however, these courts left the task of defining the specifics of their State's educational systems to their legislative and administrative bodies. For example, the Supreme Court of Washington declared specific portions of that State's education funding scheme unconstitutional and went on to

These guidelines accord with our Constitution's emphasis on educating our children to become free citizens on whom the Commonwealth may rely to meet its needs and to further its interests. As Horace Mann, the first secretary of the Board of Education, stated many years ago: "In regard to the application of this principle of natural law,—that is, in regard to the extent of the education to be provided for all, at the public expense,— some differences of opinion may fairly exist, under different political organizations; but under our republican government, it seems clear that the minimum of this education can never be less than such as is sufficient to qualify each citizen for the civil and social duties he will be called to discharge, such an education as teaches the individual the great laws of bodily health; as qualifies for the fulfillment of parental duties; as is indispensable for the civil functions of a witness or a juror; as is necessary for the voter in municipal and in national affairs; and finally, as is requisite for the faithful and conscientious discharge of all those duties which devolve upon the inheritor of a portion of the sovereignty of this great republic." *The Massachusetts System of Common Schools: Tenth Annual Report of the Massachusetts Board of Education* 17 (1849).

The content of the duty to educate which the Constitution places on the Common-wealth necessarily will evolve together with our society. Our Constitution, and its education clause, must be interpreted "in accordance with the demands of modern society or it will be in constant danger of becoming atrophied and, in fact, may even lose its original meaning." *Seattle Sch. Dist. No. 1 v. State*, 90 Wash. 2d 476, 516 (1978). Justice Holmes aptly captured this principle of constitutional jurisprudence:

> "When we are dealing with words that also are a constituent act, like the Constitution of the United States, we must realize that they have called into life a being the development of which could not have been foreseen completely by the most gifted of its begetters. It was enough for them to realize or to hope that they had created an organism; it has taken a century and has cost their successors much sweat and blood to prove that they created a nation. The case before us

---

declare broad guidelines with respect to the nature of the State's constitutional duty to educate children. Nonetheless, the Washington court made clear that the legislative branch had the responsibility to "define and give substantive content" to education. See *Seattle Sch. Dist. No. 1*, supra. Similarly, the Supreme Court of Texas held that State's Constitution "does not allow concentrations of resources in property-rich school districts that are taxing low when property-poor districts that are taxing high cannot generate sufficient revenues to meet even minimum standards [of education] . . . . Districts must have substantially equal access to similar revenues per pupil at similar levels of tax effort." *Edgewood Indep. Sch. Dist.*, supra at 397. In spite of this relatively specific holding, the Texas court declared that it did not "instruct the legislature as to the specifics of the legislation it should enact; nor do we order it to raise taxes. The legislature has primary responsibility to decide how best to achieve an efficient system. We decide only the nature of the constitutional mandate and whether that mandate has been met." Id. at 399.

As did these courts, we have declared today the nature of the Commonwealth's duty to educate its children. We have concluded the current state of affairs falls short of the constitutional mandate. We shall presume at this time that the Commonwealth will fulfil its responsibility with respect to defining the specifics and the appropriate means to provide the constitutionally-required education.

must be considered in the light of our whole experience and not merely in that of what was said a hundred years ago."

Missouri v. Holland, 252 U.S. 416, 443, 64 L. Ed. 641, 40 S. Ct. 382 (1920).

Thus, we leave it to the magistrates and the Legislatures to define the precise nature of the task which they face in fulfilling their constitutional duty to educate our children today, and in the future.

These cases are remanded to the county court for entry of a judgment declaring that the provisions of Part II, c. 5, sec. 2, of the Massachusetts Constitution impose an enforceable duty on the magistrates and Legislatures of this Commonwealth to provide education in the public schools for the children there enrolled, whether they be rich or poor and without regard to the fiscal capacity of the community or district in which such children live. It shall be declared also that the constitutional duty is not being currently fulfilled by the Commonwealth. Additionally, while local governments may be required, in part, to support public schools, it is the responsibility of the Commonwealth to take such steps as may be required in each instance effectively to devise a plan and sources of funds sufficient to meet the constitutional mandate. No present statutory enactment is to be declared unconstitutional, but the single justice may, in his or her discretion, retain jurisdiction to determine whether, within a reasonable time, appropriate legislative action has been taken.

So ordered.

O'Connor, J., concurring in part and dissenting in part:

I agree with the court that "the Commonwealth has a duty to provide an education for *all* its children, rich and poor, in every city and town of the Commonwealth at the public school level, and that this duty is designed not only to serve the interests of the children, but, more fundamentally, to prepare them to participate as free citizens of a free State to meet the needs and interests of a republican government, namely the Commonwealth of Massachusetts" (emphasis in original). I also agree that an educational program that is reasonably calculated to provide the children of the Commonwealth with the capabilities set forth in the Supreme Court of Kentucky's guidelines (*Rose v. Council for Better Educ., Inc.,* 790 S.W.2d 186, 212 [Ky. 1989]), would satisfy the constitutional mandate. I do not agree, however, that the record establishes that the Commonwealth has failed to provide public education in keeping with those guidelines. Therefore, I do not agree that the plaintiffs have proved that the defendants have violated the plaintiffs' constitutional entitlement to an education.

In support of its conclusion that children in the Commonwealth's less affluent communities or parts of communities are not receiving the education to which they are constitutionally entitled, the court states that it "need look no further than the parties' stipulations and the record appendix.". . . .In deciding whether the plaintiffs have established that their constitutional rights have been violated, it is critically important to understand that (1) the opinions contained in the aforementioned reports and affidavits do not purport to employ the Supreme Court of Kentucky guidelines (*Rose,* supra) or any other articulable standards of educational adequacy, and (2) the parties have not stipulated to the truth of any assertion or to the validity of any opinion stated in the reports and affidavits. The mere inclusion of those documents in a jointly filed appendix establishes nothing.

In addition to the aforementioned reports and affidavits, the court focuses on the opinions of four superintendents of schools . . . . Just as it is important to understand that the parties have not stipulated to the merit or validity of the opinions expressed in the reports and affidavits included in the joint appendix, it is also important to understand that, although the parties "have stipulated to the opinions of the superintendents of four of the plaintiffs' districts," as the court says, they have done so only in the sense that they have agreed that the stated opinions are indeed the four superintendents' opinions and the superintendents are competent to render them. The parties have not stipulated to the merit or correctness of the opinions. On the contrary, in a supplemental stipulation, the parties have expressly agreed that "there is no consensus among education experts as to what constitutes an adequate education." Therefore, whether standing alone or in conjunction with the reports and affidavits discussed by the court, the superintendents' opinions do not establish any constitutional violations.

The court states: "The parties have stipulated that students in the plaintiffs' districts are offered 'significantly fewer educational opportunities and lower educational quality than' students in the 'comparison' districts of Brookline, Concord, and Wellesley. The stipulations outline specific deficiencies in the plaintiffs' schools, such as: large classes; reductions in staff; inadequate teaching of basic subjects including reading, writing, science, social studies, mathematics, computers, and other areas; neglected libraries; inability to attract and retain high quality teachers; lack of teacher training; lack of curriculum development; lack of predictable funding; administrative reductions; and inadequate guidance counseling." If that passage is intended to say that the parties have agreed that, in the plaintiffs' schools, basic subjects such as reading, writing, science, social studies, mathematics, and others are "inadequately" taught, or that the teaching in those subjects does not comply with the Supreme Court of Kentucky guidelines or similar standards, I respectfully disagree with the court. The parties have not stipulated to those facts. Those facts have not been established, and it is of no constitutional significance that more educational opportunities are provided in wealthy communities than in poor ones. Therefore, I am unwilling to join the court insofar as it declares that the defendants or the Commonwealth have failed to fulfil their constitutional obligations.

Notes and Questions

1. To what extent has the court abdicated its role by leaving it to "the magistrates and the Legislatures to define the precise nature of the task which they face in fulfilling their constitutional duty to educate our children today, and in the future"?

2. The local nature of school finance has exacerbated the intractable problems of school integration. Families who have moved to the suburbs or placed their children in private schools are unlikely to support tax increases to improve inner-city school systems, and lack of funding decreases the attractiveness of these schools to parents who can send their children elsewhere. This situation led to an extraordinary order in *Jenkins v. Missouri*, 855 F.2d 1295 (8th Cir. 1988), *aff'd in part and rev'd in part*, 495 U.S. 33 (1990), which grew out of more than a decade of litigation concerning the Kansas City Metropolitan School District. To effectuate its desegregation order, a federal district court ordered local officials to levy a property tax in excess of state constitutional limits, a decision subse-

quently upheld by the Eighth Circuit. The Supreme Court unanimously held that the court could not itself impose the tax, but by a vote of 5 to 4 held that federal courts may "authorize or require local officials to levy property taxes at a rate adequate to fund the desegregation remedy and may enjoin the operation of state laws that otherwise would limit or reduce such a tax levy." Justice Kennedy charged that this "casual embrace of taxation imposed by the unelected, life-tenured federal judiciary disregards fundamental precepts for the democratic control of public institutions." This issue is discussed by several authors.[26]

3. To what extent did the wording of the Massachusetts constitution support the specific conclusions reached by the court in *McDuffy*? An article by D. Yarab[27] compares the relevant provision of the Texas constitution (Art. VII, sec. 1: "A general diffusion of knowledge being essential to the preservation of the liberties and rights of the people, it shall be the duty of the Legislature of the State to establish and make suitable provision for the support and maintenance of an efficient system of public free schools") to the very similar wording found in other state constitutions, with particular reference to Ohio.

4. On recent school finance litigation generally, see, for example, articles by J. Banks, K. Stark, and others.[28]

---

26. See D. B. La Pierre, "Enforcement of Judgments Against States and Local Governments: Judicial Control Over the Power to Tax," *George Washington Law Review* 61 (1993):301; D. Brocker, "Note, Taxation Without Representation: The Judicial Usurpation of the Power to Tax in *Missouri v. Jenkins*," *North Carolina Law Review* 69 (1991):741; and L. Gunn, "*Missouri v. Jenkins*: The Expansion of Federal Judicial Power," *Georgia State University Law Review* 7 (1991):495.

27. D. Yarab, "Comment, *Edgewood Independent School District v. Kirby*: An Education in School Finance Reform," *Case Western Reserve Law Review* 40 (1990):889.

28. J. Banks, "State Constitutional Analyses of Public School Finance Reform Cases: Myth or Methodology? *Vanderbilt Law Review* 45 (1992):129; K. Stark, "Note, Rethinking Statewide Taxation of Nonresidential Property for Public Schools," *Yale Law Journal* 102 (1992):805; "Note, The School Finance Reform Movement, A History and Prognosis: Will Massachusetts Join the Third Wave of Reform?" *Boston College Law Review* 32 (1991):1105; and "Note, Unfulfilled Promises: School Finance Remedies and State Courts," *Harvard Law Review* 104 (1991):1072.

BIBLIOGRAPHY

1. Books.

Aaron, Henry J. 1975. *Who Pays the Property Tax: A New View.* Washington, DC: Brookings Institution.

Advisory Commission on Intergovernmental Relations. 1990. Updated annually. *Significant Features of Fiscal Federalism 1990.* Washington, DC: Advisory Commission on Intergovernmental Relations.

American Institute of Architects (AIA), New York Chapter. 1988. *AIA Guide to New York City.* 3d ed. Eds. Elliot Willensky and Norval White. New York: Macmillan.

American Institute of Real Estate Appraisers. 1980. *Golf Courses: A Guide to Analysis and Valuation.* Chicago: American Institute of Real Estate Appraisers.

Appraisal Institute. 1992. *The Appraisal of Real Estate.* Chicago: The Appraisal Institute.

Aronson, J. Richard, and John Hilley. 1986. *Financing State and Local Governments.* Washington, DC: Brookings Institution.

Blake, Peter. 1960. *Mies van der Rohe: Architecture and Structure.* Harmondsworth, England: Penguin Books.

Bonbright, James C. [1937] 1965. *The Valuation of Property: A Treatise on the Appraisal of Property for Different Legal Purposes.* Reprint. Charlottesville, VA: Michie.

Ehrman, Kenneth A., and Sean Flavin. 1979 (2d ed.); 1988 (3d ed.). *Taxing California Property.* Deerfield, IL: Callaghan. Loose-leaf service with updates.

Fisher, Ronald C. 1988. *State and Local Public Finance.* Glenview, IL: Scott, Foresman.

Fjellman, Stephen M. 1992. *Vinyl Leaves: Walt Disney World and America.* Boulder, CO: Westview Press.

Friedman, Edith J., ed. 1978. *Encyclopedia of Real Estate Appraising.* 3d ed. Englewood Cliffs, NJ: Prentice-Hall.

George, Henry. [1879] 1990. *Progress and Poverty.* Reprint. New York: Robert Schalkenbach Foundation.

Gold, Steven D., and Judy A. Zelio. 1990. *State-Local Fiscal Indicators.* Washington, DC: National Conference of State Legislatures.

Goldberger, Paul. 1979. *The City Observed: A Guide to the Architecture of Manhattan.* New York: Random House.

Graduate School of Public Administration, New York University. 1980. *Real Property Tax Policy for New York City*. Report to the Department of Finance, City of New York.

Hellerstein, Jerome, and Walter Hellerstein. 1993. *State Taxation*. 2d ed. Boston: Warren, Gorham & Lamont. Loose-leaf service with updates.

International Association of Assessing Officers. 1990. *Property Appraisal and Assessment Administration*. Chicago: International Association of Assessing Officers.

International Association of Assessing Officers. 1978. *Improving Real Property Assessment: A Reference Manual*. Chicago: International Association of Assessing Officers.

Jensen, Jens Peter. 1931. *Property Taxation in the United States*. Chicago: The University of Chicago Press.

Kayden, Jerold. 1978. *Incentive Zoning in New York City: A Cost-Benefit Analysis*. Cambridge, MA: The Lincoln Institute of Land Policy.

Kuttner, Robert. 1980. *Revolt of the Haves: Tax Rebellions and Hard Times*. New York: Simon and Schuster.

Lindholm, R., and Arthur Lynn, eds. 1982. *Land Value Taxation: The Progress and Poverty Centenary*. Madison, WI: The University of Wisconsin Press.

Logan, Carol J. 1986. *Slash Property Taxes. Born Free—Taxed to Death*. Peckslip Station, New York: Western Search.

Malme, Jane H. 1992. *Assessment Administration Practices in the U.S. and Canada*. Chicago: International Association of Assessing Officers. Updated periodically.

Manvel, Allen D. 1986. *Paying for Civilized Society: A Fiscal Chart Book*. Arlington, VA: Tax Analysts.

Mills, Edwin S., and Wallace E. Oates, eds. 1975. *Fiscal Zoning and Land Use Controls, the Economic Issues*. Lexington, MA: Lexington Books.

Musgrave, Richard A., and Peggy B. Musgrave. 1989. *Public Finance in Theory and Practice*. 5th ed. New York: McGraw-Hill.

Newhouse, Wade J. 1984. *Constitutional Uniformity and Equality in State Taxation*. 2d ed. Buffalo, NY: W.S. Hein.

Pearce, David W., ed. 1992. *The MIT Dictionary of Modern Economics*. 4th ed. Cambridge, MA: Massachusetts Institute of Technology Press.

Ring, Alfred, and James H. Boykin. 1986. *The Valuation of Real Estate*. 3d ed. Englewood Cliffs, NJ: Prentice-Hall.

Rohan, Patrick J. 1984. *Real Estate Tax Appeals*. New York: Matthew

Bender. Loose-leaf service with updates.

Rohan, Patrick J., and Melvin A. Reskin. 1965 and supplements. *Condominium Law and Practice.* Loose-leaf service. New York: Matthew Bender.

Rosen, Harvey S. 1985 (1st ed.); 1992 (3d ed.). *Public Finance.* Homewood, IL: Irwin.

Sears, David O., and Jack Citrin. 1985. *Tax Revolt: Something for Nothing in California.* Cambridge, MA: Harvard University Press.

Seligman, Edwin R. A. 1931. *Essays in Taxation.* 10th ed. New York: Macmillan.

Shoup, Carl Sumner. 1969. *Public Finance.* Chicago: Aldine Pub. Co.

Stocker, Frederick D., ed. 1991. *Proposition 13: A Ten Year Retrospective.* Cambridge, MA: The Lincoln Institute of Land Policy.

Swords, Peter deL. 1981. *Charitable Real Property Tax Exemptions in New York State: Menace or Measure of Social Progress?* New York: Association of the Bar of the City of New York (distributed by Columbia University Press).

Tiffany, Herbert Thorndike. 1939. *The Law of Real Property.* 3d ed. Ed. B. Jones. Chicago: Callaghan & Company. Updated with annual supplements.

U.S. Bureau of the Census, U.S. Department of Commerce. 1993. *Government Finances: 1990–91.* Washington, DC: U.S. Government Printing Office.

U.S. Bureau of the Census, U.S. Department of Commerce. 1976. *Historical Statistics of the United States, Colonial Times to 1970.* White Plains, NY: Kraus International Publications.

U.S. Bureau of the Census, U.S. Department of Commerce. 1988. *1987 Census of Governments.* Vol. 2, *Taxable Property Values.* Washington, DC: U.S. Government Printing Office.

U.S. Department of the Treasury. 1984. *Tax Reform for Fairness, Simplicity, and Economic Growth: The Treasury Department Report to the President.* Washington, DC: Government Printing Office.

Wellford, Harrison W., and Janne G. Gallagher. 1988. *Unfair Competition? The Challenge to Charitable Tax Exemption.* Washington, DC: National Assembly of National Voluntary Health and Social Welfare Organizations.

Whyte, William H. 1988. *City: Rediscovering the Center.* New York: Doubleday.

Whyte, William H. 1980. *The Social Life of Small Urban Spaces.* Washington, DC: The Conservation Foundation.

Woolery, Arlo. n.d. *Valuation of Railroad and Utility Property.* Published in cooperation with the Lincoln

Institute of Land Policy and the Wichita Public Utility and Railroad Workshop.

2. Periodicals.

American Journal of Economics and Sociology. New York: American Journal of Economics and Sociology.

American Law Reports. Series 1–4. Rochester, NY: Lawyers Co-operative Publishing Company.

The Appraisal Journal. Chicago: Appraisal Institute.

Assessment and Valuation Legal Reporter. Chicago: International Association of Assessing Officers.

Assessment Journal. Chicago: International Association of Assessing Officers.

Intergovernmental Perspective. Washington, DC: Advisory Commission on Intergovernmental Relations.

Journal of Economic Literature. Nashville: American Economic Association.

Journal of Multistate Taxation. New York: Warren, Gorham & Lamont.

Journal of Political Economy. Chicago: University of Chicago Press.

Journal of Public Economics. Amsterdam: North-Holland Publishing Company.

Journal of State Taxation. New York: Panel Publishers.

Journal of Taxation. New York: Warren, Gorham & Lamont.

National Tax Journal. Columbus, OH: National Tax Association.

State Tax Notes. Arlington, VA: Tax Analysts.

State Tax Review. Chicago: Commerce Clearing House.

The Survey. Albany, NY: New York State Division of Equalization and Assessment.

The Tax Lawyer. Chicago: American Bar Association Section of Taxation.

INDEX OF SUBJECTS

Note: Material within cases has not been indexed. For cases, see the Index of Cases, p. 287. For names, see the Index of Names, p. 283. For states, see also the Index of Cases by State, p. 295.

INDEX OF NAMES

INDEX OF STATUTES

INDEX OF CASES

Note: Cases in boldface are reprinted in the text.

INDEX OF CASES BY STATE

Note: Cases in boldface are reprinted in the text.

APPENDIX

Table 1
Percentage of Tax Revenue
Derived from the Property Tax, 1957–2003

Level of goverment	1957	1990	2003
State and local governments	44.6	31.0	31.6
State governments	3.3	1.9	1.9
Local governments	86.7	74.5	73.4
Cities	72.7	50.9	*
Townships	93.6	92.4	*
Municipal & township governments	*	*	55.9
Counties	93.7	73.3	69.5
School districts	98.6	97.5	96.2
Special districts	100.0	70.0	71.9

* Census data formerly collected for cities and townships is now grouped as data for municipal and township governments.

Note: See original table 1, page 5.

Sources: ACIR, *Significant Features of Fiscal Federalism 1992* (1992), vol. 2, table 65. U.S. Census Bureau. State and Local Government Finance by Level and Type of Government: 2002–2003. http://www.census.gov/govs/www/estimate03.html

Table 2
The Property Tax in Local Government Finance, 1990 and 2002

	Percentage of local government general revenue		Percentage of local government tax revenue	
	1990	2002	1990	2002
United States average	29.2	27.1	74.5	72.9
New England	49.0	47.1	98.0	97.2
Mideast	31.7	29.8	66.7	66.6
Great Lakes	35.2	30.1	81.1	81.2
Plains States	31.4	27.8	82.9	77.8
Southeast	23.4	23.7	70.2	69.1
Southwest	32.0	32.3	78.7	76.1
Rocky Mountain States	30.7	25.5	76.4	67.4
Far West	20.8	18.6	70.0	66.8
Selected states				
New Hampshire	71.1	48.5	99.3	98.0
Connecticut	56.2	56.1	98.5	98.4
New Jersey	50.8	50.6	98.1	98.4
Oregon	42.3	25.7	89.5	81.1
Michigan	40.6	23.2	92.6	90.0
Iowa	36.4	31.6	95.9	86.6
Colorado	30.7	25.8	68.7	59.7
New York	29.5	25.5	61.0	58.8
Georgia	25.2	24.5	69.2	64.0
California	19.7	17.7	69.1	66.3
Washington	18.1	20.4	59.7	62.9
Louisiana	15.7	15.1	43.4	39.5
New Mexico	11.9	13.6	56.1	56.3

Note: For region definitions, see ACIR, *Significant Features of Fiscal Federalism 1991* (1991), vol. 2, table 103. See original table 2, page 5.

Sources: ACIR, *Significant Features of Fiscal Federalism 1992* (1992), vol. 2, tables 92 and 102. U.S. Census Bureau. State and Local Government Finances by Level of Government and by State: 2001–2002. http://www.census.gov/govs/www/estimate02.html

Table 3
State and Local Property Tax Revenue, 2003

	Revenue (thousands of dollars)	Percentage
State property tax revenue	10,470,510	3.5
Local property tax revenue	286,212,675	96.5
Total	296,683,185	100

Note: See table 4, page 16 for comparison to 1986 data.

Source: U.S. Census Bureau. Summary of State and Local Government Finances by Level of Government: 2002–2003. http://www.census.gov/govs/estimate/03sl00us.html

ABOUT THE AUTHOR

Joan Youngman is senior fellow and chairman of the Department of Valuation and Taxation at the Lincoln Institute of Land Policy in Cambridge, Massachusetts. An attorney, she specializes in state and local taxation and legal problems of valuation for property taxation. She has published many articles and is coeditor of the books *The Development of Property Taxation in Economies in Transition: Case Studies from Central and Eastern Europe* (2001) and *An International Survey of Taxes on Land and Buildings* (1994). She is a regular contributor to *State Tax Notes,* and has served as research fellow at the Harvard Law School International Tax Program; chairman of the National Tax Association Property Tax Committee; North American editor of the *Journal of Property Tax Assessment & Administration*; and a member of the editorial board of the International Association of Assessing Officers.

ABOUT THE
LINCOLN INSTITUTE
OF LAND POLICY

The Lincoln Institute of Land Policy is a nonprofit and tax-exempt educational institution founded in 1974 to improve the quality of public debate and decisions in the areas of land policy and land-related taxation. The Institute's goals are to integrate theory and practice to better shape land policy and to provide a nonpartisan forum for discussion of the multidisciplinary forces that influence public policy. Inspired by the work of Henry George as expressed in the book *Progress and Poverty* (1879), the Lincoln Institute introduces his thinking and ideas into the contemporary land and tax policy debate to advance a more equitable and productive society.

The work of the Institute is organized in three departments: Valuation and Taxation, Planning and Development, and International Studies. We seek to inform decision making through education, research, dissemination of information, and demonstration projects in the United States and internationally. Our programs bring together scholars, practitioners, public officials, policy advisers, and involved citizens in a collegial learning community. The Institute does not take a particular point of view, but rather serves as a catalyst to facilitate analysis and discussion of land use and taxation issues—to make a difference today and to help policy makers plan for tomorrow.

L LINCOLN INSTITUTE
OF LAND POLICY

113 Brattle Street
Cambridge, MA 02138-3400 USA

Phone: 1-617-661-3016 x127 or 1-800-LAND-USE (800-526-3873)
Fax: 1-617-661-7235 or 1-800-LAND-944 (800-526-3944)
E-mail: help@lincolninst.edu
Web: www.lincolninst.edu